Cultural Landscapes of North-east Scotland

Collaborative Research in History and Archaeology

edited by

Colin Shepherd

I0895718

OXBOW | books
Oxford & Philadelphia

Published in the United Kingdom in 2025 by
OXBOW BOOKS
81 St Clements, Oxford OX4 1AW

and in the United States by
OXBOW BOOKS
1950 Lawrence Road, Havertown, PA 19083

Paperback Edition: ISBN 979-8-88857-157-6
Digital Edition: ISBN 979-8-88857-158-3

A CIP record for this book is available from the British Library

Library of Congress Control Number: 2024952490

Printed in the United Kingdom by Short Run Press
Typeset in India by DiTech Publishing Services

For a complete list of Oxbow titles, please contact:

UNITED KINGDOM
Oxbow Books
Telephone (0)1226 734350
Email: oxbow@oxbowbooks.com
www.oxbowbooks.com

UNITED STATES OF AMERICA
Oxbow Books
Telephone (610) 853-9131, Fax (610) 853-9146
Email: queries@casemateacademic.com
www.casemateacademic.com/oxbow

Oxbow Books is part of the Casemate Group

Front cover: Excavating at Pittodrie (Photograph: Nadine Ralston)
Back cover: Tea-break at Pittodrie (Photograph: Iain Ralston)

The Publisher's authorised representative in the EU for product safety is Authorised Rep Compliance Ltd., Ground Floor, 71 Lower Baggot Street, Dublin D02 P593, Ireland.
www.arccompliance.com

Contents

Bailies of Bennachie Acknowledgement

The Bailies of Bennachie are a voluntary conservation society whose objectives are to encourage and stimulate the public's interest of Bennachie: its natural environment, history and culture – protecting this unique landscape for future generations. Part of this is understanding the impacts the cultural landscapes of north-east Scotland have had on the hill and its inhabitants over the millennia. The Bailies of Bennachie are proud to have supported this publication by also making it Open Access and we do hope you enjoy reading it.

Allan Will, Trustee and Deputy Chair,
Bailies of Bennachie

List of corresponding authors (in order of appearance)

Colin Shepherd
Honorary Research Fellow,
University of Aberdeen

Bruce Mann
Senior Historic Environment Officer,
Aberdeenshire Council

Andrew Wainwright
Independent Researcher

Samantha Jones
Research Fellow, University of Aberdeen

Nicholas Evans
Research Fellow, University of Aberdeen

Alexander Forbes
Independent Historian

Charlotta Hillerdal
Reader in Archaeology, University of Aberdeen

Penelope Dransart
Honorary Reader, University of Aberdeen

Jeff Oliver
Reader in Archaeology, University of Aberdeen

Louise Smith
Research Postgraduate, University of Aberdeen.

Sandra Davison
Independent Researcher/Post-graduate, UHI

Christine Foster
Independent Researcher

Iain Ralston
Independent Researcher

Jo Vergunst
Senior Lecturer, University of Aberdeen

List of figures

List of tables

List of plates

Foreword

Colin Shepherd

This collection of papers derives from a weekend conference held in September 2023 at the Garioch Heritage Centre, Inverurie in Aberdeenshire, entitled 'Cultural Landscapes of North-east Scotland'. It was a joint enterprise of the Bailies of Bennachie – a local conservation group of 50 years standing – and the University of Aberdeen (of almost 550 years standing!). Together, they conceived and have undertaken work on the 'Bennachie Landscapes Project' since 2011.

For those unfamiliar with its topography and history, Bennachie is the iconic hilltop visible from all parts of the north-east. Whilst it must always have been a prominent landmark, the division of it as a 'commonty' in the mid-19th century (see Oliver, this volume) caused socio-political ructions across the region that resulted in an increase in its perceived importance to the people of the north-east. The division of the commonty was (and often still is) widely viewed as theft. Plate 0.1 shows a copy of the Division of the Commonty of Bennache held by the Bailies of Bennachie. Note the different colours indicating the portions allotted to the various heritors who held land around the Commonty. Plate 0.2 shows the same map with the coloured portions converted to greyscale. The red line marks the area perceived by many in the north-east to be the land that had been stolen from them and from which they were now legally excluded. The boundary marked by the red line is far less obvious on the original where the internal divisions of the lands allotted are given pride of place. This, however, did not accord with widespread public perceptions of the day. Amongst 19th-century enclosure awards the Division of Bennachie was unremarkable. For its endurance within the regional psyche, it is remarkable. Ultimately, the perception of its removal from public-use led to the formation of the Bailies as a group, intent on ensuring and promoting future public accessibility and continued protection for the hill.

The speakers at the conference were invited to reflect on their own individual research and to present papers reflective of how their findings helped to inform a view of the development of the cultural landscapes of the north-east. Some of the speakers have worked together on the Bennachie Landscapes Project, sometimes as individual researchers, sometimes as more embedded 'collaborators'. As this book demonstrates, all have added to the sum of total knowledge of the area and respond to each other in a variety of ways: professionally, academically, practically, and socially. From whatever backgrounds the contributors come, a simple desire to learn more about the landscape underpins their research.

What makes the contents of these studies different to so many other inter-disciplinary and collaborative projects? Interdisciplinarity is the life-blood of archaeology and, arguably, the latter cannot exist without it. Community collaboration is now well-embedded in a wide range of archaeological projects, so much so that funding frequently relies upon its inclusion (Oliver *et al.* 2022, 1–2). However, since the twilight of the 'heroic era' of British rescue archaeology (Buteux 2006, 41; Morel 2019, 161), it has been argued, an increasing professionalisation of the discipline has shunted community partners from being a driving force to passive participant (Neal and Roskams 2013, 153). Whether the situation is now as clear-cut as it was in 2013, when that statement was made, it remains the case that the public are often kept at arms-length from many archaeological operations, especially in the field of developer-funded archaeology. Academic institutions, however, have proven more accepting and even desirous of increased levels of collaboration. Within the arena of the Bennachie Landscapes Project, the Bailies of Bennachie, the University of Aberdeen along with many others are collaborators who equally 'actively define research agendas and priorities' (*ibid.*) jointly. In this they are unusual.

More commonly, project organisers – professional and academic (I use this clumsy distinction to distinguish archaeological company employees from academic institutional employees) – 'invite' participants from adjoining communities to collaborate. This usually (and there are exceptions) results in collaboration across a certain timeframe, dependant upon funding constraints and duration of the project. Participants then go their own ways. The overriding constraints are, therefore, financial, leading to time. This clearly represents a traditional capitalist mode of operation: capital is invested in a project and a return is expected. Once 'returns' dry up, a new project is sought. I will refer to this type of collaboration as 'top-down'.

Seemingly tangential to this, it is worth remembering the background to the Bailies' creation. They were formed as a result of an historic antipathy to what was perceived to have been a momentous occasion of rampant 'mercantilism' – the 'theft' of a local commonty. (The number of papers in this volume that touch upon the issue of the capitalisation of the countryside – almost half – further suggests this does not remain a side-issue across the north-east.) This capitalisation saw 'subsistence' farms supplanted by larger, capitalised ones. 'Subsistence', it should be pointed out, does not mean living hand-to mouth with no end-of-year 'profit'. It involved numerous small tenant families working for family-sized profits. Their lands were then 'engrossed' during the industrialisation of the countryside in the late 18th and 19th centuries so that these family-sized profits were combined and split between single, large tenants and landowners. The former small tenants became waged labourers on the newly enlarged farms. This process of appropriation included the enclosure and division of former commonties, upon which the former small tenants had relied as part of their resource-base.

Perhaps, as a continuing Bailies 'psychological' reaction to this process, the Bennachie Landscapes Project evolved in order to try to consciously break with the capitalised 'top-down' tradition of project management. As I hope this book will demonstrate, there are other modes of operation that can function perfectly well outside of an institutional capitalised one. In order to break the cycle of 'boom and bust' – a large lump of funding followed by nothing – a 'non-institutional' approach is required that permits the community total control, *i.e.* free of all outside interference, including significant financial input. This is the model of the 'Common-pool Resource' (CPR) outlined so magnificently by Elenor Ostrom (1990). Furthermore, it is the model on which commons and commonties were organised in the pre-industrialised age. Is it, therefore, any surprise that the Bennachie Landscapes Project, with its 'anti-capitalist' 'origin myth' has followed that path!

It has been suggested by Di Giovine and Cowie (2014) that this 'top-down' model of project funding mechanisms derives from an association with a concept of 'heritage as 'property'. In other words, the only way that a capitalist world view (as presently underpins western society) can conceive of any 'asset' is by means of associating it with 'ownership'. This, in turn, permits such institutional bodies as Historic Environment Scotland, English Heritage, etc. to quantify those heritage assets. It also permits funding bodies (NERC, AHRC, etc.) to apportion resources to, what they believe to be, the most deserving of cases. But, this process, inevitably, involves a large degree of institutional control over the recipients as well as an inclination to adhere to an 'authorised heritage discourse' (Smith 2006), *i.e.* what has become socially accepted as 'how history should be understood/taught'. In other words, what is likely to receive funding are those projects that are associated with a pre-determined set of ideas concerning what is of greatest importance. Chapter 13 discusses this in further detail in regard to the Pittodrie excavations. Clearly, this subjectivity affects the fundees with respect to how they manage their projects and imposes certain limitations on their projects.

Crucially, what is demanded is a model that does not require large inputs of capital (as was the case in small, family-run subsistence farming enterprises). Conveniently, community projects can work from a very small budget, primarily because there is no wage bill. 'Low-tech' working methodologies may be slow and not cost-effective industrially, but they can function very efficiently in a low-cost environment with minimal time constraints. Within this world, volunteer groups and individuals can flourish and are free to set their own agendas and priorities. Half of the papers in this book derive from academic research, constrained by certain cost and time constraints. The other half arise from other individuals and groups not so institutionally constrained. The papers presented here reflect a wide range of projects, designed by a variety of individuals, groups and 'sub-groups'. All of the papers are inter-connected through the geography and cultures of the north-east of Scotland and all share some debt, either directly or indirectly to all of the others, irrespective of funding flows (see Figure 0.1 for project locations across the north-east). What is of note, however, is the 'bottom-up' nature of some of the projects. Issues of time constraint and a need to conform to some outside influence have been circumvented by utilising a low cost, 'subsistence' approach to project management and design. As with Ostrom's CPRs, and late medieval commonty management regimes, outside interference is minimised and the community/individual remains self-governing. This is, as Ostrom notes (1990, 90), essential for the survival of such structures. It also, I believe, makes these projects stand out as distinctive from most other collaborative community projects.

This issue of perceptions of 'ownership' and 'property', with regard to historical resources, will be returned to in the concluding chapter. As previously noted, it is particularly pertinent with respect to the origin story of the Bailies of Bennachie rehearsed briefly above. That historic angst felt across the north-east is directly related to a perceived theft of common property and its assimilation into a capitalised world. In other words, whether we like it or not, whether we wish it wasn't the case, questions of 'property' and 'ownership' are part and parcel of notions of cultural heritage, which forms the core of this volume. To some degree, overtly or otherwise, 'cultural heritage' is generally perceived as a form of 'property' and access to it is restricted on a daily basis. Sometimes this is for the safety and protection of the 'asset' – sometimes for less benign reasons. The success of the projects recorded here reflect, to varying degrees, the relinquishing of feelings of 'ownership' by many players in this pageantry. It should become clear who they are – even when un-named – throughout the course of the book. Grateful thanks are extended to all those people.

Part One highlights a range of individual studies carried out across the north-east. Each reflects one individual's journey of discovery into a certain aspect of the north-east landscape. Most have grown out of the broader Bennachie Landscapes Project, from which the individual – academic or otherwise – has been inspired to research in greater detail. Some of these relate to the Bennachie Landscapes Projects whilst others do not. Part Two showcases three projects, reliant upon much greater collaborative effort. None of the three follows the conventional 'top-down' model noted above.

'Setting the scene' for this series of studies is an actor of fundamental importance to any archaeological research, but who too frequently sits 'outside' the literature related to community and institutional collaborative processes. This is the 'county archaeologist'. He or she surveys all with regard to the institutionalised legality of the whole process. This 'grey eminence' is perfectly situated to contextualise all such research agendas within the long duree of more economically motivated landscape developmental processes.

Bruce Mann, Senior Historic Environment Officer (Archaeology) at Aberdeenshire Council (as well as overseeing Moray, Aberdeen City, and Angus), has had occasion to interact with all of the authors, usually in a professional capacity. His overview of the landscape of the north-east is tempered by an appreciation of planning law, juxtaposing the realities of the commercial sector with the acquisition of new knowledge and the protection of vulnerable heritage assets. Most of us represented here have had numerous occasions to be grateful for his unique perspective and help, as well as relief for not having his multifarious and, at times, contradictory burdens.

Bruce introduces us, in Chapter 1, to the cultural landscapes of north-east Scotland using the medium of a Bronze Age axe. In doing so, he slides us into a discussion of how present-day people in the north-east connect with their contemporary and past landscapes. Andrew Wainwright's perceptive questioning of the commonly

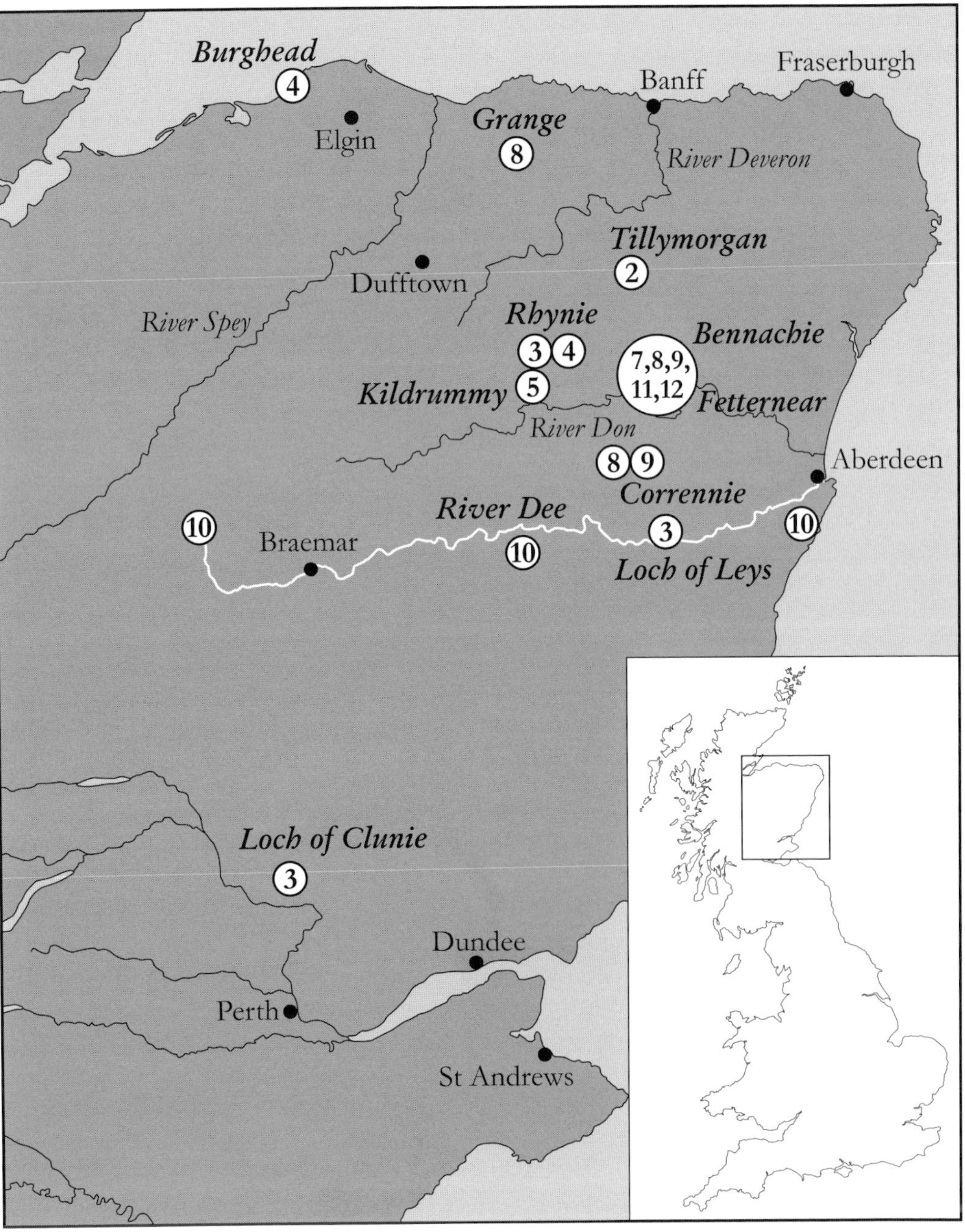

Figure 0.1. Locations of the research discussed in this book. Numbers indicate chapters.

accepted role of glaciation in the north-east demonstrates subtle links of interpersonal networking by showing how the development of commercial infrastructure, in this case the laying of a gas pipeline and wind turbine groundworks, can be used as 'surrogate geological excavations' for the building and subsequent testing of hypotheses. The importance of personal relationships is at once in evidence in the necessity of seeking permissions from contractors with strict timeframes and no reason to grant access to their sites. During the 'heroic age' of rescue archaeology, this was the only way of gaining access to archaeology and it is nice to see that the approach can still work!

Samantha Jones' investigations into Roman influences in the landscape of the north-east has developed from her collaborative work on the 'Comparative Kingship' Leverhulme funded project (e.g. Jones *et al.* 2021). Areas of destruction revealed in the pollen record demonstrate how some areas were more adversely affected than others and suggest mechanisms of change that reverberated into later Pictish times. This thread is maintained by Nicholas Evans' work on the development of Pictish power centres across the north-east and the creation of a vibrant post-Roman culture with long-distant links to the Mediterranean. His consideration of ecclesiastical power centres resonates with Alex Forbes' consideration of a possible early Christian '*banchor*' site at Kildrummy. This slightly 'phenomenological' landscape exploration has developed from Alex Forbes' ancestral interest in his own line of descent and related kindreds. It utilises family myth, local folklore and place-name evidence to suggest the former existence of an early Christian centre at Kildrummy. The Forbes family derived their lordship from the Earls of Mar, themselves based at Kildrummy. Nick and Alex's Pictish enquires are rounded off by Charlotta Hillerdal's questioning of how a Viking presence might present itself within this Pictish environment of north-east Scotland. She suggests comparison with Orcadian Viking settlement may help to answer that knotty problem.

This compendium of diverse Pictish-period studies speak to one another and, whilst they are personal journeys in an academic sense, they are mutually supportive and collaborative in a broader way. As a group they create a multi-disciplinary view of Pictish settlement and cultural practices across the north-east. The following papers move the story into and through the late medieval period towards the present day.

Penny Dransart's excavations at the episcopal palace of Fetternear sparked a detailed consideration of the economic and cultural connections of the Bishops of Aberdeen, both near and far. Although part of the wider Christian world, with which they engaged economically and spiritually, the bishops were also fully embedded within their own ancient cultural landscape of the north-east. Penny shows how they utilised the cultural symbolism inherent in that landscape as a means of expressing their spiritual and social power. The former royal forest of Bennachie provided the backdrop to that display.

A social and temporal jump takes us forward to Jeff Oliver's consideration of 19th-century 'informal' communities in the north-east. Jeff's research has evolved from his previous work delving into the story and material assemblages of the 'Colonists' on Bennachie. He presents a picture of communities sitting 'apart' whilst 'a part' of their wider social network. Marginal in one sense, but integrated in another, these communities create an interesting paradox within the world of 'improved' farming in the 19th century. Complementing this social perspective, Louise Smith demonstrates how these communities changed the ecologies of the landscapes in which they lived. Her comparison with pre-crofting flora is achieved by recourse to ecological sampling of the present biodiversity. In many ways, Louise's work is a perfect complement to Samantha Jones' Pictish palynological work and permits us to ponder the dramatic changes wrought in the pollen and ecological records across that long historic timescale.

Part Two comprises three case studies of community-led ('bottom-up') collaborative research. The first returns us to earlier times, just post-dating Andrew Wainwright's tentative hypotheses on the glacial background of the north-east. 'Mesolithic Deeside' is a completely independent community project from the Bennachie Landscapes Project. (But we all know each other well and share stories!) Sandra Davison presents a brief overview of their substantial corpus of work and demonstrates how 'low tech' approaches, harnessed with state-of-the-art technology melds a hardy team of enthusiasts to professional technicians in a remarkably successful collaboration of landscape-scale archaeology. As with Andrew Wainwright's and most community projects, social-networking and landowner permissions are critical for accessing the sought-after data. The project contains material gathered in the 1990s and has been adding to that corpus ever since, creating an ever-wider view of settlement dynamics in the early prehistoric periods of the north-east.

Introducing an 'experimental' aspect of the Bennachie Landscapes Project, Christine Foster discusses the evolution of the Shepherds Lodge kailyard ('kitchen garden') on Bennachie. This 'squatter' house was excavated as part of the project, approximately 10 years ago, by Jeff Oliver and a team comprising members of the University of Aberdeen and the Bailies of Bennachie. Inevitably, when faced with the small kailyard annexed to the house, questions concerning what was eaten and how it was maintained arose. This experiment into creating and managing the kailyard provided the setting for a wide range of further research and educational possibilities involving local school children. The kailyard is still producing and is regularly visited by hundreds of people wandering around the 'Colony Trail'.

The final study takes the form of a short report into excavations on a multi-period site on the edge of Bennachie on the Pittodrie Estate. The project grew out of the historically confusing accounts concerning a particular monument – the 'Bede House' – that stood in what was, until recently, a coniferous plantation. Subsequent research and questioning of its wider landscape have unearthed the archaeological remains of a multi-period landscape. This paper gives an assessment of the interdisciplinary and multi-disciplinary research carried out thus far and demonstrates the efficiencies in combining collaborators from a range of backgrounds to co-produce a comprehensive landscape study.

The three case studies contained in Part Two describe collaborative projects that have involved most of the authors represented here in this volume at one time or another. All three may be said to demonstrate projects in which the project design and agendas have been set, not by recourse to a hierarchical institutional structure but developed from the bottom up. The driving forces have been three groups of practitioners who wished to carry out particular pieces of research and 'actively define(d) their research agendas and priorities' (Neal and Roskams 2013, 153).

As a final 'Afterword', the Editor and Jo Vergunst suggest an anthropologically nuanced assessment of 13 years of the Bennachie Landscapes Project, university-community collaboration and co-production. They consider what has been learnt, what is still to learn and how this increased knowledge may help in charting new directions. Co-production through collaboration has not only resulted in developing new approaches to doing research, it has provided a framework in which co-producers, of whatever shape and form, feel comfortable to work at their own pace within their own points of reference. In fact, a new 'research (-with-fun)' community has, unwittingly, been created. Over the years, this community has comprised co-producers aged from five to over 90 years of age. Whilst activity in a professional environment may last 40 years, the participatory lifetime within this community might potentially span twice that.

Acknowledgement

Many thanks to Jeff Oliver for reading this Foreword and making many astute observations and recommendations, all of which have been included.

Bibliography

Buteux, S. (2006) Thirty Years of Birmingham Archaeology: A Career in Ruins. In *Rosetta* 1, 41–50.

Di Giovine, M.A. and Cowie, S.E. (2014) The Definitional Problems of Patrimony and the Futures of Cultural Heritage. In *Anthropology News* 7/5/2014.

Jones, S.E., Evans, N., Martinez Cortizas, A., Mighall, T.M. and Noble, G. (2021) Settlement, landscape and land-use change at a Pictish Elite Centre: Assessing the palaeoecological record for economic continuity and social change at Rhynie in N.E. Scotland. In *The Holocene* 31(6), 897–1067.

Morel, H. (2019) Policy and Practice of London's Historic Environment. In *The Historic Environment: Policy and Practice* 10(2), 152–77.

Neal, C. and Roskams, S. (2013) Authority and Community: Reflections on Archaeological Practice at Heslington East, York. In *The Historic Environment: Policy and Practice* 4(2), 139–55.

Oliver, J., Armstrong, J., Curtis, E., Curtis, N. and Vergunst, J. (2022) Exploring co-production in community heritage research: Reflections from the Bennachie Landscapes Project. In *Journal of Community Archaeology & Heritage* 9(3), 196–215. Doi. https://doi.org/10.1080/20518196.2021.2014659

Ostrom, E. (1990) *Governing the Commons. The Evolution of Institutions for Collective Action*. Cambridge, Cambridge University Press.

Smith, L. (2006) *Uses of Heritage*. New York, Routledge.

Chapter 1

Introducing the cultural landscapes of north-east Scotland

Bruce Mann

Introduction

Bennachie is a prominent hill range sitting in the heart of north-east Scotland. While not particularly high when compared to the nearby Cairngorms, its isolated position and unique ridgeline make it a striking feature. Of its multiple peaks, the most popular for visitors is that of the Mither Tap. Here, the striking granite tor, surrounded by stone fortifications from the early medieval period (Noble and Evans 2022, 106), provides an ideal location for observing the landscapes at the heart of Aberdeenshire (see Plate 1.1). The patchwork of fields, woodland, and settlement seen from this vantage point are a snapshot in time of the physical landscape of the north-east. The landscape is, of course, the product of millennia of change, with the influence of climate, geology and nature being coupled latterly by human interventions. William Alexander (1892, 102), when discussing the making of Aberdeenshire, described later landscape change as being

> the development of its agriculture, and related social progress of its inhabitants; the conversion of the county from a bleak, comparatively treeless, wholly roadless region, abundantly dotted with undrained swamps and dominating stretches of heather and stony waste, to one of the most skilfully cultivated counties of Scotland.

While Alexander's description is somewhat disparaging of what existed prior to the 18th and 19th centuries, the point about the related social progress of the region's inhabitants as being part of this change is key to not only understanding the physical landscape as found today, but also the cultural landscape with which it has a symbiotic existence.

The term 'cultural landscapes' was first coined by Otto Schlüter (1908) as a means of distinguishing between the 'urlandschaft' (original landscape) and the 'kulturlandschaft' (cultural landscape), to emphasise the changes humans make to natural landscapes. Today the term embodies the values, beliefs, and practices of human activity that have developed over time, reflecting the interactions between people and their environment. In the context of research in Scotland, 'cultural landscapes' has often focused on how the natural environment has been modified by historical and contemporary Scottish society. This includes the study of land use, architecture, traditional practices, and how these elements have contributed to the identity of the Highlands and other regions, including the north-east. The results from this research, and how they have been portrayed in popular literature and media, have left an embedded legacy within communities of how they think the landscape defines who they are. Thus, in the north-east in particular, what it means to be a fisherman rather than a farmer, or a country 'teuchter' (DSL 2005) rather than a city dweller. Or in other words, how the landscape that surrounds their communities influences their thinking when defining their sense of who they are.

An overview of the cultural landscapes of the north-east

This public understanding of landscape, or rather their perception of landscape, is also heavily influenced by their own personal experiences. If landscape is viewed through the lens of identity and memory, then deep connections are formed, often subconsciously. These connections are generally only realised and expressed when the landscape experiences change. Current focus in expressing and debating these connections around the pedestrianisation of the thoroughfare of Union Street in Aberdeen demonstrate the deep-seated feelings people have when presented with change. Their perception of what constitutes original and authentic, and the value of that which then justifies conserving and protecting, is a theme we shall return to later.

For now, the cultural landscapes of the north-east can be considered as fragmentary tapestries, some parts interwoven, but all overlying a physical landscape that spans high mountains to coastal dunes. The earliest evidence for human activity dates to the Late Upper Palaeolithic (LUP), *c.* 12,000 BC, shortly after the end of the last ice age during the Late Glacial Interstadial, and then subsequently during the colder Younger Dryas (Loch Lomond Stadial). The initial warm climatic period during this time saw the establishment of stable soils, open birch and juniper woodland, and comparatively low levels of water discharge in the rivers, before there was a sharp return to cold conditions with small glaciers forming in the Cairngorms. Prior to 2015 there was no recognised evidence for humans in the region at this time before the Mesolithic, but a developer-led excavation that year at Greenacres, Wester Clerkhill, on the outskirts of Peterhead led to the discovery of a large, well-executed flint broad-blade (73 mm × 32 mm × 14 mm), which could be tentatively dated to the LUP (Cameron and Ballin 2018). Further discoveries and research at that time, including re-examination of previously collected assemblages (Ballin and Wickham-Jones 2017) confirmed that groups of reindeer hunters representing the Humburgian, Federmesser-Gruppen, and the Ahrensburgian tool industries were present in the north-east, visible now only through either isolated finds or small assemblages. The landscape of the north-east at this point was not part of a separate island, but rather part of the larger European continental landmass, connected by the still dry Doggerland. Culturally the land was most likely perceived by these early nomadic groups as a fertile hunting ground, but one on the periphery of the more familiar.

The transition to the Mesolithic at the start of the Holocene, *c.* 9800 BC, is represented by further scatters of stone tools, in particular flint, and the debitage from their creation across the region. They were left by small mobile groups still reliant on hunting, gathering and fishing. Short-lived structures with a central hearth, such as that excavated at Standingstones, Dyce (Dingwell *et al.* 2019, 207–23), and dated to 7070–6600 cal BC, represent emerging evidence of how these groups had started to stay for longer periods, changing the landscape from one that was visited to one that was lived in. Camps were located based on convenience to resources such as hazel nuts, firewood, water, and for more ephemeral reasons such as views and strategic positioning along key routeways. The excavation of a pit-alignment at Warren Field, Crathes (Murray *et al.* 2009), dated to 8210–3650 cal BC, showed that 12 substantial pits dug in the Mesolithic were placed with an awareness of existing topography and intended longevity of visibility. The alignment acted as a focus for activity over an initial 2,500-year span before being revisited and recut at the start of the Neolithic, *c.* 4000 BC, for a further period of activity over several centuries. The augmentation of the physical landscape with tangible cultural landmarks and traces had begun.

The arrival of small groups of farmers from northern France around 3950 BC (Sheridan 2007, 440–92) saw a rapid change in how culture impacted the landscape. The processes of growing crops such as naked barley and emmer wheat, animal husbandry of cattle and sheep, and new technologies such as pottery and stone axes led to the landscape being cleared and exploited on a scale not seen before. With this Neolithic package came new ways of expressing beliefs around life, death and the wider world in which people lived. Physical structures start with large, rectangular timber halls at the heart of the new communities, such as at Balbridie (Fairweather and Ralston 1993, 313–23) dated to 3800–3600 BC. These halls, along with the smaller domestic structures that spread out across the landscape as colonisation took hold are now only visible through either cropmarks or excavation. One such example of these smaller homes is the Early Neolithic small ovoid building at Garthdee, Aberdeen dated to 3850–3610 cal BC (Murray and Murray 2014, 1–64). Subsequent connection to the landscape by these new arrivals was reinforced through massive funerary long cairns built of stone and earth such as the one at Dalladies (Piggott 1974, 23–47), designed to curate and display the dead while maintaining an ancestral connection to, and overt statement of ownership of, the land by the living.

Reacting to this shared cultural expression within architecture across the British Isles, the first evidence of regionalisation happening in the north-east is found during the Early Neolithic with the rapid development of Modified Carinated Bowl Ware pottery (*c.* 3800–3600 BC), and the subsequent regional variants of Impressed

Ware pottery (Sheridan 2007, 440–92). This variation seems to change once again by the Late Neolithic. Settlements at this time, comprising more than one building, are scarce in the region, but the excavated site of Greenbogs, Monymusk (Noble *et al.* 2012, 135–71), dated to 2890–2490 cal BC, demonstrates the presence of roundhouse structures with a distinctive setting of four posts at their centre. The implication is that this form of domestic building type is common across Britain and Ireland (*ibid.*), while the adoption of the ubiquitous Grooved Ware pottery that came out of Orkney enforces a sense of new cultural consistency encountered by those travelling to and from the region. Unique in Scotland, the flint mines exploited at Den of Boddam, Peterhead (HER NK14SW0003, NRHE NK14SW3), would have been a visual and auditory exception to this uniformity, with digging in what became hundreds of shaft-pits providing a significant resource that could be traded, either as raw material or finished tools.

In the middle of the 3rd millennium BC society was transformed once again by further arrivals from continental Europe, this time bringing with them metalworking technology and its associated traditions and cultural ritual. Beginning with copper, the Chalcolithic heralded change for people, ranging from the finely decorated Beaker pottery through to the proliferation of different funerary practices. As with the arrival of farming, the arrival of metal was quickly adopted by those living in the north-east of Scotland, and there is a notable concentration of early stone moulds for casting from the area, one of which we shall look at in more detail below. By the Early Bronze Age, *c.* 2200 BC, the landscape of the north-east saw burial of individuals in stone-lined cists become commonplace practice. Other forms of funerary monument include cremations placed within pots buried in pits in either isolation, within small groups, or within burial cairns. One new funerary monument was the henge, a burial enclosure defined by ditches with external banks such as that at Broomend of Crichie, dated to 2140–1500 cal BC (Bradley 2011, 61). The most remarkable additions to the cultural landscape however, that still survive today, are the recumbent stone circles. Unique to the north-east, this regional form of the stone circle comprises a ring of stones paired across the circle, reducing in height away from the dominant recumbent stone on the south-western side, itself flanked by two tall stones. The circles typically enclose a ring-cairn, of which white quartz stone played an important component. While Easter Aquhorthies (see below) is perhaps the best known, others from the surviving *c.* 70 examples have helped to confirm the complicated sequence of their construction: for instance Hillhead, Tarland (Figure 1.1), dated to 2290–1980 cal BC (Bradley and Nimura 2016, 20–21). Lastly, the complex mortuary site of Sculptor's Cave, Hopeman, on the Moray Firth coastline also needs to be added to the list of new ritualistic sites. Starting in the Late Bronze Age and continuing to the start of the early medieval, the cave saw practices ranging from the storing of mummified bodies of children through to excarnation and, later, systematic beheadings and display of the severed parts (Armit and Büster 2020).

Figure 1.1. Hillhead Recumbent Stone Circle being excavated in 2013. These monument types, initially developed in phases, see reuse over a considerable span of time (Photograph: Bruce Mann).

From the mid-2nd millennium BC the landscape changes within the surviving archaeological record from one dominated by funerary monuments to one dominated by agriculture and the ubiquitous roundhouse in which people lived and worked. This form of circular architecture continues into the Iron Age (and indeed beyond into the early medieval), ranging from 5 m up to a suggested maximum of 18 m in diameter. Materials used in their construction varied with the design, with excavated examples from across the region encompassing stone and turf, turf only, turf and wattle, or timber-only construction. This variation probably reflects the availability of the local resource for the raw materials. Other characteristics, such as the commonly found ring-ditch around the inside of the outer wall, would have been formed by repeated wear from animals for instance, corralled safely within the building next to the human occupants. Generally, a central hearth provided heat and light, while wattle and daub partitions would have divided the internal space into functional zones. The 47 roundhouses excavated between 1996 and 2006 ahead of development in Kintore (Cook and Dunbar 2008) ably show an unenclosed settlement sequence of such buildings spanning from 1800 BC to AD 1000.

Adjacent to many Iron Age roundhouses are the ancillary structures known as souterrains, a form of subterranean long-passage or chamber that can be timber-lined or stone-lined, with a stone or timber and earth roof. Debate continues as to their function, but increasingly the hypothesis is that these are for storage, primarily of food, and in use until the 3rd century AD. An example at Inverboyndie, Banff, excavated in 2019 (Savory 2020, 6) was judged to have been located deliberately on the more manageable, free draining soils, an observation supportive of the conjectured function. Interestingly, this example also revealed that the capping stones sat on top of a buried soil, indicating that the top of the souterrain probably stood proud of surrounding ground surface, and was therefore a visible structure rather than an intentionally hidden vault. The presence of souterrains also suggests that the farming landscape was now widespread and successful, capable of producing surpluses.

Beyond the roundhouse the landscape saw the building of hillforts (a somewhat loaded term whose implied meaning may not always accurately reflect the original function of the site), promontory forts, palisaded enclosures, enclosed settlements, and crannogs. These are all indicative of an increasingly volatile society, one active in warfare, competition, and conspicuous consumption. The best known hillforts and enclosures from this period dominate the core north-east landscape, from the small, thick stone-walled enclosures such as Maiden Castle, Chapel of Garioch, dated to AD 420–650 (Cook 2011a, 25–35), to the multivallate forts such as the Hill of Barra, Oldmeldrum, dated to 560 BC–AD 580 (Cook 2011b, 215–16) (see Plate 1.2), to the large oblong timber-framed forts of Dunnideer, Insch, dated to 550–250 BC (Cook *et al.* 2010, 79–91). The construction of these monumental statements in the landscape would have required the coordination of a large number of people, and it is easy to envision local elites overseeing a network built on power and social status. The cultural landscape of the region had firmly moved from one revering the past to one firmly focused on the challenges of the present.

Those challenges came no larger than the arrival of the Roman Empire in AD 79 under the command of Agricola, governor of Britain. While the location of Mons Graupius, fought in AD 83, is still debated, it has traditionally been associated with the north-east. The campaigns undertaken by Agricola in the 1st century AD, and then those by Severus in the 3rd century AD, have left a series of marching camps running across the region from Balmakewan, Marykirk, in the south (HER NO66NE0004, NRHE NO66NE5) to Bellie, Fochabers in the north (HER NJ36SE0007, NRHE NJ36SE8). The impact of the Romans, who only campaigned within the north-east rather than subjugated and colonised, is still unclear. The 4th century AD Vettweiss-Froitzheim dice tower from Germany contains the translated Latin text on one face, 'the Picts are beaten, the enemy annihilated, let us play without care' (Hunter 2007, 4). The remains of a sequence of Roman bread ovens beside the River Dee, Milltimber, dated to the Flavian campaigns of the late AD 70s and 80s (Dingwell *et al.* 2019, 135), with no identified ditches or banks as yet, suggests a very rare undefended camp deep within enemy territory, and hints at the extent of the impact the invasions had on the local populace. Certainly, between the later 3rd century AD and the 5th century AD, there is a gap in the archaeological evidence, indicating a significant decline in the number of settlements, a complete cessation in the use of souterrains or the construction of new hillforts, and the disappearance of regional cultural identifiers such as massive iron armlets. At the Tap O'Noth, Rhynie, new evidence suggests significant centralisation of settlement from the late 3rd century to the 6th century AD (Noble and Evans 2022 66–67). Here, below the vitrified upper fort, a lower enclosure encompassing an area 21 ha in size contains the remains of approximately 800 house platforms interlinked with trackways. This scale of urbanisation can be compared to that of a small town, and perhaps offers a plausible explanation for what was happening in the wider landscape at this time.

Unquestionably, by the 5th century AD, the cultural landscape is now dominated by the Picts. Originally named so by the Romans – 'Picti' meaning the 'the painted ones' (Eumenius 297) – the Romans targeted the Picts specifically during the campaigns of the 3rd and 4th centuries AD. Following the retreat of the Romans, the north-east sees the formation of powerful regional centres during the early medieval period, between the 5th and the 9th century AD. It is during this period that the citadel on Mither Tap (the granite tor on Bennachie where we began this paper) was established, with the main phase of occupation running from the 7th to the 8th centuries AD (Noble and Evans 2022, 107). The high-status metal-working and ritual site around the Craw Stane, Rhynie, provides evidence of post and beam settings for rectangular buildings, while the artefacts demonstrate the reach of the trade networks, including 6th century AD *amphorae* (B ware) from southern Italy and drinking glass from western France (Noble *et al.* 2013, 1142–3). The dead were buried in barrows, cairns, and field cemeteries containing multiple stone-lined long cists. This period also saw the establishment of the early churches at locations that became such critical focal points for communities over the following centuries.

The most distinctive cultural legacy from this period, beyond the establishment of Christianity, are the unique Pictish symbol stones. These stones are now categorised into two main classes: Class I stones, which are unshaped standing stones bearing incised symbols (see Plate 1.3), and Class II stones, which are shaped cross-slabs with symbols and Christian imagery. There are also two further classes comprising the simpler cross-slabs and the cross-marked stones. The symbols, numbering around 50 in form and often paired together on the stones, can be grouped into three categories: 'animals', 'geometric designs', and 'everyday objects' (Henderson and Henderson 2004). While their exact meanings remain elusive, it is believed that they served various functions such as territorial markers, memorials for individuals or clans, and possibly even recording marriage treaties. Over time, as the Picts converted to Christianity, these symbols began to merge with Christian iconography, reflecting the cultural and religious shifts of the period.

By the 10th century, the Picts had been absorbed into the expanding Gaelic kingdom of Alba. The death of Macbeth after the battle of Lumphanan in AD 1057, followed by his stepson's Lulach's death at Essie, Strathbogie in AD 1058, paved the way for royal dominance over the north-east, starting with Malcolm III. From the mid-AD 1200s castles became the prevalent expression of lordship, ranging from motte and bailey timber fortifications such as the 13th-century Peel of Lumphanan (HER NJ50SE0002, NRHE NJ50SE2), to stone-built buildings such as Dunnideer Castle, Insch (built on top of the previous Iron Age oblong fort referenced above). These stone-built towers and castles continue today to be some of the most significant elements of the landscape, including the iconic 15th- and 16th-century fortress of Dunnottar Castle, Stonehaven (HER NO88SE0007, NRHE NO88SE11), perched on a rocky headland, and the Scottish Baronial style of the 17th century epitomised by the tower house of Craigievar Castle, Alford, completed in AD 1626 (HER NJ50NE0005, NRHE NJ50NE6).

The demarcation of royal forests and deer parks as reserved areas for hunting by the elite was an already established practice that predated the Norman arrival (Gilbert 1979). However, as the Norman influence reached Scotland after their conquest of England in AD 1066, some hunting parks were enhanced as part of wider landscape designs. The example associated with Kincardine Castle, Fettercairn (HER NO67NE0040, NRHE NO67NE10), shows how extravagant the scale of the earthworks could become, with the enclosing dyke ranging between 3 m and 4.5 m wide, and an internal ditch averaging 2 m in width. Kincardine was possibly created by William the Lion in the second half of the 12th century (Hall and Malloy 2016, 29) who, along with his brother Earl David of Huntingdon, were virtually 'as rich in French royal blood as Henry II of England' (Stringer 1985, 10–11). Their integration into the wider European 'chivalric' lordly environment of the time directly influenced the physical landscape changes at Kincardine (Creighton 2009, 135, 151). Most parks and forests were, however, slowly dismantled from the 14th century when they were given over to the plough, as occurred at Enzie in 1327 (Shepherd 2021, 117–18).

As villages and towns grew around the ruling and ecclesiastic centres from the 12th century onwards, so the wider landscape became ever-more farmed. Estates with, originally customary and, subsequently, leasehold tenant landholders, created focused townships (fermtouns) consisting of small groups of houses, outbuildings and walled enclosures, beyond which lay largely unenclosed areas of arable and pasture. Rig and furrow agriculture, a technique of ploughing that forms parallel ridges and troughs, surrounded these townships. The most spectacular surviving example of this underlies Aboyne Golf Course (see Figure 1.2) where S-shaped rig and furrow adds an unexpected complexity to the physical landscape. Shepherd (2021, 34) notes the Reformation of the 16th century as marking a key boundary in agricultural practice within the region, with a significant, renewed, shift to even greater arable cultivation, the loss of extensive areas of forestry and upland grazing, and the introduction of new building techniques to offset the lack of timber.

The best townships, made so by being situated on the most fertile and well-drained soils with southerly aspects, and next to a water source, became the natural focus in the lowland areas during the post-medieval and early modern land improvements. The pattern of these townships is echoed today having been replaced by 18th- and 19th-century farmsteads which maintain the old place names. As farms grew bigger

Figure 1.2. Aboyne Golf Course overlying the remains of medieval and post-medieval rig and furrow agriculture. Photographed in 2006 (Photograph: Aberdeenshire Council Archaeology Service).

and lands merged, the estates shifted focus in the upland areas away from subsistence crofting to the more profitable sheep rearing, leading to wholesale removal of people from the glens, and the abandonment of their homes. The ruins seen today across the landscape are reminders of how quickly changes in land management can radically change an area's sense of place, and the cultural identity derived from it. The landscape was further altered by making it more accessible through the introduction of the toll-road network in the 18th century, through the arrival of the railways in AD 1853, and the industrialisation and expansion of the coastal harbours.

The last cultural landscape to touch on in this brief overview is that from the First and Second World Wars. The anti-invasion remains from the Second World War in particular form highly visible vestiges from this period, with long lines of anti-tank blocks along the coastline and the strategically located pillboxes. While people today will see these concrete structures as a reminder of a war they know about, having heard stories directly from relatives who experienced them first-hand, a new generation of connections are being made in relation to the threat of climate change. A recent survey observes, 'the concrete anti-tank cubes and associated structures, installed to defend Britain from invasion, may now be playing a secondary role as a kind of coastal defence, trapping sediment, and slowing erosion of mobile beach strands and dunes' (Boyd and Hambly 2023, 10).

Using an artefact to ask questions of the landscape

Taking each of these cultural landscapes and overlaying them in turn, across what is also an ever-changing physical landscape, creates a complexity of time-depth survival that can be daunting to understand. The rate of ongoing archaeological discoveries within the region, and the continuing progress of our nuanced understanding of how these remains relate to human activity in the past, show that that complexity will only continue to increase for decades to come.

Taking one artefact discovery as an example, and using that to pose, and then answer, questions about the complexity of the cultural landscape it was once part of, is a useful method to inform our perceptions of the time-depth behind the landscape we see today; what was it like then compared to now, what remains in the landscape today from that past, and how have people's ideas of culture and identity changed over time. The artefact in this instance was found by chance in 1902 during ploughing on a farm on the south side of Foudland Hill, a heather clad hill sitting to the north of and in parallel to Bennachie. Foudland is most easily recognised nowadays for the remains of the 18th- and 19th-century slate quarries across large swathes of its flanks, the produce of which accounts for the majority of traditional slate roofs seen across the region, including Balmoral Castle itself (Dean 1998, 17–19). The artefact is a red sandstone mould for the casting of flat bronze axes and ingots, dating to the Early Bronze Age, *c.* 2400 BC–1800 BC, and measuring approximately 210 mm by 176 mm (see Plate 1.4). The moulds have been carved into four faces of the block of stone, allowing for a total of four flat axes, three smaller axe-like tools, and two bars or ingots to be cast in differing sizes (Callander 1904, 487–9).

Callander (1904, 494) observed

> Stone moulds for flat bronze axes are by no means common in the British Isles and are less so on the Continent. ... They are, indeed, less numerous than might have been expected from the large number of flat bronze axes that have been found. That clay moulds were more often used might be suggested as a possible reason for this, but no clay moulds for flat bronze axes have been recorded; besides, it is not to be expected that an itinerant bronze-founder, as probably was the proprietor of this mould, would carry about a heavy stone mould if he could secure the less heavy one of clay.

The insight contained within the observation immediately connects the object with a person against a backdrop of trade, travel and opportunity within a wider landscape. Callander made the assumption that this individual would have found it necessary to travel over the country for the purposes of their craft. Indeed, if they 'had had his place of manufacture fixed in one locality, it is to be expected that he would have had his various moulds all on the top surface of several moulding stones, and not on the four sides of the same stone, as is in this case' (Callander 1904, 504). Callander goes on to also argue that a further indication that the mould travelled to where it was needed was because no bronze founder or merchant would carry finished articles with them owing to the scarcity of bronze in Scotland at this time. This latter justification becomes weaker with each new discovery, but the essence of the point Callander was making was evidence of one individual travelling around a dispersed community within the area. He concludes, 'Bronze Age man has left behind him some typical utensils, as well as numerous graves which have from time to time turned up, all which is clear testimony to his once having dwelt in the glens of Foudland' (Callander 1904, 505).

Not to be overlooked is the underlying bias, typical of the time, of the male role within the past suggested by Callander's wording. This in itself skews how past cultural landscapes are perceived, something that modern research is now correcting. We cannot fully understand the past by excluding sections of human society from our considerations, especially one as significant as gender (see Shepherd 2012 for a prime example of the value of an all-inclusive approach). For the purpose of this paper, we will merely consider the mould as being with an individual, in order to focus on the role landscape had to play in that person's life.

The arrival of bronze technology into Scotland *c.* 2200 BC required specialist knowledge to transform raw materials into valuable objects. It necessitated the development of new trade and exchange networks, not just within the British Isles, but also Europe. These specialists would have built on the small-scale movements established by people from various parts of mainland Europe to the British Isles which occurred during the preceding Chalcolithic period, and the Neolithic before that. The impact of the 'Beaker package', the catch-all term for a combination of new material goods, beliefs and practices that accompanied the metal, varied between regions (Bradley 2007, 143–4; Sheridan 2008) with some, such as the north-east of Scotland, quickly embracing and adopting this foreign cultural change.

The cultural package resulted in new monument forms being created, one form of which, the recumbent stone circle, is the most recognised and celebrated today within the region. The recumbent stone circles were themselves not freestanding structures but rather represented the end point in a protracted sequence of activity on each site, taking different forms over time (Bradley and Nimura 2016). Indeed Bradley notes that these 'rings of stones remained a significant feature of the landscape for such a long time that they were associated with renewed activity in four different phases: the later Bronze Age, the Early Iron Age, the Roman Iron Age, and the Pictish period' (Bradley and Nimura 2016, 122). That renewed focus of activity continues today where examples of these monuments that survive in the landscape act as visitor attractions. They remain a draw for the public, acting as a narrow window into the past. Easter Aquhorthies at Inverurie (HER NJ72SW0009, NRHE NJ72SW12) for instance is made accessible with its own visitor signposting, carpark, and interpretation boards; an arrangement that facilitates the average sightseer connecting with the Bronze Age, albeit through a tendency for mystical musings rather than everyday relatability towards those who lived around such monuments.

To return to the humble mould itself, we can use it as an artefact to expand on Callander's original thoughts about who was taking it across the landscape during this period of cultural transition. That person would have had to think about where to access resources within that landscape. Where were they going to get the wood for charcoal to achieve the necessary temperatures to begin the casting process? Where were the water sources needed for cooling and shaping the metal objects? How did they find out about potential consumers for their expertise? What were the communities that they encountered as they travelled like, did they share the same needs, were they in fact hostile towards the new technology? Then there is the how of navigating through the landscape; was it easy, were there established routes and friendly guides, or was it a lonely and harsh environment with the occasional oasis of civilisation? Answering these questions, through the archaeological evidence, allows for a far more nuanced understanding of how the physical and cultural landscape of that moment in our past affected the everyday lives of our ancestors. This in turn brings an altered perception of what the surviving elements of that cultural landscape represent today, a critical step in making cultural landscapes relevant and relatable to those living and working in the north-east.

Describing a Middle Bronze Age landscape

The Aberdeen Western Peripheral Route (AWPR), opened in 2018, provided an excellent opportunity to study a large swathe of landscape within the region. While there have been numerous large linear infrastructure projects resulting in archaeological discoveries previously in the north-east, the scale of this road development is one of the largest to date. The route's 58 km length was archaeologically investigated through a targeted programme of works, from 2012 to 2017, consisting of non-invasive surveys (geophysical, topographical, palaeoenvironmental, and building recording), systematic trial trenching, and targeted excavations. The resulting monograph (Dingwell *et al.* 2019) celebrates the resulting discoveries by aptly borrowing a phrase from 'Sunset Song' (Gibbon 1932, 119) for its title, 'The Land Was Forever'.

Of the new sites identified through these mitigation works, a number of Bronze Age settlements uncovered to the west of Aberdeen are of particular relevance to the questions posed by Callander and his itinerant bronze worker, albeit the features are later in date than the axe mould itself (Middle Bronze Age rather than Early Bronze Age). Along a 10 km stretch of the road line as it travels from the new bridge over the River Dee at Milltimber, up and over the higher ground overlooking Aberdeen, and down into the river valley of the Don, three settlement sites were identified at Nether Beanshill, Gairnhill, and Chapel of Stoneywood respectively.

The first of these, at Nether Beanshill, consisted of a Middle Bronze Age roundhouse (dated to 1600–1310 cal BC) and a contemporary cremation cemetery on the plateau of a hill slope at *c.* 110 m AOD. The next, at Gairnhill, lies 2.3 km to the north of Nether Beanshill, and while a multi-period site, the key remains were of one Middle Bronze Age roundhouse (dated to 1490–1270 cal BC) and six Late Bronze Age roundhouses (dated to 1150–800 cal BC) on a hill slope at *c.* 120 m AOD overlooking a small tributary of the River Dee. A further 6.8 km to the north of Gairnhill is the last site at Chapel of Stoneywood, again consisting of a single Middle Bronze Age roundhouse (dated to 1410–1210 cal BC) on a slope at *c.* 107 m AOD. It should be noted that prior to these sites being found and excavated, no other archaeological work had been undertaken within their general vicinity, and as such the landscape was somewhat of an unknown quantity beyond the visible remains of post-medieval and early modern agricultural practices.

Taking the radiocarbon dating into consideration, the landscape in the Middle Bronze Age (MBA) for this small transect of the north-east can be used as a proxy for that potentially encountered by our itinerant bronze-worker in the preceding period. Starting at the River Dee, and proceeding northwards along the same route as the modern bypass now takes, an individual would have first encountered Nether Beanshill, a post-built roundhouse approximately 8.3 m diameter, with a south-east facing entrance covered by a porch, sitting a short distance away from an outcropping of bedrock. The entranceway had a metalled surface, formed by small pebbles pressed into the natural deposits, presumably to help keep the space tidy and useable. Near to the entrance sat a small raised four-post structure, possibly used to keep grain off the ground and safe from pests. Roughly 50 m away lay the cremation complex consisting of three cremations, two within miniature ring-gullies and one marked by a horseshoe shaped arrangement of posts. While the cemetery is in close proximity to the roundhouse, the low rocky outcrop lies between them, affording a partial visual separation between the spaces. As speculated by the excavators,

> It is tempting to interpret this as a small family cemetery directly linked to the adjacent roundhouse. The presence of the burials so close to the house also suggests a certain concern with permanence in the landscape, not often associated with roundhouses that may have only been in use for a generation. (Dingwell *et al.* 2019, 203).

Moving northwards from this small family settlement, the contemporary community of Gairnhill was within an easy walk. Initially this site consisted of a single roundhouse nearly 10 m in diameter, again built using the post-ring architecture with a porch-entrance facing south. By the Late Bronze Age, the roundhouse had fallen out of use and six new ones constructed just to the north-west. The radiocarbon evidence from the four most closely clustered of these later buildings overlap in date to such an extent that they can be considered contemporary to one another (Dingwell *et al.* 2019, 157). Depending on when you arrived at this location, you would have seen it as a single building, or, later, as a small rural hamlet.

A longer walk this time, still continuing northwards, would take an individual to the third settlement along this route. The Chapel of Stoneywood site is again made up of a single post-built roundhouse, at least 6.5 m diameter in this instance. Owing to the steeper slope on which the roundhouse had been built, the post-holes upslope had survived owing to the deeper depths to which they had been dug, whereas the south-western part of the building was largely destroyed by later ploughing. It can be assumed, however, that like the other roundhouses, the entrance faced southwards, with a large projecting porch providing both shelter from the elements and an opportunity to impress visitors.

The environmental evidence from these three sites is in keeping with our understanding of the wider landscape during this period. Walking across the land, the natural woodland encountered would have been dominated by birch and hazel, with lesser amounts of oak and other species (Tipping 1994, 29). Alder would have been present along the waterways, while areas of heather moorland would cover higher ground. The impact of agriculture and grazing animals would have created open pasture and cultivated areas around each roundhouse dotted across the land, with light fencing providing functional divisions where required. All three of the singular roundhouse sites were constructed between 1550 BC and 1300 BC, and all abandoned by 1150 BC when the larger settlement at Gairnhill was formed (Dingwell *et al.* 2019, 194). Each roundhouse, a home for a small community (whether that be a family unit, an extended family unit, or something larger still), was within easy reach of each other, with the walk being no more than an hour between each.

Furthermore, the evidence goes beyond just the implication that these 'islands of settlement' were connected owing to their physical proximity to each other. All three of the MBA roundhouses produced assemblages of domestic pottery. One vessel from Nether Beanshill (Vessel 03-V09) has a T-shaped rim with a convex top. On the exterior two shallow grooves run horizontally around the pot. Lochrie (Dingwell *et al.* 2019, 183) notes, 'the shaping and smoothing of the rim has been carried out with a flat squared end, like a small spatula'. A similar vessel from Chapel of Stoneywood (Vessel 01-V04) displays the same characteristic shape, with two exterior grooves creating the same ridged upper body of the pot. Comparable ridges also appear on two vessels excavated from a contemporary roundhouse 17 km to the north at Oldmeldrum (Johnson 2010, 12–15). This points towards a shared cultural identity between these sites, with movement of both people and ideas between settlements.

While previously caveating the Foudland flat axe mould as dating to the Early Bronze Age, and these three contemporary sites revealed by the AWPR investigations are from the Middle Bronze Age, the cultural landscape evidence is one which we can usefully use to begin to answer Callander's questions. Evidence for Early Bronze Age settlement is rare within the north-east, but we can assume that any itinerant metal worker of the period would have met a scatter of roundhouses across the landscape as they travelled between potential consumers of their skills and products. They would have encountered people who knew their neighbours. As time went on, the physical landscape became more densely populated with more and more settlement, each with their own extended footprints of resource requirements. By the Late Bronze Age, this preference for individual homesteads declines, changing instead to more clustered groupings of roundhouses.

Throughout this period, the cultural landscape was one that was coherent within the north-east. Architecture through to pottery styles shared a common language at each stage of development. People moving within the region would encounter familiarity, while those arriving from outwith would experience a homogeneity that they could quickly understand and connect with. Callander's metalworker with his mould would have thrived within such a landscape, seizing upon the opportunities of local introductions between neighbouring communities, while contributing a key part of the cultural toolkit of the time. This simplified visualisation of a Bronze Age cultural landscape at a local level, one which sets aside the ongoing debates around expected lifespans of roundhouses and whether they were maintained structures or single-use (Pope 2015), allows for an easily relatable connection for those living in the north-east today as they commute past the individual farms and small townships that pepper the modern landscape.

Connecting past cultural landscapes to our current sense of place

The aim of the conference, and this subsequent publication, is to foster further connections between academics and local communities, and to realise the value of co-production when researching these landscapes of north-east Scotland. As touched on earlier, the public's perception of what constitutes original and authentic heavily influences their sense of who they are, and where they come from. The fact that landscape, and the cultural landmarks within it, have always helped people to define their identity is of course a shared trait that should resonate with each new generation.

As demonstrated with the Foudland axe mould, we have moved beyond the restrictive nature of just identifying and classifying site types and artefacts to a point where we are attempting to understand a more rounded context for those who once lived in the north-east. This also involves unpicking the complexity of how people experienced their landscapes, and how that led to the expressions of regional individuality seen time and again in the north-east when compared to the rest of Scotland or indeed the British Isles.

Taking the Neolithic monuments as an example, Brophy (2004, 145) eloquently captures the complexity of place, activity and memory when writing

> monuments are looking less and less like the monolithic icons of the age we once thought they were... All that remains of our 'monuments' are the places in which they are built. Because it is to the places people return again and again, not the monument. It is places that help recall the memories that sustain their importance, that make possible certain activities, and act as points or passages within wider patterns of movement.

The millennia of activity seen at the Mesolithic pit-alignment at Warren Field, continuing on into the Neolithic, is a prime example of this point.

Phenomenology, as applied in archaeology, offers a unique lens through which we can interpret these landscapes beyond just the physical remains of sites. It posits that our sensory experiences – what we see, hear, and feel – are integral to understanding the significance of places and spaces. Tilley's (2004) seminal work underscores this point, suggesting that our movement through space, the sounds we hear, and the memories we hold, contribute to a layered comprehension of our surroundings. Using this perspective for a more holistic approach to understanding our cultural landscapes acknowledges the subjective nature of human experience. However, phenomenology is not without its detractors (Brück 2005, 45–72). Critics argue that it lacks the empirical rigor of other methodologies and risks projecting contemporary perceptions onto ancient peoples, potentially distorting our understanding of their lived realities. Despite these criticisms, the phenomenological approach has enriched the archaeological discourse, encouraging consideration of the 'Archaeology of the Senses' (Hamilakis 2014) and the pivotal role of memory in how we experience our environment.

The integration of cognitive science into this approach addresses some of the concerns around the lack of empirical rigor. By marrying the subjective insights of phenomenology with the objective data of research and fieldwork, the combined approach can better describe the ways in which personal experiences shape people's perception of the world around them. Recently, in support of national heritage policy in Scotland, a pilot project based loosely around this combined methodology, titled 'Your Historic Place lens', has been developed for a modern-day society (Historic

Figure 1.3. Nigg Bay, Aberdeen in the early 1920s when it was used for recreation and escape from the city (Photograph: Adelphi Series No 573 © Charles Helmrich & Sons).

Environment Scotland 2023). As a tool, its intention is to help initiate and support conversations with local communities as they examine connections between people, place and the historic environment. It challenges people to consider what historic elements of their area shape the place it is today, and how they can help it be a successful place for the future.

This idea works well when people are aware of the cultural legacy contained within the landscapes they live, work and relax in. The jarring change at Nigg Bay, Aberdeen, from a popular green cove where the residents of the city once traditionally escaped to over a weekend (Figure 1.3), to the concrete industrial landscape of the new harbour opened in 2023 (Figure 1.4), is one that happened quickly, within a single lifetime, and is clearly transformative of the landscape.

Isolated pockets of the past, such as the ruins within the bay of St Fitticks (HER NJ90SE0001, NRHE NJ90SE1), first established in AD 1189, allow for remnant connections through memory and place with the previous version of the landscape. The rest is an entirely new landscape, and somewhat alien one, for everyone, waiting for fresh connections to be established.

Contrast this to the village of Insch in rural Aberdeenshire, where an individual's perception of the extent and scale of change will depend on their age and how long

Figure 1.4. Nigg Bay, Aberdeen in 2024 with the new harbour, representing a radically transformed landscape (Photograph: Bruce Mann).

they have known the village. Urban expansion has occurred in phases since the horse-shoe shape of the two halves of the village, Insch and Rothney respectively, were photographed in 1885 (Clemo n.d., 3). Suburbs are obviously modern in date, while the view down Commercial Street from the railway station is essentially unchanged since that seen in early photographic postcards taken in the early 1900s. This sense of timelessness reinforces a perception that this part of the village is unchanged, it represents the 'original'. The value then placed on the protection of this part of the community's heritage is elevated at a local level. That is why it is important that research uses all the tools available to it, including investigating people's perceptions of landscape. Oral histories and local narratives offer valuable information that may not be captured in the archaeological or historical record. They can provide personal and communal perspectives on the cultural significance of landscapes and sites.

Conclusion

Each epoch of the past has left an indelible mark on the north-east of Scotland, creating a patchwork of survival and influence that is as diverse as it is fascinating. Together they serve as a combined cultural heritage that continues to shape the identity of the region today, one which gives the landscape a 'soul'. Exploring these landscapes, and the monuments within them, allows us to connect with the myriad of stories that have unfolded across this ancient land.

Of course, the need to balance conservation of the historic environment with the demands of modern life presents ongoing challenges. Initiatives like the Bennachie Landscapes Project, which aims to engage the community in taking an active role in exploring, investigating and preserving both the cultural and the natural heritage of the region, highlights the importance of sustainable management of the landscape. The landscape helps inform our identity not only through individual experience of the present, and how we value that which lies around us, but also through offering insights into where we have come from.

Looking ahead, the landscape will continue to evolve. Climate change, population growth, and technological advancements, will all shape the future appearance of the land. The public's role in this evolution is crucial, as their perceptions and actions will influence the direction of landscape management and inform conservation efforts for what should be saved. We all need to encourage interdisciplinary collaboration to enrich the research process and outcomes when examining our past. Including community voices in the study of their own cultural heritage is essential, not only to foster a sense of ownership and engagement, but critically because that heritage is part of them, of who they are, and what it means to be from the north-east of Scotland.

Acknowledgments

I would like to begin by thanking the organisers of the conference, including the Bennachie Landscapes Project, the University of Aberdeen, and the Bailies of

Bennachie, on which this publication is based, and for inviting me to give the opening key-note address. In particular, I would like to thank Colin Shepherd, not only for being the driving force behind the conference and this resulting publication, but also for his invaluable contributions to landscape archaeology in the region over the years. The papers that follow represent a myriad of different research across the entire stretch of human activity here in north-east Scotland since the end of the last ice age. I would like to thank each author of those papers for continuing to ask questions of the landscapes around us. Finally, I would like to thank my former colleagues, Moira Greig and the late Ian Shepherd, from whom I learnt so much when looking at what surrounds us, whether at ground level or from above, and my current colleague, Caroline Palmer, for kindly reviewing this paper.

Sources

DSL, Various (2005) *Dictionary of the Scots Language*. SND Vol IX. Doi. www.dsl.ac.uk/entry/snd/teuchter

HER, Aberdeenshire Council Archaeology Service (2024) *Aberdeenshire Historic Environment Record (HER)*. Aberdeen, Aberdeenshire Council. Doi. www.online.aberdeenshire.gov.uk/

Historic Environment Scotland (2023) Your Historic Place lens. Available at: https://www.historicenvironment.scot/archives-and-research/publications/

NRHE, Historic Environment Scotland (2024) National Record of the Historic Environment (NRHE) (Edinburgh, Historic Environment Scotland). Doi. www.canmore.org.uk/site/

Bibliography

Alexander, W. (1892) The Making of Aberdeenshire. In *Transactions of the Aberdeen Philosophical Society* 2, 102–22. Aberdeen, University of Aberdeen.

Armit, I. and Büster, L. (2020) *Darkness Visible: The Sculptor's Cave, Covesea, from the Bronze Age to the Picts*. Edinburgh, Society of Antiquaries of Scotland.

Ballin, T.B. and Wickham-Jones, C. (2017) Searching for the Scottish Late Upper Palaeolithic: A case study from Nethermills Farm, Aberdeenshire. In *Journal of Lithic Studies* 4(1). Doi. www.doi.org/10.2218/jls.v4i1.1907

Boyd, S. and Hambly, J. (2023) *Coastal Zone Assessment Survey Aberdeenshire and City of Aberdeen: Cullen to Milton Ness*. St Andrews, The SCAPE Trust, University of St Andrews.

Bradley, R. (2007) *The Prehistory of Britain and Ireland*. Cambridge, Cambridge University Press.

Bradley, R. (2011) *Stages and Screens: An investigation of four henge monuments in Northern and North-Eastern Scotland*. Edinburgh, Society of Antiquaries of Scotland.

Bradley, R. and Nimura, C. (2016) *The Use and Reuse of Stone Circles*. Oxford, Oxbow Books.

Brophy, K. (2004) Ruins in the landscape: modern monuments. In Hunter, F. and Ralston, I.B.M. (eds) *The Later Bronze Age and Iron Age of Scotland from a European Perspective*, 143–54. Oxford, Oxbow Books.

Brück, J. (2005) Experiencing the past? The development of a phenomenological archaeology in British prehistory. In *Archaeological Dialogues* 12, 45–72.

Callander, J.G. (1904) Notice of a Stone Mould for Casting Flat Bronze Axes and Bars found in the Parish of Insch, Aberdeenshire; with Notes on the occurrence of Flat Axe Moulds in Europe. In *Proceedings of the Society of Antiquaries of Scotland* 38, 487–505.

Cameron, A. and Ballin, T. B. (2018) Artefacts of Buchan flint from Greenacres, Wester Clerkhill, Peterhead, Aberdeenshire. In *Archaeological Reports Online* 32. Doi. www.archaeologyreportsonline.com/reports/2018/ARO32.html

Clemo, M.G. (n.d.) *Historic Insch*. Insch, Mrs Margaret G. Clemo.

Cook, M. and Dunbar, L. (2008) Rituals, Roundhouses and Romans. Excavations at Kintore, Aberdeenshire 2000–2006. Volume 1: Forest Road. In *Scottish Trust for Archaeological Research Monograph 8*. Edinburgh, Scottish Trust for Archaeological Research.

Cook, M., Kdolska, H., Dunbar, L., Engl, R, Sagrott, S., Druce, D. and Cook, G. (2010) New light on oblong forts: excavations at Dunnideer, Aberdeenshire. In *Proceedings of the Society of Antiquaries of Scotland* 140, 79–91.

Cook, M. (2011a) Maiden Castle, Insch, Aberdeenshire: Choice and Architecture in Pictland. In *Tayside and Fife Archaeological Journal* 17, 25–35.

Cook, M. (2011b) New evidence for the activities of Pictish potentates in Aberdeenshire. In *Proceedings of the Society of Antiquaries of Scotland* 141, 215–16.

Creighton, O.H. (2009) *Designs Upon the Land. Elite landscapes of the Middle Ages*. Woodbridge, The Boydell Press.

Dean, A. (1998) *Foudland: Slate Quarriers and Crofters in Aberdeenshire*. Aberdeen, Dean.

Dingwall, K., Ginnever, M., Tipping, R., van Wessel, J. and Wilson, D. (2019) *The Land was Forever: 15,000 years in North-East Scotland*. Oxford, Oxbow Books.

Eumenius (297) Pro restaurandis scholis. In *Panegyrici Latini IX*.

Fairweather, A.D. and Ralston, I.B.M. (1993) The Neolithic timber hall at Balbridie, Grampian Region, Scotland: the building, the date, the plant macrofossils. In *Antiquity* 67, 313–23.

Gibbon, L.G. (1932) *Sunset Song*. London, Jarrolds Publishing.

Gilbert, J.M. (1979) *Hunting and Hunting Reserves in Medieval Scotland*. Edinburgh, John Donald.

Hall, D. and Malloy, K. (2016) Always chasing deer – further excavations at Buzzart Dykes and Kincardine Park and new excavations at Kincardine Castle in 2013. In *Tayside and Fife Archaeological Journal* 21/22, 25–34.

Hamilakis, Y. (2014) *Archaeology and the Senses: Human Experience, Memory and Affect*. Cambridge, Cambridge University Press.

Henderson, G. and Henderson, I. (2004) *The Art of the Picts: Sculpture and Metalwork in Early Medieval Scotland*. London, Thames and Hudson.

Hunter, F. (2007) *Beyond the edge of the empire – Caledonians, Picts and Romans*. Rosemarkie, Groam House Museum.

Johnson, M. (2010) Prehistoric Pottery. In White, R. and Richardson, P. (eds) The Excavation of Bronze Age Roundhouses at Old Meldrum, Aberdeenshire. *Scottish Archaeological Internet Reports (SAIR)* 43. Edinburgh, Society of Antiquaries of Scotland.

Murray, H.K., Murray, J.C. and Fraser, S.M. (2009) *A Tale of the Unknown Unknowns: A Mesolithic Pit Alignment and a Neolithic Timber Hall at Warren Field, Crathes, Aberdeenshire*. Oxford, Oxbow Books.

Murray, H.K. and Murray, J.C. (2014) Mesolithic and Early Neolithic activity along the Dee: excavations at Garthdee Road, Aberdeen. In *Proceedings of the Society of Antiquaries of Scotland* 144, 1–64.

Noble, G. and Evans, N. (2022) *Picts: Scourge of Rome, Rulers of the North*. Edinburgh, Birlinn.

Noble, G., Greig, M., Millican, K., Anderson, S., Clarke, A., Johnson, M., McLaren, D. and Sheridan, A. (2012) Excavations at a Multi-period Site at Greenbogs, Aberdeenshire, Scotland and the Four-post Timber Architecture Tradition of Late Neolithic Britain and Ireland. In *Proceedings of the Prehistoric Society* 78, 135–71.

Noble, G., Gondek, M., Campbell, E. and Cook, M. (2013) Between prehistory and history: the archaeological detection of social change among the Picts. In *Antiquity* 87, 1142–3.

Piggott, S. (1974) Excavation of the Dalladies long barrow, Fettercairn, Kincardinshire. Edinburgh. In *Proceedings of the Society of Antiquaries of Scotland* 104, 23–47.

Pope, R.E. (2015) Bronze Age architectural traditions: dates and landscapes. In Hunter, F. and Ralston, I.B.M. (eds) *The Later Bronze Age and Iron Age of Scotland from a European Perspective*, 159–84. Oxford, Oxbow Books.

Savory, G. (2020) *Moray East Offshore Wind Farm, Onshore Cable Route, Aberdeenshire: Section 1, Archaeological Excavation Report No. 3919*. Musselburgh, CFA Archaeology Ltd.
Schlüter, O. (1908) *Über den Begriff der Kulturlandschaft*. Halle, Verlag von Gebauer-Schwetschke.
Shepherd, A. (2012) Stepping Out Together: men, women and their Beakers in time and space. In Allen, M.J., Gardiner, J., Sheridan, A. and McOmish, D. (eds) The British Chalcolithic; place and polity in the later 3rd millennium. In *Prehistoric Society Research Papers* 4, 257–280. Oxford, Oxbow Books.
Shepherd, C. (2021) *The Late Medieval Landscape of North-East Scotland*. Oxford, Windgather Press.
Sheridan, A. (2007) From Picardie to Pickering and Pencraig Hill? New information on the 'Carinated Bowl Neolithic' in northern Britain. In Whittle, A. and Cummings, V. (eds) *Going Over: The Mesolithic-Neolithic Transition in North-West Europe*. London, British Academy.
Sheridan, A. (2008) Towards a fuller, more nuanced narrative of Chalcolithic and Early Bronze Age Britain 2500–500 cal BC. In *Bronze Age Review* 1, 57–78.
Stringer, K.J. (1985) *Earl David of Huntingdon, A Study in Anglo-Scottish History*. Edinburgh, Edinburgh University Press.
Tilley, C.Y. (2004) *The Materiality of Stone: Explorations in Landscape Phenomenology*. Oxford, Routledge.
Tipping, R. (1994) The form and fate of Scotland's woodlands. In *Proceedings of the Society of Antiquaries of Scotland* 124, 1–54.

Chapter 2

A major glacial lake in north-east Scotland

Andrew Wainwright

Introduction

This study looks at the evidence for a major ice-dammed lake covering much of north-east Scotland with a maximum elevation of about 250 m above mean sea level (amsl). The story of discovery is one of serendipity and luck. It begins with the excavations

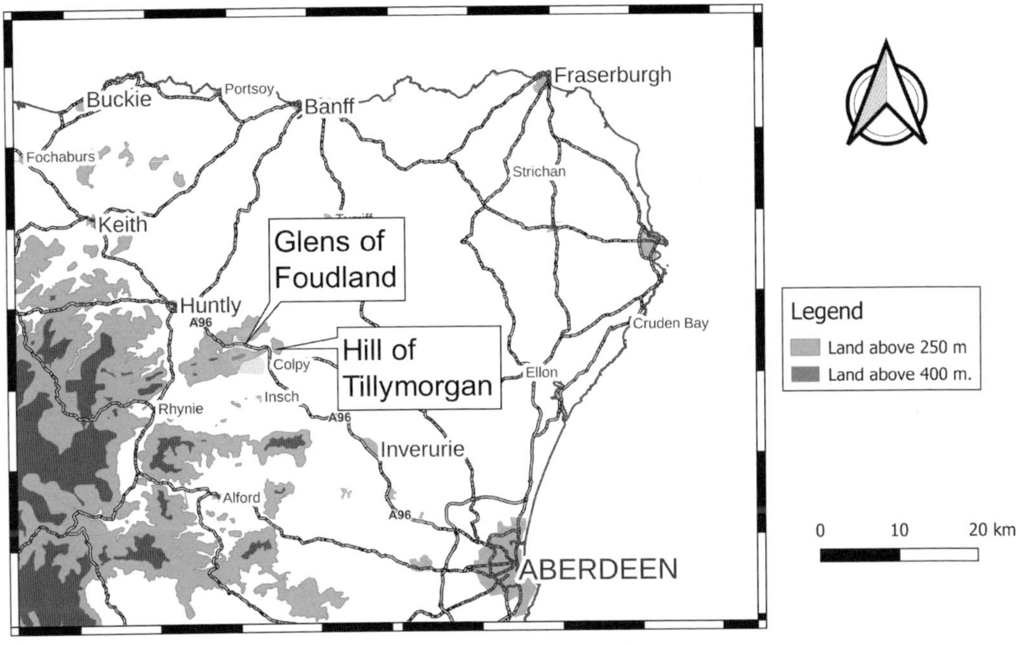

Figure 2.1. Location map of north-east Scotland showing the Hill of Tillymorgan, and Glens of Foudland. Land above the 250 m contour is the approximate western and southern limit of the proposed lake (Drawn from Ordnance Survey Open Data).

of the Bennachie Landscape Group at Druminnor Castle, whilst looking at fragments of slate collected from destruction layers of the castle and from adjacent field-walking. The author, being a geologist, was asked to investigate whether the samples could all be derived locally from the slate belt running from Hill of Tillymorgan to Gartly or, alternatively, imported from the better-quality slate-workings on the west coast. It was, therefore, decided to visit the slate-workings at the top of the Hill of Tillymorgan in order to try to discover the answer. At the time, it was noticed that three wind-turbines were being erected near there, the groundworks for which, it was hoped, would provide a good view of the underlying geology. Access was granted by the landowners and at the top of the road, fortuitously, there was a trench that had recently been dug for the power cables of the turbines.

Tillymorgan section

Within this trench at the top of the road was a band of well-sorted gravel with a sharp and nearly horizontal basal contact with unsorted slate debris below. The gravel consists of pebbles of slate up to about 50 mm diameter and is rounded or sub-rounded. The individual pebbles are in contact with each other with little clay or silt matrix between them. This structure might be described as 'clast- supported'. As a result, they are porous and permeable and water was seen flowing out of the gravel at a steady rate (see Plate 2.1). The underlying slate debris is an unsorted mix of fragments of slate of all sizes up to about 150 mm and angular in shape. The clasts are supported in a mud matrix and there is no significant porosity or permeability in this material. The whole sequence is overlain by further slate debris. A comparison between the clasts from the proposed 'beach' and the slate debris is shown in Plate 2.2.

An initial interpretation of this gravel was that it appeared to be a beach deposit. However, it is located at about 240 m amsl, which is much higher than any other beaches in north-east Scotland. Consequently, further evidence was sought to strengthen this interpretation. The electrical cables extended down the hill below this exposure but the trench had already been filled-in. However, the trench also extended uphill towards the turbines and was still open. A brief examination was made before it too was in-filled. Gravels were seen up to about 260 m

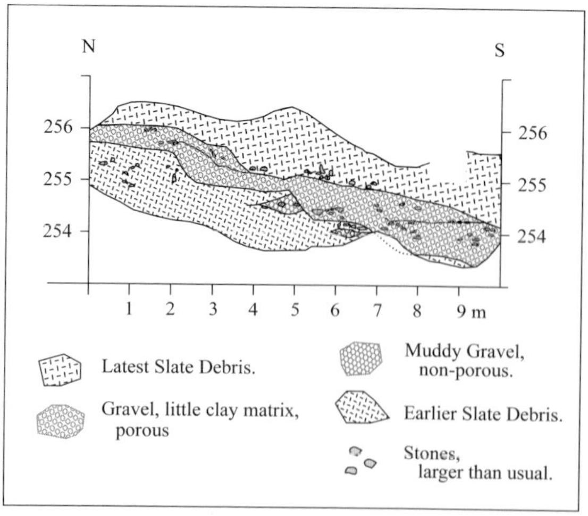

Figure 2.2. Drawing of gravels seen in a small temporary quarry on the Hill of Tillymorgan. Several postulated beaches are seen with near horizontal basal contacts with underlying slate debris.

but not beyond. A small quarry was found where gravel had been extracted for the engineering works. This exposed a good sequence of gravel and slate debris showing a form that is a better example of stacked beaches, all extending out into the valley and pinching out towards the hillside (Figure 2.2).

Whilst looking for further evidence of these beaches at a similar elevation, it was noticed that Scottish Gas Networks (SGN) were laying a gas pipeline to the west of the A96, from the village of Colpy to a farm at Jericho. Unfortunately, by the time this was noticed the trench had also been filled in and no further information was available from that site.

Bogs of Foudland section

In 2019 further serendipity ensued and it was noticed that SGN were extending their pipeline from Jericho down to the Bogs of Foudland. Subsequently, the author visited the site and permission was kindly given to examine their trench as it was dug and lay open. Obviously, these visits had to comply with SGN's Health and Safety rules

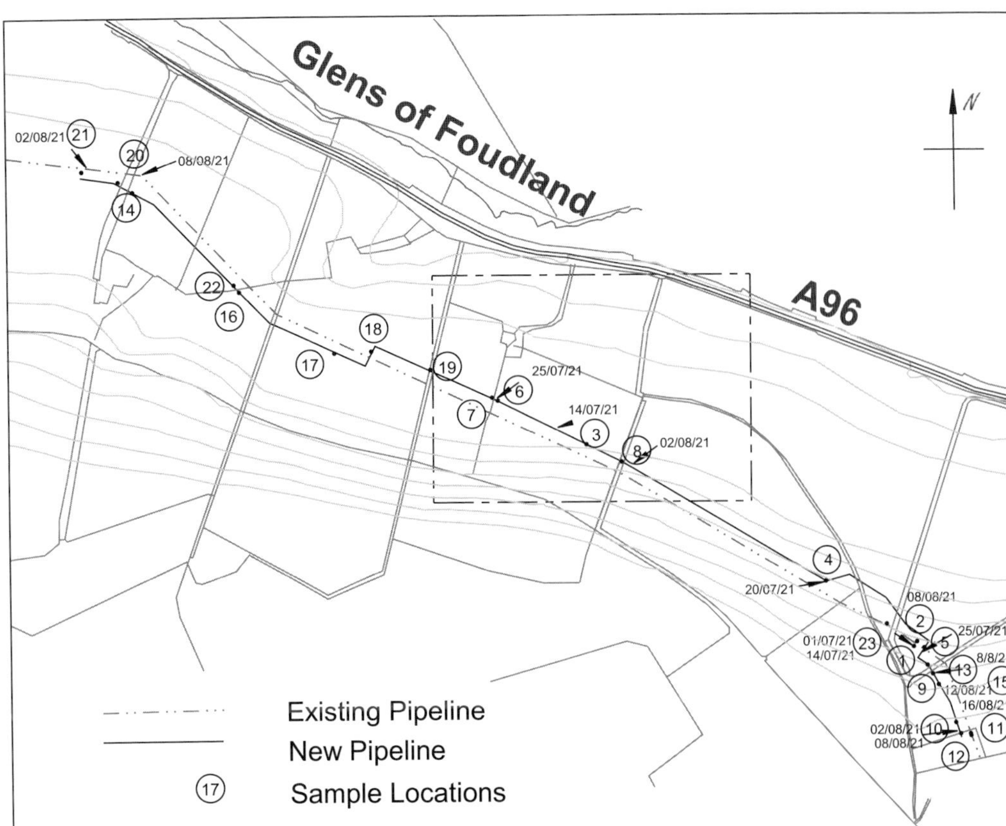

Figure 2.3. Plan of the pipeline from Jericho to the Glens of Foudland. Numbers in circles show the locations examined and sampled.

and an employee was required to accompany the author on all occasions. This placed serious constraints on the time available for visits: sections of the trench were only open for a day or two and, consequently, it was never possible to go back to double-check an observation or to improve on drawings or photos. However, almost the entire section was examined.

The pipeline runs down the north flank of the Hill of Foudland from the pass over from the farm of Jericho in the east to the farm of East Bog in the west (Figure 2.3). The hillside is underlain by Pre-Cambrian metamorphosed sediments of the Dalradian Supergroup. The higher levels are mapped by the British Geological Survey as the Hill of Foudland Pelite Member of the Macduff Formation, consisting of poor-quality slates, while the lower slopes are mapped as undifferentiated Macduff Formation, which contains metamorphic sandstones as well as the slates.

During the later part of the glacial period, when this part of north-east Scotland was not completely buried under ice, the surface rocks would have been frozen solid for several hundred metres and so completely impermeable to any liquid water. During this time the principal form of sediment transport and deposition would have occurred by a process called 'solifluction' or 'freeze-thaw'. This is illustrated on Figure 2.4. During the winter, water in the top metre or so of the sediment freezes and expands, so that the material is driven upwards, perpendicular to the ground surface. In the spring it melts and falls back down vertically, so moving slightly downhill each year. In this way the sediment gets steadily more mixed-up while moving downhill, eventually becoming an unsorted muddy 'melange'. The consequence of this is seen along most of the pipeline trench, resulting in a melange of slate clasts in a matrix of sand, silt and mud. The resulting sediment has been referred to here as 'slate debris'.

Other lithologies were seen along the trench (see Figure 2.5). Thin beds of well-sorted slate clasts up to approximately 10 mm in diameter occur at various levels. They are more rounded than the slate debris and are clast-supported, *i.e.* the individual fragments are in contact with very little intervening muddy-matrix. They show porosity and permeability, and occasionally water was seen flowing from them. They have been interpreted here again as beach deposits. The best one was seen at an elevation of 240 m, which is similar to that of the first beach seen on the south side of the Hill of Tillymorgan. However, this latter one is not as thick and the clasts are smaller and less well-rounded. Whilst these were being deposited in

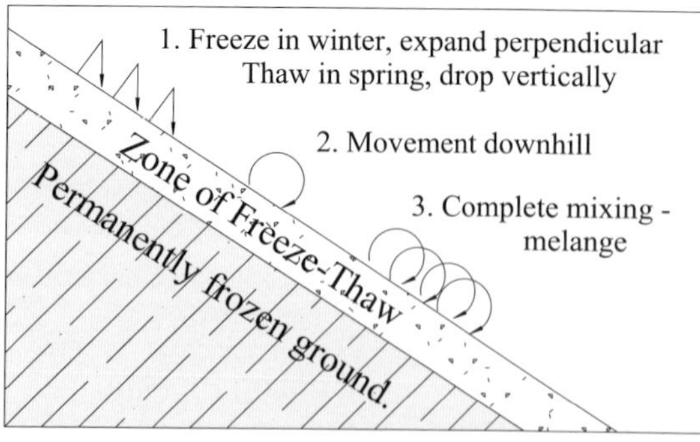

Figure 2.4. Illustration of solifluxion. sediment freezes and expands in winter. Then in spring and summer it thaws and contracts. As a consequence, it flows downhill and forms a melange of 'slate debris'.

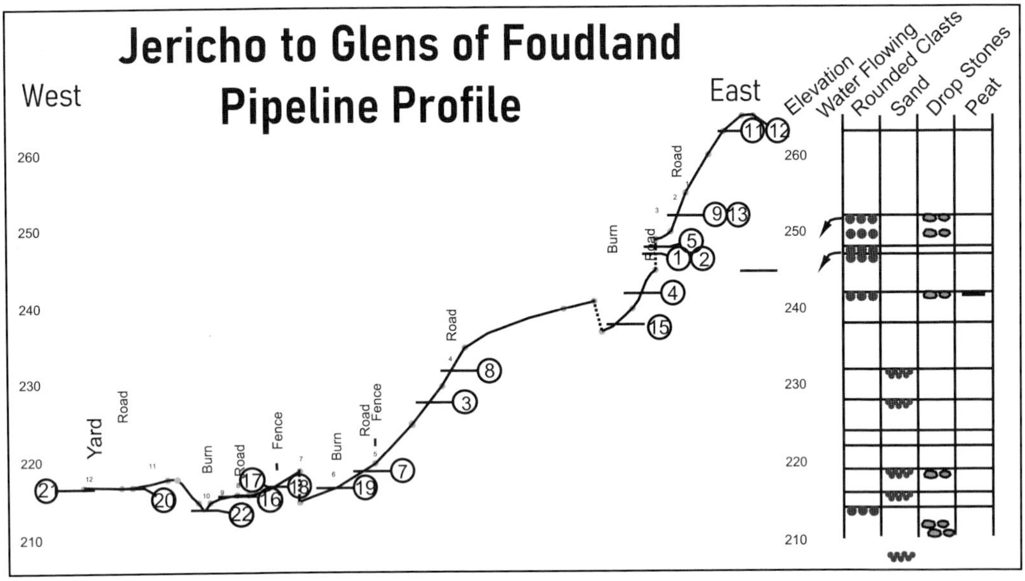

Figure 2.5. Profile of pipeline showing examined and sampled locations (in circles), occurrences of various lithologies and where water was observed flowing from the sediments.

the dim geological past, the prevailing wind was probably from the south-west and so the beach on this north side of the hill, may have been sheltered and the beach, consequently, less well-developed.

Beds of silt or fine sand were also seen at various locations. These are usually tens of centimetres thick but occasionally they may be up to a metre. They have a muddy matrix and are commonly yellowish in colour; they are not porous. They are very uniform in structure and no bedding or banding has been recorded. Isolated stones of a totally foreign lithology are sometimes seen in these sediments and these beds are sometimes in close proximity to the porous beds of sorted fine slate clasts. These stones are totally out of context with the surrounding material in that they are of a different lithology, indicating that they did not originate from this area. They are rounded and smooth or even polished (Plate 2.4). They may be isolated or arranged along a horizontal plane, presumably a bedding plane (Plate 2.5). At many points along the trench the slate debris rests on slate bedrock in its original position. This slate is somewhat rotten and weathered and the bedding has been rotated and broken up. This is normal for rock exposed to erosion for considerable periods of time.

Interpretation

The slate debris consists of the same material as that outcropping on the top of the hill. It is highly likely that it was brought down by solifluction processes which resulted in the very poor sorting along with large amounts of muddy matrix. Along most of the section it is homogeneous and unbedded; only towards the base of the valley is a poor layering visible (see Plate 2.6).

At places the slate debris has been subject to mechanical abrasion and the finer clasts (5 to 15 mm range) are rounded or sub-rounded, and the matrix has almost been removed. The resulting sediment is clast-supported. However, larger clasts of slate are still present either in the same bed or very close to it. These sediments are interpreted as beach deposits formed alongside a lake at that elevation. However, the poor degree of sorting and rounding would suggest that the energy along this shoreline was less than that seen on the south side of the Hill of Tillymorgan, most likely because it was protected from the prevailing south-westerly winds, or that it was located in a sheltered bay (Figure 2.1).

Wave action along a shoreline of a lake would have winnowed the slate debris and washed out the finer material. This would have been carried into deeper water and deposited as silts and sands. The fact that they are more common and thicker towards the base of the section would agree with this interpretation. Normally, fine sediments deposited in glacial lakes show fine laminations, called varves. In the summer, silts, which are pale in colour, are deposited. Then, in the winter when the lake is frozen over and sediment input is reduced, darker coloured mud settles out of the water column. On other local sites where the author has worked on possible glacial lake silts, varves have not been seen. However, very fine banding due to grain size or porosity variation has occasionally been seen after a well-cleaned section has been exposed for a week or two. Because of time constraints this was not possible to observe on this site.

The origin of the exotic stones seen in many parts of the section needs an explanation. They are of a completely different lithology from all other rocks in the neighbourhood. Usually, they are very hard, metamorphic or igneous rocks, commonly rounded, very smooth and often of a very different size to the material around them. As such they could be referred as 'lone stones', which is a term carrying no suggestion concerning place of origin or method of transport – just that they are 'out of place'. However, the formation of such foreign material has been described in the literature (Hartley *et al.* 2020) as due to a wide range of causes: volcanic action, 'rafting' in tree roots or other organic material, mass gravity flows, or 'ice-rafting'. In this area, during the Ice Age, with glaciers and ice caps in the area, 'ice-rafting' is seen as the most likely explanation. As such they almost fit the definition of 'drop-stones', except that they are not seen to disturb varves or other layering in the sediments, possibly because no varves have been recognised in this section. They are most likely fragments of rock caught up in icebergs floating on the lake surface and being dropped when the ice melted in summer (Figure 2.6). The source of the ice might have been lake-ice that either incorporated beach material when it froze in winter or acted as the recipient of rocks falling off adjacent hills in winter. Alternatively it may have been glacier ice retaining incorporated rocks from its source area. The latter explanation is preferred here because the stones are exotic to the local area, commonly very smooth or even

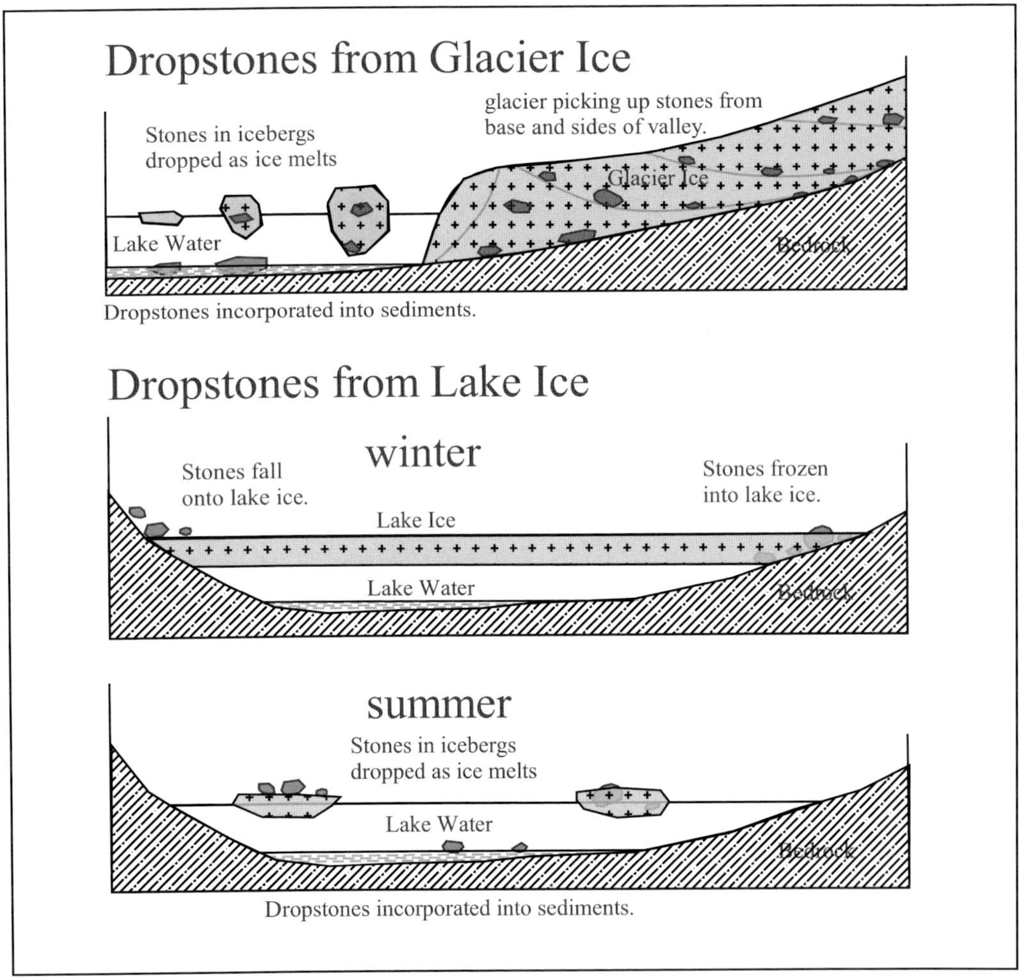

Figure 2.6. Diagram to illustrate the deposition of 'drop-stones' from glacier ice or lake ice.

polished. This is more likely to be expected in the dynamic situation within glacier ice than along a beach where a rougher, less rounded, surface would be expected.

So, all the lithologies and features seen on Hill of Tillymorgan and along the pipeline section are consistent with the hypothesis of deposition in a glacial lake with a maximum elevation of around 250 m amsl. However, categoric proof of such an environment has not so far been seen and other methods of deposition might still be considered.

If such a lake existed it would have been bordered on the south by the Bennachie massif, and on the west by the Cabrach and the hills of the Clashindarroch (Figure 2.1). To the north and east there are no hills of sufficient height to provide even a partial barrier. Instead, it is proposed that the limits to the lake in these

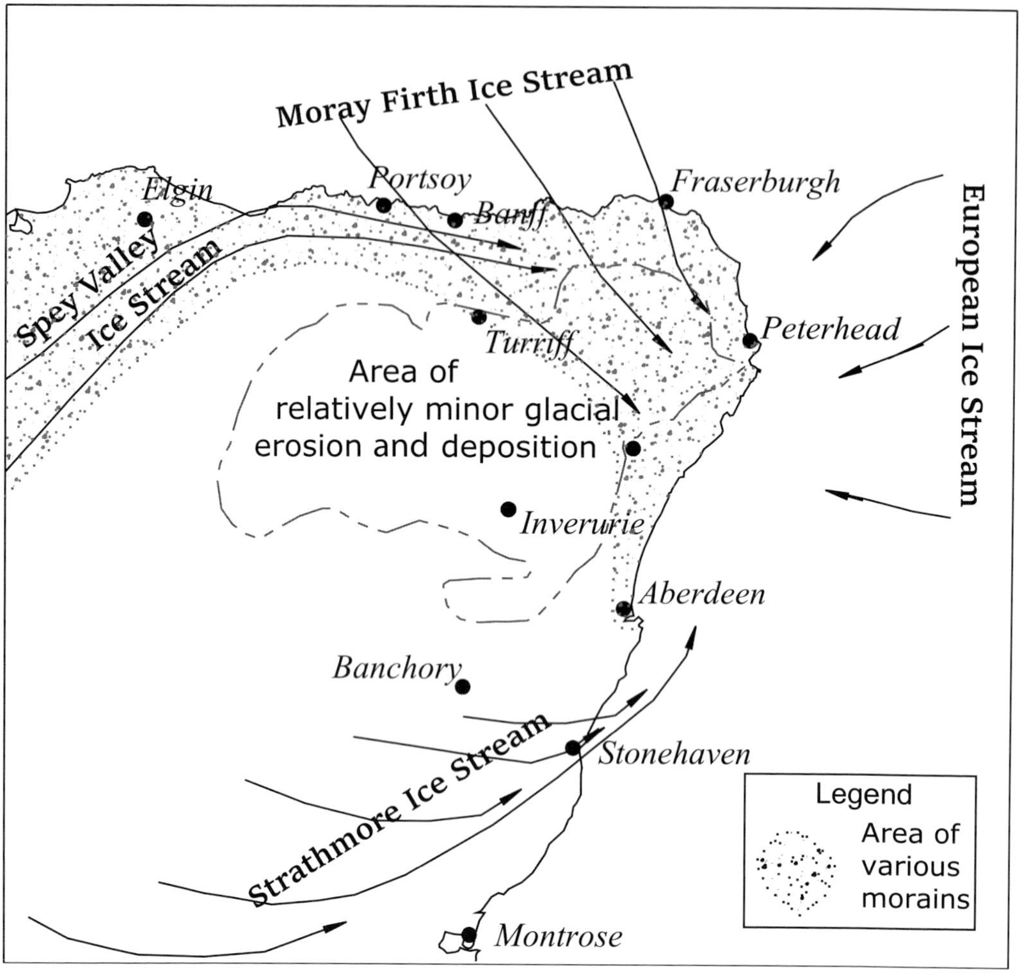

Figure 2.7. Map showing the various ice streams affecting the north-east of Scotland and the area where little evidence of glacial action has been recorded (Data after Merritt et al. *2017).*

directions was provided by ice which, at that time, filled the North Sea Basin. A full discussion of the distribution of ice during this period is given by Merrett *et al.* (2003). A major ice-stream came up from Strathmore, bringing with it red-stained debris from the red Devonian sediments in that area (see Figure 2.7). This is now recognised as red till or boulder clay along the Aberdeenshire coast almost as far north as Peterhead. Similarly, ice-streams flowed out of Strath Spey and Loch Ness, bringing debris from the hard metamorphic rocks of the Highlands, which is now seen as grey boulder clays along the coast from Inverness to Portsoy. Finally, ice also came out of the Northern Highlands and Moray Firth, bringing the dark muds of the Kimeridge Clay Formation, now seen as a dark or black boulder clay between Elgin and Peterhead. These ice-streams were pushed onto the Scottish coast by a further, major ice-stream flowing out of northern Europe, over Denmark and southern Sweden.

Merritt has mapped the glacial sediments for the British Geological Survey (BGS) (Merritt *et al.* 2003) and has recorded most of the principal locations of these boulder clays and other indications of glacial action. It is noticeable that they all occur near to the coasts with none in the area south and west of Turriff or Ellon. Merritt also illustrates the locations of glacial moraines (*ibid.*, fig. 8) over north-east Scotland. They are similarly noticeably absent over the same area. Furthermore, Synge (1956) mapped an area almost coincident with the proposed lake as an area of minor glacial erosion. This area is also almost devoid of stone dykes, suggesting that it is underlain by fine-grained sediments, such as those deposited from a lake, and not by boulder clay with the accompanying large blocks of glacially produced rock.

Age of the lake

It is known that at the peak of the glacial period this whole area was totally covered by ice with only a few mountain tops still showing, known as nunataks. As the weather ameliorated the ice gradually wasted away, probably by melting from the top-down rather than by moving en masse into the North Sea. Eventually, the top of Mither Tap of Bennachie was uncovered. This has been dated by cosmogenic nuclide techniques as reported by Ballantine and Small (2019, fig. 19) as 20.6 ka (thousand years) before present. Also, marine shells have been found near St Fergus and radiocarbon-dated to between 18 and 17.5 ka (*ibid.*, fig. 24). By this time, the ice-dam must have disappeared in order to allow the sea to invade the area. Thus the age of the lake must be between these two extreme dates, or in the region of 19 ka. This would relate to the later Palaeolithic period in Britain.

Conclusions

Evidence has been presented to support the hypothesis of a major glacial lake covering much of north-east Scotland at an elevation of about 250 m amsl. At this level, clast-supported gravels, interpreted as beach deposits, have been seen. 'Drop-stones' or 'lone stones' have been seen at many elevations and interpreted as having been dropped from melting ice floating on the lake. The lake was limited to the west by the hills of the Clashindarroch, to the south by the Bennachie massif, but to the north and east it was damned up by ice-streams flowing out of western Europe, the Moray Firth and Strathmore. The age of the lake is estimated at between 18 and 19 ka as Mither Tap was ice-covered until 20.6 ka and marine molluscs dated at between 18 and 17.5 ka have been recovered from St Fergus. The lake would therefore have been present during the late Palaeolithic (the Mesolithic is generally regarded as starting around 9000 BP soon after the final disappearance of the ice) when the climate would have been extremely cold, probably similar to the area surrounding the present arctic ocean. People are able to exist in such parts today and there is no reason why they should not have done so then. Pederzani *et al.* (2024) have shown that *Homo sapiens* was able to survive in northern Germany 45,000 years ago when conditions would have been similar to those envisaged here.

Acknowledgements

Without the help and enthusiastic support of Scottish Gas Networks and their staff this project would not have been possible. Thanks are due to Dr Jessica Pugsley of Aberdeen University for help with an early draft and for helpful comments from Dr Jon Merritt of the British Geological Survey. The support of members of the Bailies of Bennachie are also recorded with gratitude.

Bibliography

Ballantyne, C.K. and Small, D. (2019) The Last Scottish Ice Sheet. In *Earth and Environmental Science Transactions of the Royal Society of Edinburgh* 110(1/2), 93–131.

Hartley, A., Kurjanski, B., Pugsley, J. and Armstrong, J. (2020) Ice-rafting in lakes in the early Neoproterozoic: dropstones in the Diabaig Formation, Torridon Group, NW Scotland. In *Scottish Journal of Geology* 56, 47–53.

Merritt, J.W., Auton, C.A., Connell E.R. *et al.* (2003) *Cainozoic Geology and Landscape Evolution of North-East Scotland.* Edinburgh, British Geological Survey.

Merritt, J.W., Connell, E.R. and Hall, A.M. (2017) Middle to Late Devensian glaciation of north-east Scotland: implications for the north-eastern quadrant of the last British-Irish ice sheet. In *Journal of Quaternary Science* 32(2), 276–94.

Pederzani, S., Britton, K., Trost, M., *et al.* (2024) Stable isotopes show *Homo sapiens* dispersed into cold steppes ~45,000 years ago at Ilsenhöhle in Ranis, Germany. In *Nature Ecology & Evolution.* Doi. https://doi.org/10.1038/s41559-023-02318-z

Synge, F.M. (1956) The glaciation of north-east Scotland. In *Scottish Geographical Magazine* 72, 129–43.

Chapter 3

Beyond the north-western frontiers of the Roman Empire: exploring the impacts of the Romans on farming communities in north-eastern Scotland

Samantha Jones and Gordon Noble

Introduction

Hadrian's Wall is often considered the most north-westerly frontier of the Roman Empire and indeed it was for almost 300 years between *c.* AD 122 and *c.* AD 410, but, for albeit very brief periods of time, there were two other frontiers in northern Britain located 178–240 km further north: 1, the Antonine Wall (~178 km further north), which was constructed (taking 6–12 years to build) and occupied between AD 142 and AD 165, and 2, less well known – the Gask Ridge frontier (~240 km further north, located between Dunblane in Stirling and the Tay in Perthshire), which was constructed and occupied between *c.* AD 79/80 until AD 86 during the Flavian campaigns (Woollisroft and Hoffman 2006) and consisted of a series of towers, forts, and fortlets along a Roman road as well as a secondary line of forts, incorporating the legionary fort of Inchtuthil.

The location of the Gask Ridge and other temporary camps constructed within north-eastern Scotland during this period would have sent a strong signal to local communities highlighting the military might of the Roman army and the potential consequences of local resistance. It would equally have brought local farming communities living beyond the frontier regions into more frequent contact with the Roman military, compared to the later Roman Iron Age when the frontier was more firmly situated behind Hadrian's Wall. This is perhaps most strongly evident in the archaeological records where a higher proportion of luxury Roman items across north-eastern Scotland have been found at Iron Age settlements dating to the Flavian and Antonine periods compared to the later Roman Iron Age (Robertson 1983; Hunter 2001; 2007; Fraser 2009, 42; Stratigos 2017). However, despite the snippets of historical data and archaeological finds, very little is known about the everyday farming communities living beyond the most north-westerly frontiers of the Roman Empire whose engagement with the Roman Empire would have varied both temporally and spatially. In September 2022 a five-year Leverhulme project began, entitled: 'Coming into the Light: Exploring the Dark Age Societies of Northern Britain'.

The project consists of a collaboration of historians, archaeologists and palaeoenvironmental experts from the Universities of Aberdeen, Glasgow, Queen's University, Santiago de Compostela in Spain and the National Museum of Scotland. One of the major focus points of this project is to explore the potential impacts and interactions of the Roman army with communities living beyond the northernmost frontiers of the Roman Empire and, in particular, north of the Antonine Wall. To achieve this, several sites have been selected beyond the Antonine Wall from different locations on a south to north trajectory (including in Fife, Angus, Perth and Kinross, and Aberdeenshire) for multi-proxy, high resolution and interdisciplinary analyses. The analyses include pollen, non-pollen microfossils (NPPs), high resolution radiocarbon dating and Bayesian modelling, geochemistry, and other types of sedimentary analyses, closely compared with available historical and archaeological archives.

This chapter presents some of the recent findings so far completed from this new project, but also incorporates some of our previous research findings from: the 'Comparative Kingship' Leverhulme project (2017–2022); a project aimed at exploring the environmental and social changes taking place in Scotland as the early kingdoms of Scotland emerged and took shape. In this chapter, however, we will only be exploring those findings that are relevant to understanding the Roman Iron Age. The sites that will be discussed include Loch Clunie, Perthshire and two locations from Aberdeenshire – Loch of Leys, Banchory and the Craw Stane valley mire at Rhynie. All three sites have already been or are in the process of being published in detail (Jones *et al.* 2021; 2022; forthcoming). The aim of this chapter, therefore, is not to go over these findings in detail but instead to tease out new information related to regional variability and economic patterns at different temporal scales of the Roman Iron Age, with particular emphasis placed on how farming communities may have been impacted by Roman interactions beyond the north-western frontier(s) of the Roman Empire. It should be emphasised, however, that the 'Coming into the Light Project' is still in its infancy and the results presented here are the preliminary findings so far achieved. At least five more sites will be analysed by the completion of this project, which will allow a more comprehensive synthesis to be published at a later date.

Site selection

The sites selected for this chapter are all based in north-eastern Scotland, beyond the Antonine Wall (Figure 3.1) and include:

1. Loch Clunie (56° 34′54.4″N 03° 27′07.4″W) – a large, freshwater mesotrophic lake in Perthshire, located only 5.4 km north of the river Tay and 3 km west of Blairgowrie, Perth and Kinross. Loch Clunie has been selected because it is surrounded by a combination of Iron Age settlements and nearby Roman camps close to the Gask ridge. The Iron Age settlements include two crannogs (artificial lake settlements)

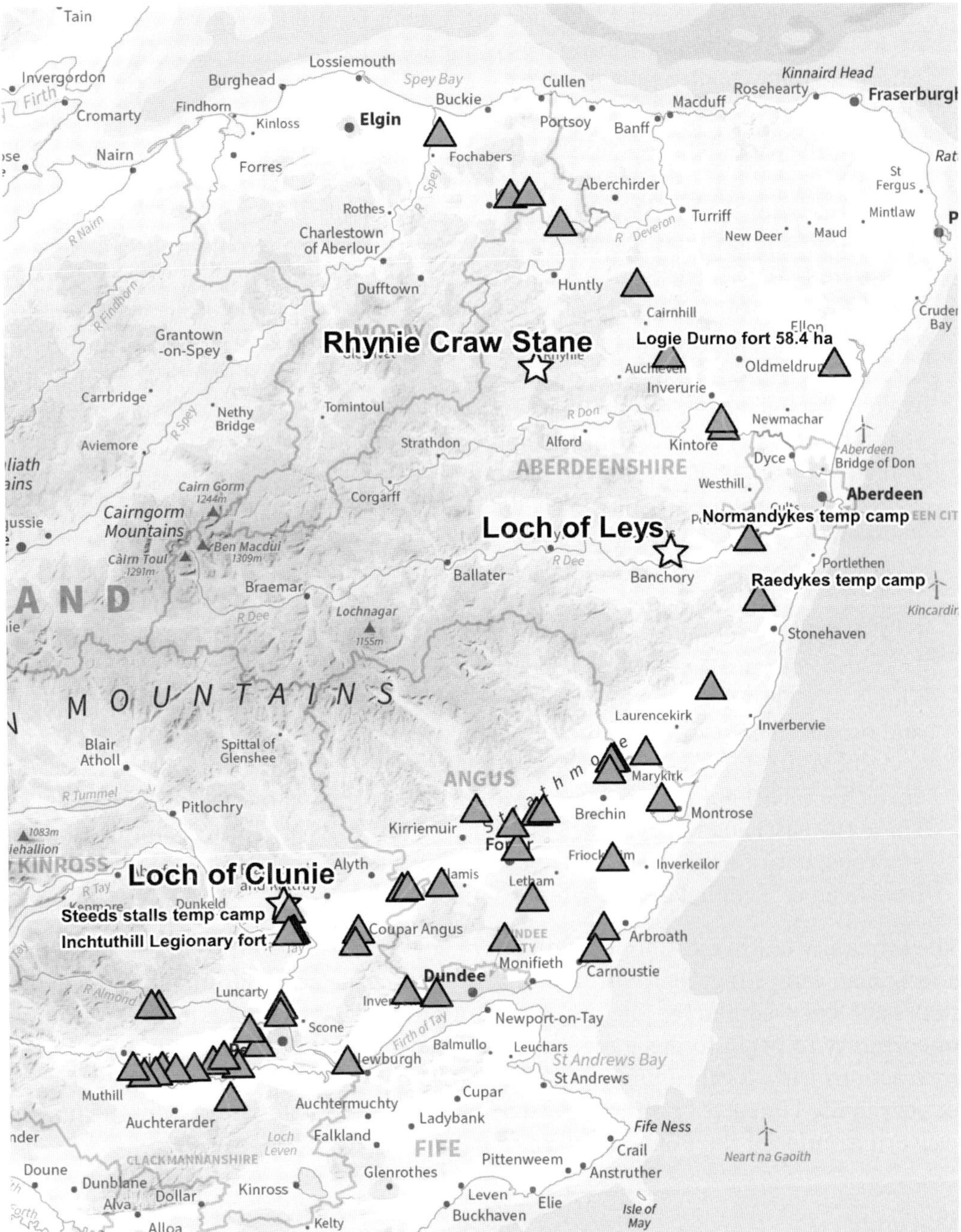

Figure 3.1. Map of sites analysed (stars) and Roman camps (triangles) (Data courtesy of Ordnance Survey MiniScale data).

of unknown age, a potential lake side settlement of unknown age, and a probable early medieval hillfort (Hudson 1998; Shelly 2013; Canmore 2024). The Roman camps include Steeds Stalls Roman temporary camp (only 1 km to the south of the loch) and Inchtuthil, the main legionary base in Scotland, located 5.4 km to the south (Richmond 1943; St Joseph 1951; Woolliscroft and Hoffman 2006).

2. Rhynie-Craw Stane valley mire (57° 19′ 26.3″N and 2° 49′ 59.3″W) is located 900 m south-east of the village of Rhynie and 300 m south-east of the early medieval enclosure complex at the Craw Stane, in Aberdeenshire (Noble and Evans 2019; Noble *et al.* 2019a). This site was selected because it was occupied before the end of the Roman Iron Age and became a major post-Roman central place. In relation to Roman sites, the valley is located around 25 km to the west of Logie Durno, the largest Roman temporary camp (959 × 653 m or *c.* 58.6 ha) north of the Antonine Wall. Logie Durno and the surrounding landscape is one of the key contenders for the battle of Mons Graupius, a major confrontation between Iron Age warriors and the Roman army during the Flavian period. Excavations were undertaken in 1975–1977 by St Joseph (St Joseph 1978) and more recently in 2016 and 2018 by Cameron Archaeology as part of a Watching Brief, but no radiocarbon dates or finds have so far been recorded from the camp (Cameron and Lenfert 2016; Lenfert 2018).
3. Loch of Leys is a drained loch located about 2 km north of the town of Banchory in Aberdeenshire (57° 04′ 12.9″N and 2° 29′ 19.2″W). Like Loch Clunie the Loch of Leys also contains a crannog, but whilst the chronology of the crannogs at Loch Clunie remain unknown, the crannog at Loch of Leys has been radiocarbon dated and produced a 1st-century AD initial construction date (Stratigos 2017; Stratigos and Noble 2018). The site was selected because the chronology of local occupation spans the early Roman Iron Age. Two Roman temporary camps – Normandykes (13 km to the east) and Raedykes (15 km to the south-east) are located in the broader environs; both camps were likely occupied during Agricola's campaigns but may have been reoccupied during later incursions.

The proximity of Rhynie, Clunie, and Loch of Leys to both local Iron Age settlements and Roman camps together with the high resolution palaeoenvironmental analyses that have been conducted on the sediments from all three sites offers a unique opportunity to begin to piece together the impacts of Roman incursions upon, and interactions with, local communities. These sites were once believed to have had no or very limited impacts or interactions, being considered so far away from the north-western frontier of the Roman Empire.

Methods

The sediment cores were extracted using a Russian peat corer. At Loch Clunie a 3.15 m core was extracted from terrestrialised lake sediments, although only 1.4 m was selected for analysis since this covered the period needed for the research project. Similarly, for the Loch of Leys, a 3.5 m core was extracted from the former lake, but only 2.1 m was needed for analysis. At Rhynie a 1.86 m core was extracted from a valley mire, but here the complete core was analysed. The sites analysed in this investigation were subsampled at high resolution (2 cm resolution) and Bayesian modelling conducted using OxCal (Bronk Ramsey 2009; 2020; Bronk Ramsey and Lee 2013) and Bacon (Blaauw and Christen 2011), which has allowed us to differentiate between the early, mid- and late Roman Iron Age; however, 0.5–1 cm resolution would be recommended for increased chronological accuracy and has already been achieved with a specialised industrial bone saw on frozen sediments for some of our other sites (analysis still in progress).

Multi-proxy analysis pollen, non-pollen microfossil, Loss-On-Ignition (LOI) and geochemical analysis was then undertaken on these sediments, whilst an additional step of Colour and Vibrational spectroscopy (FTIR–ATR) was conducted on the Loch of Leys and Loch Clunie sediments. These results have been published elsewhere, so this chapter predominantly focuses on the pollen and non-pollen microfossil findings, which were prepared using the standard chemical procedures outlined in Moore *et al.* (1991). A count of 500 total land pollen (TLP) was achieved where possible. Cereal pollen grains were identified using the procedures outlined in Jones *et al.* (2022) adapted from Andersen (1979), Fægri and Iverson (1975) and Albert and Innes (2019). Based on the size dimensions, the cereal-type grains identified likely belong to either *Hordeum*, *Triticum*, or *Avena*, although it should be acknowledged that some wild grasses can be incorporated into this group as well (Tweddle *et al.* 2005). *Secale cereale* was also identified. For a detailed account of the procedures and reasoning behind these different types of analyses, please refer to Jones *et al.* (2021; 2022; forthcoming).

Findings to date

This section provides an overview of the most significant results that will form the focus of the discussion in this chapter. Table 3.1 displays the radiocarbon and calibrated ages for all three sites. Figure 3.2 displays and compares temporal and spatial variations in cereal production across the three sites whilst Figure 3.3 provides a summary of the most significant pollen and NPP taxa. All dates described in the results and discussion are based on calibrated ages.

Loch Clunie (for more detail see Jones *et al.* forthcoming)

Sediments have been analysed from the Middle Iron Age *c.* 350–105 BC at 2 cm intervals until the present day. During the Middle Iron Age, and well before the first Roman campaigns into Scotland the environment at Loch Clunie was relatively open with herbaceous taxa representing 30–40% TLP between *c.* 300–190 BC, trees 15–22% and tall shrubs 7–8%. Most of the trees and shrubs likely belonged to wet woodland surrounding the loch. The woodland identified consisted of a mixture of birch (*Betula*), alder (*Alnus*), hazel or bog, myrtle (*Corylus/Myrica*), some oak (*Quercus*), elm (*Ulmus*),

Table 3.1. Radiocarbon dates; Cl: Clunie, L: Loch of Leys, CS: Crawstane-Rhynie; P: Peat, G: Gyttja; tw: twig, R.wood: roundwood. Dates have been calibrated using the INTCAL20 calibration curve (Stuvier and Reimer 1993; Stuvier et al. *2022).*

Lab code	*Location*	*Sample Type*	*Depth (cm)*	*^{14}C age BP*	*Error +/-*	*δ^{13}C (‰)*	*AD age (2.sigma)*
SUERC-99242	Loch Clunie	Peat humic acid	40	609	24	-31.1	AD 1301–1401
SUERC-84657	Loch Clunie	Peat humic acid	58–60	1174	34	-29.4	AD 774–976
SUERC-99243	Loch Clunie	Peat humic acid	68–70	1530	24	-28.4	AD 437–601
SUERC-83359	Loch Clunie	Peat humic acid	85	1788	29	-28.8	AD 210–350
SUERC-99244	Loch Clunie	Peat humic acid	95	1877	24	-29.5	AD 86–232
UBA-49370	Loch Clunie	Peat humic acid	117	2042	27	–	150 BC–AD 59
UBA-49371	Loch Clunie	Birch twig	136–137	2161	23	–	353–105 BC
SUERC-82572	Loch of Leys	Peat-humic acid	48	1715	30	-28.8	AD 250–390
SUERC-82571	Loch of Leys	Roundwood	73–74	886	30	-27.4	AD 1040–1220
Poz-91194	Loch of Leys	Peat-humic acid	115–116	1435	30	–	AD 571–655
Poz-91196	Loch of Leys	Peat-humic acid	155–156	1535	30	–	AD 428–592
Poz-91197	Loch of Leys	gyttja-humic acid	205–206	2390	30	–	730–400 BC
SUERC-8041	Craw Stane	Peat (bulk)	89–90	1.0931 ± 0.004	–	-30.6	Modern
SUERC-81223	Craw Stane	Peat (bulk)	110–111	593	21	-30.7	1303–1408
SUERC-80414	Craw Stane	Peat (bulk)	131	1171	30	-29.5	770–960
SUERC-81224	Craw Stane	Peat (bulk)	156	1092	24	-29.6	892–1011
SUERC-76891	Craw Stane	Peat (bulk)	181–182	1686	24	-25.0	260–415

pine (*Pinus*), and willow (*Salix*). There is strong evidence of an agricultural economy during the Middle Iron Age. Cereals (predominantly barley types, and one wheat/oat grain) were recorded between ~190 BC to AD 30 as well as a burnt grass and a burnt cereal glume, and one parasitic worm egg belonging to *Capillaria*, which has a wide range of hosts. The other herbaceous plants identified include a range of plants often associated with disturbance (*e.g.* Apiaceae, *Artemisia,* Chenopodiaceae, Brassicaceae), arable (*e.g. Polygonum aviculare, Rumex acetosella*), and pastoral farming (*e.g.* Asteraceae, Caryophyllaceae, Chenopodiaceae, Lactuceae, *Plantago lanceolata,* Ranunculaceae, *Rumex acetosa and acetosella*); grass (Poaceae) represented 30–40% TLP between *c.* 350–105 BC, but likely consisted of a mixture of species associated with both the natural fen environment as well as disturbance-agricultural activity from nearby field systems. Coprophilous fungi HdV-55A *Sordaria,* HdV-113 *Sporomiella,* HdV-368 *Podospora*, and HdV-1112 *Cercophora* were also present. These are often associated with large herbivores and although wild deer may account for some of these fungal spores the presence of pastoral indicators in the pollen record support the presence of domesticated herbivores associated with a pastoral economy.

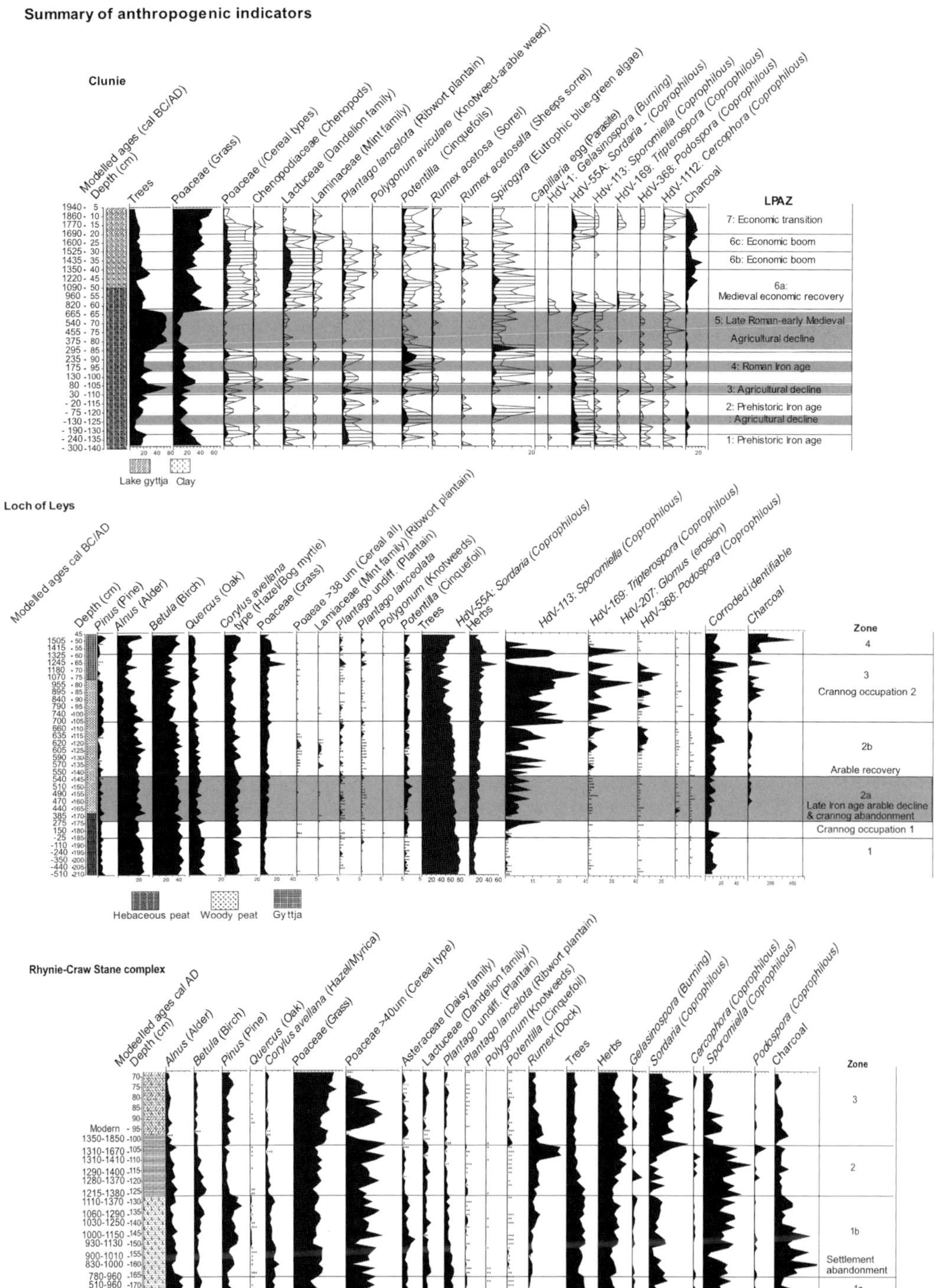

Figure 3.2. Comparison of cereal fluctuations during the early–mid and late Roman Iron Age, and early medieval period at Loch Clunie, Loch of Leys and Rhynie Crawstane.

Main findings from Loch Clunie during the Roman Iron Age

The most significant findings at Loch Clunie include continued economic activity during the early Roman Iron Age as well as three periods of economic downturn before and between the early to late Roman Iron Age. The first downturn may be linked to taphonomic changes rather than actual economic downturn and is relatively brief between ~AD 30–80, evidenced by a pronounced but brief decline in cereal types, general decrease in herbaceous taxa and by a recovery in tree taxa. The cause of the event appears to be linked to a sudden drop in organic content from 47% to 17% (LOI), which suggests either a brief rise in the water-table or an erosional in-wash event. However, if this was a true economic downturn then the arable economy quickly recovered, as shown by an increase in barley types and by a decline in trees (below 20% TLP) in the pollen sequence thereafter. After *c.* AD 80 rye also appears for the first time, whilst other microfossils often associated with disturbance or pastoral farming become more consistent in the pollen and NPP records (*e.g.* Lactuceae, *Rumex acetosa*, *Potentilla*, *Plantago lanceolata Gelasinospora*, *Glomus* sp., Chlamydiospores, *Sordaria*, and *Cercophora*). This recovery lasted until *c.* AD 130–175.

A second decline in barley is represented between *c.* AD 130–175; pastoral and disturbance indicators (*Plantago lanceolata*, *Rumex acetosa*, and Asteraceae) decrease whilst birch and alder trees increase. This event is not linked to changes in LOI.

The third decline is the most pronounced and prolonged from *c.* AD ~210–350 (cal. ^{14}C age range: note the actual date could fall anywhere between this range but is still likely to be later than the Septimus Severus and Carcalla campaigns between AD 208–211). This event is represented by a sudden reduction to almost complete disappearance of all cereals and pastoral indicators (*e.g. Potentilla*, *Rumex* (all), Lactuceae, Chenopodiaceae, and *Plantago lanceolata*); herbaceous taxa generally decrease from 79% to 42%, tree taxa increase (from 18% to 33–50%), particularly alder but also, pine, birch, oak, and elm as well as the tree fern *Polypodium*. LOI decreases to 23% between 85–76 cm, potentially linked to a rise in the water table, but then increases to 44% by 62 cm and thus it remains unclear whether the decline in cereals here might be linked to that aberration.

There is no evidence of economic recovery immediately after the end of the Roman Iron Age. It is not until after *c.* AD 660–700 (~400 years later) that Loch Clunie experienced not only an economic recovery but also a change in crop cultivation, from barley cultivation, to increased diversification including some rye, oats/wheat as well as barley, which remained the dominant crop. At the same time trees decreased to below 20% and herbaceous taxa increase to 54–83%.

Loch of Leys (for more detail see Jones *et al.* 2022)

The start of the Loch of Leys sequence dates to the prehistoric Iron Age from *c.* 510 BC. The prehistoric environment differs from Loch Clunie by being less open; vegetation surrounding the loch was dominated by trees and tall shrub taxa (70–80%) including alder (*Alnus*), birch (*Betula*), oak (*Quercus*), hazel (*Corylus avellana* type), willow (*Salix*), elm (*Ulmus*), ash (*Fraxinus*), beech (*Fagus*), the rose family (Rosaceae undiff.), and *Prunus*, which can include cherry, plum, or blackthorn. There is sporadic evidence of cereals (two grains) at *c.* 490 BC the occasional presence of coprophilous fungi *Sporormiella*, *Tripterospora*, and *Sordaria*, which might be associated with wild deer or livestock, but generally evidence of human activity is poorly represented during this period.

Main findings at Loch of Leys during the Roman Iron Age

Between *c.* 25 BC and AD 275 the microfossil record shows a rise in disturbance, pastoral and arable indicators (this includes the fungal spores *Podospora, Sporormiella, Sordaria*, and *Tripterospora* and the herbaceous taxa Apiaceae, *Artemisia*, Chenopodiaceae, Asteraceae, Caryophyllaceae, Lactuceae, *Plantago lanceolata*, *Potentilla*, Ranunculaceae, *Rumex*, and the presence of the agricultural weed *Polygonum* – knot weed). Cereal type pollen (Poaceae >38 µm) is present at: ~25 BC (four grains) and ~AD 275 (three grains).

After ~AD 275 an economic downturn is potentially represented by the disappearance of not only cereal type pollen (except for a sporadic occurrence at ~AD 490), but also by the disappearance/decrease of some herbaceous taxa often linked to disturbance and pastoral farming including *Potentilla*, *Rumex*, *Plantago lanceolata*. Coprophilous fungi (*Podospora*, *Sordaria*, *Sporormiella*, and *Tripterospora*) increase initially but then also decrease after ~AD 275.

This economic downturn lasted between 200–300 years. Disturbance indicators begin to increase from *c.* AD 450, evidenced by a first appearance and then consistent representation of charcoal shards, coinciding with a peak in corroded unidentified pollen, and small increases in the herbaceous taxa Chenopodiaceae, *Rumex*, *Plantago lanceolata*, *Potentilla*, and the fungal spore *Gelasinospora*. Previous studies suggest *Gelasinospora* type are carbonicolous and are either an indicator of fire or representative of drier conditions (Van Geel 1976). After *c.* AD 550 cereal type pollen recover and become more consistent.

Rhynie-Craw Stane (for more detail see Jones *et al.* 2021)

The sediment core from Rhynie-Craw Stane starts at *c.* AD 260–415 until modern and represents the beginning of occupation at the Craw Stane complex. The early Roman Iron Age is missing; the beginning of this sediment sequence, however, does span the mid–late Roman Iron Age.

Main findings at the Craw Stane valley mire during the Roman Iron Age

The main findings at Rhynie are of agricultural continuity throughout and after the mid–late Roman Iron Age. Herbaceous taxa indicative of pasture and disturbance are well represented including Asteraceae, Lactuceae, *Plantago* undiff., *Potentilla*, *Ranunculus*, and *Plantago lanceolata*. Coprophilous fungi often associated with herbivore dung include *Podospora* type, *Tripterospora* type, *Cercophora* type, *Sporormiella* type, and possibly *Sordaria* type, although fluctuations in fungal spores have been attributed to some extent to terrigenous in-wash (Jones *et al.* 2021). Evidence of arable farming is strongly visible throughout the record as cereal type pollen is consistently present

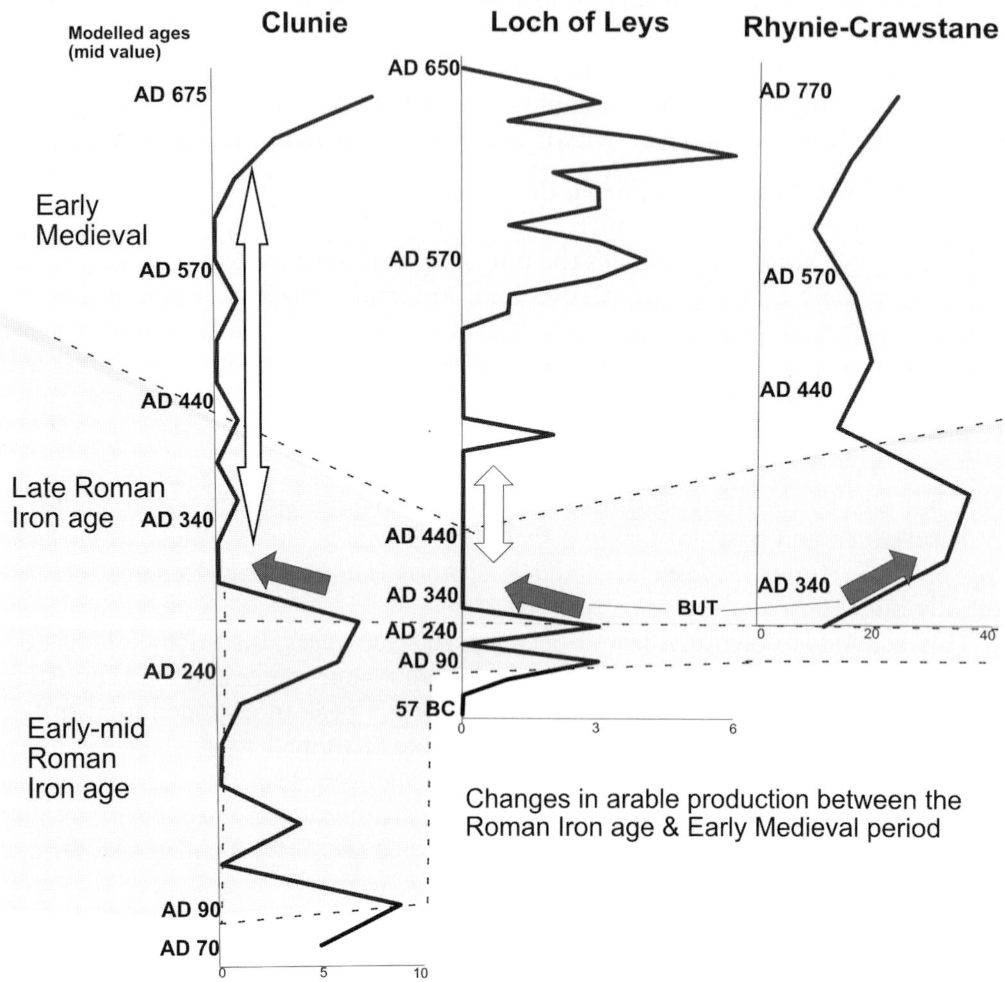

Figure 3.3. Pollen and Npp diagrams of selected taxa associated with disturbance, pastoral and arable farming from Clunie, Loch of Leys and Rhynie Crawstane.

and generally greater than 2% although some of the grains could potentially belong to *Glyceria fluitans*. Measurements of the annulus diameter and long diameter suggest the majority likely belong to *Hordeum vulgare*, whilst small amounts of *Avena/Triticum* may also have been present. There is no evidence of economic downturn during the Roman Iron Age until the abandonment of the Craw Stane complex after *c.* AD 550.

Discussion

The impacts of Roman campaigns on local communities living within and beyond frontier regions of the Roman Empire would have varied both temporally and spatially.

Yet our understanding of this period and the impact on Iron Age communities is still relatively piecemeal, relying on snippets of literary material, limited excavations, and a limited number of palaeoenvironmental studies. Roman palaeoenvironmental investigations have in the past focused their attention on the areas centred along and between the Antonine Wall and Hadrian's Wall including the works of Dumayne (1994); Dumayne and Barber (1994); Manning *et al.* (1997); Dumayne-Peaty (1998a; 1998b; 1999); Tipping and Tisdall (2005); and more recently Fernández-Götz *et al.* (2022). Despite some spatial and temporal variability represented in these publications, a general pattern of woodland clearance has been detected during the early–mid Roman Iron Age and linked to timber demands required to construct military structures between Hadrian's Wall and the Antonine Wall; woodland regeneration has at some locations been linked to the withdrawal of Roman troops at the end of the Roman Iron Age.

Agricultural production itself tends to show continuity rather than intensification between the 1st–2nd centuries AD although, in some areas, there is a reduction in cereals and expansion of pastoral farming, which, it has been suggested, could represent local adaptation to a new market. It has also been suggested that Roman withdrawal may have caused an agricultural recession. These findings, however, are with regards to locations that were in closer proximity of the Roman frontier and the supply demands of the Roman army in that region. Beyond the Roman frontier different factors would have been at play. It must also be said that much of the existing palaeoenvironmental work for this time period lacks much in the way of robust chronological resolution and are generally low resolution – the patterns for the area around the frontier need further work and clarification.

North of the Antonine Wall there has been much less focus with regard to the environment. High resolution palaeoenvironmental investigations targeting this period are almost non-existent and that is what the current project aims to address. Those studies that are available, again, tend to lack both sampling resolution and/or chronological accuracy, including at Gartlea Bog close to Loch Lomond. This, it is argued, spans the Roman period, but there are no radiocarbon dates (Ramsay 1995). Black Loch in Fife and Lochs Davan and Braeroddach in Aberdeenshire, both likely span the Roman Iron Age but, at both sites, interpretations are problematic due to low sampling resolution and wide ^{14}C error margins (Whittington and Edwards 1993). Fannyside Muir is another site near to Cumbernauld that likely spans the Roman Iron Age, although interpretations are based on only two radiocarbon dates (Dumayne-Peaty 1999). Whilst Letham Moss in Stirlingshire has slightly better chronological control for the late and post-Roman Iron Age, it does not for the early Roman Iron Age (Dumayne-Peaty 1999).

To be able to fully understand Rome's impact on local communities at different temporal and spatial scales, particularly beyond the frontier regions of the Roman Empire, a multitude of high-resolution site comparisons are needed. The findings so far emerging from the 'Coming into the Light' and 'Comparative Kingship' projects mark a start towards reducing this knowledge shortfall. Findings so far produced from these investigations are discussed below and have been divided into the sub-categories: 1. The early Roman Iron Age (Agricola campaigns); 2. The early–mid Roman Iron Age (Antonine campaigns); 3. The mid–late Roman Iron Age (Severus, sons and later campaigns).

Early Roman Iron Age during the Flavian dynasty and Agricola campaigns of AD 78–84

Pollen results from both Loch of Leys in Aberdeenshire (further away from the Gask ridge) and Loch Clunie (adjacent to the Gask ridge) in Perthshire (Jones *et al.* 2022; forthcoming) show no evidence of major impacts or evidence of a social-economic crisis during the early Roman Iron Age, as has been suggested in the past by Whittington and Edwards (1993) for Aberdeenshire. Some caution is needed as a short-lived crisis, such as an invasion and relatively rapid withdrawal, might not necessarily be detectable in the palaeoenvironmental record even at higher (2 cm) resolution sampling. At Lochs Davan and Braeroddach in Aberdeenshire, an episode of woodland recovery and agricultural decline has been tentatively attributed to the impacts of warfare (*e.g.* the battle of Mons Graupius of AD 83/84) and the ravaging of communities during the Agricola campaigns (Whittington and Edwards 1993), but this evidence is based on low sampling resolution (5–10 cm resolution) and wide C14 age error margins (200–500 years for some of the dates). Thus the decline observed here could in fact have occurred much later, which the authors acknowledge. At Fannyside Muir in Cumbernauld, no such decline is evident. Instead Dumayne-Peaty (1999) proposes an increase in human activity, in particular woodland clearance. However, this could be linked to deforestation by the Roman military (for construction purposes or indeed other factors) during the early Roman Iron Age. Whilst at Letham Moss in Stirlingshire, agricultural continuity is also suggested, with a potential agricultural decline later around *c.* AD 107 (Dumayne-Peaty 1999). This interpretation is based on estimated ages, not actual; however, at both Loch Clunie and Loch of Leys, the more chronologically accurate findings also seem to reflect agricultural continuity and not a decline. More comparative studies are needed to understand these patterns of continuity or spatial variability, but findings so far are intriguing.

In Aberdeenshire there are currently over 24 finds of Roman material, according to Curtis and Hunter (2006), which suggest that, despite lying so far to the north of long-term Roman occupation, there was Roman interaction with local communities or, at least, Roman material finding its way to local sites through down-the-line exchange. Many Roman finds found at Iron Age sites in north-eastern Scotland belong to the Flavian and Antonine period (Hunter 2007, 20). At Loch Kinord, which is only 26 km to the west of Loch of Leys, a Roman perfume bottle was discovered from the loch, close to the edge (Stratigos, 2017). To the east and south-east of Loch of Leys (only 13–15 km) lie the Roman temporary camps of Normandykes and Raedykes, believed to have been occupied during the Flavian period, although these may have been reoccupied during the later Antonine and/or Severus campaigns. There are no radiocarbon dates for these camps; however, 90 Roman bread ovens have been discovered at nearby Milltimber, 4 km to the east of Normandykes, and this site produced calibrated dates between AD 40–170 (Dingwall and Shepherd 2018). At Kintore 20 km further north, the Roman camp is likely to date to Agricola's campaigns, but it may have also been reoccupied during either the late 2nd or early 3rd century AD (Cook and Dunbar 2008; Cook 2012).

The process of invasion in the Flavian period undoubtedly included violent conquest, but there may also have been sustained efforts to make peace and to begin to establish networks of communication, administration, and trade with local Iron Age communities as part of 'Empire-building'. The Agricola campaigns were specifically aimed at conquering northern Scotland, which would eventually have required local elites to manage local affairs on behalf of the Roman Empire. This would have placed a strong emphasis on diplomacy and establishing peace treaties following conquest. Some communities may have submitted more easily than others, splitting into pro- and anti-Roman contingents. The establishment of trade networks between the camps and surrounding environs, the need for local supplies and particularly the need for grain to feed the army (to supplement what could not be imported) would also have facilitated diplomatic ties, promoting the continuity of regional-local agricultural production. Hence for this period, despite the Agricola campaigns, the evidence is for relative continuity in environment and economy.

Mid-Roman Iron Age and Antonine Scotland (*c.* AD 139–165)

By the early 2nd century AD, the Roman army would have been predominantly based behind the Tyne-Solway line. Between AD 139–165 Antonius Pius attempted to recapture southern Scotland. Construction for the Antonine Wall began in AD 142 and consisted of a turf rampart that ran along the central belt of Scotland between the Firth of Clyde and the Firth of Forth. In the pollen record from Loch Clunie a brief period of agricultural decline is represented between *c.* AD 130–170, which does not appear to be related to taphonomic changes (Jones *et al.* forthcoming). This period of decline coincides with the timing of the Antonine campaigns into Scotland, but whether this agricultural decline might be related to these renewed interventions by the Roman military remains inconclusive. It could simply represent a period of shifting cultivation (*e.g.* Tipping and Tisdall 2005) to allow soils to recover.

Previous investigations have not been able to detect an Antonine horizon due to lower chronological resolution combined with the wide potential age ranges. Loch Clunie is no exception with the problem of wide potential age ranges. At 95 cm the radiocarbon age could be anywhere between *c.* AD 86–232 whilst 85 cm could be between *c.* AD 210–350. However, the cereal decline takes place between these two dates (95–90 cm), which is clearly after the Agricolan and before the Severan campaigns. Recent advances of age-depth modelling, using high sampling resolution, can also help narrow down the potential time frame. At Loch Clunie, Bacon Age-depth modelling which uses Bayesian statistics (Blaauw and Christen 2011) was used, incorporating seven radiocarbon dates from 1.36 m of sediment (high resolution). The model suggests the decline occurred between *c.* AD 130–170. Further comparative studies are still needed to determine if this is an isolated case, perhaps linked to local environmental or social change or if this might represent a more regional pattern of change in areas situated close to the Antonine frontier.

Mid–late Roman Iron Age: Severus, sons and others (AD 208–410)

After the abandonment of the Antonine Wall (by AD 164–165) and the withdrawal once more of the Roman Army to the Tyne-Solway line and Hadrian's Wall, the various campaigns into north-eastern Scotland after AD 160 appear to have been mainly aimed at quelling unrest rather than invasion. Here, impact on the local landscape may have been more dramatic – aimed at disrupting local societies and economies (Hanson 2006, 136–8; Fraser 2009, 22–29).

In the palaeoenvironmental record a substantial change is represented in the palaeoenvironmental records during the mid–late Roman Iron Age at both Loch Clunie, and Loch of Leys. Both sites show a prolonged period where arable and pastoral farming substantially declined or even disappeared, lasting several hundred years, until a recovery in the 5th–7th centuries AD. Historical sources suggest the campaigns of Septimius Severus and his sons in Scotland between AD 208–210 may have been particularly brutal with genocide an element of Roman doctrine specially mentioned in the sources (Reed 1978, 99; Fraser 2009, 28). The palaeoenvironmental results may belong to this period, but there is a strong probability that the findings reflect a slightly later period. Caution is also needed with the Loch Clunie findings – some of the lithological datasets suggest a rise in the water table concurrently with the agricultural regression (*e.g.* a pronounced decline in LOI, as well as changes in colour and geochemistry described in Jones *et al.* forthcoming). There is general agreement that western Europe experienced warmer and more stable conditions between 100 BC and AD 200, and that this was followed by climatic instability between AD 200 until AD 600 (McCormick *et al.* 2012). Increased rainfall is a possibility to consider for the rise in the water table at Loch Clunie, but the evidence is far from conclusive; warm-cool and wet-dry fluctuations have been reported in Britain and western Europe spanning this period (McCormick *et al.* 2012). Snow-ice melt is an alternative possibility to consider and is known to have caused a rise in water-depth at Clunie before in 1788 (Shelley 2013). Whether the rise in the water table is in some way connected to the agricultural decline equally remains unclear. This needs further investigation. What is significant about both the Loch Clunie and the Loch of Leys findings is that these findings do support previous arguments, not only made by Whittington and Edwards (1993), but also by Dumayne-Peaty (1999) for a prolonged period of agricultural regression beginning in the late Roman Iron Age–post-Severus (either mid–late 3rd and/or 4th centuries AD). This brings the total number of sites, north of the Antonine

Wall with similar findings, to at least seven across six different regions, ranging from: Cumbernauld, Fife, Perth and Kinross, Stirlingshire, and Aberdeenshire.

During the late Roman Iron Age, not only are there profound changes now evident in multiple palaeoenvironmental records, but these findings coincide with substantial changes taking place in the archaeological record, where a general trend of abandonment of unenclosed settlement included the demise of the tradition of earth-fast timber roundhouse construction, which had endured for more than 2,000 years (*e.g.* Hunter 2007, 48–50; Cook and Dunbar 2008; Hodgson 2014, 48; Stratigos 2017; Jones *et al.* 2022; Noble and Evans 2022, 32). The abandonment of both agriculture and settlement could well be linked to more brutal and directly detrimental Roman campaigning.

More punitive and hostile campaigning may have prompted some Iron Age groups to coalesce to resist Roman hostility for, as elsewhere on Roman frontiers (Heather 2009, 36–93), one result of Roman presence may have been the amalgamation of polities bordering Roman Britain, into fewer but larger units. Indeed, while describing the major Roman campaigns under Septimius Severus and Caracalla north of Hadrian's Wall from AD 208–211, against the Maiatai and beyond them the Caledonii, Cassius Dio, in the mid-3rd century, noted that 'the names of other British groups had been merged' into these two main polities (Cary 1927, 262–3; Fraser 2009, 15–17, 23–29). However, given the traditional sparsity of the archaeological evidence for the late Roman Iron Age the opposite has been argued – that this was a period of socio-economic collapse (Hunter 2007, 42–44). Both might be true: the environmental evidence certainly suggests major discontinuities in environment, but on the other hand, the discovery of Rhynie and Tap o' Noth – the latter a 17 ha hillfort with hundreds of dwellings – may also represent some form of centralisation within certain regions at least. Radiocarbon dating suggests the origins of this central landscape was in the 3rd century AD (Noble and Evans 2019; Noble *et al.* 2019a; 2019b; 2019c). Evidence from the pollen record suggests a prosperous agricultural community who cultivated predominantly barley during this period. Most importantly, there is no evidence of crisis during the late Roman period here (Jones *et al.* 2021).

There may have been important long-term repercussions of these patterns. Roman administration ended in Britain for good at the beginning of the 5th century AD, and it took some landscapes (and, by implication, communities) time to recover from this late Roman Iron Age regression in the economy. At the Loch of Leys, agricultural recovery did not take place until the 6th century AD, at Loch Clunie from the 7th century AD. These results are also comparable with Black Loch in Fife, with recovery evidenced here from the 7th century AD, whilst recovery of agriculture to previous levels at Loch Davan in Aberdeenshire potentially did not take place till the 12th century AD (Whittington and Edwards 1993). At Letham Moss, agriculture is more evident from the 7th century AD and, at Fannyside Muir, it did not appear again until the 10th century AD (Dumayne-Peaty 1999). An argument proposed by Dumayne-Peaty (1999) is that frequent conflicts between different local groups may have prevented agricultural recovery even in the post-Roman period. Equally, the changes in the late

Roman Iron Age may have been so profound that it took centuries for population levels and an agricultural economy to recover.

Conclusion

Recent findings from the Leverhulme funded projects are beginning to shed new light on the Roman Iron Age in Scotland. Findings not only help to confirm that local communities, despite living beyond the north-westernmost frontier of the Roman Empire, were impacted (directly or indirectly) by Roman policies and campaigns, but equally highlight substantial differences between early Roman and late Roman Iron Age environments north of the Antonine Wall. Early evidence tentatively suggests that the initial Roman campaigns did not lead to widespread economic crisis, and local agricultural productivity may have been maintained. The campaigns themselves may have been violent, but the agenda of Rome was not to decimate local communities. Local communities would have been needed to administer local rule, for trade, for resources and to maintain peace and, therefore, agricultural productivity may have been encouraged.

A small downturn in arable productivity is recorded at Loch Clunie spanning the Antonine period but whether this is a local event or representative of more widespread changes along the Antonine frontier is uncertain as currently there are no other high resolution comparative studies. In contrast to the early Roman Iron Age, the late Roman Iron Age pollen records show a significant and prolonged agricultural downturn at Loch Clunie in Perthshire and Loch of Leys in Aberdeenshire, and these are not isolated cases. Despite poorer chronological and temporal resolution from earlier comparative investigations and some caution needed with the Clunie interpretations, a regional pattern is beginning to emerge that strongly suggests wide-scale environmental regression or abandonment beyond the Antonine frontier encompassed the regions of Fife, Stirlingshire, Cumbernauld, Perth and Kinross, and Aberdeenshire.

The agricultural decline coincides with a general trend in settlement change across north-eastern Scotland and may be representative of major social/political restructuring spanning this period. In some regions, at least, this may have entailed the abandonment of smaller, less-protected settlement units, and the centralisation of settlement into larger, enclosed settlements, giving rise to the formation of major power centres in Scotland. Rhynie may be one such centre. Rhynie shows no evidence of crisis. Here agriculture continued through the late Roman Iron Age and into the post-Roman era with a major power centre developing. Rhynie and Strathbogie is one such example of centralisation, but others will undoubtedly emerge.

After Roman withdrawal from Britain in the early 5th century AD, many regions show no immediate sign of recovery until after the 6th century AD. Recovery was not uniform but instead happened at different temporal and spatial scales. The fight for territories after Roman withdrawal from Britain, the formation of new kingdoms and the frequently shifting borders would have made for uncertain times and frequent conflict may well have prevented communities from returning to their former way of life and the expansion of their economy. Nonetheless, despite these initial findings many questions still remain:

1. During the early–mid-Roman campaigns can patterns of economic continuity, downturn or variability be detected at other sites? If so, can these be linked to short-term periods of diplomacy or unrest?
2. Does settlement and economic abandonment during the late Roman period reflect the violent nature of the later Roman campaigns into Scotland? Or, might these changes reflect increasing unrest, such as territorial change amongst local Iron Age communities? Or something else (e.g. What role does natural environmental change play?)
3. Questions also remain regarding the temporal and spatial scale of late Roman economic decline, prosperity and continuity. If small settlement units across Scotland were abandoned due to out-migration, where did people migrate to and why? To what extent might centralisation have been a factor in other landscapes – *e.g.* are there other Rhynies out there?

More multi-proxy and high-resolution site comparisons are needed to understand these patterns of change better, but initial results are promising. We are currently in the process of investigating two new locations: Blairdaff, close to Bennachie and Flanders Moss, near to Stirling. By the end of this current project, it is hoped that at least five more sites in total will be incorporated into this list, including the two aforementioned sites, but also with new analyses from the Lomond Hills, Fife; Inchtuthill, Perth and Kinross; and Dundurn, Perth and Kinross.

Acknowledgements

Special acknowledgements to the Leverhulme Trust for funding the: 'Comparative Kingship: the Early Medieval Kingdoms of Northern Britain and Ireland' (Grant: RG13876-10) and 'Coming into the Light Project' (Grant: RG16612-10). Special acknowledgements also go to the various people who assisted in the sediment coring, particularly to anybody who had holes in their wellies or fell over: Gordon Noble, Tim Mighall, Michael Stratigos, James O'Driscoll, and Edouard Masson-Maclean.

Bibliography

Albert, B.M. and Innes, J.B. (2019) On the distinction of pollen grains of early varieties of Hordeum from Glyceria species: addressing the early cereal cultivation problem in Palynology. In *Palynology* 44(2), 369–81.

Andersen, S.T. (1979) Identification of wild grass and cereal pollen. In *Danmarks Geologiske Undersøegelse Årbog* 1978, 69–92.

Blaauw, M. and Christen, J.A. (2011) Flexible paleoclimate age-depth models using an autoregressive gamma process. In *Bayesian Analysis* 6(3), 457–74.

Bronk Ramsey, C. (2009) Bayesian analysis of radiocarbon dates. In *Radiocarbon* 51(1), 337–60.
Bronk Ramsey, C. (2020) OxCal 4.2. Available at: Doi. https://c14.arch.ox.ac.uk/oxcal.html.
Bronk Ramsey, C. and Lee, S. (2013) Recent and planned developments of the program OxCal. In *Radiocarbon* 55(2–3), 720–30.
Cameron, A. and Lenfert, R. (2016) *N of Kirkton Farm, Colpy, AB52 6XD to Blackhall Road (adjacent to Westburn Gardens), Inverurie, AB51 5SN.* Cameron Archaeology. Unpublished Data Structure Report: https://i.rcahms.gov.uk/canmore-pdf/WP00005772.pdf
Canmore (2024) Clunie, Perthshire archaeological finds at: https://canmore.org.uk/search/. Cluny Castle: https://canmore.org.uk/site/28970/clunie-castle-hill; Cluny crannog 1: https://canmore.org.uk/site/28959/loch-of-clunie; Cluny crannog 2: https://canmore.org.uk/site/28944/loch-of-clunie; Clunie lake shore settlement: https://canmore.org.uk/site/28969/craigie. Accessed August 2024.
Cary, E. (1927) *DIO CASSIUS.* In *Roman History* 77, 238–77. Translated by Cary, E. and Foster, H.B. Loeb Classical Library, 177. Cambridge, MA, Harvard University Press.
Cook, M.J. (2012) Romans, Picts, and Development: Continuity and Change in Aberdeenshire's Archaeology and Informed Planning Decisions. In *Stirling International Journal of Postgraduate Research* 1(1), 1–13.
Cook, M.J. and Dunbar, L. (2008) *Rituals, Roundhouses and Romans: Excavations at Kintore, Aberdeenshire 2000–2006.* Volume 1, Forest Road. Edinburgh, Scottish Trust for Archaeological Research, 31–40.
Curtis, N. and Hunter, F. (2006) An unusual pair of Roman Bronze vessels from Stoneywood, Aberdeen and other Roman finds from north-east Scotland. In *Proceedings of the Society of Antiquaries of Scotland* 136, 199–214.
Dingwall, K. and Shepherd, J. (2018) Iron Age and Roman. In Lowe, C., Craddock-Bennett, L. (eds) *Highway through History: An archaeological journey on the Aberdeen peripheral route*, 71–86. Edinburgh, Headland Archaeology Ltd. http://publications.aberdeenshire.gov.uk/
Dumayne, L. (1994). The effect of Roman occupation on the environment of northern Britain: pollen data from Fozy Moss, Northumbria. In *Britannia* 25, 217–24.
Dumayne, L. and Barber, K.E. (1994) The impact of the Romans on the environment of northern England: pollen data from three sites close to Hadrian's Wall. In *Holocene* 4, 165–73.
Dumayne-Peaty, L. (1998a) Forest clearance in northern Britain during Romano-British times: re-addressing the palynological evidence. In *Britannia* 26, 315–22.
Dumayne-Peaty, L. (1998b) Human impact on the environment during the Iron Age and Romano British times: palynological evidence from three sites near the Antonine Wall. In *Journal of Archaeological Science* 25, 203–14.
Dumayne-Peaty, L. (1999) Continuity or discontinuity? Vegetation change in the Hadrianic-Antonine frontier zone of northern Britain at the end of the Roman occupation. In *Journal of Biogeography* 26, 643–665.
Fægri, K. and Iversen, J. (1975) *Textbook of Pollen Analysis.* Revised 3rd edn. Hafner Press, New York.
Fernández-Götz, M., Cowley, D., Hamilton, D., Hardwick, I.J. and McDonald, S. (2022) Beyond Walls: Reassessing Iron Age and Roman Encounters in Northern Britain. In *Antiquity* 96(388), 1021–9.
Fraser, J.E. (2009) *From Caledonia to Pictland Scotland to 795. The new Edinburgh history of Scotland.* Edinburgh, Edinburgh University Press.
Hanson, W.S. (2006) Scotland and the northern frontier: second to fourth centuries AD. In Todd, M. (ed.) *A Companion to Roman Britain*, 9, 136–61. Oxford, Blackwell Publishing.
Heather, P. (2009) *Empires and Barbarians, the Fall of Rome and the Birth of Europe.* Oxford, Oxford University Press.
Hodgson, N. (2014) The British Expedition of Septimius Severus. In *Britannia* 45, 31–51.

Hudson, B.T. (1998) (eds) Danari uastauerunt Pictauiam ad Cluanan et Duncalden. In *The Scottish Chronicle. Scottish Historical Review* 77, 129–61.
Hunter, F. (2001) Roman and Native in Scotland: New approaches. In *Journal of Roman Archaeology* 14, 289–309.
Hunter, F. (2007) *Beyond the Edge of Empire: Caledonians, Picts and Romans*. Inverness, Groam House Museum Trust.
Jones, S.E., Evans, N., Martínez-Cortizas, A., Mighall, T.M. and Noble, G. (2021) Settlement, landscape and land-use change at a Pictish power centre: assessing the palaeoecological record for economic continuity and social change at Rhynie, N.E. Scotland. In *Holocene* 31(6), 897–914.
Jones, S.E., Martínez-Cortizas, A., Mighall, T.M., Noble, G., López-Costas, O. and Stratigos, M. (2022) Lake and crannog: A 2500-year palaeoenvironmental record of continuity and change in NE Scotland. In *Quaternary Science Reviews* 285, 107532. Doi. https://doi.org/10.1016/j.quascirev.2022.107532
Jones, S.E., Blauuw, M., López-Costas, O., Martínez-Cortizas, A., Mighall, T., Noble, G. and O'Driscoll J. (forthcoming) Farming in the shadows of Rome: A multi-proxy palaeoenvironmental record from Loch Clunie – Perthshire. In *Journal of Archaeological Science* (Submitted).
Lenfert, R. (2018) *Report on an Archaeological Watching Brief Land to The Southeast of North Lodge Logie Pitcaple, Inverurie AB51 5EH*. Cameron Archaeology. Unpublished Data series. Doi. https://doi.org/10.5284/1048496
Manning, A., Birley, R. and Tipping, R. (1997) Roman impact on the environment at Hadrian's Wall: precisely dated pollen analysis from Vindolanda, northern England. In *Holocene* 7(2), 175–86.
McCormick, M., Büntgen, U., Cane, M.A., Cook, E.R., Harper, K., Huybers, P., Litt, T., Manning, S.W., Mayewski, P.A., More, A.F.M., Nicolussi, K. and Tegel W. (2012) Climate Change during and after the Roman Empire: Reconstructing the Past from Scientific and Historical Evidence. In *Journal of Interdisciplinary History* 43:2, 169–220.
Moore, P.D., Webb, J.A. and Collinson, M.E. (1991) *Pollen Analysis*. London, Blackwell Scientific.
Noble, G. and Evans, N. (2019) *The King in the North: The Pictish Realms of Fortriu and Ce*. Edinburgh, Birlinn.
Noble, G. and Evans, N. (2022) *PICTS Scourge of Rome, Rulers of the North*. Edinburgh, Birlinn.
Noble, G., Gondek, M., Campbell, E., Evans, N., Hamilton, D. and Taylor, S. (2019a) A powerful place of Pictland: Interdisciplinary perspectives on a power centre of the 4th to 6th centuries AD. In *Medieval Archaeology* 63(1), 56–94.
Noble, G., Maclver, C., O'Driscoll, J. and Masson-Maclean, E. (2019b) *Cairnmore* (Data Structure Report). Aberdeen, University of Aberdeen (Unpublished report).
Noble, G., Maclver, C., O'Driscoll, J. and Masson-Maclean, E. (2019c) *Excavations at Tap O'Noth 2019* (Data Structure Report). Aberdeen, University of Aberdeen (Unpublished report).
Ramsay, S. (1995) *Woodland clearance in West – Central Scotland during the past 3000 years*. University of Glasgow. Unpublished PhD Thesis. Doi. https://theses.gla.ac.uk/71679/1/10391313.pdf
Reed, N. (1978) The Scottish campaigns of Septimus Severus. *Proceedings of the Society of Antiquaries of Scotland* 107, 92–102.
Richmond, I.A. (1943) Recent Discoveries in Roman Britain from the air and in the field. In *Journal of Roman studies* 33, 47–49.
Robertson A.S. (1983) Roman coins found in Scotland, 1971–82. In *Proceedings of the Society of Antiquaries Scotland* 113, 405–48.
Shelly, M. (2013) The Isle of Loch Clunie: the key to the see of Dunkeld. In *The Innes Review* 64(1), 39–65.
St Joseph, J.K. (1951) Air reconnaissance of north Britain. In *Journal of Roman studies* 41(1–2), 52–65.
St Joseph, J.K. (1978) The Camp at Durno, Aberdeenshire, and the site of Mons Graupius. In *Britannia* 9, 271–87.

Stratigos, M.J. (2017) *Crannogs in North-East Scotland: Understanding the Resource.* PhD Thesis (Aberdeen, University of Aberdeen). Doi. http://ethos.bl.uk/OrderDetails.do?uin=uk.bl.ethos.731628

Stratigos, M.J. and Noble, G. (2018) A new chronology for crannogs in north-east Scotland. In *Proceedings of the Society of Antiquaries of Scotland* 147, 147–73.

Stuiver, M. and Reimer, P.J. (1993) CALIB rev. 8. In *Radiocarbon* 35, 215–30.

Stuiver, M., Reimer, P.J. and Reimer, R.W. (2022) CALIB 8.2. Doi. http://calib.org.

Tipping, R. and Tisdall, E. (2005) The landscape context of the Antonine Wall: a review of the literature. In *Proceedings of the Society of Antiquaries Scotland* 135, 443–69.

Tweddle, J., Edwards, K. and Fieller, N. (2005) Multivariate statistical and other approaches for the separation of cereal from wild Poaceae pollen using a large Holocene dataset. In *Vegetation History and Archaeobotany* 14, 15–30.

Van Geel, B. (1976) *A Palaeoecological Study of Holocene Peat Bog Sections Based on the Analysis of Pollen, Spores and Macro- and Microscopic Remains of Fungi, Algae, Cormophytes and Animals.* Amsterdam, Academisch proefschrift. Huego de Vries laboratorium, Universiteit van Amsterdam.

Whittington, G. and Edwards, K.J. (1993) Ubi solitudinem faciunt pacem appellant': the Romans in Scotland, a palaeoenvironmental contribution. In *Britannia* 24, 13–25.

Woolliscroft, D.J. and Hoffman, B. (2006) *Rome's First Frontier: The Flavian Occupation of Northern Scotland.* Stroud, Tempus.

Chapter 4

Identifying early medieval secular and ecclesiastical landscapes of power and community around Rhynie and Burghead

Nicholas Evans

Introduction

All early medieval societies were the result of a complex web of local, regional and international connections and relationships that intrinsically linked people living throughout the country with the more mobile nobles, kings, clerics, craftsmen and clerics who controlled and transformed resources. However, understanding how local societies in Scotland operated in practice is difficult. We are often forced to make very general statements based on fragmentary evidence or to rely heavily on wider parallels, for example with Ireland, England or the Continent, where sources are more abundant.

The 'Comparative Kingship' project led by Professor Gordon Noble aimed to surmount obstacles to understanding early medieval Scotland by adopting an interdisciplinary approach, including environmental analysis of core samples (see Samantha Jones and Gordon Noble, this volume) and archaeological investigation of two areas, one around Burghead in Moray and another around Rhynie in Aberdeenshire. When combined with the evidence of texts, place-names and territorial units such interdisciplinary research enables us to reconstruct the development of local landscapes of power and local society from the 5th century to the early 12th century more effectively.

In this period, while there is little specific textual evidence relating to the environs of Rhynie and Burghead, these localities can be placed in a broader framework (see Figure 4.1). At the start of the medieval era, the population spoke primarily Pictish, a Celtic language that was a Brittonic language closely related to the ancestral language of Welsh (Rhys 2015). In the late 4th century, Ammianus Marcellinus referred to the Verturiones as one of the two most powerful Pictish peoples (Noble and Evans 2022, 8). Closely related to this population name was the early medieval territory and kingdom

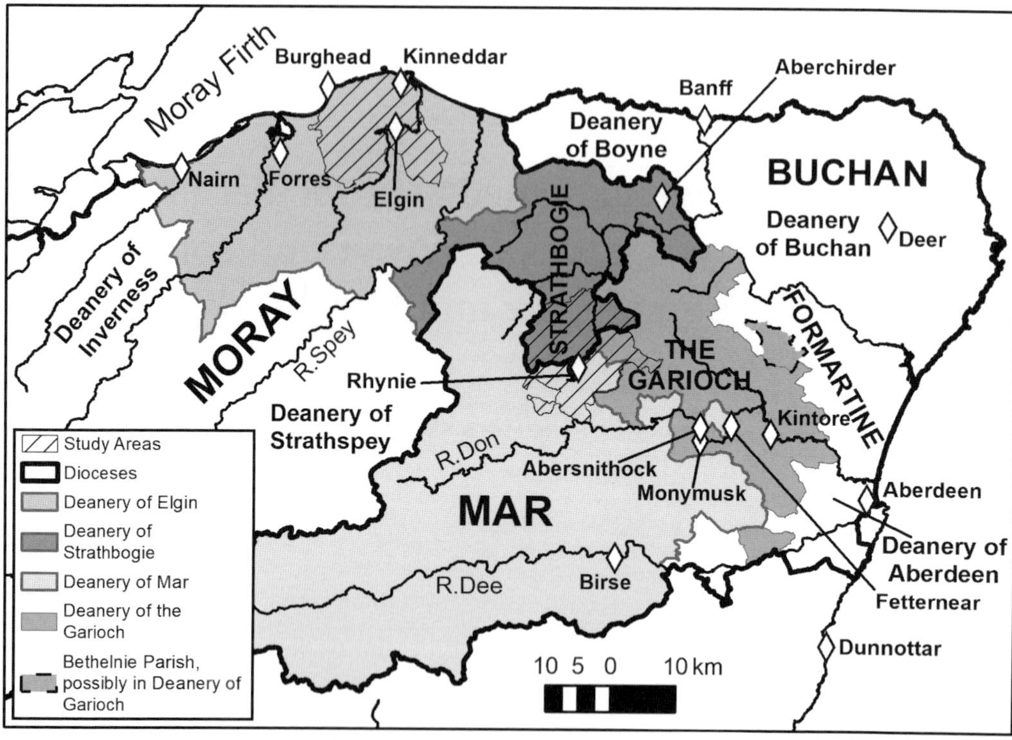

Figure 4.1. Case study areas, regions, dioceses, deaneries and places in north-east Scotland (Contains OS data © Crown copyright and database right 2024, and NRS data © Crown copyright and database right 2024).

probably based around the Moray Firth called Fortriu in Gaelic (Woolf 2006), which became the most powerful Pictish kingdom in the late 7th century, taking over lands south to the Firth of Forth after the Battle of Dún Nechtain in 685 (Evans with Taylor forthcoming). The main centres and extent of Fortriu before its apogee are uncertain, but it is very likely that Burghead and possibly Rhynie were included.

By 1000, this Pictish kingdom had largely been Gaelicised and was called Alba, *Scotia* in Latin, though there was considerable continuity from the Pictish era (Woolf 2007). In the 12th century we start to get detailed information from charters and other documents about local societies. Such sources indicate that people had key relationships with lords of their settlements and with members of their own kindred (Broun 2015; Taylor 2016, esp. 59–60, 146–7, 150–1). While the names and details are likely to have been different, the meagre evidence that survives shows that early medieval Pictland was similar. Adomnán's 'Law of the Innocents', adopted in the Pictish kingdom as well as the Gaelic world in 697, makes it clear that social stratification and kindreds were fundamental to the functioning of society, since the wider kin group was liable if a member did not pay compensation (Márkus 2008; Noble and Evans 2022, 93).

In the kingdom of Alba there were a variety of rights and responsibilities that connected local people to each other and to those with higher social status. In Alba generally, these included the produce and hospitality renders called *cáin* and *coinnmed*, provided by households and settlements to local secular or ecclesiastical lords, such as the *toísech* (plural *toísig*), sometimes also called a *thanus*, 'thane', and the *mormáer* (plural *mormáir*), a regional lord who by the 12th century was 'first among equals' in a province and was called an 'earl' in English (Broun 2015; forthcoming, a; Taylor 2016, 33–113). In the late 12th century or early 13th century the role of the *mormáer*/earl changed, so that their jurisdiction no longer extended over the whole province. Instead, it was largely confined to the lands of the *mormáer* and this leader's own kindred, where their lordship became more intensive (Broun 2015; Taylor 2016, 81), with the implication that later earldoms do not represent the full extents of earlier provincial *mormáer*doms, which had included the territories of other kindreds and institutions.

In the north-east, property records mainly in Gaelic (plus one in Latin) added in the mid-12th century to a small gospel book, the *Book of Deer*, provide us with valuable details that can be compared with evidence from elsewhere in Alba (Forsyth 2008). Adapting pre-existing sources covering *c.* 950–1150, these texts were written by clerics at the monastery of Deer in Buchan because they wanted to establish, in a sacred book, their immunity from exactions by local lords, especially the *mormáir* of Buchan, and the area's *toísig* (Broun 2008, 342–9; Forsyth *et al.* 2008). While primarily focused on the interests of a substantial local ecclesiastical establishment (Taylor 2008), and containing different vocabulary to other sources in Latin, the *Book of Deer* records present a similar picture overall to that found elsewhere (Broun 2008; 2015, 19–24). The clerics of Deer frequently referred to the *mormáer* and *toísech* in general terms and in particular to the *mormáer* of Buchan and the *toísig* of Clann Morgainn and Clann Chanann, the two kindreds from whose leaders the *mormáer* was selected (Broun 2008, 351–4; 2015, 17–18). Clearly high status was rooted in kinship relations in Buchan. In addition, the ecclesiastical community of Deer itself, kings and members of the royal dynasties of Alba and Moray all appear as lords, though Broun (2008, 352, 355–6) has argued that by the 12th century royal landholding in Buchan could have been minimal.

The property records include not only grants of land, but also donations of the *cuit* ('share, portion') of a king, *mormáer*, or *toísech*, which were the equivalent to the annual *cáin* render, as well as cases where the burdens attached to grants to Deer are described as being 'extinguished' (Broun 2008, 329–53). Sometimes the records related these transactions to a small unit called the davoch. Most notably, Text VI states that the *mormáer* of Buchan, his wife, and the *toísech* of Clann Morgainn extinguished all the burdens on the donations that would apply to four davochs throughout the chief settlements or districts of Alba (*ard-mandaidib Alban*) and its chief churches (*ard chellaib*) (Broun 2008, 340; Forsyth *et al.* 2008, 140–1).

The davoch varied in nature, but usually consisted of multiple settlements, lands and water, leading Alasdair Ross to regard it as a territory that provided all the necessary resources for a functioning local society (Ross 2015, 175–6). By the 12th century the three 'royal service' common burdens of providing men for the army, labour service, and 'aids' (renders to supply the army) were imposed on the davoch (Ross 2015, 151–60; Taylor 2016, 91–101). Davoch is Scots, a borrowing of the Gaelic word *dabach*, meaning 'a large tub or vat with two handles' (eDIL, *s.v. dabach*). *Dabach* is attested in Scotland by the 11th century, the *Book of Deer* probably providing an early example with its record of a donation by King Máel Coluim son of Cináed (1005–1034) of *dá dabeg uactair Ros a[n] Bard*, 'two davochs of the upland of Ros in Baird' (a place meaning 'promontory of the poet'), likely to include modern Auchnavaird in Old Deer parish (II.7c: Forsyth *et al.* 2008, 138–41; Taylor 2008, 297–8; Ross 2011, 27). However, the davoch unit probably originates in the Pictish era, perhaps in the late 9th century, building on pre-existing local units of varied origins and types (Woolf 2017; Broun forthcoming, b). Indeed, *Doldauha*, 'haugh of the davoch', in Braemar in the St Andrews Foundation Account B could even represent a preceding phase when the davoch had a more restricted meaning and usage (Taylor with Márkus 2009, 571, 591–2; Broun forthcoming, b).

By the late 12th century the kingdom of the Scots was also divided into parishes, whose priests ministered to the community and obtained revenues, in particular teinds (tithes), to support the Church. Ross argued (2011, 26–7) that, since parish boundaries in northern Scotland corresponded to those of their constituent davochs, the parishes were created by combining the territories of multiple davochs. Alternatively, it has been argued that parishes often were based on and thus reflected lordships (Rogers 1997), but the degree to which parishes and local lordships coincide has been called into question (Broun 2015, 35–41), as can be seen in Aberchirder (also known as Marnoch) parish in Banffshire, which contained two lordships, Netherdale and Aberchirder (Ross 2015, 200). We therefore should not assume that each parish had corresponding secular and ecclesiastical centres, though many in our areas did. Parishes were not secular units, so various factors, including half a millennium of local Christian life, could have influenced their boundaries when these were formalised in the 12th century, and some change is even evident in subsequent centuries.

At the same time as parishes were formed, we gain greater evidence for related larger Church structures, most notably dioceses led by bishops, often divided into deaneries for more effective administration. It has been suggested that in Scotland such dioceses and deaneries often reflected the earlier religious landscape (Barrow 1975, 126–7; Stringer 1985, 65–6). Church possessions, sometimes detached from the core, were often kept with their parent establishment when these became diocesan centres, vying with another tendency, that of having dioceses coinciding broadly with secular lordships (as seen, for example, in the dioceses of Dunblane and Glasgow). This was also the case for the subdivisions of the diocese, the deaneries.

In the north-east, the diocese of Moray broadly matched, albeit with some differences, the extent of the large secular province of Moray as it was before the independent ruling line there ended in 1130 (Ross 2011, 64–80). The lordship of Strathbogie, in existence by the 1220s, is one area of uncertainty; it was part of the diocese of Moray (in the deanery of Strathbogie), but was not in the post-1312 earldom, so it is unclear whether it had been in Moray before 1130. Rather than coinciding with a single secular territory, the diocese of Aberdeen included a number of lordships: the earldoms of Mar and Buchan, and by the early 13th century the lordship of the Garioch, alongside a number of other landholdings, such as the substantial 13th-century royal thanage of Kintore (Grant 1993, 74). Some of the diocese's deaneries were named after the lordships of Mar, the Garioch and Buchan, though they also included other parishes, such as those dominated by the bishops of Aberdeen. It is likely that administrative concerns, such as geographical proximity, as well as earlier provinces and patterns of lordship decided which deanery a particular parish was in; there is no reason to assume that deaneries preserved archaic social or political conditions from the early medieval era.

In the north-east evidence survives for *mormáir* of Buchan, Mar, and Moray. *Mormáir* of Buchan, some active in the 11th century, appear in the *Book of Deer* records (Texts II.2, II.3a, II.14, VI; Forsyth *et al.* 2008, 136–41; Broun forthcoming, a). The title *mormáer* of Mar first appears applied to Domnall son of Eimen son of Cainnech, in the Irish chronicles' lists of dead leaders at the Battle of Clontarf in Ireland in 1014 (AU 1014.2, CS 1014.2). Mar's extent is uncertain, but it may originally have been confined to Deeside, later expanding to include Donside, and presumably northwards to Clova, Auchindoir and perhaps the Cabrach (Broun forthcoming, a; Evans with Taylor forthcoming).

Mormaír of Moray also appear in Irish chronicles in the early 11th century, but then the same ruling dynasty produced two kings of Alba, MacBethad and Lulach, probably with legitimacy through their descent and inheritance from one branch of the royal dynasty (McGuigan 2021, 57–64, 85–9, 109–12, 132–8). After their deaths in 1057 or 1058, their successors appear as kings of Moray, until King Óengus was killed in battle in 1130 and the separate Moravian power base was dismantled by King David I (1124–53) (Barrow 1988, 1–7, 10; Oram 2004, 89–110). David I placed William fitz Duncan in a position of power there, but after his death *c.* 1147 there was no earl/*mormáer* of Moray until it was re-created as an earldom by Robert I (the Bruce) in 1312 (Barrow 1988, 1–2; Oram 2004, 93–6; Ross 2011, 67, 78).

Reconstructing from the Church diocese of Moray and the re-established earldom of Moray, it is clear that Moray was a very large secular and ecclesiastical province stretching from at least the Spey to the Atlantic seaboard (Ross 2011, 64–80), including Burghead, but probably not Rhynie. Nevertheless, given that the rulers of Moray were making donations in Buchan to Deer in the 11th century (II.8, II.9, also possibly II.6: Broun 2008, 331, 356 n. 71; Forsyth *et al.* 2008, 136–9), it is possible that they also were involved elsewhere in the north-east, at least before the very late 11th century (McGuigan 2021, 344–8).

The situation outside Mar, Buchan, and Moray before the late 12th century is pretty obscure. In regions like Strathbogie, the Garioch, Formartine and coastal Banffshire (roughly the deanery of Boyne in the diocese of Aberdeen) it may be that kings of Alba and their dynasty more generally were dominant, as indicated by royal lordships in the late 13th century at Kintore, Aberchirder and elsewhere (Grant 1993, 73–4), as well as royal grants to create the lordship of the Garioch. However, it is likely that other lords held dominions in these regions, though the lack of early medieval references make this difficult to assess.

Therefore, as is shown in the Book of Deer records, by the early 12th century there were complex webs of interactions in and between local society and the wider realm. Can we trace any of this to the Alba or Pictish periods in the north-east, especially in our two case study areas around Rhynie and Burghead?

Rhynie and its environs

The case study region of Rhynie and its immediate environs incorporates parishes later in Aberdeenshire and Banffshire, now all in the Aberdeenshire Council area (see Figure 4.2). The area contains uplands, valleys, mosses, and a mixed arable and pastoral landscape (Jones *et al.* 2021; Shepherd 2021, esp. 88–92). Archaeologically, the project has identified significant 1st millennium sites at Rhynie, but also Tap o' Noth (dating from the 3rd to 7th centuries), Rhynie (late 4th century to mid-6th century), and Cairn More in Kearn parish (5th to 7th century) (Noble *et al.* forthcoming). However,

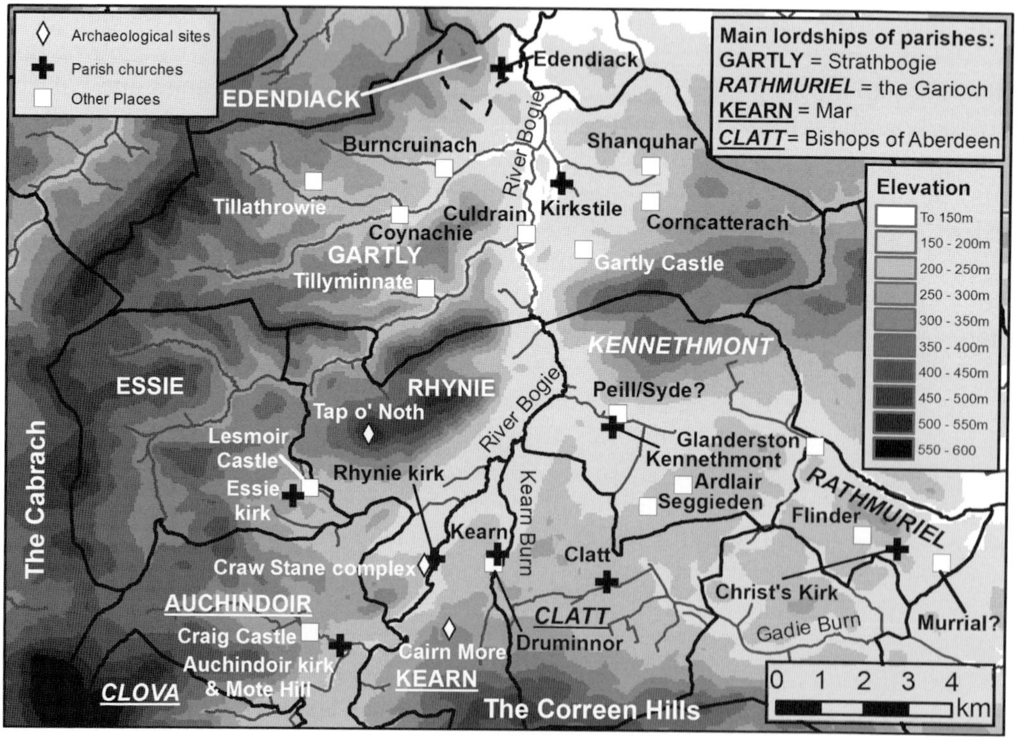

Figure 4.2. Places, medieval parishes and lordships in the environs of Rhynie (Contains OS data © Crown copyright and database right 2024, and NRS data © Crown copyright and database right 2024).

our first reference to the area appears in an early 12th-century note added to a king-list of Alba, which stated that King Lulach was killed (in 1057 or 1058) in Strathbogie, at Essie, a medieval parochial centre to the west of Rhynie.

By the early 13th century the environs of Rhynie were divided ecclesiastically between the dioceses of Aberdeen and Moray (see Figure 4.1), and in secular terms (see Figure 4.2) between the earldom of Mar, the lordships of Strathbogie and the Garioch, as well as lands of Aberdeen's bishops including the nearby parishes of Clatt and at least part of Clova (which also encompassed the Cabrach) (RCAHMS 2007, 142–4; Evans with Taylor forthcoming). While not central to these lordships and bishoprics, the area contained nodes for important routeways, providing it with a strategic significance (Simpson 1930, 48–52).

However, Rhynie might have been more at the centre of an earlier Strathbogie polity. The place-name Rhynie is Celtic, meaning 'place of or associated with a great/divine king' (Noble *et al.* 2019, 61), fitting with the archaeological evidence that it was a significant palisaded site, with symbol stones, manufacturing and a large building (Noble *et al.* forthcoming). The Water of Bogie and its catchment were more peripheral to the later lordship of Strathbogie than the River Deveron, beside which its caput, Huntly Castle, was located (Evans with Taylor forthcoming). Perhaps the original lordship of Strathbogie was more focused on the Bogie, including more southerly and easterly lands within the later parishes of Auchindoir, Kearn, Clatt, Kennethmont and Clova in its catchment area, and Rhynie as a centre, which might explain the later name of the lordship.

The organisation of secular resources is difficult to establish in detail for much of the study area in the 12th to 14th centuries. We know that there was a shire of Clatt, as part of the lordship of the bishop of Aberdeen (*RRS* ii, no. 398, from the reign of William I, 1165–1214; RCAHMS 2007, 142–3). Extending a little beyond Clatt parish, this would correspond to the small shires found elsewhere in the realm from which a *toísech* (in Gaelic), otherwise called a thane, extracted dues such as *cáin*, Clatt itself perhaps being the collection point here.

In the Garioch, in Rathmuriel parish, the name Flinder (*flandres c.* 1208 × 1214; Stringer 1985, no. 14 [*Lind. Cart.* no. CXXIX]) reflects Flemish settlement in the area, though nearby Glanderston derives from a *Gillandres Buch* (Gaelic Gilla Andréis with probably an error for Gaelic *buidhe*, 'yellow, blond') active in the early 13th-century Garioch lordship (RCAHMS 2007, 140, 185). In Kennethmont parish, by the 16th century, not far from Kennethmont kirk was the main secular centre called Peill or Syde, located very close to its 17th-century successor, Leith Hall (Alexander 1952, 348). However, two late 12th-century grants by David, Lord of the Garioch, one of Ardlair to the Bishop of Aberdeen (and thus incorporated in the shire of Clatt), in return for David not paying second teinds to the bishop, the other of Seggieden to St Andrews Cathedral Priory (RCAHMS 2007, 143), indicate something of the complexity and changeable nature of lordship.

In the earldom of Mar, the evidence in our study area is somewhat later. It is only in about 1271 that we gain some idea of lordship in Kearn parish, as that is when the Forbes family were established in a barony there and in Forbes (*RRS Handlist/ Alexander III*, no. 198), but a drying kiln excavated at Druminnor indicates that the later castle (near to Kearn parish kirk) was already a site for processing cereals in the mid- to late 12th century (Shepherd 2018). Similarly, at Auchindoir, though the nature of secular lordship before the late medieval era is uncertain, the existence near the parish kirk of a mound – probably a motte (maybe used earlier) – means that secular and religious centres in the 12th or 13th centuries were located close together, before the later establishment of Craig Castle a short distance to the west (Simpson 1930, esp. 54–62).

In the lordship of Strathbogie, local leadership below those based at Huntly is often imperceptible, but in Essie parish Duncan of Frendraught granted to Archibald of Aberchirder the land of Essie called *Kyrketoun*, presumably near the parish kirk (poms.ac.uk/record/source/4758, probably 1296 × 1314). Near to this was Lesmoir, probably the main secular centre for the parishes of Essie and Rhynie, its Gaelic meaning (*lios*, 'enclosure, enclosed settlement', but with local importance, plus *mór*, 'big') indicating that it was probably a significant early medieval centre (Evans with Taylor forthcoming). In addition, in the 1220s, after a dispute with the lord of Strathbogie, the bishops of Moray were granted half-davoch portions in various places in the lordship, mainly around the parish churches (*Moray Reg.* no. 30).

Overall, we do get some evidence for the existence of shires, local secular lords, lower in status than the regional magnates, and of some smaller landholdings in the Rhynie area. The main centres do seem to indicate that significant secular and ecclesiastical sites were located close together, and it is possible to discern some interesting patterns, including perhaps the movement of people and goods eastwards through the Garioch, though caution is needed as the evidence is not clear-cut (Evans forthcoming). If there was a trend, especially in the second half of the 12th century, towards the creation of more consolidated lordships, where one person was lord of both the settlement (and its inhabitants) and controlled renders like *cáin* (Broun 2015, 46–53), then we might expect the earlier pattern of ownership, rights, and responsibilities to be in some ways more complex than later.

However, we can gain some idea of change over time reaching back into the early medieval era, with the davoch. This unit appears in the names of two of our medieval parishes, Edendiack (Old Gaelic étan, now *aodainn*, 'face, slope of hill', plus *dabach*, so 'a davoch on a hillside or slope'; Alexander 1952, 269) and the earlier name of Auchindoir, *Dauachendor* (*Abdn. Reg.* ii, 52, 1270 × 1279). This supports Alasdair Ross's argument (2011, 26–7) that the davoch unit was earlier than parishes, though not necessarily that davochs were the building blocks employed to create parochial boundaries. We find half-davochs in our first charters referring to the lordship of Strathbogie in the 1220s and davochs in the Gordon rental for the Lordship of Strathbogie in 1600 (*Huntly-Strathbogie Rental*; Ross 2015, 100). Clearly, the davoch was a durable unit in this area, though in many cases other land units, like ploughgates, are found in our documents. Can we go further, as Ross did (2015, 60–64, 195–6), and argue that the davochs of the early modern era are survivals, even down to their boundaries, from the Pictish period *c.* 800?

The answer is 'no'. The archaeological excavations in the Rhynie area, when combined with the place-name and other documentary evidence, enable us to create a more reliable chronological sequence at a sub-parish level than would be possible otherwise (see Figure 4.3). We are lucky to have late 18th-century estate plans for much of the Rhynie area, which include boundaries for 'possessions' or 'farms', comprising multiple settlements and fields (for instance, RHP2254). Often these 'possessions' were divisions of earlier, larger units. For instance, Simon Taylor has argued (Taylor and Evans 2021) that there was once a large Noth unit, including all Noth names in the parish, both hills like Tap o' Noth and Hill of Noth and low-lying names like Old Noth, New Noth, Milton of Noth, and Smithston, which earlier was called 'Smithston of Noth'. Noth is probably a Pictish, or less likely a Gaelic, word meaning 'bare, exposed', maybe referring to woodland clearance for agriculture or to the upland area around Tap o' Noth (Taylor and Evans 2021). It is likely that the Noth area reflects to some extent the immediate hinterland that could provide provisions that helped to support the 1st millennium site at Tap o' Noth (see Plate 4.1).

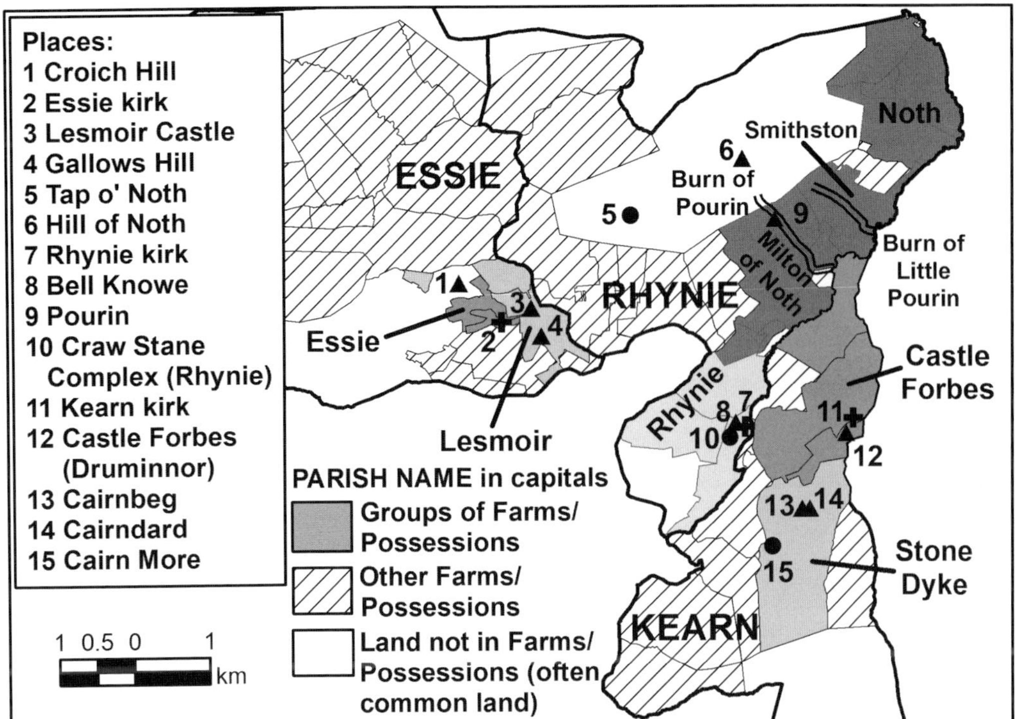

Figure 4.3. The medieval parishes of Rhynie, Essie and Kearn utilising RHP2254 (1776) and RHP260/1 (c. 1771) (Contains OS data © Crown copyright and database right 2024, and NRS data © Crown copyright and database right 2024).

The sub-divisions of Noth are also instructive. According to Ross (2015, 284), two of these, Smithston and Old and New Noth (together), were identified as davochs, and were thus regarded as early, but this description seems to only be based on statements by Macdonald (1891, 252–3, 274). However, the use of Scots in these cases, as with others, indicates that these units were created in the late medieval period, not in the Pictish era. It might be objected that these were simply older units renamed or translated into Scots from Pictish predecessors, but there are other names in Gaelic and a few, probably in Pictish, in the same area. On the first edition Ordnance Survey maps there is a settlement called Pourin, Burn of Pourin and Burn of Little Pourin in the areas of Smithston and Milton of Noth. Pourin includes the word *pòr*, 'cropland', a Gaelic loanword from Pictish, plus a diminutive suffix, so it means 'at the cropland' (Evans with Taylor forthcoming). Cutting across the later 18th-century possessions, they represent a Pictish or Gaelic phase of naming inside Noth before that part of the unit was divided.

What we get, therefore, with Noth is a Pictish unit, which potentially was the immediate supplying-hinterland of Tap o' Noth in the 4th to 7th centuries AD. By 1200 the Noth area was combined with other units, including those around Rhynie, to create the parish of Rhynie, the church representing a degree of continuity from the Craw Stane complex. The Pourin names represent part of the early medieval division (at least in terms of function) of this landscape, but they were not the basis for the later davochs into which Noth was divided. Some davochs existed in Rhynie parish by the 1220s, but certainly others were later creations, the result evolving into the possessions of the 18th century.

In Kearn parish we cannot identify developments in such depth, but there is a similar overall trajectory of a move to lower-lying power centres. There, excavations have shown that Cairn More ('big cairn'), situated on a hill on the northern side of the Correen Hills, was a significant settlement that fell out of use in the 7th century (Noble *et al.* forthcoming). Cairn More (see Plate 4.2) was located *c.* 1771 in a farm unit called Stone Dyke (RHP260/1), where to the north there are other place-names containing Gaelic *càrn* 'cairn, heap of stones, burial mound' (Taylor with Márkus 2012, 322): Cairndard, 'cairn of the height', beside which the Ordnance Survey 6 inch first-edition map (1870) had a Cairnbeg, 'little cairn' settlement (Evans with Taylor forthcoming). These might represent Cairn More's hinterland, but by the 12th century Druminnor and Kearn were the locality's key places. Kearn probably comes from Old Gaelic *cern*, 'angle, corner, recess' (modern Gaelic *ceàrn*), and Druminnor may mean 'the ridge of the confluence', with Gaelic *druim*, 'ridge, back' plus *inbhear* 'river-mouth, confluence'. Therefore, both names seemingly relate to the narrowing land between the Bogie and Kearn burns in the north of this parish, reflecting a shift to lower locations for elite sites (Evans with Taylor forthcoming).

Local relationships with lords meant that people had various obligations, as individuals, members of families, kindreds, settlements (with related land), davochs, parishes and shires. The most forceful and fearful presentation of power relates to local justice, embodied in Essie parish in the place-names Gallows Hill, to the south-east of Lesmoir Castle, and in Croich Hill, the Gaelic equivalent further to the west (Alexander 1952, 244), but it is unclear how old this usage was. However, decision-making would often have entailed negotiation (with or without a lord being represented), which was most easily undertaken at meeting places. Their locations often are obscure, though pre-existing monuments, like the prehistoric cairn at Bell Knowe (Canmore ID 17195) near Rhynie provides one potential site. We can assume in some cases that the davoch provided locations for parochial meeting places, as at Auchindoir, where these were presumably held around the kirk and the nearby Mote Hill.

In Gartly parish, though they require further investigation, place-names might sometimes indicate the significance of these meeting places for local society (see Figure 4.2). Three significant places there, already present by the 16th century, contain Gaelic *tulach*, 'hillock, mound', often used for significant secular sites in the east of Scotland (Taylor with Márkus 2012, 519–20). Gartly itself (*Garentuli* 1232 × 1237, *Lind. Cart.* no. 18), corresponding to Grandtully in Perthshire, comes from (unexplained) *garen* or similar plus *tulach* (Alexander 1952, 287). The existence of an earlier high-status site nearby is indicated by two other names, Shanquhar (Gaelic *seann* plus **cair*, 'old fort': Taylor with Márkus 2012, 316–18; *cf.* Alexander 1952, 370) and Corncatterach (Gaelic *coire* + *na* + *cathrach*, 'Corrie of the seat/fort': Watson 1926, 222), so here it is possible that Gartly was established or came to the fore after the demise of the earlier centre.

Two other places, Tillathrowie and Tillyminnate, both in western Gartly, also contain *tulach*. Tillathrowie's lands covered a substantial area and included a chapel and well dedicated to St Finnan, whose cult is found elsewhere in Aberdeenshire (Clancy 2008, 370–5). Macdonald (1891, 104) suggested that Tillyminnate had Gaelic *mennat* (eDIL *s.n. mennat*, 'A place of abode in wide sense (of locality or district, not of dwelling-house)', as its specific (*Tollemenat* 1545 *RMS* iii. 3103; *Tullemenett* 1600 *Huntly-Strathbogie Rental*, 272; Alexander 1952, 392), but there are other possibilities (*e.g.* Jackson 1972, 78). Interestingly, an estate plan from 1776 (RHP2240) has 'Cairn a Ruin' marked on 'Castle hilloc' beside the settlement, which could be the focus, and also a nearby field called 'Finands Burn shade' (shade is 'a strip of land, a distinct or separate piece of land': Taylor with Márkus 2012, 492), probably referring also to the same St Finnan venerated at Tillathrowie. Intriguingly, if we include Gartly, with its relatively close parochial church at Kirkstile, all three *tulach* places here were associated with Christian religious sites, though it should be noted that Tillathrowie and Tillyminnate could actually once have been in Edendiack parish.

It is interesting to speculate whether other potential meeting places in Gartly parish were different in nature or date. There are other possible place-names containing references to assembly. Culdrain could derive from Gaelic *comhdail*, meaning 'assembly place' and Gaelic *droigheann*, 'thorn', both of which are more certainly found in Coldrain in Fossaway parish, Kinross-shire (Barrow 1992, esp. 234; Taylor 2020, 401–3, 412). Burncruinach (attested in the 18th-century RHP2289 as *Burn Cruinach*), probably containing Gaelic *cruinneachaidh*, 'meeting, assembly', and Coynachie (*Connachie* 1535 *RMS* iii no. 1453; *Conzeauchye* 1600 *Huntly-Strathbogie Rental*, 272), possibly containing Gaelic *coinneachadh* may be other examples, but they have been interpreted to have referred instead to the confluences of watercourses (Macdonald 1891, 97–98; Alexander 1952, 191, 234) and alternative words may underlie these names. Leaving aside uncertain cases, there still is substantial evidence overall for multiple centres in Gartly parish where medieval communal events took place.

Burghead and its environs

Our second case study is focused around Burghead and Kinneddar near the Moray Firth (see Figure 4.4). This coastal area has undergone substantial environmental change, which can be correlated with archaeological, place-name and other textual sources (Stratigos 2020). The sea level has gradually fallen over millennia, which combined with drainage programmes, has resulted in the loss of nearly all the wetlands in the area, reducing Loch Spynie to a tiny loch next to Spynie Castle. In the medieval period Loch Spynie was much larger and connected to the sea, while inland from Burghead

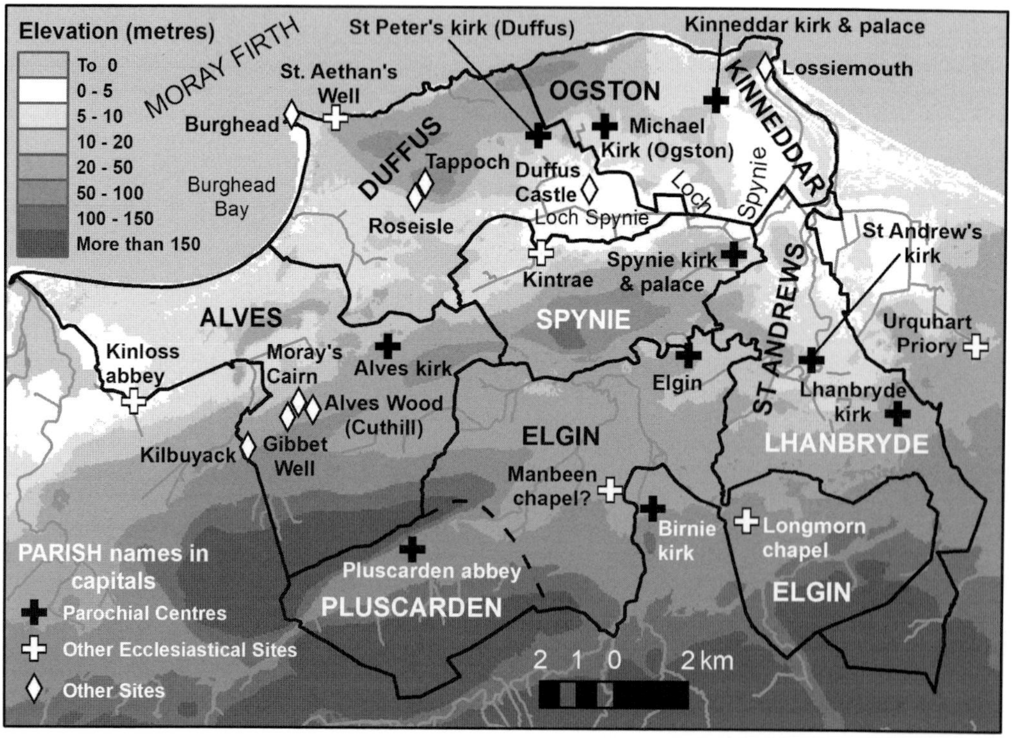

Figure 4.4. Places and medieval parishes in the environs of Burghead (Contains OS data © Crown copyright and database right 2024, and NRS data © Crown copyright and database right 2024).

Bay there were many lochs, bogs and mosses (Stratigos 2020). Thus the area from Burghead, a major Pictish fort from the 6th to the late 9th or early 10th century, to the ecclesiastical centre at Kinneddar, near to Lossiemouth at the eastern end of the headland, was a distinct peninsula with limited land access in a way that is difficult to visualise today.

Burghead and Kinneddar were clearly two important Pictish centres of Fortriu, but the case study area continued to be significant in subsequent centuries. After 1130 we can gradually build up a picture of settlements, landholdings and rights in the area. Royal burghs were established near to the Moray Firth, Elgin and Forres being the closest to Burghead and with associated royal officers called 'grieves' allocated lands in the area (Duncan 1975, 189–91; Barrow 1988, 2). There were also royal 'forests' (which were not primarily woods) in the area at *Kelbuthac* (Kilbuiack, Alves parish) (*RRS* ii, no. 159, 1173 × 1177, probably 1176), Longmorn and Pluscarden (Elgin parish) (*Moray Reg.* no. 29, from 1226; *Records of Elgin* I, 10–11, from *c.* 1303). Moreover, just outside our study area, by the 1150s, David I had established a Cistercian priory at Urquhart, and inside the study area at Kinloss, with a later Premonstratensian abbey founded inland at Pluscarden in the early 1230s (Barrow 2003, 167; Oram 2011, 358).

Among the most prominent lords in the area were the bishops of Moray, who had residences at Kinneddar, Spynie (in addition to Birnie just south of the project area), while from the early 13th century Elgin was the seat of their bishopric, with an established chapter (Noble *et al.* 2018, 115). After 1130 the Flemish Freskin family also settled in the area, controlling Duffus Castle by Loch Spynie and coming to be known as *de Moravia* as a result (Duncan 1975, 189; Barrow 1988, 2–3). It has plausibly been suggested that many of their lands were those of the former rulers of Moray (Barrow 1988, 3), which is particularly likely in Duffus parish, which contained the former major stronghold at Burghead.

Yet, as elsewhere, the pattern of lordship and how that impinged on local communities and the landscape could be complex (see Figure 4.5). Inverlochty, west of Elgin, was granted in the 1150s by King David I to Kinloss Abbey (*Moray Reg.* CO no. 3; CO no. 5 = *Kinloss Recs.* no. 6), but by 1226 a certain Archebald of Inverlochty was a significant local figure, witnessing charters and holding lands in the fief of Spynie from the Bishop of Moray by the River Lossie, over which he built a bridge (*Moray Reg.* nos. 27, from 1224 × 1242, 31 and 120, both from 1226). The exact situation eludes us, but it is possible that Archebald administered Inverlochty for the monastery of Kinloss and nearby lands in the fief of Spynie for the Bishops of Moray, while retaining a high personal social status.

King David I presumably held Inverlochty before its grant to Kinloss, but the Freskins also had rights in this land. In 1263 'Lord Freskin of Moray' collected 3 marks annually in Inverlochty, and so clearly also had a pre-existing status in this area (*Moray Reg.* no. 125). Similarly, in Spynie parish, in 1226 a dispute arising from claims by Walter (Freskin) *de Moravia* to rights to the resources of the woods and

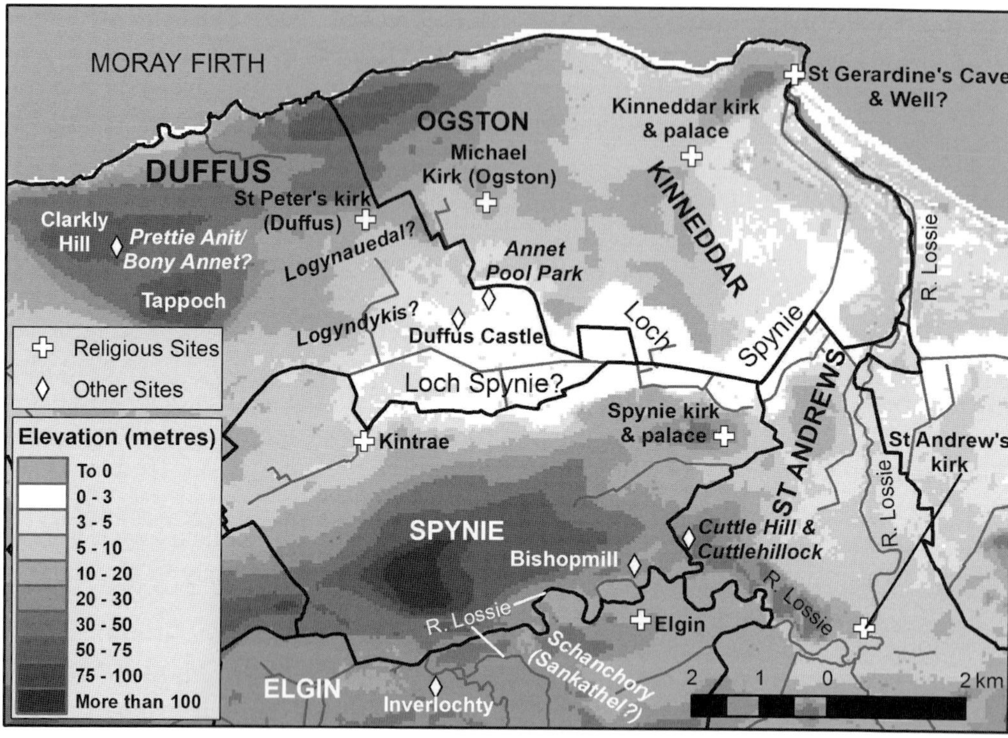

Figure 4.5. The area around Loch Spynie (Contains OS data © Crown copyright and database right 2024, and NRS data © Crown copyright and database right 2024).

moors of Spynie and Findrassie on the south side of Loch Spynie were resolved by stipulating his rights in detail (*Moray Reg.* 120). In these cases, it could be speculated that the Freskins had maintained the rights of the *mormáir*/kings of Moray in places that had come to be dominated by ecclesiastical institutions and the kings of Alba. So, in Inverlochty we get a glimpse of a picture of varied recipients of produce and multiple layers of lordship with which local people would need to negotiate.

When attempting to reconstruct the early medieval social landscape in this area, we face considerable obstacles, because no shires and few davochs appear in our sources, and it is often difficult to date sites. An example is the area's *cuthill* names, which refer to assembly sites (Taylor 2020; Evans forthcoming). One *Cuthill* was a name for Alves Wood in 1567, in which there is Moray's Cairn (Canmore ID 16248), a cluster of sites located on a ridge relatively central to Alves parish including Gallows Hill and Gibbet Well just to the west (*Moray Reg.*, 393; Barrow 1992, 231). Other cases occur in Spynie parish where a *villa* of *Cuthilfeld* was mentioned in 1389 (*Moray Reg.*1837, 199; Barrow 1992, 235), a *Cuthilbyrnie hill* (perhaps with Sc. *birny*, adj. of *birn*, 'pasture on dry heathy ground': Taylor with Márkus 2012, 297) near *Bischoppis mylne* (now Bishopsmill) is referred to in 1567 (*Moray Reg.* 1837, 395; Barrow 1992, 235), possibly either the *Cuttle Hill* or *Cuttle hillock* depicted on Spynie parish's south-eastern border on an estate plan of 1764 (RHP11823). Located on raised ground away from parish churches, they were clearly significant, but the Scots specifics of many of these names make it less likely that they are early medieval (Taylor 2020, 398–404).

However, there are place-names and fragments of evidence in post-1100 sources that enable us to discern change and to identify aspects of the earlier medieval landscape. For instance, in the fief of Spynie there was also a *Sankathel* (*Moray Reg.* no. 27, 1224 × 1242), from Gaelic *seann + cathair*, 'old seat' (Barrow 2003, 54; Taylor with Márkus 2012, 317), on the east bank of the River Lossie close to the aforementioned bridge built by Archebald of Inverlochty. This name indicates that in the Gaelic-speaking period there was a substantial disused site, perhaps outside Spynie parish but inside the secular Spynie lordship. Since *cathair* and **cair* could be substituted for each other in eastern Scotland, it is tempting to connect it to the places variously named *Sanchory*, *Schancory* or *Sanquary* wood, *Sanquare* or *Schanchory* hill, and *the Sanquhary*, probably including Gaelic *seann* and Gaelic **cair*, 'fort, fortification', a loan-word from Pictish (Watson 1926, 365–71; Taylor 2011, 100–1). These were located to the west of Elgin, according to the burgh's attempts to regulate its usage as attested in the 16th-century Burgh Court Book (*Records of Elgin* I, 62, 63, 97–98, 117, 121, 125, 258). Perhaps further investigation will discover whether *Sankathel* and *Schanchory* were the same place, and to what feature(s) they were related.

On the ecclesiastical side, there is some evidence for ongoing change throughout the medieval period. Pluscarden was probably part of Elgin parish before the foundation of the monastery there in the 1230s led to it becoming a new parish. Moreover, Kintrae at the western end of Loch Spynie (hence its Gaelic name, *ceann + tràigh*, 'end of the shore'), was described as an 'old church' (*vetus ecclesia de Kyntra* in *Moray Reg.* no. 211) in 1203 × 1222, and was incorporated into Spynie parish (Cowan 1967, 205). Presumably, its position in the landscape became less nodal as Loch Spynie and other wetlands receded, encouraging the use of other routeways to and from the Burghead to Lossiemouth area and diminishing its importance.

However, the Gaelic names of nearly all the area's parishes, except perhaps Ogston and Spynie, whose origins are uncertain, would fit the view that the post-1100 ecclesiastical landscape was often considerably older. Indeed, in the cases of Duffus kirk and Kinneddar, Pictish sculpture indicates that they had earlier origins, their Pictish names perhaps supplanted or Gaelicised. The former process may have taken place at St Peter's, Duffus, since some charters refer to the lands of *Logynauedal* and the *Logyndykis* (*Moray Reg.* no. 119; *SEA* I, no. 113, 15 March 1187 × 1203, possibly 1190) in the vicinity. No longer extant, *Logynauedal* is described as by or near Duffus kirk (see Plate 4.3), while *Logyndykis* includes the Germanic word *dyke*, 'ditch, wall, dyke', most likely relating to drainage ditches (Clancy 2016, 61) around the lower, boggy wetlands extending south to Loch Spynie and south-west to the Unthank mosses and muirs. Both place-names contain **login*, from Latin *locus*, 'place, ecclesiastical site, holy place', used for Pictish churches, leading Thomas Clancy (2016, 49–51, 61) to suggest that the **login* here was St Peter's Kirk, the name supplanted by Duffus (probably Gaelic *dubh*, 'black', plus *-as*, *-us*, 'place'). If so, then probably the name Duffus first related to the castle's site, before this fort's significance resulted in the name's application to Duffus parish's kirk.

Given our patchy evidence base, it is difficult to move beyond the identification of early medieval places to a wider understanding of the cultural landscape. Kinneddar is a clear example of continuity, with evidence for activity commencing there AD 585–655 (95% probability), ditches cut implying the beginning of ecclesiastical use in the 7th century. A high-status in the Pictish era is indicated by surviving sculpture found in the vicinity, with occupation continuing after the 1st millennium, when it was an episcopal seat for the bishops of Moray (Noble *et al.* 2018). Once the cathedral was established at Elgin, the bishops built a palace at Kinneddar (Dransart 2016, 73–74). The place-name Kinneddar includes Gaelic *ceann* 'head, end' and *foithir*. *Foithir* probably had a range of meanings over many centuries, so no single explanation will fit all the evidence, but in former Pictland it is often found in parish names, so it is perhaps a Gaelic rendering of Pictish **uotir*, literally 'under' plus 'land', used for administrative units (Taylor with Márkus 2012, 376–8). *Foithir* first appears in Scottish place-names in 680 (AU 681.5), for a siege of *Dún Foither* ('fort of the *foithir*', Dunottar in the Mearns), so it is possible that the name Kinneddar dates to the ecclesiastical establishment's foundation or earlier. It might be speculated that Kinneddar may have begun as the central place of a *foithir* that was originally subordinate to an elite site elsewhere, perhaps Burghead. In a similar way Fetternear in Aberdeenshire was possibly the *foithir* of nearby Ner (now no longer identifiable), which had a monastery by AU 623.2 and was perhaps located at Abersnithock or Monymusk (Clancy 2008, 367–75). In the cases of *Foderbirse* and *Fothrif*, the *foithir*s were constituent parts of, respectively, Birse in Aberdeenshire and Fife, so a *foithir* was not necessarily geographically separate from its superior site (Taylor with Márkus 2012, 72–89, 377). The extent of Kinneddar's *foithir* is unknown, but it may partially have been preserved, with changes over many centuries, in the medieval parish of Kinneddar, which was later combined in the 17th century with neighbouring Ogston to form the modern parish of Drainie (Figure 4.5; Ross 2015, 271).

It is possible that early medieval Kinneddar had wider interests in the area. In Duffus parish two extinct place-names, *Prettie Anit*, roughly at NJ13803868234 between Clarkly Hill and Tappoch (RHP2016, from 1749; *Bony Annet* RHP2004, from 1773) and *Annet Pool Park* located at NJ193586750 north-east of Duffus castle (RHP427, from 1783), contain Gaelic *annat* (Old Gaelic *andóit*). On its own this refers to a mother church, or, when it was the specific part of a name (*eg.* X of the annat), it meant land they held (Clancy 1995; Ross 2003, 59–60). In the case of *Prettie Anit*, the adjective may represent an interpretation of different place-name elements (Taylor, pers. comm.), and there is no evidence for a church at this location. Annet Pool Park at about 1–3 m above sea level, would have been dry (ish) in the 12th century (see Plate 4.4). In the preceding centuries from *c.* 800 to 1100 when we would expect Gaelic *andóit* place-names to have been coined, it would have been dry or at the edge of the tidal range (Stratigos, pers. comm.; *cf.* Stratigos 2020, 217). Nevertheless, its shoreline location makes it an unlikely church location. Both annat place-names probably relate to lands of a church located elsewhere, possibly the kirks of Duffus and Ogston, but another possibility is that Kinneddar was this church, superior to Duffus and Ogston, and holding lands in what became these other parishes. The now-supposed lost well and hermitage of St Gerardine (*i.e.* Gartnait) in Lossiemouth and the graveyard and well of St Aethan (*i.e.* Áedán) around Burghead were also significant parts of this early landscape. The former was perhaps closely connected with Kinneddar (whose patron saint Gartnait may have been), the latter providing a Christian dimension to the Pictish fort (Grant and Leslie 1798, 122; Dransart 2003, 241–2; Noble *et al.* 2018, 139–41).

As with Tap o' Noth, it is possible to identify an immediate hinterland for the stronghold at Burghead. When 18th-century land units are reconstructed and related to earlier charters, it is likely that much of western Duffus parish contains Roseisle names or areas regarded as part of Roseisle (see Figure 4.6). *Rossile* appears as a landholding in a 12th-century charter (1166 × 1171, *RRS* ii, no. 116). This name does

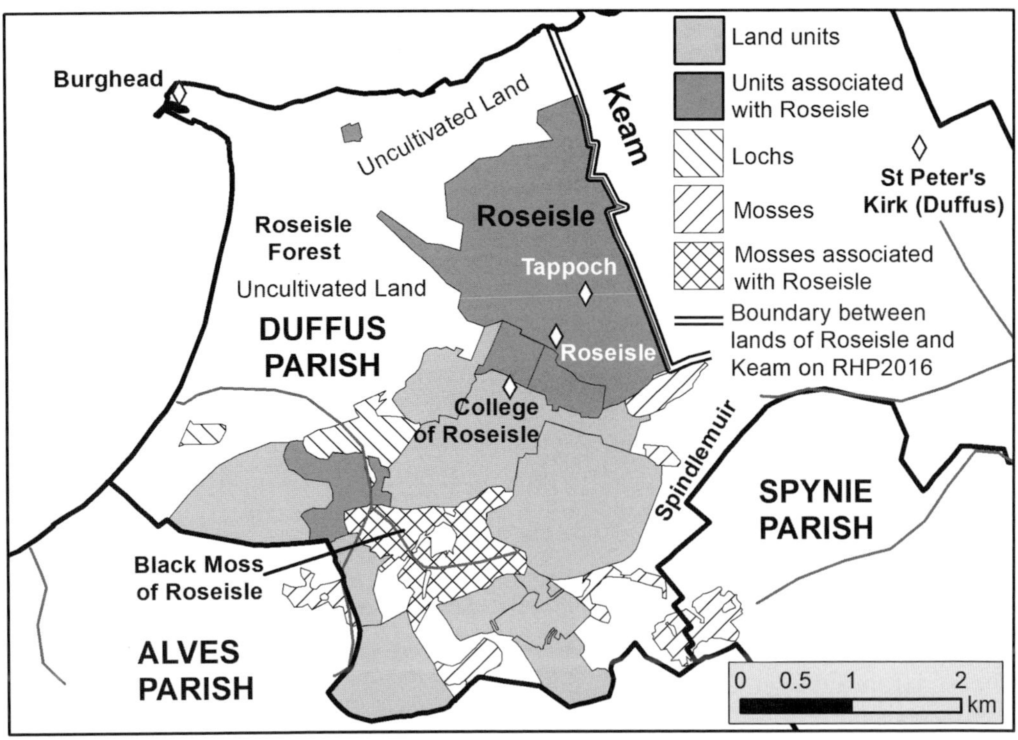

Figure 4.6. Places and units associated with Roseisle, utilising RHP2004 (1773) and RHP2016 (1749) (Contains OS data © Crown copyright and database right 2024, and NRS data © Crown copyright and database right 2024).

not refer to an island of roses, but probably includes **ros*, meaning 'promontory' in Pictish (Taylor with Márkus 2012, 73, 481; Simon Taylor, pers. comm.) and maybe the personal name or element *–Ilei*. Since the Scots name Burghead first appears as *Bruchsey* as late as 1572 (Keillar 1994, 3), it is plausible that Roseisle was originally the Pictish name for Burghead, the inhabitants of the wider Roseisle area perhaps part of a territory providing resources to support this Pictish fortress (Simon Taylor, pers. comm). When Burghead declined, presumably the name Roseisle came to be primarily attached to this hinterland's main settlement by Tappoch and the unit's other lands, whereas the former fort came to have a new name. Some continuing medieval activity and occupation at Burghead is plausible if poorly understood. For instance, the Doorie, a mound in the Burghead fortifications used since 1655 for Hogmanay celebrations, could be a potential meeting site (Canmore ID 16168). Nevertheless, the transformation of the local landscape of power by 1200 was such that Burghead and Roseisle area became part of a Duffus parish whose centres at Duffus Castle and St Peter's Kirk were located far away by its eastern border, well placed to interact with the bishops of Moray and the rising burgh of Elgin.

Conclusion

The overall trajectories of the Burghead and Rhynie areas were quite different, with Burghead's wider locality maintaining its importance, while the environs of Rhynie became a borderland, divided into different lordships and dioceses. However, there are some similarities, for instance in the survival of sites like Kinneddar and Rhynie as central places, but also the demise of early secular foci at Burghead, Tap o' Noth, and Cairn More.

It is possible to also discern dimly the wider territories of important Pictish sites reflected in Roseisle, Noth and Cairn- place-names and sub-parochial land units, though Pourin in Rhynie parish indicates that such large units were never monolithic. By the 12th century these large units had been combined with others to form parishes and were divided up over centuries to create davochs before becoming 18th-century 'possession' farm units. However, with Kinneddar, a development sequence from being the centre of a *foithir* unit, to a powerful mother church, to an episcopal and parochial centre with probably some degree of estate continuity can be discerned.

The earliest davochs, probably dating from the late Pictish era, and with associated military and work obligations, were significant for the lives of their inhabitants. However, they were adaptable, not set in stone, with new davochs created in later centuries. We can only guess whether neighbourhood solidarity or obligations imposed from above created each davoch, but these case studies generally confirm the picture developed elsewhere that lordship was based on a web of rights, obligations and relationships between lords and clients, members of kindreds, families, and neighbourhoods, connecting kings to the poorest labourers and slaves, those with the lowest social status. Assembly sites, where people of different social statuses could interact and be involved in decision-making, can be found, particularly for the period from the 9th century onwards, when Gaelic and then Scots were dominant in these areas. What is clear is that it has only been through an interdisciplinary analysis, here linking textual and place-name evidence to the archaeology, that a very fragmentary picture of change over time has been constructed. Similar research combining different approaches can enable us to investigate the profusion of remaining questions that remain about the development of local society in medieval Scotland.

Acknowledgements

I would like to thank Simon Taylor, Michael Stratigos, and Colin Shepherd for comments on aspects of this piece, along with Gordon Noble and Dauvit Broun, for discussing issues and showing me work before publication.

Sources

Abdn. Reg. = Innes, C. (ed.) (1845) *Registrum episcopatus Aberdonensis*, 2 vols. Spalding and Maitland Clubs.

AU = Mac Airt, S. and Mac Niocaill, G. (eds and trans.) (1983) *The Annals of Ulster (To AD 1131) Part I Text and Translation*. Dublin, Dublin Institute for Advanced Studies.

CS = Hennessy, W. (ed. and trans.) (1866) *Chronicum Scotorum*. London, Rolls Series.

Huntly-Strathbogie Rental = *The Rentaill of the Lordschipe of Huntlye alias Strauthbogye* (1600) (ed. 1849) in *Miscellany of the Spalding Club*, vol. 4. 260–83. Aberdeen, Spalding Club.

Kinloss Recs. = Stuart, J. (ed.) (1872) *Records of the Monastery of Kinloss*. Edinburgh, R & R Clark.

Lind. Cart. = Dowden, J. (ed.) (1903) *Chartulary of the Abbey of Lindores 1195–1479*. Edinburgh, Scottish History Society.

Moray Reg. = Innes, C. (ed.) (1837) *Registrum Episcopatum Moraviensis*. Edinburgh, Bannatyne Club.

Records of Elgin I = Cramond, W. (ed.) (1903) *The Records of Elgin, vol. I*. Aberdeen, Aberdeen University.

RHP427 = Kinnaird, H. (1783) *Plan of the loch of Spynie and adjacent grounds*. National Records of Scotland.

RHP2004 = Taylor, A. (1773) *Plan of the runrig lands in the west end of the Parish of Duffus*. National Records of Scotland.

RHP2016 = Anderson, W. (1749) *Plan of the Duke of Gordon's and Sir Robert Gordon's Estate and Mosses in the West end of the Parish of Duffus*. National Records of Scotland.

RHP260/1 = Anon. (*c.* 1771) *Plan of the lands of Forbes comprehending the parish of Kearn*. National Records of Scotland, courtesy of Lord Forbes.

RHP2240 = Milne, T. (1776) *Plan of Tillyminnate and Strone*. National Records of Scotland.

RHP2254 = Milne, T. (1776) *Plan of part of the Lordship of Huntly lying in the Parishes of Rhynie, Essie and Gairtly and County of Aberdeen*. National Records of Scotland.

RHP2289 = Anon. (18th century) *Plan of the lands of Artlich and part of Braes of Gartly*. National Records of Scotland.

RHP11823 = May, P. (1764) *Plan of the lands of Myreside and Linksfield*. National Records of Scotland.

RMS = Thomson, J.M. *et al.* (eds) (1882–1914), *Registrum Magni Sigilli Regum Scotorum*, 11 vols. Edinburgh, H.M. General Register House.

RRS ii = Barrow, G.W.S. (ed.) (1971) *The Acts of William I King of Scots 1165–1214*. Regesta Regum Scottorum vol. II. Edinburgh, Edinburgh University Press.

RRS Handlist/Alexander III = Simpson, G.G. (1960) *Handlist of the Acts of Alexander III, The Guardians and John (1249–1296)*, Regesta Regum Scottorum. Edinburgh, Department of Scottish History, University of Edinburgh.

SEA I = Shead, N.F. (ed.) (2015) *Scottish Episcopal Acta Volume I. The Twelfth Century*. Woodbridge, Scottish History Society and Boydell.

Bibliography

Alexander, W.M. (1952) *The Place-Names of Aberdeenshire*. Aberdeen, Spalding Club.

Barrow, G.W.S. (1975) The pattern of lordship and feudal settlement in Cumbria. In *Journal of Medieval History* 1, 117–38.

Barrow, G.W.S. (1988) Badenoch and Strathspey, 1130–1312. 1 Secular and Political. In *Northern Scotland* 8, 1–15.

Barrow, G.W.S. (1992) *Scotland and its Neighbours in the Middle Ages*. London, The Hambledon Press.

Barrow, G.W.S. (2003) *The Kingdom of the Scots*, 2nd edn. Edinburgh, Edinburgh University Press.

Broun, D. (2008) The property records in the Book of Deer as a source for early Scottish society. In Forsyth, K. (ed.) *Studies on the Book of Deer*, 313–60. Dublin, Four Courts.

Broun, D. (2015) Statehood and lordship in 'Scotland' before the mid-twelfth century. In *The Innes Review* 66(1), 1–71.

Broun, D. (forthcoming, a) The origins of the *mormaer*. In Brown, M. (ed.) *Earls and Earldoms in Medieval Scotland*. Woodbridge, Boydell.

Broun, D. (forthcoming, b) *Doldauha* and the origins of the *dabach* in Pictland. In Clancy, T.O., Hough, C. and Williamson, E. (eds) *Onomastications: A Festschrift for Simon Taylor*. Glasgow, Clò Gàidhlig Oilthigh Ghlaschu.

Clancy, T.O. (1995) Annat in Scotland and the origins of the parish. In *The Innes Review* 46(2), 91–115.

Clancy, T.O. (2008) Deer and the early church in North-Eastern Scotland. In Forsyth, K. (ed.) *Studies on the Book of Deer*, 363–97. Dublin, Four Courts.

Clancy, T.O. (2016) *Logie*: an ecclesiastical place-name element in eastern Scotland. In *Journal of Scottish Name Studies* 10, 25–88.

Cowan, I.B. (1967) *The Parishes of Medieval Scotland*. Edinburgh, Scottish Record Society.

Dransart, P. (2003) Saints, stones and shrines: the cults of Sts Moluag and Gerardine in Pictland. In Cartwright, J. (ed.) *Celtic Hagiography and Saints' Cults*, 232–48. Cardiff, University of Wales Press.

Dransart, P. (2016) Bishop's Palaces in the Medieval Dioceses of Aberdeen and Moray. In *Transactions of the British Archaeology Association* 40, 58–81.

Duncan, A.A.M. (1975) *Scotland. The Making of the Kingdom*. Edinburgh, Oliver and Boyd.

Evans, N. (forthcoming) Identifying the development of local power centres in Pictland and Alba. In Geddes, J., Hall, M., Plumb, O and Sanmark, A. (eds), *Places of Royal Power and Ritual in Early Medieval Scotland and Europe*. Leiden, Sidestone Press.

Evans, N. with Taylor, S. (forthcoming) Exploring the historical and place-name evidence. In Noble, G. (ed.) *Rhynie*. Edinburgh, Society of Antiquaries of Scotland.

Forsyth, K. (ed.) (2008) *Studies on the Book of Deer.* Dublin, Four Courts.

Forsyth, K., Broun, D. and Clancy, T.O. (2008) The property records: text and translation. In Forsyth, K. (ed.) *Studies on the Book of Deer*, 131–44. Dublin, Four Courts.

Grant, A. (1993) Thanes and Thanages, from the Eleventh to the Fourteenth Centuries. In Grant, A. and Stringer, K.J. (eds) *Medieval Scotland. Crown, Lordship and Community. Essays presented to G.W.S. Barrow*, 39–81. Edinburgh, Edinburgh University Press.

Grant, J. and Leslie, W. (1798) *A Survey of the Province of Moray; Historical, Geographical, and Political.* Aberdeen, Isaac Forsyth.

Jackson, K. (1972) *The Gaelic Notes in the Book of Deer*. Cambridge: Cambridge University Press.

Jones, S.E., Evans, N., Martínez-Cortizas, A., Mighall, T.M. and Noble, G. (2021) Settlement, landscape and land-use change at a Pictish power centre: assessing the palaeoecological record for economic continuity and social change at Rhynie, N.E. Scotland. In *Holocene* 31(6), 897–914.

Keillar, I. (1994) *Place-Names and Settlement Patterns in Part of the Laich of Moray*. Elgin, unpublished.

Macdonald, J. (1891) *Place Names in Strathbogie*. Aberdeen, D. Wyllie and Son.

McGuigan, N. (2021) *Máel Coluim III 'Canmore'. An Eleventh-Century Scottish King*. Edinburgh, John Donald.

Márkus, G. (trans) (2008) *Adomnán's 'Law of the Innocents – Cáin Adomnáin* (Kilmartin, Kilmartin House Trust).

Noble, G. and Evans, N. (2022) *Picts: Scourge of Rome, Rulers of the North*. Edinburgh, Birlinn.

Noble, G., Cruikshanks, G., Dunbar, L., Evans, N., Hall, D., Hamilton, D., MacIver, C., Masson-MacLean, E., O'Driscoll, J., Paskulin, L., & Sveinbjarnarson, O. (2018) Kinneddar: a major ecclesiastical centre of the Picts. In *Proceedings of the Society of Antiquaries of Scotland* 148, 113–45.

Noble, G., Gondek, M., Campbell, E., Evans, N., Hamilton, D., and Taylor, S. (2019) A Powerful Place of Pictland: Interdisciplinary Perspectives on a Power Centre of the 4th to 6th Centuries AD. In *Medieval Archaeology* 63(1), 56–94.

Noble, G. with Cruickshanks, G., Evans, N, Gondek, M., MacIver, C., Masson-Maclean, E., O'Driscoll, J. & Taylor, S. And contributions by Britton, K., Campbell, E., Czére, O., Davis, M., Leanne Demay, L., Fawcett, J., Gerrard, J., Hamilton, D., Hunter, F., Jones, S., Koster, L., Mainland, I., McGibbon, F., McManus, E., Niehaus, S., Oxenham, M., Prado, S., Ramsay, S. and Roshem, E. (forthcoming) *Rhynie*. Edinburgh, Society of Antiquaries of Scotland.

Oram, R. (2004) *David I. The King who made Scotland*. Stroud, Tempus.

Oram, R. (2011) *Domination and Lordship. Scotland 1070–1230*. Edinburgh, Edinburgh University Press.

RCAHMS (2007) *In the Shadow of Bennachie. A Field Archaeology of Donside, Aberdeenshire*. Edinburgh, Society of Antiquaries of Scotland.

Rhys, G. (2015) *Approaching the Pictish language: historiography, early evidence and the question of Pritenic*. Unpublished PhD thesis, University of Glasgow.

Rogers, J.M. (1997) The formation of parishes in twelfth-century Perthshire. In *Records of the Scottish Church History Society* 27, 68–96.

Ross, A.D. (2003) *The Province of Moray, c. 1000–1230*, 2 vols. Unpublished PhD thesis, University of Aberdeen.

Ross, A. (2011) *The Kings of Alba c. 1000–c. 1130*. Edinburgh, John Donald.

Ross, A. (2015) *Land Assessment and Lordship in Medieval Northern Scotland*. Turnhout, Brepols.

Shepherd, C. (2018) A 12th-century 'bowl-fired' grain- drying kiln at Druminnor Castle, Aberdeenshire. Implications for social change, agricultural productivity and landscape development in north-east Scotland. In *Studia Celtica* 52, 1–32.

Shepherd, C. (2021) *The Late Medieval Landscape of North-East Scotland. Renaissance, Reformation and Revolution*. Oxford, Windgather Press.

Simpson, W.D. (1930) Craig Castle and the Kirk of Auchindoir. In *Proceedings of the Society of Antiquaries of Scotland* 64, 48–96.

Stratigos, M. (2020) Landscape Reconstruction. In Armit, I. and Büster, L. (eds) *Darkness Visible. The Sculptor's Cave, Covesea, from the Bronze Age to the Picts*, 215–20. Edinburgh, Society of Antiquaries of Scotland.

Stringer, K.J. (1985) *Earl David of Huntingdon 1152–1219*. Edinburgh, Edinburgh University Press.

Taylor, A. (2016) *The Shape of the State in Medieval Scotland 1124–1290*. Oxford, Oxford University Press.

Taylor, S. (2008) The toponymic landscape of the Gaelic notes in the Book of Deer. In Forsyth, K. (ed.) *Studies on the Book of Deer*, 275–308. Dublin, Four Courts.

Taylor, S. (2011) Pictish Place-names Revisited. In Driscoll, S., Hall, M. and Geddes, J. (eds) *Pictish Progress. New Studies on Northern Britain in the Early Middle Ages*, 67–118. Leiden: Brill.

Taylor, S. (2020) *Coldon/Cowden*-place-names: trees, coos, fuel or assembly-sites? In Kidd, S.M., Clancy, T.O. and Ó Maolalaigh, R. (eds) *Litreachas, Eachdraidh agus Cànan: Rannsachadh na Gàidhlig* 7, 398–427. Glasgow, University of Glasgow.
Taylor, S. and Evans, N. (2021) Rhynie and Noth: the Names and the Archaeology. In *Scottish Place-Name News* 51(2), 6–8.
Taylor, S. with Márkus, G. (2009) *The Place-Names of Fife. Volume Three. St Andrews and the East Neuk.* Donington, Shaun Tyas.
Taylor, S. with Márkus, G. (2012) *The Place-Names of Fife. Volume Five. Discussion, Glossaries and Edited Texts.* Donington, Shaun Tyas.
Watson, W.J. (1926) *The Celtic Place-Names of Scotland*. Edinburgh.
Woolf, A. (2006) Dún Nechtain, Fortriu and the geography of the Picts. In *Scottish Historical Review* 85, 182–201.
Woolf, A. (2007) *From Pictland to Alba, 789–1070*. New Edinburgh History of Scotland 2. Edinburgh, Edinburgh University Press.
Woolf, A. (2017) Review of Alasdair Ross, *Land Assessment and Lordship in Medieval Northern Scotland*. In *Scottish Historical Review* 96(1), 110–12.

Websites

Canmore: https://canmore.org.uk/
eDIL = *Dictionary of the Irish Language*, https://dil.ie/
poms.ac.uk = Amanda Beam, John Bradley, Dauvit Broun, John Reuben Davies, Matthew Hammond, Neil Jakeman, Michele Pasin and Alice Taylor (with others) (2019) *People of Medieval Scotland: 1093-1371*. Glasgow and London, https://poms.ac.uk

Chapter 5

'The *banchor* of Kildrummy': a forgotten religious landscape?

Alexander Forbes

Introduction

This paper began as an informal presentation, to illustrate a walk in the places around the origin myths of the Forbes family, noting the monuments and places of interest passing by. It is a landscape rich in history, but abounding in contradictions. As a result of rewriting it as a paper for publication it has become more serious. However, my qualifications for writing it have not changed. I am not a historian of Celtic Scotland, nor a philologist, not even a Gaelic speaker. I therefore ask for indulgence from those who are any of these things, and hope the paper will stimulate others better qualified to pursue these threads.

The thesis is that, while the rich historical and archaeological landscape of the Kildrummy basin can convincingly be explained by the fertility of the soil and the intersection of the east–west and north–south corridors of trade and travel – perhaps the most important cross-roads in the province of Mar (Simpson 1943, 9, 11, 143), there may be another factor. The overlapping threads of legends and, in particular, the religious traditions and associations of the district, can be followed back through the Middle Ages, and the Pictish era, and even into pre-history. They are evidence of enduring religious significance: but is this just the inevitable result of good soil and trade routes? Or did the Kildrummy basin very early acquire a special religious status, and sustain it over millennia?

The 'duthus' of Forbes

The Forbes family emerges into the dimmest of daylights in 1271/2 with their earliest surviving charter, granting or confirming the barony of Forbeys to Duncan de Forbeys (Illus. AB, iv, 372). Before this there is nothing, and no certainty about

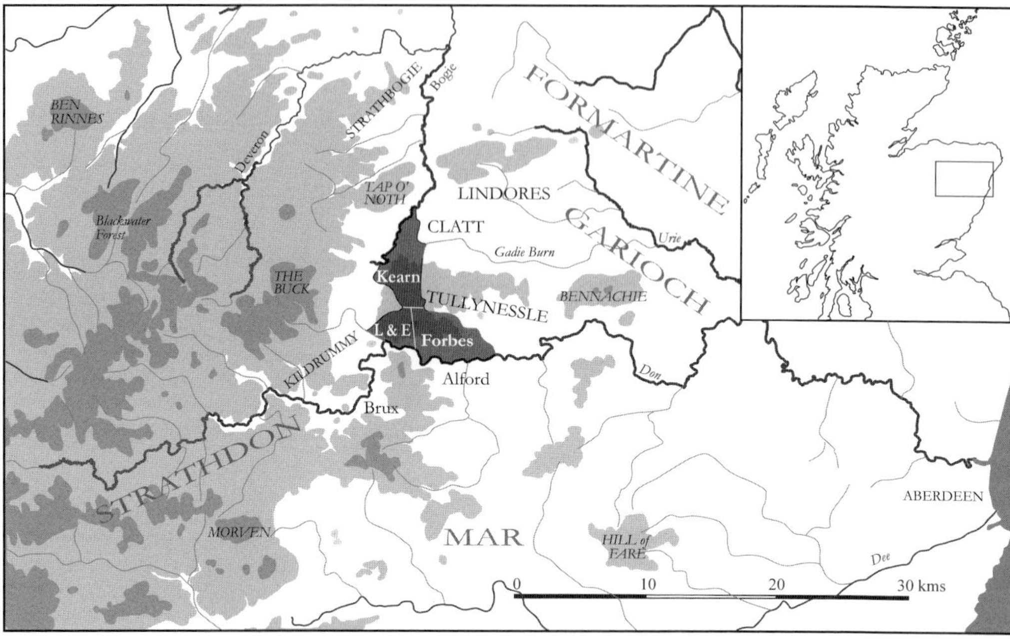

Figure 5.1. Map showing the barony of Forbes as it was from 1272 (or before) until 1429 – comprising the lands (and parishes) of Forbes and Kearn, held of the Crown in barony; plus the lands of Logie and Edinbanchory, held as feudal tenants of the earldom of Mar.

the family's origins. This dispiriting obscurity has been compensated by a plethora of legends and myths, carrying the family story back to the reign of King Gregory the Great in the 9th century, or still further back to the 6th century and King Comgall of Dalriada.

Looking only at proven facts, the most plausible thesis is that the Forbeses were originally cadets of the Earls of Mar (part of Clan Morgund, ultimately of the *Cenel Loarn*, *i.e.* of Dal Riatan/Irish origin). Some such connection is essential to explain the flourishing of the family in the generations following the extinction of the comital line in 1373. Even if they were not male line cadets of the earls, the early Forbeses were undoubtedly closely related to them by marriage. None of the legends are based on such a link – meaning that if this is the true origin, there would be little or no truth in any of the legends.

The Forbes origin myths are many, and are set out in Tayler (1937, 1–12). For convenience, they can be gathered into three bundles, which flatly contradict each other: (i) they were aboriginal Picts; (ii) they were Irish immigrants around AD 800; (iii) they were Irish immigrants around 1300. Story (iii) was the one commonly believed in the 16th century.

The most popular and enduring legend (or bundle of legends) runs as follows. Once, there was an Irish prince, called Ochonchar like his famous father. 'Inspired with a sprightly fire, and desirous to gain honour,' he came over and fought for the King of the Picts against the Danes, who were then 'infesting' Scotland. He was rewarded with the castle of Urquhart on Loch Ness and its lands: but was slain by 'those merciless and insulting barbarians'. He left a posthumous son, also Ochonchar, who grew up in Ireland. Twenty years later young Ochonchar came back to Scotland, visited the King of the Picts and claimed his father's lands of Urquhart. Unfortunately, in the intervening years the King had granted the lands to other heroes and to the church. However, in recognition of Ochonchar the father's valuable service, the King knighted the boy and gave him 'the lands of Logie upon the bank of the river Done, which in the Lord Forbes ancient evidents, are thus bounded between Essack, Massach, Bogie and Done' (Tilliecairn 1900, 4; Tayler 1937, 7).

The new Knight of Logie soon came to take possession of his new land and received a nasty shock. The King had been able to give him the land of Logie only because it was uninhabitable. It had become the *terroir* of 'a Bear of a monstrous and huge bulk', which had devoured half the inhabitants, and the rest had fled. No one would help young Ochonchar for terror of the bear, so he had to deal with it on his own. He stalked it for a long time, deep into the wild woods of Logie, and found it at last by the Nine Maidens' Well, where, after a ferocious battle he 'couped' its head off with his mighty sword. (The Nine Maidens were sisters who used to live near the Well with their aged father, Saint Donald. They had fallen victim to the bear one by one, since unlike their neighbours, they had neglected to flee.)

In memory of the young Knight's stunning victory, a large stone near the scene of the ursicide was carved into a likeness of the bear, and called the Bear Stone. The people called the hero *forbais*, 'the man of courage' (Tayler 1937, 2). The land of Logie

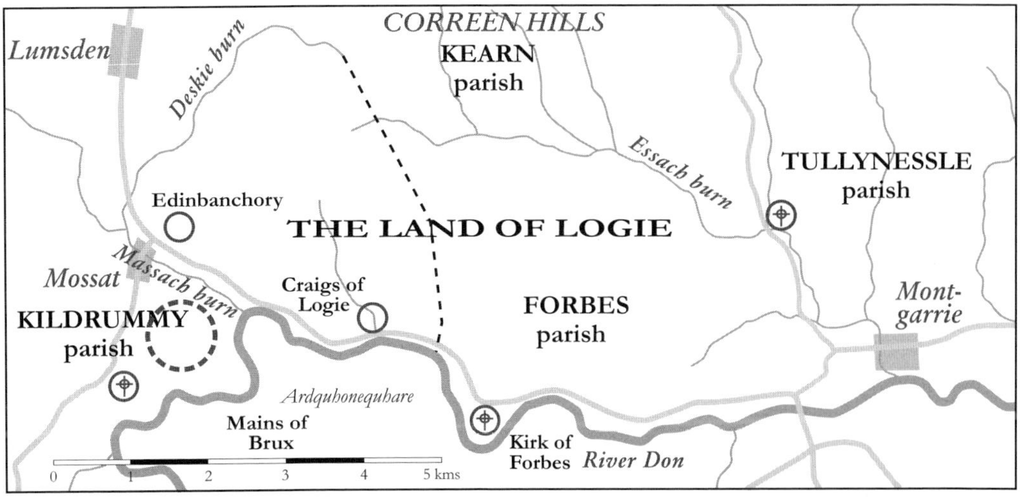

Figure 5.2. Map of the land of Logie, the duthus of Forbes, bounded by the four burns of Essachie and Mossat, Deskie and Don. The dotted line divides the eastern portion of Logie (the lands and parish of Forbes, half of the barony of Forbes) and the western portion (the lands of Edinbanchory and Craiglogie in Kildrummy parish, held by the Lords of Forbes as tenants of the earldom of Mar).

came to be called the land of *forbais* in memory of 'he who killed the Bear', and the hills above the Nine Maidens' Well were called the Braes of *forbais*. The King gave him a coat of arms: three bear's heads *couped*, in tribute to his victory. Strangely, however, Ochonchar the *forbais* did not live on the land of Logie which he had so bravely won and which was now named after him. Traditionally, he lived at Ardhuncart, also named after him – close by but on the land of Kildrummy.

So runs the most popular myth of the origins of the Forbes family. It has little historical value, except: (i) the association of Forbeses with bears; (ii) the marches of the early barony of Forbes; and (iii) the idea that the land was named 'Forbes' after its owner rather than the reverse (but this is still moot). However, it contradicts the most basic origins tradition of the family, *viz.*: 'No one either in fable or history owned the land of Forbes before us' (the 13th Lord Forbes, writing in 1730 to his supposed cousin, the Marquis de Forbin: Tayler 1937, 246). Clearly, this legend tells that Ochonchar was not the first owner of the land of Logie. Nor was he a native Pict: he was a newly arrived immigrant from Ireland.

Geographically, the land of Logie is in the province of Mar and must originally have been within the earldom of Mar. It follows that, when two-thirds of it was erected into a barony of the Crown independent of the earldom, it must have been carved out of the earldom for the benefit of the original grantee. This may be what the 1271/2 charter recorded, *i.e.* the creation of the barony for Duncan, the original grantee. Alternatively, the charter may record the merger into one barony of two previously existing but separate baronies or feudal tenements, Forbes and Kearn. Or, it may simply be a succession charter, confirming Duncan as holder of an existing barony. Lord Lyon Innes of Learney suggested that the earliest charter, probably this one of 1271/2, may record the transition of the Forbes *allodium* (ancient tribal territory) into the feudal system (Tayler 1937, 12). Unfortunately, the only surviving record of the charter, a summary written in 1593, is such a redaction that it is not possible to be more certain.

Places and monuments in the land of Logie

Logie

Logie is quite a common name in Scotland. In the north-east there are, or were, three parishes with the name, called to distinguish them: Logie-Mar or Logie-Ruthven (now merged with Coldstone to form Logie-Coldstone); Logie-Talargy (now Logie-Buchan); and Logie-Durno (now Chapel of Garioch). 'Logie' occurs in a dozen other places in the region, including here at Logie (Forbes). Prof. Thomas Clancy has established firstly that the name was probably originally Pictish, secondly that it is almost always associated with a church, usually an early and important one (Clancy 2016). Thus the name Logie probably indicates an ancient religious centre.

Despite its religious name, Logie (Forbes) appears to have no religious associations, except with St Donald and the Nine Maidens. On the other hand, no secular centre was ever built on Logie – no castle, fortress, manor house, hall, or homestead (see Simpson 1943, 37). Given that Forbes was the first known Crown barony in Mar, and its lords shared their name with the land of Forbes, this requires explanation.

At an unknown date in or before 1272, the land of Logie was divided in two. The eastern two-thirds was renamed the land of Forbes. The land of Forbes was formed into its own parish, probably simultaneously. The parish church was dedicated to the Nine Maidens of St Donald (Scott 1928, vi, 144). The land of Forbes was then combined with the adjacent land of Kearn and erected by the Crown into the barony of Forbes, with its caput at Druminnor, in Kearn. The parishes of Forbes and Kearn, separate in *c.* 1280, had become united by 1325 when Forbes (with Kearn) was made a prebend of the See of Aberdeen (*REA*, *ii*, 52, 55, 252; Illus. AB, iv, 371).

The western third of Logie was not included in the new barony and parish of Forbes. This comprised Craig-Logie and Edinbanchory, with the Bear and Boar Stones and the Nine Maidens' Well. These lands remained in the earldom of Mar and the parish of Kildrummy. They were also held by the Lords of Forbes hereditarily, but as feudal tenants of the earldom. More than 150 years later, in 1429, this western third of Logie was subtracted from the earldom and added to the barony of Forbes, meaning that the whole of the original land of Logie was now in the barony of Forbes (*RMSS, ii*, #134, 26–27). The parishes were unchanged: the land of Logie remained split between the parishes of Forbes and Kildrummy (until the 18th century, when the Kildrummy portion was transferred to Auchindoir parish; Scott 1928, vi, Kildrummy).

Forbes

By local tradition *forbais* means 'the super-strong (or super-brave) man' (Tayler 1937, 2), happily matching the name to the legend. This would mean the land was named after the man without adding an element of 'place', which is unusual.

The dictionaries give no clear definition of '*forbais*' but several options. One is 'victory', plausible in the context of the Ochonchar legend. Alternatively, 'glebe land', *i.e.* the priest's land (*Am Faclair Beag*). This would tie into the ecclesiastical associations of 'Logie', and echo the strand in the Ochonchar myth that the King had given his father's lands to the church and others. Moncrieffe thought the stem was *forba*, Gaelic for 'field' or 'district'. Macdonald suggested *fuar bhathais*, 'the cold brow'.

The name is often given as '*Forbhasach*' (*e.g.* Tayler 1937, 2), which literally means 'person bearing the name Forbes', or 'having Forbes characteristics', and is perhaps best translated as 'Forbesy', 'Forbes-like' (*Am Faclair Beag*). *Forbhasach* can also mean 'treacherous', which may explain a meme much used by Forbes detractors: 'as if [this family] had always been monstrously disloyal, false and treacherous' (Tayler 1937, 5).

'Duncan names': Ochonchar and Ardhuncart

Ochonchar is a form of the name O'Conor, one of the greatest Irish dynasties. There is no known connection between them and Forbes – except that both families have legends in which their founding ancestor killed a ferocious beast. In O'Conor's case, he saved the King of Ireland's life by killing a huge boar. Several other family-founders saved other kings' lives in much the same way, including FitzGerald (a stag), Mackenzie (the same stag), Haliburton (another boar), Gordon (yet another boar) (Mackenzie 1894, 10–11; Douglas' Peerage: Gordon).

Ardhuncart was the legendary abode of Ochonchar *forbais.* In 1508 the spelling was *Ardquhonquhar* or *Ardquoneqhare* ('*ard+conquhar*') (*RMSS*, #3251; Illus. AB, iv, 220–1). The '*conquhar*' element in Kilconquhar in Fife is a form of *Donchadh, i.e.* Duncan. Kilconquhar parish is dedicated to St Duncan (11th abbot of Iona, died AD 717). (See Taylor and Markus 2012, iv, 304–5; also Watson 1973, 409: 'Pitconnoquhoy, the old name of Rosehaugh in the Black Isle, is "Donnchadh's [Duncan's] share"'.) It follows that '*ard+ conquhar*' means 'Duncan's hill'. And 'Ochonchar' means 'son (or descendant) of Duncan' – which of course all Forbeses are.

If the Gaelic name of the Forbes family before 1300 was 'mac Donchadh' or 'mac Conchar' or 'mac Connochie' (or in Irish Gaelic 'O'Conchar'), then it would be an easy step to borrow the legends in the Irish mythologies associated with O'Conchar/O'Conor. This would answer the difficult question: why did the Forbeses decide that their founder was called O'Conor? It has been assumed that, because the killing of the beast is an exploit of O'Conor/Ochonchar in the Irish legends (*e.g.* in 'The Four Masters') – therefore, the early Forbeses reasoned, Ochonchar must be the Forbes progenitor – despite the fact his beast was a boar not a bear. Perhaps the truth is the other way round – *i.e.* the MacDuncan/MacConnochie lords of Forbes appropriated the legend of the killing of the beast because it was an exploit of Ochonchar, Duncan's son.

The Nine Maidens' Well

Named after the nine saintly daughters of St Donald: examined below.

The Bear Stone

For centuries 'a bear roughly cut in flinty stone and unpolished' stood near the Nine Maidens' Well (Tayler 1937, 8). About 300 years ago the stone was uplifted by Lord Forbes for its own protection and built into 'the wall above the back gate of the old house of Putachie' (Tayler 1937, 285). Putachie was demolished in 1815. In the new Castle Forbes that replaced it, the Bear Stone was given a place of honour above the fireplace in the entrance hall. In 1869 the stone was described as 'a rude representation of a boar's head', by James Forbes, a former tenant of Lord Forbes (Tayler 1937). Surely Ochonchar's beast was supposed to be a bear? If it was a boar, all the neat associations between the Ochonchar myth and Forbes heraldry evaporate.

The Boar's Stone

A second large stone remains in its original place, traditionally marking the spot where Ochonchar killed the Bear. It is called the Boar's Stone, confusingly. (Note: there were two ancient stones in this one place commemorating the termination of monstrous beasts, a bear and/or a boar. It is implausible that there were two quite separate beast terminations in exactly the same spot.)

It seems there were once more than just these two stone monuments at Logie: 'the wood of Logie, nigh which are "several old monuments in stone", one of which is the effigies of a bear, said to have infested that country, *etc*; and not far from it is a well, called The Nine Maidens' Well, where nine virgins were slain by him' (Description of the parish of Auchindore, c. 1725, in Macfarlane's Geographical Collections, quoted in Colls., 613–14).

Figure 5.3. Sketch of the Boar's Stone in the 1865 OS Name Book. This shows a plan of the stone lying on the ground, measuring 5'6" long by 3'9" wide. The heavy line across the middle is a deep groove. This and the other two lines are, we are told, 'the marks of its fearful tusks' (bears do not have tusks).

Inchdonald

A field beside the Don near the Boar's Stone. 'Inch' indicates it was once an island in the river. Was this believed to be the island home of St Donald and his water-loving daughters?

The Nine Maidens Green (at Invermossat)

'Tradition points to this, as being the burial place of the Nine Maidens who were killed by a ravinous boar near Logie' (OSNB 1865). Once again: was Ochonchar's beast a bear or a boar?

The parish church of Forbes

The parish church of Forbes was dedicated to the Nine Maidens of St Donald (Scott 1928, vi, 144). Was this peaceful spot in fact their burial place, rather than the Green

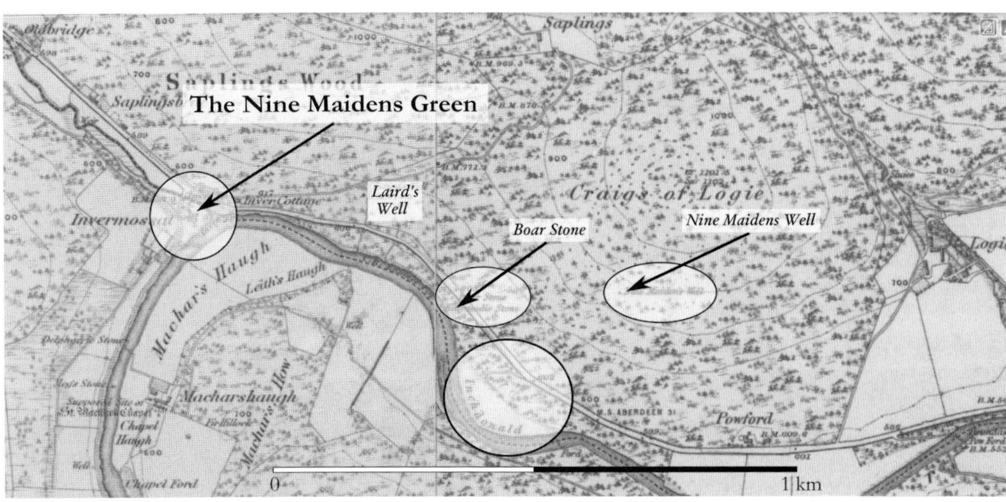

Figure 5.4. Map of the woods of Logie, showing the places associated with the forbais, the Nine Maidens and Arthur the Bear (and/or the Boar).

at Invermossat? It is sited at the south-west corner of the parish of Forbes, but this is the central point of the land of Logie. The only other parish churches in Scotland with this dedication as recorded by Mackinlay (1906) are Tough (near Alford) and Finavon (Angus), though there are many chapels and even more wells.

Saints in the Landscape: the Nine Maidens and St Bride

The Nine Maidens

They were the daughters of St Donald. Their main achievement was to be eaten by the Bear. Even legend is silent on the question of whether the bear ate St Donald as well. It may have preferred maidens. (Sources for St Donald and the Nine Maidens: Forbes 1872; Mackinlay 1906; 1914; Baring-Gould 1914, 358; Briggs 2007, 7–44; Taylor and Marcus 2012, v, 457–8; McHardy 2023.)

In the Middle Ages, St Donald and his nine (sometimes seven) daughters were popular saints, particularly the Maidens, but only in the shires of Aberdeen, Forfar, and Perth. They were most strongly associated with the Glen of Ogilvy in Glamis parish. After St Donald's death in that place, his nine saintly daughters, intact and undevoured, were invited by the King of the Picts to live at Abernethy under his protection. They lived there, piously but not long, in an immense hollow oak tree apparently. They were buried at the foot of the tree – which continued to be an object of pilgrimage as late as the 17th century (Baring-Gould 1914, 358; Mackinlay 1914, 16).

The Nine Maidens were venerated in many other places, and were variously devoured by bears, dragons and serpents. They were associated with water – sometimes as water-spirits – and their usual association with springs and wells reflects this. There were Nine Maidens' Wells and/or Chapels dedicated to them at Glamis, Cortachy, Finavon, and Strathmartin (all in Angus); at Mid-Calder (Edinburgh) and Newburgh (Fife); and in the north-east, at Drumblade, Tough, Old Aberdeen, Tomintoul and Logie (Forbes) (Taylor and Marcus 2012, v, 457–8; OSNB; Mackinlay 1906; 1914, 16–18). There is, or rather used to be, a famous Nine Maidens' Well at Pitsligo, with a Chapel of the Nine Maidens (also known as 'the Chapel in the Sands') and a Nine Maidens' Hill nearby (O.S. First Series maps). A mile to the south was the ancient church of Tyrie, 'the "White Church" of Buchan' (Canmore website – http://canmore.org.uk/site/20826). The dedication to the Nine Maidens may have been imported by Sir William Forbes of Kynaldy after he acquired Pitsligo in 1423. However, such a voluminous spring must always have been an important feature, and probably the association with the Nine Maidens was much older. In either case, the name at least shows the importance of their legends to the Forbes family. It also supports the hypothesis that the church of Forbes was dedicated to the Nine Maidens.

Three of the Nine – Mazota/Mayoca the eldest, Fincana the second, and Findoca – were named saints in their own right. Mayoca had one parish dedicated to her: Dalmaik (now Drumoak – evocatively): near the church is St Maik's Well. The adjacent parish of Echt is dedicated to Fincana (St Fink), and the adjacent parish of Skene is dedicated to St Bride (Mackinlay 1914).

The land of Logie was originally in the parish of Kildrummy (Simpson 1943, 3). The parish church of Kildrummy was dedicated to St Bride (Scott 1928, vi).

St Bride

Bride (or Brigit in Ireland) was the most important female saint of the Celtic world. 'St Brigit's cult is, I believe, the most widespread of all cults in Scotland outside that of the Virgin Mary' (Clancy 2013). In Ireland traditionally, Brigit was a princess who founded the nunnery of Kildare ('the church of the oak tree'), was its abbess, and died there in AD 525. Kildare was the first nunnery in Ireland and remained always the greatest. St Brigit of Kildare is probably not a historical figure: she may be an example of Christian absorption of pagan cults and traditions. (Sources for St Bride: Forbes 1872; Mackinlay 1914, 116–18; Clancy 2013; Cushnie website.)

Darlugdach, Brigit's favourite pupil, became the second abbess of Kildare but died a year later. According to the *Pictish Chronicle* (Skene 1867, 6), Nectan King of the Picts (457–481) founded a nunnery at Abernethy, and invited Darlugdach to bring nuns from Kildare to establish it and dedicate it to Bride/Brigit of Kildare. It was the first nunnery in Scotland and remained the greatest. Later generations believed that Abernethy was founded by St Brigit of Kildare herself: and that she brought her faithful attendants, the Nine Maidens, to be the first nuns there. They lived and were buried in the great oak tree at Abernethy, mirroring Kildare.

In the Celtic world, St Bride shared many of the attributes of Mary the mother of God. Indeed the overlap between their cults sometimes approached merger (Clancy 2013). Bride was the inheritor of many pagan legends and cults. She was said to 'preside over fire, over art, over all beauty, beneath the sky and beneath the sea' (Mackinlay 1914, 117). Candlemas, Lady Day, Michelmas, and Christmas, the four pillars of the medieval calendar, marked the annual cycle of rebirth and death: they were milestones in the legend of St Bride, particularly the first two (McNeill 1959, 20–21; see also Dransart, this volume). St Bride was also closely associated with cattle, their health and the healing of their sicknesses (cattle played a central role in Celtic culture). She was sometimes depicted with a cow, or even in the form of one. The flame on Brigit's shrine at Kildare was kept alight for a thousand years by a team of nine nuns, with a brief extinction in 1220 when the Archbishop of Dublin tried to stamp out the cult: Rome did not do fire worship (Mackinlay 1914, 117).

St Bride was directly associated with nine maidens only at Kildare and Abernethy, though they are central to her stories in those places. Bride's nine maidens, however, were not the Nine Maidens of St Donald: St Donald's maidens arrived at Abernethy independently of Bride and were saints in their own right. But it is notable that the other legend of St Donald's maidens, the ones devoured by Arthur the Bear, was located in Kildrummy parish, which is dedicated to St Bride.

In pagan times, the Nine Maidens were fearsome witches with unlimited supernatural powers. They terrorised mankind and were placated by prayers and sacrifices. In Arthurian legend, the Nine under their Queen, Morgan-la-Faye, morphed into more-or-less benevolent, but still 'perilous', enchantresses. Their home was the Isle of Avalon, where they cared for King Arthur after his death. There is a tantalising association here. Morgan-la-Faye was the leader of Nine Maidens. She was King Arthur's half-sister, and ultimately both his nemesis and his protector. 'Arthur' means 'a bear' or 'son of a bear' or 'bear-like', with the subtext of great strength and courage, and leadership and nobility. Probably it was borrowed from Latin into Welsh/Pictish, and then into Irish Gaelic (Zimmer 2009, 131–6).

> The Bear certainly had a sacred significance among the ancient Celts; and 'King Arthur' (whom some scholars think to have been a god-spirit) was identified sometimes with the constellation of the Great Bear, for his name was derived from the Old Celtic *arth*, a bear. So it is interesting that, long after such derivations were forgotten, Arthur was a popular Forbes name (Moncrieffe 1967, 177–8).

Indeed, Arthur and Duncan were the Forbes family's distinctive names – its 'Ur-names' (names recalling the family's foundation myths). Arthur is rare in other Scottish families, the Campbells and Galbraiths excepted.

Like Bride, the Nine Maidens were absorbed into the Christian world and made harmless. The terrifying demons of the pagan world became saintly maidens living piously in an oak tree, on occasion being devoured by a beast.

Places in Kildrummy parish with religious names

St Bride's church, Kildrummy

A superb site: a ruined church on the summit of a graceful mound, in the centre of a broad, fertile basin. An old name, 'the Chapel of the Lochs' or 'the chappell in the loch' (Colls., 589), suggests it was once surrounded by water. Perhaps odd for the abode of a fire goddess, less so for her water-loving Maidens (see Plate 5.1).

'Kildrummy ... signifies the little Burial Mount. ... The little green mount, the only burial ground in the parish, upon which also the church is built, has no doubt given the parish its name' (OSA). It is interesting that it was commonly believed in 1792 that the defining feature of Kildrummy parish was not its great medieval castle but the so-called 'Chapel' on its little green mound. The medieval 'burgh' of Kildrummy extended from near St Bride's Well as far as the river Don, where the Norman motte castle was built, with tollbooth, school, and mill. No trace of the burgh is evident today. The annual fair held at Kildrummy was called 'Bride's Fair' (OSA; Colls., 589).

St Bride's Well

At the foot of the 'little green mount' is, or rather was, St Bride's Well, 'famous for curing diseases in Cattle' (Macfarlane 1907, 30; Mackinlay 1914, 131). There are a large number of springs and wells named after St Bride, many with rituals and associations which have little to do with Christianity:

> The tradition of a bride washing at a well is by no means uncommon. Farther up the valley there is another well called Bride's Well, which was long the resort of all the brides of the district on the eve of their wedding. Accompanied only by their 'maidens' they paid their visit 'atween the sun and the sky', the maidens bathing the bride's feet and breasts. This ensured that she should be no childless wife. On leaving, she dropped bread and cheese into the well, and her children were safe from want (McConnachie 1901, 90).

McConnachie's source was the OSA (Strathdon parish), describing Bride's Well at Corgarff, near St Machar's Well (*cf.* Mackinlay 1893, 319).

'Banchory' *names*

Edinbanchory is a mile or so north of St Bride's church. It was part of the land of Logie, and ran up to the watershed of the Correen Hills, with the two peaks of Edinbanchory Hill and Lord Arthur's Cairn.

Corbanchory lies a mile or two south of the church. Close by the farm of the name there was a chapel in the Middle Ages: dedication unknown.

These '*+banchory*' names are surely connected. There has never been a satisfactory translation of the uncommon word-element *banchor*, though much discussion of 'pale corries' and 'horn-settings' (interpreted as bends in rivers) (*e.g.* MacDonald 1899, 123; Watson 1973, 481; Taylor and Markus 2012, v, 338, 347). There were other, much better known, *banchorys*: *e.g.* Banchory-Ternan and Banchory-Devenick, both on the river Dee and both coupled with the names of their founding saints. Banchory-Ternan was arguably the cradle of Christianity in the north-east. Banchory-Devenick was founded soon after by another important missionary saint. There are a few other *banchors*: (i) on the Findhorn in Nairnshire; (ii) at Kingussie in Badenoch, close to St Bride's church; (iii) at Tullybole in Clackmannanshire – in the parish of Fossoway, whose church is also dedicated to St Brigit.

Much more important and famous was the monastery of Bangor in Ulster. Its abbots sent missionaries across Europe, including to Germany, France, Wales, and Scotland, and founded monasteries in all of those countries. It was one of the greatest Christian centres of Europe, claiming 3,000 monks across all its houses in the 6th–7th centuries. Traditionally, when King Alfred decided to found a seat of learning at Oxford, he invited monks from Bangor to establish it (Lewis 1837). Another Bangor, almost as important, is near Anglesey. It was the second most important Christian centre in Wales after St David's and was founded in the 6th century. Bangor today is the smallest city in Britain, but has a cathedral and a university (Lewis 1834). 'Bangor in Wales is called by the annals *Benncoir Moer in Britannia* (s.a. 631), and *Bennchair Brittonum* (s.a. 671), to distinguish it from Bangor in county Down' (Anderson 1973, 15, fn 64. See also Anderson 1990, i, 181).

The meaning of *banchor* seems to be 'the White Church', with the '*chor*' element borrowed from Latin, perhaps controversially ('Bangor, signifying the "White Church," or "Fair Choir"' (McLeod 1898, 13; Lewis 1837)). A 'White Church' indicated one built of stone, and probably lime-washed – *i.e.* it was a major building. St Ninian's '*candida casa*' at Whithorn has the same meaning – 'white house'. So does '*whit+horn*'. The Venerable Bede noted: 'there was a time when there was not a stone church in all the land, but the custom was to build them all of wood; and therefore when a church was built of stone, it was such a rarity and unusual thing among the Britons that they called the place "*Candida Casa*" or "White-Church"' (Bede, III, *c.* 4). The land belonging to the White Church would be its *banchor+y*. Edinbanchory would then mean 'the hill-face (*edin*) of the land of the White Church'. Corbanchory: 'the end/corner/edge (*cul*) of the land of the White Church'. Both of these interpretations correspond to the topography.

From the two Bangors, internationally famous centres of Christianity and missionary activity, the name *banchor* seems to have acquired a secondary meaning as an important religious teaching centre, akin to a university (Cushnie website: Machar). With Edinbanchory and Corbanchory in Kildrummy parish, the *banchor* in question seems likely to have been St Bride's church, the heart of this religious landscape. Edinbanchory would be the northern end of the *banchory*, and Corbanchory its southern corner or edge.

Culispik

'The bishop's corner or patch'. The location is lost: the name is known only from the 1508 crown charter granting the barony of Kildrummy to the Elphinstones (Macdonald 1899; *RMSS* #3251; Illus. AB, iv, 220–1). The place does not occur in *REA* – presumably it had ceased to be church land before 1508.

Seven other chapels

There was a chapel at Drumallachie south-west of Corbanchory, and Chapel Ronald in Glenkindie (OS maps; MacKinlay 1914). In the adjacent parish of Towie 'there are ruins of chapels at Nether Towie, Kinbattoch, Belnaboth, Ley and Chapel of Sinnahard' (Colls., 612).

The Monastery of Clova

St Moluag of Lismore and Rosemarkie was one of the most important missionaries to the Picts. He died in 592 AD at Rosemarkie on the Black Isle, having founded important monasteries at his base on Lismore (Argyll), at Rosemarkie on the Black Isle, and at Mortlach near Dufftown, with a daughter house at Clova, all dedicated to himself (posthumously of course) (Simpson 1922, 1943, 89; Dransart 2003, 237). The monastery of Clova was established two miles to the north of St Bride's church, but still in Kildrummy parish (Plate 5.2). Arguably the site was chosen because it is close to the hallowed *banchor*. The traditional foundation date falls within the period of occupation of the 'high status' Pictish palace at the Craw Stane, Rhynie, during the 5th and 6th centuries (Noble and Evans 2022, 99). Clova was endowed with the surrounding land, presumably donated by the local king/chieftain. Traditionally, the north-east was ruled by the Pictish kingdom of Cé, with its caput at Bennachie. However, there is a case for supposing that the Picts based at Bennachie and Tap o' Noth were rival,

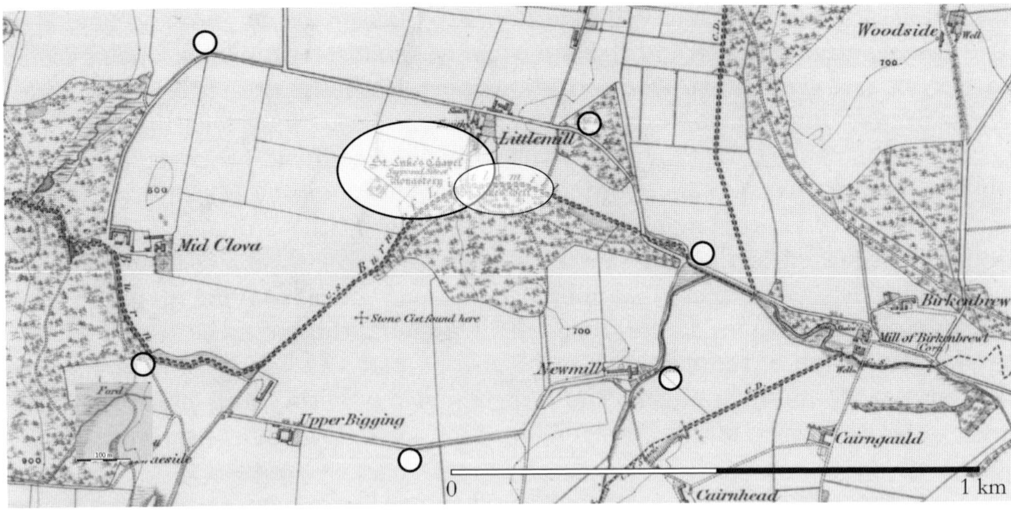

Figure 5.5. Map of Clova monastery. The OS map (1865) records 'St. Luke's Chapel', 'Monastery', and 'St Luke's Well'. A conjectural perimeter of the monastery's precinct is marked by circles.

or at least adjacent, tribes or kingdoms; and the Kildrummy landscape clearly looks to Tap o' Noth as its nearest major hillfort.

Clova and Monymusk (and its predecessor Nér) were the only pre-Reformation monasteries in the province of Mar, as far as we know. Banchory-Ternan and Banchory-Devenick should probably be added to the list. Other important ecclesiastical centres in Mar – *e.g.* Kinkell, Kincardine, and Tullich – may also have comprised or included monastic establishments before the 'Canmore reforms' of the late 11th and 12th centuries. Clova gradually decayed and was closed, five centuries after its foundation, when Bishop Nechtan moved his *cathedra* from Mortlach to Aberdon, around 1130. Nevertheless, locally it continued to be an important place of worship for another half millennium: 'Macfarlane's Topographer, writing in 1725, speaks of a "chapel dedicated to St Luke called Sommiluak's Chappel, formerly much frequented by all the northern pariochs"' (Simpson 1922, 6; Mackinlay 1914, 161). Simpson (1943, 89) also uses the spelling, 'Simmerluak'. These are corruptions of St Moluag, and by the 19th century it had evolved into 'St Luke' (see the OSNB).

Monymusk, a house of Culdees, was founded two or three centuries later than Clova. It possibly took the place of the monastery of Nér, which was probably at Abersnithack, and may have been pre-Columban like Clova (Noble and Evans 2022, 170). The Culdees were supplanted in the 1220s when Monymusk was refounded as an Augustinan priory, dedicated to St Mary, and given to St Andrews: the bishop duly appropriated most of the luckless Culdees' former possessions.

Lulach's Stone

A shapely monolith once 11 ft high, dating to the Bronze Age, *i.e.* it is three or four thousand years old (Simpson 1943, 51–52). Its name comes from a late (in its own history) association with Macbeth's stepson, King Lulach '*fatuus*', who was killed in 1058 at Essie around the foot of the Tap o' Noth – almost within sight of this stone. He was the last King of Scotland of the northern House of Moray (Clan Morgund) (Simpson 1943, 108; 1949, 67–8). How Lulach came to be associated with this stone is a complete blank. Is 'Lulach' here a corruption of or a confusion with 'Luaig' – *i.e.* St Moluag? (Thanks to Colin Shepherd for this thought.) Simpson (1943, 51) observed that there is another local monolith called Lulach's or Luath's Stone, in Tough parish (which is dedicated to the Nine Maidens). Luath was the favourite boar-hound of the mythical Irish super-hero Cuchullin. He was in the habit of tying up his gigantic hounds to suitable stones across the Gaelic world, and these may be two of them – *i.e.* 'the conversion of the name to Lulach's stone may be a comparatively modern piece of pseudo-antiquarianism. The Kildrummy monolith seems always to have been associated with Lulach' however (Simpson 1943, 52). Note the return of the boar-hunt theme.

The purpose of such stones is unclear. They may have been grave markers, or boundary markers, or places of worship in their own right. Here, it is tempting to speculate that the stone may have played a part in the annual drama of the goddess Bride and the Cailleach (see below). Perhaps it merely marked the northern edge of the *banchory* of Kildrummy – though, of course, that would add another millennium or two to the period during which the 'little green mount' of Kildrummy was the centre of a sacred district, a holy land.

Cnoc Cailleach

There are many hills with this name across Scotland. The Cailleach was a monster in the form of a hideous old hag, who played a vital part in the annual cycle of Bride the goddess. Every year, as the year waned, the Cailleach would capture Bride and drag her down into the Underworld, the Cailleach's domain, to hold her captive there in darkness and ice. A version of the Euridice myth, without a Celtic Orpheus. Without Bride to warm it, the world slipped back into bitter cold and every living thing suffered. But, every year, indomitably, Bride escaped from the Cailleach's dismal dungeons and returned to the light. With her, spring returned bringing warmth and a new year. Meanwhile the Cailleach was turned to stone (Lulach's stone?) – until next winter. In the most atavistic forms of the legend, Bride and the Cailleach were complementary aspects, Janus-like, of a basic 'mother goddess' (McNeill 1959, 20–21). Is it a coincidence that there is a Cnoc Cailleach within sight both of the *banchor* of Kildrummy and of Lulach's stone?

St Machar's Chapel, Haugh and Ford

Across the Don from the Boar's Stone, but still in the parish of Kildrummy, was the Chapel of St Machar, long since vanished. The 1st edition OS maps mark a spot hard by the steading of Macharshaugh farm. Behind the chapel site is a low hill (named 'Fir Hillock' on the OS maps) and a dell named Machar's How. A haugh, Machar's Haugh, separates the hill from the river Don, which here describes two-thirds of a circle round the farm. Nearby are Chapel Haugh and Chapel Ford. No local legends concerning St Machar in this place have come down to us. (Sources for St Machar: Mackinlay 1914, 219–20; Forbes 1872: Maurice/ Machar, Ternan, Yrchardus; Cushnie website: Machar, Ternan, and Erchard; Illus. AB, ii, 54 [Aberdeen Breviary, June 12]).

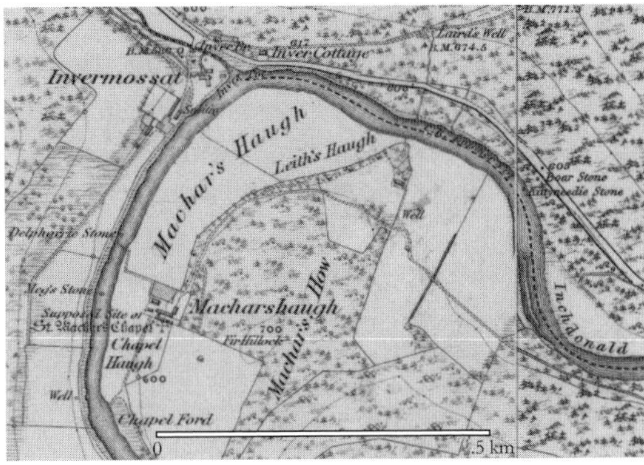

Figure 5.6. Map of Macharshaugh.

Profiling Machar is a work in progress. Erchard/Yarchardus (Mo+Erchard/Merchard, whence Machar, Machorius) was one of the earliest native saints. Traditionally he was a Pict, born before AD 500 at Tolmads and educated at Banchory by St Ternan. His own cult centre was at Kincardine Onele, where he died and of which he was traditionally the founder. Several churches were dedicated to him, all in the north-east. It is claimed that for a time he served as bishop of all the Picts. Even less plausibly, he is supposed to have visited Rome and served for a time as bishop of Tours in France (Forbes 1872, 466; Mackinlay 1914, 218–19; Cushnie website: St Machar). At Balnagowan, Aboyne, a stone with an incised cross and also a well are dedicated to St Muchrieha. His stone chair nearby was broken up for building materials about 1810. *Per* Watson (1973, 331), 'Muchrieha' is *Mo-chridhe*, 'my dear one', so 'there is nothing by which we can identify this Aberdeen saint'. Indeed: but locally it is believed that this was the 'cell' of St Machar from Tolmads.

A second saint who lived perhaps 100 years later is also called St Machar. He was an Irish prince, who became a monk at Bangor in Ulster under the great St Comgall, who named him MoChumma. MoChumma went to St Columba in Iona, where he cured seven lepers and turned a fierce boar into stone. He does not appear in the earliest lists of Columba's companions, but grew in prominence over time as he acquired the *mythos* of Merchaid/Machar of Tolmads. Their biographies apparently merged and MoChumma became St Machar (Mackinlay 1914, 43, 94–95, 156). (Machar is occasionally also called Maurice, an unhelpful distraction – *REA*, I, lxxxvi–vii: '*Mauricius, apud Scotos Machorius nominatur*'.)

The legend of the Irish MoChumma/Machar tells that Columba (*i.e.* about AD 590) sent him off with 12 companions as missionaries to the Picts. Columba told him to search for a place where a bend of a river was shaped like a bishop's crosier, and there build his church. The bend of the river Don below St Machar's Cathedral once circumvallated the whole of Seaton Park: Columba's phrase would have exactly described it. Old Aberdeen held two fairs, those of St Machar and St Luke. There were two holy Wells there, dedicated to St Machar and the Nine Maidens of St Donald (Blew 1854, vi, 18).

'A bishop's crosier' also describes the course of the Don as it curls round Macharshaugh. (As does the Don at Dyce/Fintray: these peninsular sites seem to have been attractive to missionaries to the Picts (*cf.* Blew 1854, vi, 16).) This begs questions applicable to both sites: (i) Did the myth lead to the building of a church dedicated to Machar beside this crosier-shaped loop of the river? (ii) Did the myth evolve after St Machar's church was built, exploiting the distinctively crosier-shaped course of the river? (iii) Is Machar's myth in fact substantially true? (iv) Did one of these options apply to one site, and another to the other? (v) Which came first, Macharshaugh or Aberdon?

MoChumma/Machar's adventures continued with his companion St Drostan, the other 11 missionaries having dispersed leaving not a wrack behind. Obedient to Columba's instructions, the two saints wandered about looking for a crosier-shaped bend in a river, visiting the monastery at Clova in Kildrummy parish on the way, then moving on to the similar community in Dunmeath parish (now Glass). They probably passed Macharshaugh on their way. At Dunmeath, Machar found a bell buried at the foot of a tree, as saints can do. He recognised it at once as special, and decided to ignore Columba's instructions to search for a crosier-shaped river bend – clearly having already discounted both the bend at Aberdon/Balgownie and the bend at Brux. He resolved instead to build his church wherever this holy bell rang for the third time of its own accord, which being a saint he knew it would do. His wanderings eventually brought him to the banks of Loch Ness, where the bell duly rang all by itself at three different places, the third being in Glenmoriston (close to Urquhart Castle, coincidentally), and there he established his 'cell'. He was long commemorated there as St Merchaid, with his church, his seat, his well and his famous bell, stolen by tourists in 1873.

In Glenmoriston St Merchaid was the Pictish MoErchard of Tolmads and Onele, not MoChumma of Iona. His story starts with him finding the bell, not at Dunmeath (now in Glass parish), but in Strathglass in the Aird (part of which was owned by Forbes of Pitsligo from 1400–1612). The other chapters of the Machar story, in Ireland, Mull, and Aberdeenshire, as bishop to the Picts, and in France and Rome, were unknown in Glenmoriston (Mackinlay 1914, 218–19). It seems there may have been two, possibly three, entirely separate saints' legends that have been amalgamated under the label Machar.

Traditionally, as noted, the monastery of Clova was founded by Moluag who died in AD 592. Therefore, M'Erchard cannot have visited Clova monastery and that part of the story can only apply to MoChumma. Unless of course there was an older religious community at Clova before Moluag's time – perhaps Moluag took it over and appropriated it to Mortlach.

One of the legends of MoChumma/Machar was that 'he turned a savage beast ... into stone' (Forbes 1872, 394) or 'a fierce boar' (Mackinlay 1914, 94). This incident is located in Mull, but that should not discourage us. Was the stone beast's head now in the hall at Castle Forbes originally understood to portray St Machar's lithified beast/boar?

Did the Forbeses, much later, appropriate the effigy as a memorial to Arthur, Ochonchar's monstrous Bear? Worse: was the beast originally a Boar, obliged to self-identify as a Bear when the association of boars and Gordons became problematic?

Seven centuries after M'Erchard/Machar's death, the new cathedral at Aberdon was dedicated by King David and Bishop Nectan to 'St Mary and St Machar'. The most important saint of the Roman church was yoked to an obscure local saint. No doubt the older church now being replaced by the cathedral had been dedicated to the local man, and Mary was added to provide weight and respectability. But it would be more normal simply to replace the older dedicatee entirely. It follows that the cult of St Machar was probably entrenched at Aberdon and powerful, and the founders were obliged (and perhaps desired) to preserve the old dedication, while adding another more familiar to Rome. Indeed, if Machar was a prominent local saint, that may have helped determine the location of the new cathedral – in particular the odd choice of Aberdon rather than Aberdeen. Further, the fact that Aberdeen Cathedral is universally known today as St Machar's not St Mary's suggests that local tradition and devoted loyalty have ultimately prevailed.

Why the chapel at Brux was dedicated to St Machar is unclear. The dedication does not prove that either of the possible Machars spent any time there: it may have been dedicated later, perhaps centuries later, and perhaps simply because of the crosier loop in the river there. There is no archaeological evidence that there ever was a church here, merely the evidence of the place-names. But Machar's Chapel, Macharshaugh and Machar's Howe, Chapel Haugh and Ford, the 'Boar's Stone' and the bend of the Don, together suggest that the association of Machar with this place was deep-rooted and complex. And entirely lost from memory, preserved only in place-names.

Is the Kildrummy basin an ancient religious landscape?

Today, 'Kildrummy' is most associated with the great castle built in the 13th century, the chief military fortress in the north-east for the next 500 years. As the *caput* of the earldom of Mar it was often also the most important political power-house in the north-east. Thus it seems odd to talk of the Kildrummy basin as a lost 'religious landscape'. But it is surely significant that, as far as we know, no forts, castles, or tribal strongholds were built in this densely populated, richly fertile district in the 800 years before the motte castles were made at Kildrummy and Fichlie.

Do these complex currents of legends associated with places in the vicinity of Kildrummy amount to more than accidents of time and place? Firstly, the Ochonchar story blends legends, toponyms, heraldry, ecclesiastical history, and landscape into a stimulating origins myth, animating the landscape of Logie (Forbes) and Ardhuncart. But many of the religious toponyms across the same ground – Logie, possibly Forbes, Edinbanchory and Corbanchory, the 'Machar' names, St Bride (and the Cailleach) – obviously predate that narrative. In pagan times, did Bride's mound, the Cailleach's hill and the great monolith now called Lulach's stone, provide a stage-set for the

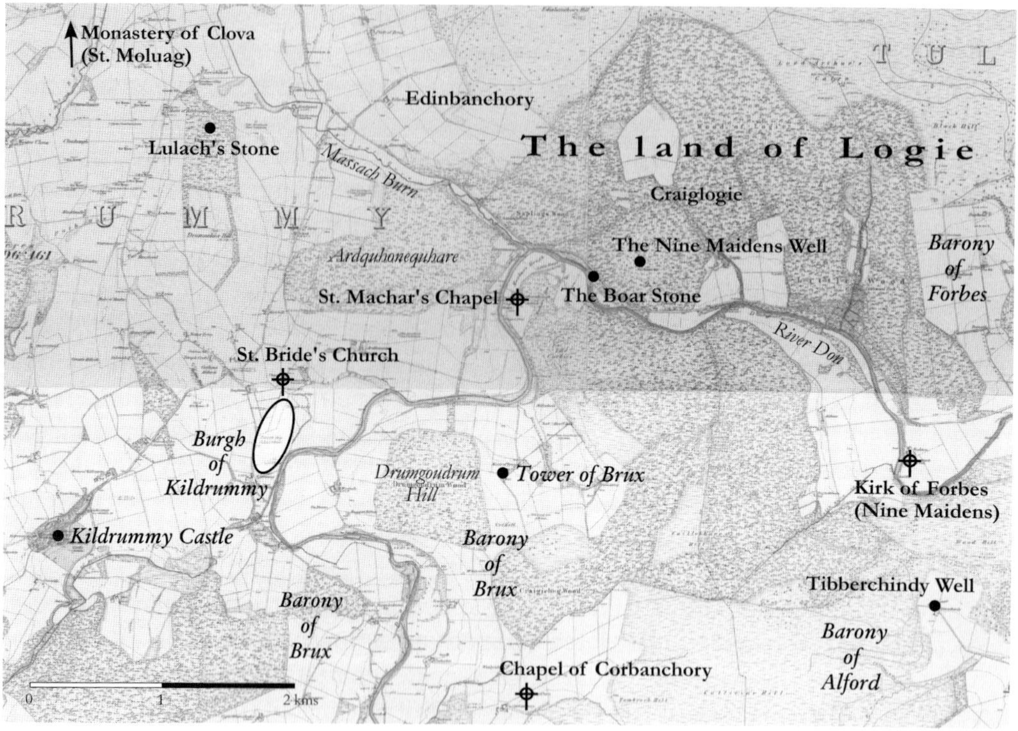

Figure 5.7. Map of the banchory of Kildrummy.

dominant drama of creation and death, all in the shadow of the Tap o' Noth? The area's religious importance continued through the Pictish era, with Simmerluak's *monasterium* at Clova and Machar's chapel at Brux, with its crosier-shaped bend and lithified boar. The landscape abounds with saints and supernatural beings: Bride (and her possible avatars, St Mary and the Cailleach), Donald and his Nine Maidens, Machar and Moluag. At the centre sits the 'Chapel of the Lochs' giving a focus for all of it, and providing the *banchory* (if there was one) with its essential stone-built church.

Finally, is it significant that the most important medieval castle in the north of Scotland was built in this parish? This densely populated landscape at the cross-roads of Mar, kept clear of any manifestation of secular power for a millennium or more, suddenly became the power-centre of Mar, and arguably of the whole north-east.

Does the palimpsest of hints and associations swirling around Bride's little green mount really amount to a religious landscape, an ecclesiastical estate, a *banchory*? If so, it is ancient and extraordinarily enduring.

Sources

Bede, *Ecclesiastical History*, III, chapter 4.

Colls. = Robertson, J. (ed.) (1853) *Collections for a history on the shires of Aberdeen and Banff.* Aberdeen, Spalding Club.

Douglas' Peerage = Douglas, R. (1764) *The peerage of Scotland: containing an historical and genealogical account of the nobility of that kingdom.*
Illus. AB. (1847–1869) *Illustrations of the Topography and Antiquities of the Shires of Aberdeen and Banff, Volumes 1-4.* Aberdeen, Spalding Club.
OSA = *Old Statistical Accounts* (1799) Aberdeenshire, www.stataccscot.edina.ac.uk.
OSNB = *Ordnance Survey Name Books* (1865–1871) Aberdeenshire, https://scotlandsplaces.gov.uk/digital-volumes/ordnance-survey-name-books/aberdeenshire-os-name-books-1865-1871
REA = *Registrum Epicopatus Aberdonensis* (1845). Edinburgh, Spalding Club.
REM = *Registrum Episcopatus Moraviensis* (1837). Edinburgh, Spalding Club.
RMSS = Paul, J.P. and Thomson, J.M. (eds) (1882–1914) *Registrum Magni Sigilli Regum Scotorum.* Edinburgh, HM General Register House.

Bibliography

Anderson, A.O. (1990) *Early Sources of Scottish History AD 500 to 1286.* Edinburgh, Oliver & Boyd.
Anderson, M. (1973) *Kings and Kingship in Early Scotland.* Edinburgh, Scottish Academic Press.
Baring-Gould, S. (1914) *Lives of the Saints.* Edinburgh, Grant.
Blew, W. (1854) *Breviarium Aberdonense.* Edinburgh.
Briggs, K. (2007) Seven Wells. In *Journal of the English Place-name Society* 39, 7–44.
Clancy, T.O. (2013) Saints in the Scottish Landscape. In *Proceedings of the Harvard Celtic Colloquium* 33, 1–34.
Clancy, T.O. (2016) Logie: an ecclesiastical place-name element in eastern Scotland. In *The Journal of Scottish Name Studies* 10, 22–88.
Dransart, P. (2003) Saints, stones and shrines: the cults of Sts Moluag and Gerardine in Pictland. In Cartwright, J. (ed.) *Celtic Hagiography and Saints' Cults*, 232–48. Cardiff, University of Wales Press.
Forbes, A.P. (1872) *Kalendars of Scottish Saints.* Edinburgh, Edmonston & Douglas.
Lewis, S. (1834) *A Topographical Dictionary of Wales.* London, S. Lewis & Co.
Lewis, S. (1837) *A Topographical Dictionary of Ireland.* London, S. Lewis & Co.
McConnachie, A.I. (1901) *Donside* (1985 edition). Aberdeen, James G. Bisset.
MacDonald, J. (1899) *Place Names of West Aberdeenshire.* Aberdeen, New Spalding Club.
Macfarlane, W. (1907) *Geographical Collections relating to Scotland*, Scottish History Society, 3 vols 1906–8. Edinburgh, T. & A. Constable at the University Press.
McHardy, S. (2023) *The Nine Maidens.* Edinburgh, Luath Press.
Mackinlay, J.M. (1893) *Folklore of Scottish Lochs and Springs.* Glasgow, William Hodge & Co.
MacKenzie, A. (1894) *History of the MacKenzies.* Inverness, W. & A. Mackenzie.
Mackinlay, J.M. (1906) Traces of the cultus of the Nine Maidens in Scotland. In *Proceedings of the Society of Antiquaries of Scotland* 40, 255–65.
Mackinlay, J.M. (1914) *Ancient Church Dedications in Scotland: vol. 2. Non Scriptural.* Edinburgh, David Douglas.
McLeod, N.K. (1898) *The Churches of Buchan and Notes by the Way.* Aberdeen, A. & R. Milne.
McNeill, F.M. (1959) *The Silver Bough, Vol.1: Scottish Folklore and Folk-Belief.* Glasgow, William MacLellan.
Moncrieffe, I. (1967) *The Highland Clans.* London, Barrie & Rockliff.
Noble, G. and Evans, N. (2022) *Picts, scourge of Rome.* Edinburgh, Birlinn.
Scott, H. (1928) *Fasti ecclesiae scoticanae; the succession of ministers in the Church of Scotland from the reformation.* Edinburgh, Oliver and Boyd.
Simpson, W.D. (1922) *A forgotten Aberdeenshire monastery.* Aberdeen, Aberdeen University Press.
Simpson, W.D. (1943) *The Province of Mar.* Aberdeen, Aberdeen University Press.
Simpson, W.D. (1949) *The Earldom of Mar.* Aberdeen, Aberdeen University Press.
Skene, W.F. (1887) *Memorials of the family of Skene of Skene.* Aberdeen, New Spalding Club.
Tayler, A. and H. (1937) *The House of Forbes.* Aberdeen, Third Spalding Club.

Taylor, S. and Marcus, G. (2012) *Place Names of Fife*, vol. iv; vol. v. Donington, Shaun Tyas.
Tilliecairn, M. Lumsden of (1900) *Historie of the Familie of Forbes*, 1580 – Newe version, in Walter Macfarlane, *Genealogical Collections concerning families in Scotland*, Vol. 2, Scottish History Society Series 3, vol. 34. Edinburgh, T. & A. Constable at the University Press.
Watson, W.J. (1973) *History of the Celtic Place-Names of Scotland*. Shannon, Irish University Press.
Zimmer, S. (2009) The Name of Arthur – A New Etymology. In *Journal of Celtic Linguistics* 13(1), 131–6. University of Wales Press.

Websites

Am Fachlar Beag. English – Scottish Gaelic online dictionary. https://www.faclair.com
Canmore website – http://canmore.org.uk/site/20826
Cushnie website – https://www.cushnieent.com/saints/stbride.html

Chapter 6

North-eastern Vikings? The presence and absence of a Norse–Scottish cultural landscape in north-east Scotland

Charlotta Hillerdal

Introduction

The Viking Age (*c.* AD 750–1050) could be seen as somewhat of a watershed moment in the history of Scotland: the time where Norse colonists change the course of history. For at least the Northern and Western Isles would, for several centuries, align themselves with Scandinavia as the Earldom of Orkney and the Kingdom of the Isles. Viking activity in Scotland is concentrated in the Western and Northern Isles and Caithness on the mainland. North-east Scotland, south of Caithness and Sutherland, is very nearly void of Norse remains. This absence of a Norse–Scottish landscape

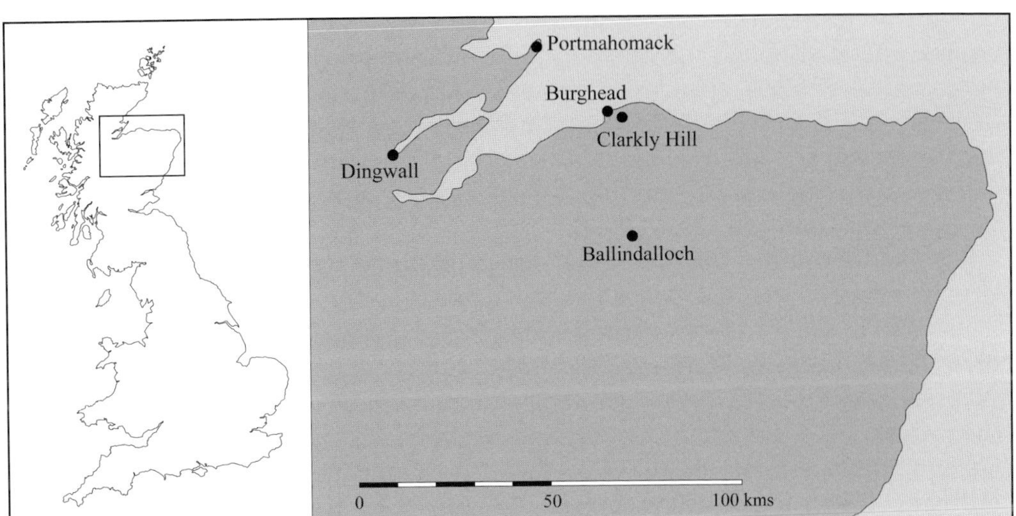

Figure 6.1. Map of the north-east as defined in the chapter showing central locations referred to in the text.

finds its easiest explanation in the early medieval Pictish Kingdom of Fortriu being centred to the Moray Firth (Woolf 2006; Noble and Evans 2019). Recent advances in Pictish archaeology have established the Northern Pictish polity as highly influential in early medieval Scotland (Noble and Evans 2022). However, the Norse influence on the north-eastern cultural landscape may be of a less direct nature. The fall of Pictish Fortriu and the rise of the Gaelic kingdom of Alba coincides with the Viking era in northern Scotland, and the intervention of the Scandinavian incomers is often referred to as a more or less significant contributing factor in this political, cultural, and linguistic change (*e.g.* Noble and Evans 2019, 172; 2022, 249–89; Woolf 2007, 275). In this chapter I review the evidence for Norse presence in the north-east, and discuss the nature of Viking and Norse interaction in Scotland.

Viking violations

The 8th-century Pictish monastic settlement of Portmahomack in the Tarbat peninsula (Figure 6.1) is suggested by the excavators to be the scene of a previously undocumented Viking attack (Carver *et al.* 2016). Parts of the settlement, interpreted as a workshop for the preparation of hides and production of parchment, was scourged by an intense fire at the turn of the 9th century, and a total of 230 shards of broken Pictish sculpture found scattered over the area has been taken as evidence of intentional destruction and desecration (Carver *et al.* 2016; Spall 2023). The sculpture fragments were deposited as part of a levelling episode for rebuilding shortly after the fire (Carver *et al.* 2016, 259). Stratigraphy, typology and ^{14}C dates place the attack between AD 780 and 810 (Spall 2023). The assumed raid appears to mark the end of the monastic function of Portmahomack. Following the destruction, a metalworking industry took over from the vellum makers, with finds indicating a trading place, though this was short lived. After AD 900 the settlement has the character of a farming estate, although the cemetery did continue in use (Carver *et al.* 2016). The settlement was finally abandoned just after AD 1000, around which time a hoard was deposited in the cemetery, suggesting these were times of turmoil (Spall 2023). The hoard comprised four penannular silver arm-rings and at least 14 coins and was placed by the cemetery wall, perhaps for safekeeping, sometime between AD 990 and 1000 (Graham-Campbell 1995, 143–4).

It should be noted that the only thing linking Vikings to the destruction of Portmahomack is that the event has been confirmed to a time-period known for Viking raiding and plunder targeting monasteries in particular. If this interpretation is correct, it would be one of the earliest Viking raids documented in northern Scotland, and predating the first clear evidence of settlement in the Northern Isles by at least half a century (see Barrett 2003). The first recorded Viking attack in Scotland is the raiding of the monastery on the Hebridean Isle of Iona in AD 795 (Jennings 1998).

Other evidence for violent encounters between Vikings and Picts in the north-east might be found at the promontory fort at Burghead. Burghead is the largest early medieval promontory fort in Scotland, with initial activity at the site dating back to the 6th or 7th century AD (Noble 2019). The burning of the rampart evidenced in archaeological excavation is traditionally linked to a 9th-ceuntury Viking attack (Shepherd 1993; Turnock 1995), with reference to the *Orkneyinga Saga* where an account of Earl Thorfinn's defeat of the Scots in Torfness has historically been placed at Burghead (MacDonald 1863; Bremner 1903, 354)

Recent excavations confirm the importance of Burghead. The settlement had evidently been a significant Pictish power centre of Fortriu, heavily fortified but also clearly functioning as an important centre for, perhaps, both pre-Christian activities, and the location of an early Christian church (Noble and Evans 2022).

Sueno's stone, a Pictish standing stone outside of Forres on the western approach to Burghead and depicting a battle scene, has often been linked to confrontations between Picts and Vikings, and maybe even the alleged attack on Burghead (Sellar 1993; Loggie *et al.* 2024). The stone bears the name of a Viking leader, Sueno – Sweyn Forkbeard of Denmark and England – to whom it has historically been linked as a commemoration of an important Scottish victory over the Danes in the 11th century (Sellar 1993, 100; Graham-Campbell 2004, 205). However, given the date of the stone and the cultural context, this association is anachronistic and originates in an 18th-century tradition of linking ancient monuments to historic events, particularly struggles against 'the Danes' (Sellar 1993, 98). Based on iconography and regional historical events, dates ranging between the 9th and 11th centuries have been suggested for the creation of the monument (Loggie *et al.* 2024). Sellar (1993) agrees with previous interpretations as the stone commemorating a real battle, but suggests, instead of Viking confrontations, that it marks the victory of the Scots over the Picts in the 9th century, and the inauguration of the King of the Scots following the final defeat of the Picts. Recent research (Loggie *et al.* 2024) establishes a likely 9th-century date for the stone based on its archaeological context, which reinforces a link to Viking assaults on Pictland in the 9th and early 10th centuries as documented in the Annals of Ulster. Loggie *et al.* (2024) find it probable that one of these battles was the event memorialised but point out that internal conflicts could also have inspired such a statement of power in a time of turmoil. Either way the monument is conspicuously linked to large-scale political developments in the north-east.

Place-names and settlement

Barbara Crawford (1986), among others, point to place-names in the Tarbat peninsula as evidence for Norse settlement, and what she refers to as 'the ebb and flow of Norse and Scottish control' (Crawford 1986, 33). These Norse place-names are concentrated around coastal farmlands (Crawford 1986), which are suggested to constitute a southern frontier of Norse settlement in Scotland (Crawford and Taylor 2003) and an interaction zone between Picts and Norse peoples (Fraser 1986). Crawford and Taylor (2003, 9) also point out that the character of place-names alludes to primarily farming settlements. Most of the argument for intervals of Norse control, or aspirations towards control, south of the Dornoch Firth and the Moray Firthlands is based on written sources, especially the Orkneyinga Saga. According to this there are three main phases of campaigns aimed at political control – the late 9th century, the late 10th to early 11th centuries, and the late 12th to early 13th centuries (Crawford 1986, 34). The Norse earls associated with control of Moray were rulers in the 11th century (Crawford and Taylor 2003, 3–11), and place-names are suggested to originate from Norse settlement in this era.

One of the most tantalising place-names is that of Dingwall, located at the head of Cromarty Firth (Figure 6.1). The name indicates a 'thing' site – an assembly site in a Norse context – and would suggest that a Norse system of administration was in place (Crawford 1986; 1987, 206). Crawford and Taylor (2003, 9) even suggest that the location of Dingwall, in relation to events inferred from the written sources, would indicate settlers here were, to a degree, independent from the authority of the earldom of Orkney. Norse presence in the area is implied by a few place-names in the vicinity such as Scatwell, further inland from Dingwall following River Conon (Crawford 1986), but no archaeological remains provide direct evidence for such settlement. Recently, O'Grady *et al.* (2016) proposed that the 'thing' site survives as a mound within Dingwall itself. Known in the medieval period as Mute hill, this was subject to excavations in 2011–2012. However, other than establishing the mound as artificial and initially created sometime in the mid-11th century, with several subsequent episodes of construction (O'Grady *et al.* 2016), there is no conclusive evidence confirming this to be a 'thing' site, or even linking it to Norse activities.

While place-names alone could suggest notable Norse influence on the Moray Firth and at least parts of the north-east, the general lack of archaeological evidence presents clear problems in tracing this influence further.

Archaeological evidence

Norse furnished graves in Scotland date between *c.* AD 850 and 950 and are one of the strongest types of evidence for early Norse settlement. The majority of furnished graves have been found on Orkney. On the Scottish mainland, seven furnished Norse graves are located in Caitness and Sutherland, part of the later Norse Earldom of Orkney, with a few isolated finds suggesting the number could be somewhat larger (Batey 1993). In north-eastern Scotland, south of Caithness, the only possible Viking grave is an antiquarian find of a man and his horse made in 1829 in Ballindalloch (Sikora 2003–2004). Despite the horse, which is one characteristic of Norse grave customs (see Pedersen and Bagge 2021), Graham-Campbell and Batey (1998, 105) refers to the grave's Viking interpretation as possessing 'considerable uncertainty'. The archaeological material is now lost, but the find was reported as that of human remains together with the remains of a horse. Artefacts reportedly recovered have been interpreted as the bit for the horse and possibly a harness, as well as a shield boss.

The burial was initially interpreted as Norse, but later described as Anglo-Saxon due to the shape of the shield boss, which has been retained in an illustration by Daniel Wilson from 1851, despite the loss of the actual artefact. The grave is sometimes included in the corpus as tentatively Norse, but a more recent study suggests that the shield boss, at least, was of 6th- to 7th-century Anglo-Saxon origin (Graham-Campbell 2004, 227–8).

The isolated find of a well-preserved sword made in Gorton, Morayshire, in 1864 is particularly notable given the general lack of Norse artefacts in the north-east. The sword has close associations with finds from Viking Age Norway (Anderson 1874, 567). There is no clear suggestion the sword would have come from a grave (Graham-Campbell 2004, 223), but this remains one possibility.

Metal detector finds from Clarkly Hill south of Burghead have produced a small assembly of artefacts with Norse association, including a Hiberno-Norse zoomorphic strap end, a Viking bell and a three-way strap distributor of 9th- to 10th-century AD date (Hunter 2010; 2014). However, the extent to which such isolated finds can pinpoint direct Scandinavian presence or the trading of material between Viking areas of settlement and those of Pictland/Alba is a moot point.

Indeed, the odd isolated and ambiguous grave find and a handful of stray finds, certainly does not paint a vivid picture of a Viking Age north-east. Looking to the artefactual evidence only, one would be inclined to agree with Keillar (1993, 25) that the 'Vikings did not linger on these shores'. Place-names and archaeology clearly tell conflicting stories about a Norse–Scottish cultural landscape and Pictish–Norse relations in north-eastern Scotland. How then, can we approach the evidence?

Breaking down the grand narrative

All cultures are subjects to generalisations, maybe the Vikings more so than most. Much nuance has been obscured under the convenient heading 'Viking', and the term wields a lot of assumptions. At first glance, some of them, may be met in the history of north-east Scotland, such as the raiding of monasteries and forts. However, even these are glossed over by the grand narrative of 'Viking conquest' and interpreted on presumptions about Viking presence, as expressed by the late David Dumville: 'But it seems sensible to me to deduce that vikings' intentions within a given period were more or less constant and therefore predictable' (Dumville 2002, 226). However, the extent to which Viking intentions and activities can be seen as predictable and indeed present in north-east Scotland is difficult to ascertain.

The earliest evidence of Norse activity in the north-east, the attack on Portmahomack, certainly seems to confirm such predictable Viking behaviour. However, notwithstanding the lack of written documentation for such a raid, the evidence for a Viking attack is rather circumstantial, despite the excavators' assertive interpretation. Narrowing down the chronology, for example, rests partially on the 'predictable intentions' of Vikings and a predicted chronology for Viking presence:

'The expectation from cross-dating with other sites is that the raid should have occurred towards the end of the 8th century, or at least in the early 9th' (Carver *et al.* 2016, 260). However, if we detach the archaeological evidence from the predictability of Vikings, although a raid is not unthinkable, there is certainly room for other interpretations.

Up until now I have purposefully been a bit careless with terminology throughout the paper, both to reflect the uncertainties surrounding Norse activities in north-eastern Scotland, and to make a point. Terminology directs thoughts and association. Just as we think we can interpret Viking activity according to their known intentions, 'Norse Scotland' alludes to a full adaptation to Scandinavian culture, and this is often the assumption behind the Viking-Age developments in northern Scotland. Maybe, in an effort to capture the cultural as well as chronological variations and intermixtures present, the rather cumbersome Hiberno-Norse might be a better term.

When looking into the archaeological material, it becomes clear that 'Viking activity' in Britain, and the people we call Vikings, were far from homogenous. Pictured in broad brushstrokes, in England Viking activity was characterised by large-scale military campaigns with clear political aims, eventually leading to the establishment of the Danelaw in the late 9th century (Holman 2016). The 'Viking ambition' in Scotland seems to come from a very different motivation, and follows a very different trajectory, despite some rather hyperbolic claims made in the Orkneyinga Saga.

The Viking history of northern Scotland has often been told from records that were either written by the enemy or are largely fictional. As pointed out by Alex Woolf (2007, 277), the Orkneyinga Saga, one of the most central of these and often treated as if written in Orkney by an Orcadian, is neither local nor contemporary, but was written in the 12th century to serve a very particular purpose. Thus, the account of events predating this century should be met with a great deal of scepticism.

The Earldom of Orkney, comprising the Northern Isles of Orkney and Shetland and Caithness and Sutherland on the mainland, was a medieval, semi-independent polity under the Kingdom of Norway until 1468–69 when it was incorporated into the Kingdom of Scotland (Morris 1985, 210). The Northern Isles assumed a Scandinavian identity including their own Scandinavian language, Norn, that was widely spoken at least into the 18th century (Barnes 1991). The islands were settled by Scandinavian incomers during the Viking Age, but the nature of this early settlement is still shrouded in uncertainty.

The written sources, the *Orkneyinga Saga* and *Historia Norwegiae* in particular, describe the Norse takeover of the Scottish Isles as hostile and final. An almost complete lack of Pictish place-names in the Northern Isles are often taken as corroboration of this (*e.g.* Smith 2001; Gammeltoft 2004). However, the archaeological material supports neither violence nor a complete eradication of Native culture. Instead, changes in culture and economy are subtle and at present suggest a slower and more gradual adaption to Norse ideals and ways of life (Owen 2004, 30; Griffiths 2020). The earliest permanent Norse settlement can be determined at no earlier than the mid-9th century (Barret 2003).

The burial record is especially telling for early Norse permanent activity in the Northern Isles. A suggested total of 223 'pagan' Norse graves have been identified in Scotland (Graham-Campbell *et al.* 2023, 300), the majority in the north. Norse graves, and not least settlements on the Isles, display a mixture of Pictish and Norse material culture and at least some continuity of Pictish customs (*e.g.* Ritchie 1977; Buteux 1997; Graham-Campbell and Batey 1998, 160–173; Hillerdal 2020;).

Rather than being unilinear and predictable, David Griffiths (2019, 468) suggests 'redefining the Viking Age as a sporadic, opportunistic and chaotic series of events and unforeseen cumulative impacts', which offers a fresh way of looking at this time period. We should not take Viking impact, settlement or presence as a given and should instead cast a critical eye on our sources. While Viking impact has been traced to the changes we see around the end of the 9th century, with the amalgamation of Pictland and Dal Riata, many other factors and processes may have been at work (Noble and Evans 2022, 249–89).

Conclusion

Barabara Crawford (1986, 33) referred to the land south of the Moray Firth as a 'disputed region'. The presence or absence of a Norse–Scottish cultural landscape in the north-east and the extent to which this really was a 'disputed region' may be dependent on how we define such a landscape, the approaches we bring to the table and the extent to which we are led by assumptions as opposed to hard evidence.

The one-dimensional treatment of 'the Vikings' in British and Scottish history results in them somehow being caught in a narrative of perpetual first encounter, with little reflection on either local variation or chronological development. If the destruction of Portmahomack indeed can be attributed to Vikings, this event would presumably belong to the earliest phase of Scandinavian intervention in the west, aimed towards acquiring insular loot (Heen-Pettersen 2019). However, the attackers of Burghead several generations later would be very different Vikings. Archaeological finds from the fort could tentatively suggest a southern link (Noble and Evans 2022, 271), which would place the invaders in an altogether different cultural sphere from their northern counterparts, with diverging expressions of internalised Hiberno-Norse culture (*e.g.* Williams 2016). The Norse place-names belong to yet another cultural context, as reminders of settling farmers from the north who probably had long-since stopped considering themselves as immigrants to the Northern Isles.

This brings attention to a type of artefact hitherto omitted from the story: ringed pins. Numbering at least 11, ringed pins are by far the largest finds category with Norse connotations in the north-east. These are a distinctive Hiberno-Norse type of artefact inspired by insular Irish pins, developed and produced in Norse Ireland, but widely popular among Norse Scots (Moldonado 2021, 118–19). Whilst sometimes found in graves, the ringed pins from the north-east are all stray finds. As low-value, everyday objects they reveal a more mundane, less-confrontational side of the history of Norse Scotland, but also that of cultural interaction and invention. Foremost, they emphasise that Hiberno-Norse Scotland is not external to the development of the north-east but part of an interconnected history.

Archaeology and place-names provide tentative evidence of Norse settlement and presence in north-east Scotland, but they are far from providing definitive accounts of the extent to which Scandinavian presence altered the trajectories of history in the north-east. Over the coming generations, hopefully, major research excavations like that at Burghead, developer-funded archaeology, and a critical overview of place-name evidence, historical evidence and material culture studies can begin to tell new stories.

Bibliography

Anderson, J. (1874) Notes on the relics of the Viking Period of the Northmen in Scotland, illustrated by specimens in the Museum. In *Proceedings of the Society of Antiquaries of Scotland* 10, 536–94.

Barnes, M.P. (1991) Reflections on the structure and the demise of Orkney and Shetland Norn. In Ureland, P.S. and Broderick, G. (eds) *Language Contact in the British Isles. Proceedings of the Eight International Symposium on Language Contact in Europe. Douglas, Isle of Man, 1988*, 429–60. Tübingen, Max Niemeyer Verlag.

Barrett, J.H. (2003) Culture contact in Viking Age Scotland. In Barrett, J.H. (ed.) *Contact, Continuity and Collapse. The Norse Colonization of the North Atlantic*, 73–111. Turnhout, Brepols.

Batey, C.E. (1993) The Viking and Late Norse graves of Caithness and Sutherland. In Batey, C.E., Jesch, J. and Morris, C.D. (eds) *The Viking Age in Caithness, Orkney and the North Atlantic. Select Papers from the Proceedings of the Eleventh Viking Congress, Thurso and Kirkwall, 22 August–1 September 1989*, 148–64. Edinburgh, Edinburgh University Press.

Bremner, R.L. (1903) Some notes on the Norsemen in Argyllshire and on the Clyde. In *Saga-Book* 3, 338–80.

Buteux, S. (1997) *Settlements at Skaill, Deerness, Orkney. Excavations by Peter Gelling of the Prehistoric, Pictish, Viking and Later Periods, 1963-1981*. BAR British Series 260. Oxford, Archaeopress.

Carver, M., Garner-Lahire, J., and Spall, C. (2016) *Portmahomack on Tarbat Ness. Changing Ideologies om North-east Scotland, Sixth to Sixteenth Century AD*. Edinburgh, Society of Antiquaries of Scotland.

Crawford, B.E. (1986) The making of a frontier: the Firthlands from the ninth to twelfth centuries. In Baldwin, J.R. (ed.) *Firthlands of Ross and Sutherland*, 33–46. Edinburgh, Scottish Society for Northern Studies.

Crawford, B.E. (1987) *Scandinavian Scotland*. Leicester, Leicester University Press.

Crawford, B.E. and Taylor, S. (2003) The southern frontier of Norse settlement in north Scotland. Place names and history. In *Northern Scotland* 23(1), 1–76.

Dumville, D.N. (2002) Vikings in the British Isles: A question of sources. In Jesch, J. (ed) *The Scandinavians from the Vendel Period to the tenth Century. An ethnographic perspective*, 209–40. Woodbridge, The Boydell Press.

Fraser, I.A. (1986) Norse and Celtic place-names around the Dornoch Firth. In Baldwin, J.R. (ed.) *Firthlands of Ross and Sutherland*, 23–32. Edinburgh, Scottish Society for Northern Studies.

Gammeltoft, P. (2004) Contact or conflict: what can we learn from the island-names of the Northern Isles? In Adams, J. and Holman, K. (eds) *Scandinavia and Europe 800–1350: Contact, Conflict, and Co-existence*, 87–95. Turnhout, Brepols.

Graham-Campbell, J. (1995) *The Viking-age Gold and Silver of Scotland (AD850–1100)*. Edinburgh, National Museums of Scotland.

Graham-Campbell, J. (2004) 'Danes... in this Country': discovering the Vikings in Scotland. In *Proceedings of the Society of Antiquaries of Scotland* 134, 201–39.

Graham-Campbell, J. and Batey, C.E. (1998) *Vikings in Scotland. An Archaeological Survey.* Edinburgh, Edinburgh University Press.

Graham-Campbell, J., Paterson, C. and Harrison, S. (2023) The 'Pagan Norse Graves of Scotland' research project. In Horne, T., Pierce, E. and Barrowman, R. (eds) *The Viking Age in Scotland. Studies in Scottish Scandinavian Archaeology*, 229–307. Edinburgh, Edinburgh University Press.

Griffiths, D. (2019) Rethinking the early Viking Age in the West. In *Antiquity* 93(368), 468–77.

Griffiths, D. (2020) How Scandinavian was the Early Viking Age in the Northern Isles? In Pedersen, A. and Sindbæk, S.M. (eds) *Viking Encounters: Proceedings of the Eighteenth Viking Congress*, 318–30. Aarhus, Aarhus University Press.

Heen-Pettersen, A.M. (2019) The Earliest Wave of Viking Activity? The Norwegian Evidence Revisited. In *European Journal of Archaeology* 22(4), 523–41.

Hillerdal, C. (2020) Negotiating narrative – An emic perspective on Norse reuse of ancient monuments on the Northern Isles of Scotland. In Hillerdal, C. and lves, K. (eds) *Re-imagining Periphery. Archaeology and Text in Northern Europe from Iron Age to Viking and Early Medieval Periods*, 157–168. Oxford, Oxbow Books.

Holman, K. (2016) Defining the Danelaw. In Graham-Campbell, J. Hall, R., Jesch, J. and Parsons, D.N. (eds) *Vikings and the Danelaw. Select Papers from the Proceedings of the Thirteenth Viking Congress*, 1–11. Oxford, Oxbow Books.

Hunter, F. (2010) Clarkly Hill, Metal detector finds. In *Discovery and Excavation in Scotland, New Series* 11, 112.

Hunter, F. (2014) Clarkly Hill, Metal detector and casual finds. In *Discovery and Excavation in Scotland, New Series* 14, 128.

Jennings, A. (1998) *Iona and the Vikings: survival and continuity*. In *Northern Studies* 33, 37–54.

Keillar, I. (1993) Man in Moray, 5,000 years of history. In Sellar, W.D.H. (ed.) *Moray: Province and People*, 25–46. Edinburgh, Scottish Society for Northern Studies.

Loggie, R., Campbell-Hower, F. and Noble, G. (2024) Reconsidering the Forres cross-slab (Sueno's Stone), part 1: dating and historical context. In *Proceedings of the Society of Antiquaries of Scotland* 153, 225–43.

MacDonald, J. (1863) Historical Notices of the 'Broch' or Burghead, in Moray, with an Account of its Antiquties. In *Proceedings of the Society of Antiquaries of Scotland* 4, 321–42.

Moldonado, A. (2021) *Crucible of Nations. Scotland from Viking Age to Medieval Kingdom*. Edinburgh, National Museums Scotland.

Morris, C.D. (1985) Viking Orkney: a survey. In Renfrew, C. (ed.) *The Prehistory of Orkney*, 210–42. Edinburgh, Edinburgh University Press.

Noble, G. (2019) Early medieval hilltop and enclosed settlements of Scotland during the first millennium AD. In Pergola, P., Castiglia, G., Hanna, E.E.K., Marietto, I. and Segura, J.-A. (eds) *Perchement et Réalités Fortifiées en Méditerranée et en Europe, Vème-Xème Siècles. Fortified Hilltop Settlements in the Mediterranean and in Europe (5th–10th centuries)*, 433–447. Oxford, Archaeopress Publishing.

Noble, G. and Evans, N. (2019) *The King in the North. The Pictish Realms of Fortriu and Ce.* Edinburgh, Birlinn.

Noble, G. and Evans, N. (2022) *Picts. Scourge of Rome Rulers of the North*. Edinburgh, Birlinn.

O'Grady, O.J., MacDonald, D. and MacDonald, S. (2016) Re-evaluating the Scottish thing: exploring a Late Norse Period and Medieval assembly mound at Dingwall. In *Journal of the North Atlantic* 8, 172–209.

Owen, O. (2004) The Scar boat burial – and the missing decades of the Early Viking Age in Orkney and Shetland. In Adams, J. and Holman, K. (eds) *Scandinavia and Europe 800–1350. Contact, Conflict, and Co-existence*, 3–33. Turnhout, Brepols.

Pedersen, A. and Bagge, M.S. (eds) (2021) *Horse and Rider in the Late Viking Age: Equestrian Burial in Perspective. Papers from a conference Skanderborg 27–28th of June 2019*. Aarhus, Aarhus Universitetsforlag.

Ritchie, A. (1977) Excavations of Pictish and Viking-Age farmsteads at Buckquoy, Orkney. In *Proceedings of the Society of Antiquaries of Scotland* 108, 174–227.

Sellar, D. (1993) Sueno's stone and its interpreters. In Sellar, W.D.H. (ed.) *Moray: Province and People*, 97–116. Edinburgh, Scottish Society for Northern Studies.

Shepherd, I.A. (1993) The Picts in Moray. In Sellar, W.D.H. (ed.) *Moray: Province and People*, 75–90. Edinburgh, Scottish Society for Northern Studies.

Sikora, M. (2003–2004) Diversity in Viking Age horse burial: a comparative study of Norway, Iceland, Scotland and Ireland. In *The Journal of Irish Archaeology* XII and XIII, 87–109.

Smith, B. (2001) The Picts and the martyrs or Did Vikings kill the native population of Orkney and Shetland? In *Northern Studies* 36, 7–33.

Spall, C. (2023) The Tarbat Peninsula in Northern Pictland: Portmahomack as a case study in Native-Norse interaction during the 9th to 11th centuries. In Horne, T., Pierce, E. and Barrowman, R. (eds) *The Viking Age in Scotland: Studies on Scottish Scandinavian Archaeology*, 43–56. Edinburgh, Edinburgh University Press.

Turnock, D. (1995) *The Making of the Scottish Rural Landscape*. Aldershot, Scolar Press.

Williams, H. (2016) Citations in stone: the material world of hogbacks. In *European Journal of Archaeology* 19(3), 497–518.

Woolf, A. (2006) Dún Nechtain, Fortriu and the Geography of the Picts. In *The Scottish Historical Review* 85(220), 182–201.

Woolf, A. (2007) *From Pictland to Alba 789–1070*. Edinburgh, Edinburgh University Press.

Chapter 7

Trodden paths: Fetternear bishop's palace and its landscape in medieval times

Penelope Dransart

Introduction

From the Loaves and Fishes café at the Kemnay Church Centre, in Aberdeenshire, from a vantage point on high ground, Bennachie stands boldly behind the trees of Fetternear across the river Don (Figure 7.1). In medieval times, Fetternear was a parish in its own right. Contained within the curves of the river Don, which marked its southern extent, the parish met with that of Logie Durno on its northern flank. On its north-eastern flank, it was separated from the parish of Inverurie by the Burn Hervey, which flows in a south-easterly direction until reaching the river Don. Monymusk lies to its west. While most of these parishes neighbouring Fetternear were located in a subdivision of the Diocese of Aberdeen known as the Deanery of Garioch, the parish of Fetternear was located in the Deanery of Mar. Early in the 17th century, the parishes of Logie Durno and Fetternear were amalgamated to form a new parish, which, since then, has been called Chapel of Garioch (Simson 1845, 560).

Fetternear was one of the properties listed by Pope Adrian IV in a charter issued in 1157, confirming that Bishop Matthew and his successors held the hamlet of Fetternear, its church and pertinents or, in the language of the text, '*villam de Fethirneir et ecclesiam cum suis pertinentibus*' (*REA*, I, 6). Its parish church was the bishop's own mensal church, meaning that

Figure 7.1. View from Kemnay looking across the parish of Fetternear towards Bennachie (Photograph: P. Dransart).

its income was intended to support the bishop and his household. The bishops maintained a moated castle residence about a mile from the church. Following the Protestant Reformation what remained was converted into the tower-house and mansion of the Leslies of Balquhain (Figure 7.2 and Plate 7.1).

Figure 7.2. Fetternear House, showing the site of the medieval bishop's palace in the fields either side of the drive (Photograph: P. Dransart).

Medieval churchmen in the diocese of Aberdeen traced the origin of their diocese from Mortlach, which had an early minster-like church and five associated subsidiary churches. Bishop Nechtan, who was active about 1131–1132, transferred the site of the diocese to St Machar's, Old Aberdeen, perhaps under pressure from Rome and as part of the reorganisation of the episcopal sees instigated by David I (Cowan 1972, 23). In 1157, when Bishop Edward received papal permission to introduce a chapter at Old Aberdeen, Fetternear was one of only four churches confirmed to him that was not appropriated as a prebend in the cathedral (Cowan 1972, 26).

Bruce Campbell used the period around 1290 in an ambitious comparative study exploring the economic situation in the British Isles (Campbell 2008). Using taxation records, he found that the spiritual wealth of the church in England was two-and-a-half times greater than that of Scotland, Wales and Ireland combined. Within Scotland, the income of the dioceses of St Andrews and Glasgow was high. The diocese of Aberdeen had a middling income. The medieval bishops of Aberdeen maintained various residences within the diocese to enable them to make pastoral visits (Dransart 2016a, 60–61). Parts of the diocese that did not have any episcopal residence included Buchan, where the abbot of Deer Abbey would have been in charge of ensuring the pastoral needs of the people, and Fyvie, at the heart of Formartine, where monks of the order of Tiron had settled (Cowan and Easson 1976, 67, 74). When the bishop visited these places, he would have been entertained by the monks.

In the following pages, I consider Fetternear in its landscape setting, giving particular attention to sites of judicial assembly and the role of the bishop's scriptorium in providing instances of how land holdings and taxation were administered. The bishop's chapel played an important role in the religious sanction it gave to the exercise of justice. My discussion also focuses on routes within the parish of Fetternear and to neighbouring parishes, through Inverurie and beyond. In addition to Fetternear, the other bishop's residences mentioned here are Rayne and Loch Goul. Activities connecting the routes between these residences took place in the context of a landscape marked by still visible sites where previous generations of people had been active.

Fetternear in an ancient and judicial landscape

In the surroundings of Fetternear, the landscape can be seen to contain a sedimentation of places from different periods of time. The schematic map in Figure 7.3, which covers the parishes of Fetternear, the southern part of Logie Durno, Inverurie and parts of Kintore and Kinkell, shows the location of the bishop's palace. It is situated at the

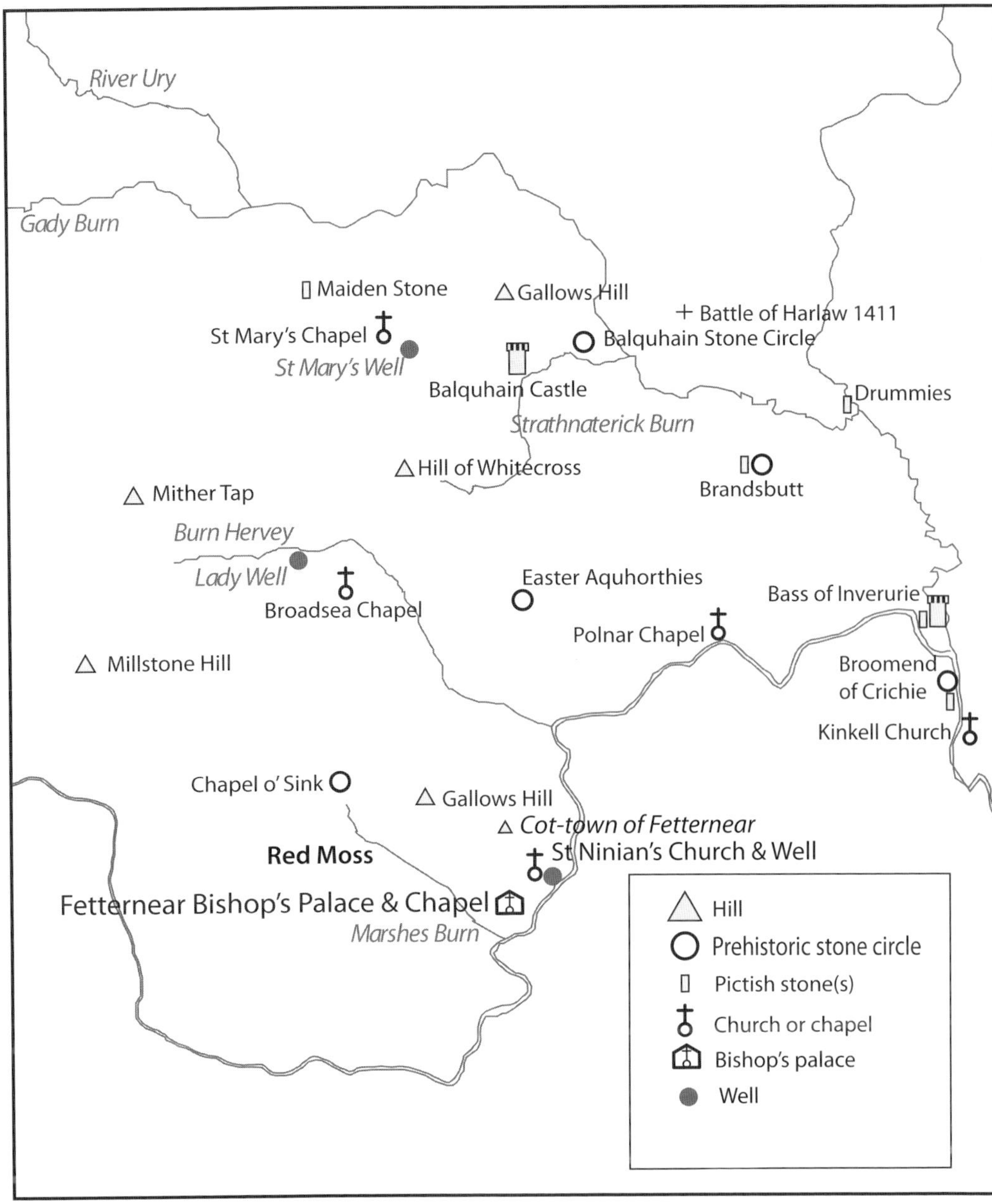

Figure 7.3. Schematic map of Balquhain and Fetternear, showing sites of archaeological interest.

southern extremity of the Red Moss, which was an important economic resource in prehistoric and medieval times, through which the Marshes Burn flows to join with the river Don.

Figure 7.3 includes some prehistoric sites, which continued to retain importance as sediments surviving from the past in the local landscape. Such materialised points of reference were reactivated and acquired different associations during the Middle Ages. Some of this evidence was revealed in post-medieval times, such as the Bronze Age axe reported in 1864 from near the source of the Marshes Burn at Westerton. It was recorded as being five inches long [127 mm], three inches [76 mm] across the mouth and 'in very good preservation' (OSNB, OS1/1/13/107). Mr James Grant, the finder, intended to present it to Colonel Leslie of Fetternear, the landowner, but its whereabouts are not now known. Because the description mentions the width at the 'mouth', I presume the axe was a metal socketed axe head. Traces of a Bronze Age settlement have been detected more recently in a field behind and on higher ground immediately north of the bishop's palace (Dransart *et al.* 2001). While the medieval inhabitants of Fetternear would not have known these particular examples of Bronze Age occupation, they must have encountered similar remains when cultivating the land and in their own building activities.

Whitecross, in the adjacent parish of Logie Durno, is recorded as Quhitecros in 16th-century charters, when it formed part of the Barony of Balquhain immediately north of the lands of Fetternear (*RMSS*, 24 James IV, 1511, no. 3600). A cairn sited on the Hill of Whitecross (NJ 7166 2255) would have been a visible monument surviving from the past in the medieval landscape. Surveyors working for the Ordnance Survey described it in the following terms:

> A large cairn of stones, situated on the Hill of Whitecross, it has never been opened, but it is supposed that it contains an urn, or stone cist – A portion of this cairn has been removed for the purpose of building stone walls (OSNB, OS1/1/13/86).

The character of the site perhaps suggests there was once a white cross planted on the cairn. If so, it would have been similar to the hill top locations studied by Colin Shepherd that once bore crosses, as mapped by Robert Gordon of Straloch in the 17th century. One of these sites was Selby Hill, on the site of a prehistoric cairn, immediately east of Inverurie (Shepherd 2016, 71). Alternatively (or additionally), the hill and its cairn denoted a different kind of crossing, a celestial one. Whitecross has a particular significance because it seems to have served as a 'marker hill for sunset on the Feast Day of Bride-Candlemas' and also at Martinmas (Youngblood 1999, citing observations made by Theodore Allan). St Bride's day falls on 1 February and the Purification of the Virgin, or Candlemas, on 2 February, while Martinmas falls on 11 November. These dates coincide with two of the four Scottish term days, which divided the calendrical year into quarters, when contracts and leases became due and people paid rent or interest on loans. Sightings focused on significant landmarks could also have been used by local people in calculating when specific dates fell in the annual cycle, whether associated with agricultural tasks or ritual celebrations (see also Forbes, this volume).

Between the Hill of Whitecross and the neighbouring Hill of Blairbowie, water rises to form the Strathnaterick Burn, which snakes its way round Blairbowie Hill and down past Balquhain Castle before joining the Ury at Drummies (also spelled Drimmies). Referring to the frequent appearance of serpents and Z-rods on Pictish stones, Marion Youngblood observed that the place-name Strathnaterick means 'valley of the serpent' (Youngblood 1999). The Brandsbutt stone is a close-by example of a Pictish stone bearing a serpent and Z-rod symbol.

Stone circles are a prominent feature in the parishes of the Garioch and Mar, and the Brandsbutt stone was found next to the location of a stone circle. Some of the stone circles included in Figure 7.3 are recumbent stone circles (Balquhain and Easter Aquhorthies), while the evidence that Brandsbutt might have had a recumbent is not proven. Adam Welfare thought it best to regard it as a plain stone circle (Welfare 2011, 498–9). In contrast, the almost circular setting of stones known as Chapel o' Sink is perhaps the remnant of a cairn, measuring 14.7 m in diameter (Welfare 2011, 505). Situated east of the summit of White Hill, it is just above the 500 ft contour line (that is, slightly over 152 m above sea level). It overlooks Westerton where James Grant found the Bronze Age axe and it is close to the source of the Marshes Burn. If the circle was once a cairn, it is likely to have presented a dominant marker of the past in medieval times as seen by people travelling through the parish of Fetternear. Since then, like Whitecross, it has been robbed of its grandeur. It owes its name to a local story that 'upon a time, attempts were made to erect a chapel here but unfortunately the part which was built during the daytime was always found on the following morning to have sunk, or have been knocked down, and hence the name' (OSNB, OS1/1/13/102).

Large stone settings in circular or elliptical formation provided particular opportunities for assembling people. An example of such a gathering is recorded in a charter dated 1439 (*REA*, I, 79–81). William de Deyn, bishop of Aberdeen, summoned William de St Michael to appear at a court held at the standing stones of Rayne in the presence of William, Earl of Ross, the King's justiciar in the north, for forcibly retaining landed property belonging to the church. This event probably took place at Candle Hill, Old Rayne, where a partially surviving recumbent stone circle is sited on the east side of a summit overlooking a public road (NJ 6798 2798; Welfare 2011, 432). The court has been discussed by G.W.S. Barrow (1992, 225–6, 236, no. 2.6) and Oliver O'Grady (2014, 110), drawing attention to the place-name element 'candle' as a derivation from the Old Gaelic *comhdhail* or 'meeting', 'tryst', or 'assembly' (Barrow 1992, 220). The judicial landscape of medieval Rayne had the moated bishop's manor at its centre, with routes radiating to the south-east to Candle Hill and, to the north-east at the junction with Barreldikes, up to the Gallows Hill, an eminence that was still covered with heathland at the time the Ordnance Survey 6-inch first edition was being surveyed in the area in 1867 (Aberdeenshire Sheet XLIV, published 1870).

Both Fetternear and Balquhain were also provided with a prominently situated Gallows Hill. At Fetternear, the summit of Gallows Hill is about 154 m above sea level, rising to a slightly greater height than the hill on which Cot-town Wood is located. St Ninian's church and its well is south of the Cot-town Wood, on the north bank of the Don. The hamlet listed in the 1157 charter is likely to have been a community of houses dispersed over the hill, now occupied by the wood. People living in this community would have been able to see any execution on the Gallows Hill from the top of their hill.

At Balquhain the Gallows Hill is about 177 m above sea level. The compilers of the Ordnance Survey Object Name Book recorded that, in 1838, the tenant farmer trenched formerly uncultivated land on the hill and in so doing uncovered human remains, including three skulls (OSNB, OS/1/1/13/68). They also cited a sentence from the Revd Simson's chapter in the New Statistical Account:

> About half a mile to the east of the Church, there is an eminence which commands an extensive view of the Garioch, and from which nine parochial Churches with as many manses may be seen (Simson 1845, 561).

This description of Gallows Hill, which Simson did not specifically name, relates of course to the view from the hill in the first part of the 19th century. It highlights the prominence of this low but eminent hill in the landscape. In a statistical analysis of the political landscapes of Buchan, as indicated by the occurrence of place-names in connection with topographical placement, Colin Shepherd found that gallows have a strong connection with hilltop locations, but are not strongly correlated with parish boundaries (2021, 190).

In a charter of David II in 1358, the monarch inspected and accepted a grant concerning a neighbouring lordship. It was issued by Thomas earl of Mar and lord of the Garioch in which Thomas granted to Robert Erskine and Christiana de Keith, his kinswoman, lands of:

> Balhalgardie, Boynds, Knockynglas [unidentified, perhaps Knockinglews], Inveramsy and the mill of Inveramsy, with the multure due and customary to the same mill from any past time, and half the land of Drumdorno, pertaining to our lordship of Garioch, and the lands of Pitscurry, Pitbee, Pettocher [probably Pittodrie - see Shepherd and Ralston, this volume)] and Newlands [of Oyne], along with four merks sterling of our annual rents due to us from the abbot and convent of Lindores from the land of Flinder [...] in one integral free barony (*RPS*, Document 1358/11/1).

The same document also specified that these lands came with the duty to maintain 'gallows and pit, toll and theame, soke and sac, infangthief and outfangthief'. In the original text, a mixture of Latin and Flemish – or at least Germanic – the conventional terms used were '*furca et fossa, tol et teme, sok et sak, infangandtheyf et utfangandtheyf*'. The phrase 'toll and theame' permitted the lord to adjudicate over a plaintiff's claim to stolen goods if a third party vouched that the plaintiff was indeed the owner of the goods. 'Soke and sac', or 'cause' and 'suit', gave the beneficiaries of the charter

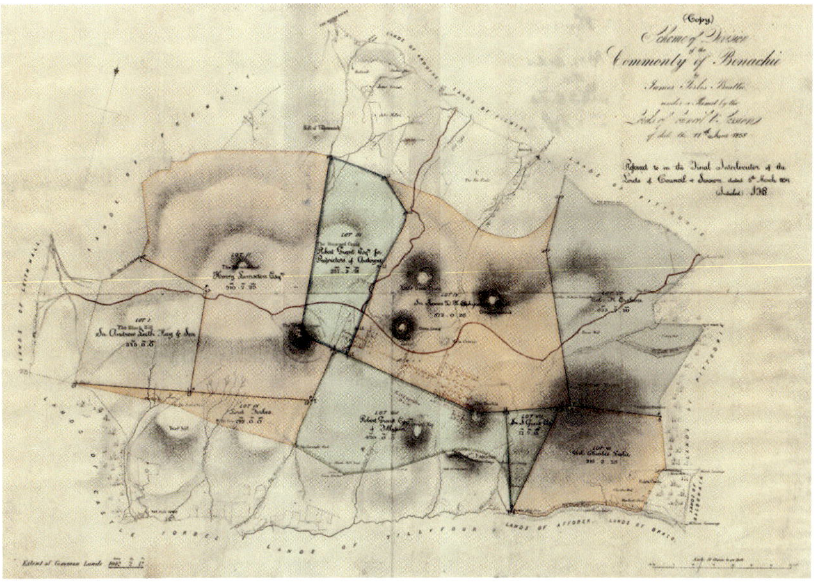

Plate 0.1. A copy of the Division of the Commonty plan of 1858. The individual lots granted to the several heritors are tinted in different colours. The internal divisions are marked clearly whilst the delineation of the area enclosed is less obvious (Courtesy of the Bailies of Bennachie).

Plate 0.2. The same plan converted to greyscale in order to suppress the internal divisions. A red line has been added to mark the commonty boundary – the land annexed by parliament for the benefit of the heritors. This boundary was of far greater significance to the people of the north-east as it demonstrated the area from which they were now excluded.

Plate 1.1. Mither Tap, Bennachie looking out from the early medieval entranceway of the citadel across rural Aberdeenshire (Photograph: Bruce Mann).

Plate 1.2. Barra Hillfort, Oldmeldrum showing the ramparts of the Iron Age and early medieval site (Photograph: Aberdeenshire Council Archaeology Service).

Plate 1.3. The most famous early medieval carved stone from the north-east, the Rhynie Man, shortly after it had been found during ploughing in 1978 (Photograph: Aberdeenshire Council Archaeology Service).

Plate 1.4. Early Bronze Age stone mould, Foudland Hill, Insch (Photograph: University of Aberdeen, ABDUA_18237_00001 © CC-BY).

Plate 2.1. Suggested beach gravel. Rounded clasts with little intervening matrix – porous with water seeping out from the bast – resting on slate debris with no porosity (Photograph: Andrew Wainwright).

Plate 2.2. Comparison between beach gravel (2.2a on left) and slate debris (2.2b on right). Note the rounded corners on the former in comparison with the angular nature of the latter, which was also associated with much matrix of sand silt and mud (Photograph: Andrew Wainwright).

Plate 2.3. Glens of Foudland from the A96 looking south-east. The Hill of Foudland is on the right with the Hill of Tillymorgan to the left. The pipeline trench ran north-westwards from beyond the pass through to Jericho Farm on the east side of the Hill of Foudland and, from there, down to the farm of Bog (north of the hill), in the middle distance. The highest lake level would have been just below the tree line on all three hills (Photograph: Penelope Shepherd).

Plate 2.4. Drop-stone of gneissic material. Note the rounded form and very smooth surface. This is in contrast to the fragments in Plate 2.1 (Photograph: Andrew Wainwright).

Plate 2.5. Layer of drop-stones that are significantly larger than the slate debris that makes up most of this section (Photograph: Andrew Wainwright).

Plate 2.6. Horizontal bedding seen in section and along the trench section at the very bottom of the hill. Small drop-stones can be seen at several locations. The higher part of the pipeline can be seen in the distance to the left of the right hand digger. Workmen ready to emplace the pipe and fill-in the trench (Photograph: Andrew Wainwright).

Plate 3.1. Loch Clunie, Perthshire (Photograph: James O'Driscoll).

Plate 3.2. Crawstane valley mire at Barflat, Rhynie (Photograph: Samantha Jones).

Plate 4.1. View of Tap o' Noth, the Hill of Noth and lands of Noth and Rhynie below taken from the north side of Hare Hill, upon which lies Cairn More (Photograph: Nicholas Evans).

Plate 4.2. View, taken from the south-west, of the walls and bank of Cairn More on Hare Hill, showing why it was called a cairn (Photograph: Nicholas Evans).

Plate 4.3. The south side of St Peter's Kirk, Duffus (Photograph: Nicholas Evans).

Plate 4.4. View north-east from Duffus Castle with Lossiemouth in the background. The further part of the large arable field was called Annet Pool Park on RHP427 (1783) (Photograph: Nicholas Evans).

Plate 5.1. The ruins of Old St Bride's Church, Kildrummy - the Chapel in the Lochs' - sit on top of its evocative green mound with Ardhuncart Hill in the background. Bride's Well lies at the foot of the mound (Photograph: Alexander Forbes).

Plate 5.2. View from Ardhuncart Hill looking across the rich farmlands surrounding the monastery of Clova (Photograph: Alexander Forbes).

Plate 7.1. Kite photograph of the excavation of the bishop's palace east of the drive, taken by Simon Harbord on 18 July 2004.

Plate 7.2. Fetternear, excavation of the sole plate of a timber bridge crossing the moat on the east side of the bishop's palace (Photograph: Scottish Episcopal Palaces Project).

Plate 7.3. Excavation of the moat on the south-west side of the bishop's palace, July 2005 (Photograph: Scottish Episcopal Palaces Project).

Plate 7.4. Excavation of the moat on the south side of the bishop's palace, July 2007 (Photograph: Scottish Episcopal Palaces Project).

Plate 7.5. An example of medieval window glass from Fetternear (Photograph: Robin Murdoch).

Plate 7.6. Styli excavated from the scriptorium at Fetternear (Photograph: Scottish Episcopal Palaces Project).

Plate 7.7. Fragment of dip pen excavated from the scriptorium at Fetternear, A6152, 47 mm long (Photograph: Iain Ralston).

Plate 7.8. Fragment of dip pen excavated from the scriptorium at Fetternear, A6212, 26 mm long (Photograph: Iain Ralston).

Plate 7.9. Medieval illumination of a scribe writing at his desk, probably Eadmer of Canterbury. Illuminated manuscript probably created for the Benedictine Abbey of Saint Martin, Tournai, Belgium. Getty Museum, Ms. Ludwig XI 6 (83.MN.125), fol. 44V, image in public domain.

Plate 7.10. Pope John XXII receiving Odoric de Pordenone in the Audience chamber near his palace at Pont-de-Sorgues, illumination dated between 1410 and 1412, Bibliothèque nationale de France, Français 2810, f. 97r, public domain.

Plate 8.1. View across the windswept uplands of Corrennie Moor with deserted colonist's dwelling in the foreground. The distant hills all contain similar examples of 19th-century settlement (Photograph: Jeff Oliver).

Plate 8.2. Community archaeologists from the Bailies of Bennachie undertake an elevation survey of Burnside cottage, the Bennachie Colony (Photograph: Jeff Oliver).

Plate 8.3. View across the slopes of Bennachie to the Pictish fort on Mither Tap. The former colony enclosures, subsequently Essons Farm, can be seen surrounded by the encroaching forestry woodland and natural regeneration (Photograph: Jeff Oliver).

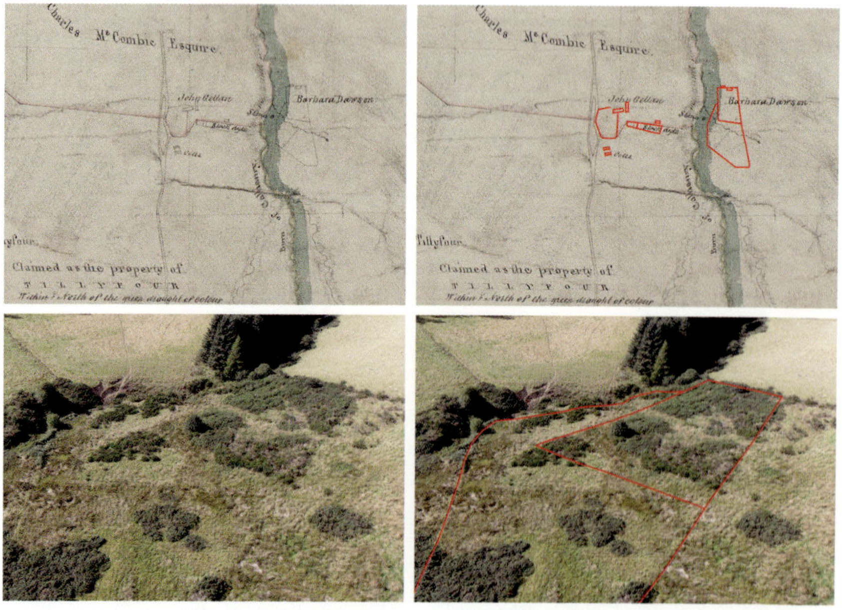

Plate 8.4. Top: detail of Corrennie Commonty Scheme of Division, 1834. At left, outlines of squatter settlement at the Hill of Tillyfour; at right, the same image with cottages and enclosures outlined in red. Provenance: MS 3860/6002 Aberdeen Special Collections. Bottom: drone photograph of the contemporary landscape, 2023. At left, the pattern of contemporary vegetation. At right, superimposed outlines of the kailyard and surrounding enclosed field as marked in the Scheme of Division (Photograph: James O'Driscoll).

the right to administer justice. 'Infangthief' was the right of the lord to apprehend and try anyone who was suspected of theft on the land specified in the charter, while 'outfangtheif' gave the lord permission to pursue someone beyond the bounds of the lordship and to take him or her back to be tried.

In Latin, *furca et fossa* was the phrase used for 'gallows and pit'. The pit – sometimes called a 'pot' by the local people consulted by the compilers of the Ordnance Survey Object Name Book – was the place where people alleged to have committed a crime were put through an ordeal. If the suspect admitted guilt and was a repeat offender, he or she might be hung on the gallows. Hence *furca et fossa* comes first in the list of the means that Robert Erskine and Christiana de Keith had at their disposal to deal with people judged to have committed crimes within their lordship. Rather than being placed as a potential outcome after a process, 'gallows' is the first term mentioned in the permissions they were given in order to pursue, arrest and try anyone suspected of criminal activity. This positioning in the text at the head of the judicial process is monitory. It is analogous to the physical prominence of Gallow Hill locations on an elevated site; both local people and travellers coming into the lordship were given a warning that they were in a place where punishment could be capital.

A charter that can only be broadly dated between 1172 and 1199 in which David, earl of Huntingdon granted the lordship of Leslie, in the parish of Leslie, to Norman, son of Bartolf – the ancestor of the Leslie family in the Garioch – contains a simplified set of means, '*cum sacca et socco cum tholl et them et infangandthef cum furca*' (Stringer 1985, 254, *Acta* no. 55). It omits 'outfangtheif', the right to pursue suspects outwith the boundaries of the lordship. In the copy of the charter transcribed in Robertson and Grub (1843, 546–7), the pit is also omitted, which is specifically excluded ('*preter fossam*'). Instead, the term *infangandthef* implies the right to hang a thief and seize his chattels (Taylor 2016, 159). The parish of Leslie indeed has a Gallow Hill. It rises north of the castle and is described as a 'Hill of considerable extent and elevation situated about a mile north of the Castle of Leslie' (OSNB, OS/1/1/54/26).

Alice Taylor notes that the phrase *furca et fossa* became more frequent after the 1180s in charters issued to beneficiaries mainly north of the Forth (Taylor 2016, 159). She explains that jurisdiction over a particular lordship was granted or confirmed by the king to the beneficiaries specified in its charter and that some beneficiaries had the right to use pit and gallows, which were the 'tools by which they could administer justice to thieves in particular' (Taylor 2016, 173). Of interest in the charter granted to Norman, son of Bartholf, at Leslie is that one of the witnesses was Bróiccín (Bròicean in modern Gaelic spelling), the *judex* (the lawmaker, in Gaelic, *breitheamh*), or '*filio Brouiss judice*', Duncan, the son of Brouiss, the *judex,* in the version presented in Leslie (1869, I, 147). Taylor argues that over the course of the 12th century, *judices*, who had been responsible for the preservation of laws, were ceasing to be the main lawmakers and the king-in-assembly was increasingly taking over that role (Taylor 2016, 131–2). Another process she outlines is that by the mid-13th century, legal prescriptions were being situated within institutional and jurisdictional structures involving the redefinition of aristocratic powers and the recasting of royal officialdom (Taylor 2016, 175). Keith Stringer thought that the style of Earl David's charter would date it to 'no later than 1185' (Stringer 1985, 255). The difference between the details and the ordering of terms used in the 12th-century charter issued to Norman, son of Bartholf, and the 14th-century charter of Robert Erskine and Christiana de Keith is a manifestation of the changes occurring in the administration of justice.

Throughout these changes, the presence of gallows remained as a warning against repeat offending. Gallows placed on hills must have been a frequent presence, distributed on low but prominent foothills surrounding Bennachie. They continued to be used into early modern times. In the Ordnance Survey Object Name Book, there is an instance of the use of an ordeal pit called Jenkins Hole. Described as a deep pot in the river Ury, it occurs in the records for both Inverurie and its neighbour Keithhall and Kinkell, implying that its location was on the boundary between the two. The entry cites a document in the possession of the Revd John Davidson, who was minister of the parish church in Inverurie:

> Alexander Fergus alias Walace, in Inverury attached be ye Shreff of theft putt to ane assyss was convickt be ye assisse & drowned in Urie in ye pott callit Ginkin Holl till he was deid. Buriet in ye kirkeyard of Inverury 4 August 1629 (OSNB, OS/1/1/44/12).

The exact location of Jenkins Hole was not exactly defined by the people from whom the Ordnance Survey compilers received their information, other than it was close to where the Sketrie Burn joins the river Don (OSNB, OS/1/1/42/46). In 1629, the execution was by drowning. In other cases, the persons accused of a criminal act might be subjected to an ordeal in the pit and then be hung on the gallows. Inverurie's Gallows Hill was at the north end of the burgh, not close to the site of judgment in the river Ury. If Jenkins Hole was used to put other suspects through an ordeal – as implied by the place name, which seems to have been named after someone other than the man executed in 1629 – the procession of people from the pit to the gallows was part of a public display in a judicial process in which the suspect was found guilty and taken through the parish to the place of hanging.

By the 14th and 15th centuries, St Ninian – the saint to whom the parish church of Fetternear was dedicated – was famous for his works of mercy, which included visiting prisoners in captivity. In one of the miracles attributed to him, an Englishman in an unnamed location found guilty three times of committing crimes was 'weilang in that py[n]ful pyt' ('wailing in that painful pit') before the sheriff came to town and condemned him to the gibbet, from which the saint miraculously saved him (Legends of the Saints, II, 331–2).

Trodden routes through the parish of Fetternear

From the foregoing section, it can be seen that the administration of justice took place over multiple but connecting sites. The parish of Fetternear differed somewhat from its neighbouring parishes in essentially containing the lordship possessed by the bishops of the medieval diocese of Aberdeen, whereas other lordships might be split between parishes, as Keithhall was between Inverurie and Kinkell, or contain more than one lordship, as in Logie Durno parish. Fetternear's parish church was about a mile distant from the bishop's palace. The route between the bishop's palace and the church follows a terrace along the south bank of the Don. It must have been well trodden in medieval times.

On crossing the parish boundary at Burnhervie, the route continued into the parish of Inverurie. It would have passed the Polnar church of Rothket or Rothkes, mentioned in late 12th-century charters with its dependent chapels at the foot of the Bass in Inverurie and Montkeigie, now known as Keithhall (Stringer 1985, 70, 94, 220). There was a ferry boat crossing over the Don near Rothket, at Rockarl.

The Roy Military Survey, produced in 1745–1755, shows the main route coming from south of the Don, across the ferry at Rockarl, to reach the north bank of the Don (Figure 7.4). Rockarl has lost its initial 'R' in the place-name recorded by the Roy map makers, who rendered it as 'Achurell'. It appears as 'Racharral' in the John Thompson map of 1826. The spelling of the place-name has been anglicised as Roquharold, but locally the more ancient pronunciation of Rockarl still survives. Roy's map makers did not extend the route from the spot where the ferry-route crossing turns eastward on the north bank of the Don. This spot must have been a junction, however, and the route must have continued westward to Fetternear and Monymusk. The main route drawn in the mid-18th century is indicated as going past Ardtannes, marked as a cluster of unnamed houses, on the approach to Inverurie (Figure 7.4). Surveyors compiling the Ordnance Survey Name Book in the 19th century listed the site of the Old Hall of Ardtannes and added a report to the effect that Mr Bisset of Ardtannes had found a platform of black oak logs, which covered a 'draw-well from which it is conjectured the people of Old Hall of Ardtannes drew their water' (OSNB, OS1/1/42/87). John Davidson, however, surmised that the route would have been somewhat higher up Corsman Hill than today's unclassified road between St James's Place in Inverurie and Burnhervie (Davidson 1878, 6–7). In the context of the places associated with judicial landscapes, it is worth noting that Davidson claimed that Alexander Stewart, as lord of the Garioch, held his courts at Ardtannes and not at the Bass of Inverurie (Davidson 1878, 2). Unfortunately, he does not back up this statement by referring to any sources.

Bishop Ralph de Lamly, former abbot of Arbroath, was consecrated bishop of Aberdeen before 20 August 1240, 'in the presence of King Alexander' (Boece 1894 [1522], 12; POMS, Permalink: poms.ac.uk/record/source/2027/). Medieval bishops were expected to participate in lavish festive occasions, but Hector Boece drew attention to Bishop Ralph's commitment to his vow of poverty as a monk, explaining that he visited 'on foot his whole diocese' (Boece 1894 [1522], 13). Bishop Ralph is likely to have walked from Fetternear, past Burnhervie and the ferry at Rockarl, to continue past Ardtannes. On reaching Inverurie, he probably turned northwards to reach his

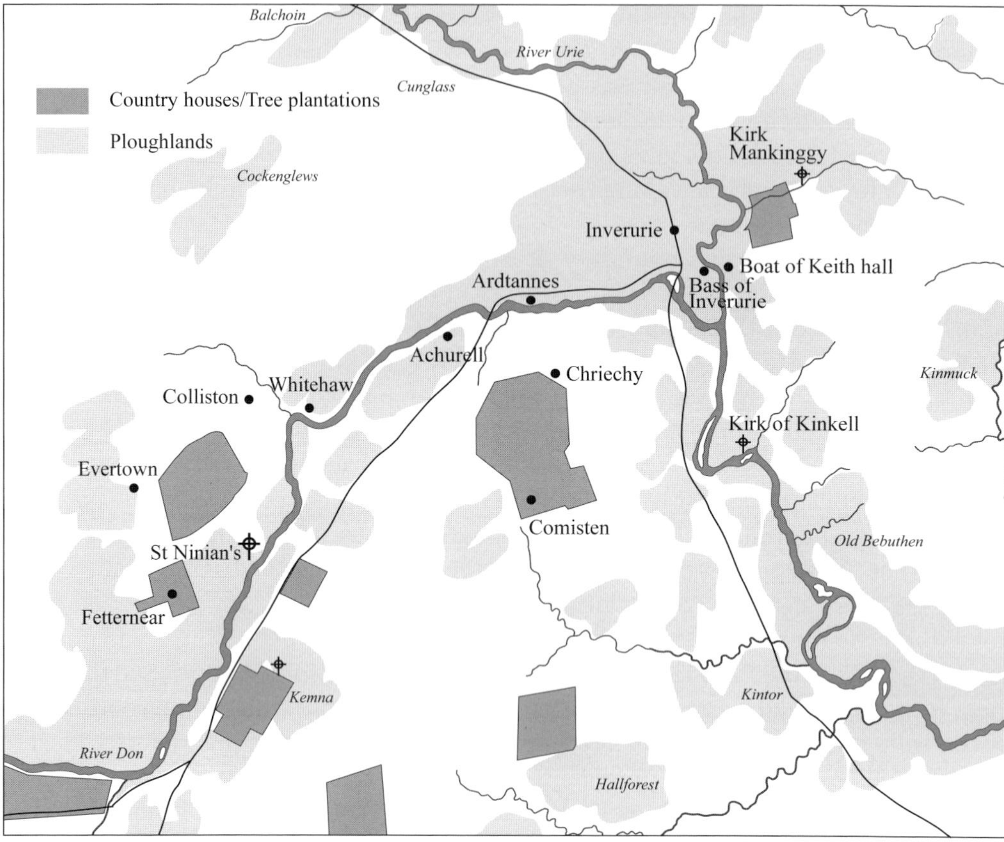

Figure 7.4. Map of routes and place names contained in the Roy Military Survey 1747–1755, drawn by Colin Shepherd.

episcopal residence of Rayne. It is also possible that Bishop Adam de Tyninghame took a similar route when travelling between Rayne and Fetternear, discussed further below in connection with the scriptorium at Fetternear.

To the frugal Bishop Ralph de Lamly and his less frugal successors, on 18 September 1242, Alexander II granted land in free forest at Brass (that is, Birse) and Fethyrnier (*REA*, I, 15–16; POMS, Permalink: poms.ac.uk/record/source/2027/). This grant formally specified that Bishop Ralph and his successors should charge the king's 'full fine of ten pounds' if anyone trespassed on the said lands without their permission. It seems that by the 14th century, the bishops had granted rights to certain people to make use of the free forest for specific purposes. The charter cited above, which was granted to Robert Erskine and Christiana de Keith, included rights to common pasture in the forest of Bennachie and the woods of an unidentified place called 'Aldclochy': *et cum communi pastura in foresta de Benethkey et in silvis de Aldeclochy* (*RPS*, Document 1358/11/1). If 'Aldeclochy' referred to the Clachie Burn on Bennachie, then the cattle of the beneficiaries of the grant would have browsed in what was then the woodlands of the free forest in the possession of the bishops of Aberdeen. (I am grateful to Colin Shepherd for this potential identification of Aldeclochy.)

In the years following the Protestant Reformation of 1560, the lands of the bishops of Aberdeen were granted to the Leslies of Balquhain, who had helped save St Machar's Cathedral from being destroyed by the reformers. These lands included the free forest of Bennachie. After the division of what, by the 19th century, had become the Commonty of Bennachie, Colonel Charles Leslie inserted a note in his three-volume family history, citing the succession of legal documents which confirmed his family's title to the forest of Bennachie (Leslie 1869, III, 681). In other words, he refuted the local accusation that he was a 'thief' who had stolen the lands on Bennachie apportioned in 1859 to Balquhain and Fetternear.

Bishop Bennum's residence in Loch Goul

One of Bishop Ralph's successors was Hugh Bennum, whose family is thought to have had lands in Benholm in Kincardineshire. He was active between 1247 and 1281 and, in 1272, he was consecrated in Orvieto, Italy (Watt 1977, 39). Bishop Hugh was especially associated with a modestly sized episcopal residence located on what used to be an island in Loch Goul, near Dyce. According to tradition, the residence had a chapel, which was dedicated to the Virgin (Moir 1845, 1029). Drainage works over the centuries have caused the site to become a peninsula.

In late medieval times, a question arose in documentary sources about how Bishop Hugh met his end. Was he murdered in his residence on the island? In a document entitled *De fundatione et translatione sedis episcopalis atque episcoporum succione*, dated *c.* 1400 and kept by the bishops of Aberdeen, the entry in Latin on Bishop Hugh is ambiguous: '*Decimus Hugo qui suffocatus fuit in lacu de Goyle*' (*REA*, II, 126). It can be translated as 'Hugh, tenth bishop, who was drowned in Loch Goul' or as 'Hugh, tenth bishop, who choked in Loch Goul'. Another version is included in a fine 16th-century manuscript produced in Antwerp for Bishop Gavin Dunbar, in which it was stated, 'Hugh of Benhame, tenth bishop, who fell in an ambush in the year of our Lord's incarnation 1282' (*REA*, II, 247).

Hector Boece, the first principal of the fledgling university of Aberdeen, tried to quash rumours concerning Bishop Hugh's death. In 1522, he wrote:

> His term of office reached to the twenty-ninth year of Alexander III. In that year he suddenly died of an excess of rheum in the island of the lake of Gowllis, where the old man found such delight in the pleasant groves adjoining that he sought no other retreat (Boece 1894, 15).

Whatever happened, after Hugh's bishopric, subsequent bishops of the diocese of Aberdeen seem to have ceased making use of Loch Goul as a residence. Despite the strong association Bishop Hugh had with Loch Goul, it is known that he also made use of his residence at Fetternear because he sealed a charter there. That he employed scribes to write documents at Fetternear implies the maintenance of a scriptorium where they could do the specialised work. Indeed, some of the finds from the archaeological excavation at Fetternear, which formed part of the Scottish Episcopal Palaces Project, provide direct evidence for scribal activities undertaken within the bishop's palace.

Fetternear bishop's palace

Fetternear was a much larger site than Loch Goul and the excavation shows that it remained in continuous use up until the Protestant Reformation. Today, visitors approaching the site see the ruins of Fetternear House, which dominates the view. After receiving the estate of Fetternear in 1566, the Leslies of Balquhain built a tower-house, which was extended twice during the 17th century to make the still-existing façade (see, again Figure 7.2). Nowadays, it is not immediately obvious that Fetternear bishop's palace was a medieval moated site. In the 19th century, however, the occupants of Fetternear House found evidence for the moat when they extended the house in about 1818 and, again, in the 1840s (Leslie 1869, I, 120; Dransart 2016a, 67).

Between 1995 and 2010, the excavation gradually revealed that the bishop's palace was like an island nearly completely surrounded by a moat. The discovery of the

Figure 7.5. Aerial photograph of Fetternear showing the alignment of the route from the direction of the parish church of Fetternear to the bishop's palace (Photograph: Moira Greig).

Figure 7.6. Excavation of the moat on the east side of Fetternear bishop's palace, July 2003 (Photograph: Scottish Episcopal Palaces Project).

Figure 7.7. Excavation of the moat at the bishop's manor of Old Rayne (Photograph: Hilary and Charles Murray).

sole plate of a trestle-type timber bridge on the south-east side of the moated area indicated that access to the bishop's palace was not from the south, as is the case now in the approach to the post-medieval mansion (Plate 7.2). Someone leaving the parish church of Fetternear would have approached the bishop's palace along a route aligned as in Figure 7.5.

After digging through late 18th- and 19th-century pits, the excavation team encountered the moat on the east side of the site (Figure 7.6). Its full width had been curtailed on the east by the construction of a more recent stone-lined drain and, on the west, by the widening of the long curtain wall that surrounded much of the area contained within the moat. This widening must have been undertaken in late medieval times and, as a result, the curtain wall encroached into the moat. By the 19th century, the lower courses of this wall were converted to serve as a garden feature. Further evidence for the moat was found on the south of the site, on both sides of the modern drive leading to the house (Plate 7.3). On the west side of the palace, which we excavated in 2005 and 2006, the moat was overlain by a diagonally trending terraced wall, which prevented us from gaining an unimpeded view of the moat.

Finally, in July 2007, we gained a good view in cross-section of the moat, on the south side of the site, east of the drive (Plate 7.4). But here the moat became more shallow as it rose to an end. Elsewhere the moat is deeper. On the north side, it was cut into the granitic bedrock with a V-shaped profile. For most of its trajectory, the moat was dug into natural, alluvial material with a U-shaped profile. At the south-eastern corner, a sluice arrangement allowed it to drain through a straight V-shaped channel into the Marshes Burn, which is a tributary of the river Don.

The bishop's manor at Rayne (now called Old Rayne) was also moated, although its ditches were dry and there was no evidence for them having been filled with water

(Figure 7.7). The moat took the form of a near double ellipse with a flattened side where it ran next to the road to Aberdeen (Murray and Murray 2012, 6–7).

Medieval bishop's residences were frequently surrounded by water in ditches or moats or, as at Loch Goul, surrounded by the waters of a loch. In a previous publication, I have suggested that bishops used such cultural features in an evocative landscape expressing the spiritual and secular dimensions of their authority (Dransart 2017, 92–93). In their writings and sermons, churchmen made use of the different elements of a castle. They put the built landscape of moats, ditches, towers, inner and outer wards to use in allegories of Christian salvation. Robert Grosseteste's poem *Chasteau d'amour*, written *c.* 1230, likened the Blessed Virgin Mary's heart to a strong castle surrounded by a moat which shielded the faithful and defended the defenceless against marauding enemies. Later in the Middle Ages, Gavin Douglas's poem *Palis of honoure* (1501) praised honour and moral purpose in an allegory of a mountain-top palace with an internal court or 'garth' as a place of sanctuary and an inner hall, where Honour reigned (Dransart 2017, 93, 97 n. 48). Both these poets became bishops later in life, Grossesteste as bishop of Lincoln and Douglas as bishop of Dunkeld.

At Fetternear, a visitor approaching the palace would have crossed the moat over the bridge and they would have seen a nicely built stone wall on either side of the entrance. Part of this wall survives and a medieval stone drain, which ran in front of the chapel within the palace led out through the wall and ran along the outside into the moat. The entrance portal in this well-built wall was perhaps quite simple. A possible comparison might be made with the lower parts of the gatehouse of Prudhoe Castle in Northumberland (Figure 7.8), ignoring the upper parts, which are more recent additions (West 2006, 15). Although the lower courses of the walling either side of the entrance survived at Fetternear, the rest of the gatehouse arrangements have been lost. The area behind the entry into the palace was severely levelled in the late 16th or early 17th century, as part of the remodelling of the site by the Leslies of Balquhain.

Examination of the small finds from within the moated area has enabled the identification of several different activity areas. The kitchen was located in the south-west corner of the site. Diagonally opposite, in the north-eastern sector, were the chapel and scriptorium. The great hall has not been located. It might have been where the present ruined mansion stands.

Figure 7.8. The entrance portal of Prudhoe Castle, Northumberland.

Hector Boece praised Alexander de Kininmund (bishop 1329–1344), the next but one bishop after Hugh de Bennum, for devoting his 'whole energies to preaching and admonition' (Boece 1894 [1522], 18). According to Boece,

> He spent the winter at Mortlach, and the spring at Aberdeen. He selected the city as his spring residence in order to be able more conveniently to instruct the crowds who assembled there in Lent, to punish in ecclesiastical fashion those that had erred from the path of virtue, and to pass the sacred season of Easter with greater solemnity and pomp. The summer and autumn he spent at Feterneyr and Rain (Boece 1894 [1522]: 18–19).

Boece attributed to Bishop Alexander the building of episcopal residences at the four places he mentioned, adding that he only completed Fetternear and Aberdeen (Boece 1894 [1522], 19). Because it is known that Fetternear already existed, perhaps Bishop Alexander strengthened the already existing arrangements rather than build on a new site. He had good reason to do so. During his episcopate, Boece reported that 30 English ships anchored by night alongside the road next to Aberdeen harbour. The following day, English soldiers attacked the city, killing many of its citizens. Boece commented on the panic caused as men, women, and children fled, while Aberdeen burned for six days (Boece 1894 [1522], 19–20). The residences of the bishop and the canons were also attacked. Stephen Boardman attributed the organisation of this 1336 attack to the English king, Edward III, in response to the strength of local support for Robert I (the Bruce) (Boardman 2002, 28). It is therefore likely that Fetternear served as a place of refuge for the bishop and his staff at a distance from Old Aberdeen.

The Fetternear scriptorium

As mentioned above, the scriptorium at Fetternear was next to the chapel. While the chapel was a masonry building and probably had a tiled floor (Figure 7.9), the scriptorium was of a timber construction and it seems to have had a timber floor, too. It was equipped with a latrine for the convenience of the scribes. These buildings were later demolished. The debris from the chapel contained small quarries of medieval glass (Plate 7.5), but similar pieces also occurred elsewhere within the moated area. One likely medieval piece found near the chapel was coloured cobalt blue and another was flashed with red (Murdoch, in preparation; see also Murdoch 2008, 53–55). The windows of the chapel were likely to have been small and narrow, and were perhaps like the

Figure 7.9. The south wall of the chapel in Fetternear bishop's palace (Photograph: Scottish Episcopal Palaces Project).

Figure 7.10. St Mary's Auchindoir, lancet window in the north wall (Photograph: P. Dransart).

lancet window in Figure 7.10, which has survived in the north wall of St Mary's Church, Auchindoir. It is dated to *c.* 1200.

In its south wall, the church at Auchindoir has a very fine main portal. The chapel at Fetternear might have had an elaborate entrance, too, because the Aberdeen architect William Kelly observed extremely fine carving at Fetternear when he undertook work to underpin the mansion in the years between 1896 and 1900. He commented,

> The foundations of extensive buildings were uncovered some years ago. In the course of excavations some perfect pieces of advanced first-pointed mouldings and tracery were discovered. The material appears to be Kildrummy freestone. The workmanship is of the finest kind, and the mouldings even more beautifully profiled than the fragment attributed to Chein's choir (Kelly 1910, 173).

These carved stones have unfortunately not been located. Kelly's comments are tantalising because his attribution of the stones to the period when 'first-pointed mouldings and tracery' were produced suggests that the carving at Fetternear might have been contemporary with the portal and lancet window that have survived at Auchindoir, from the very beginning of the 13th century. In his article, Kelly included a photograph of a 'moulded stone of advanced first-pointed character' reportedly found when a house in Old Aberdeen was demolished. The oldest part of the house, which formerly was in the possession of the Buchans of Auchmacoy, had served as the chancellor's manse. Kelly described it as being the capital from where the rear-arch of a window opening would have sprung (Kelly 1910, 172 and plate no. 2). This remnant is likely to have come from the St Machar's cathedral rather than Fetternear.

The location of Fetternear's scriptorium is significant because its proximity to the chapel would have added to the sense of authority attributed to the activities conducted within it. It is possible that the scriptorium, like the chapel, had glazed windows to provide the scribes with natural light while they undertook their tasks. Their work probably included the production of charters, but they would also have recorded tithes contributed by the people of Fetternear. In a previous publication, I referred to the building as a counting house because a token-like object, stray coins and a 15th-century jeton from Bourges, France, were also recovered from the area of the scriptorium (Dransart 2016b, 125–6).

Evidence for the activities of scribes is witnessed by the presence of writing tools, recovered from beneath the floor of the scriptorium. There were two bronze styli for writing on wax tablets, a means of making a temporary record (Plate 7.6).

Fragments of copper alloy dip pens were also found (Plates 7.7 and 7.8). It is likely these tools dropped between the floorboards of the scriptorium, preventing the scribes from retrieving them. A complete example of a dip pen can be seen in the online collections of the London Museum (accession number A2405; London Museum n.d.).

Medieval illuminations frequently depict an evangelist or other saint in the act of writing. The example in Plate 7.9, probably from the Benedictine Abbey of St Martin in Tournai, Belgium, is thought to depict Eadmer of Canterbury at his writing stand. Using his right hand, Eadmer dips his quill pen in an ink pot and he holds a knife for trimming the point of the pen in his left. Quill pens could easily have been used at Fetternear, but the feathers do not survive in the archaeological deposits. There are no survivals of ink-horns or ink-pots amongst the Fetternear finds. They would have been too bulky to fall between the floorboards. Medieval examples were made from different materials. In the collections of the London Museum, an inkwell elaborately crafted from leather is stamped with the figures of saints (A28570) and two carved from horn have incised ornament drawn with a compass (A292 and A13339) (Ward Perkins 1975, 292, 198, plates XLV and XC).

Oak is attested in the environmental analysis of deposits from Fetternear. It is possible that the scribes collected oak galls locally to make their ink. They would, however, have had to have imported another ingredient, gum arabic, probably from North Africa. Ink recipes might also contain iron sulfate and wine. The following two sections present details of the charters issued at Fetternear and which were preserved in the records of the bishops of Aberdeen. They indicate something of the range of documents relating to land-holdings and taxation, which scribes working for the bishops of Aberdeen were responsible for producing at Fetternear.

The granting of land in Ardlair

Bishop Hugh Bennum issued the first of these charters at Fetternear on the '*xj kalendas Februarij anno gratie millesimo ducentesimo septuagesimo sexto*', which is the year of grace 22 January 1277 in the calendar used today (*REA*, II, 278). It concerned two ploughgates or carucates of land in Kennethmont, which the historian Keith Stringer identified in earlier charters as Ardlair (Stringer 1985, 220 [Charter no. 1], 222–3 [Charter no. 5]; *REA*, I, 218). A carucate is the amount of land that could be ploughed in a year.

In his charter, Bishop Hugh declared,

> Let people of the present and in the future know that we have given by the agreement and consent of our chapter and confirmed by this our charter to William de Tatenell our man in fee and inheritance those two carucates of land in Kynalchmond [Kennethmont] that earl David [of Huntingdon] granted to our church and to bishop Matthew (*REA*, II, 277–8).

According to the charter's terms, William de Tatenell, as beneficiary of the grant, agreed to make a payment to the bishop and his successors of one merk on the feast of Pentecost and a further merk on feast of St Martin in winter (11 November).

Several men witnessed the grant. They were Henry le Chene, precentor, Thomas de Bennum, chancellor, Robert, treasurer, Galfrid, archdeacon, Gilbert de Stirling, master Richard Logate, Robert of Glasclogy, Gilbert, rector of Clatt, and 'many others'. Henry le Chen was to become the next bishop after Bishop Hugh. His name appears first in the list of witnesses, indicating his important status over the witnesses who followed him. His role as precentor meant that he had a pre-eminent position close to the bishop when Mass was celebrated in St Machar's cathedral. The precentor was responsible for leading the singing and chanting during religious ceremonies. Thomas de Bennum, the chancellor, was another powerful dignitary in the chapter of the cathedral and he is likely to have been a kinsman of Bishop Hugh (Watt 1977, 40). The charter was probably written in the scriptorium but the key witnesses may have appended their seals elsewhere. If everyone named and unnamed was present at the occasion they are likely to have filled the small chapel at Fetternear. Alternatively, the public pronouncement of the charter might have been performed in the Great Hall.

The lands mentioned in the charter appear in another document sealed in the year 1297 at Fetternear. On this occasion, Bishop Hugh's successor, Bishop Henry le Chen, confirmed the two ploughgates of land to Patrick de Rothnek (of Ruthven) (*REA*, I, 37–38).

Bishop Henry began the charter with a salutation to all the children of the Holy Church, wishing them eternal salvation in the Lord. He then announced his confirmation of the sale of the land made by William de Tatenell to Patrick de Rothnek, naming William's grandfather (also named William) as the man who formerly received the land in the grant of Bishop Hugh. The condition is again specified that Patrick and his heirs should pay the bishop and his successors two silver merks, one on the feast of Pentecost and the other on the feast of St Martin in winter. As a conclusion, the charter is dated *apud Fethirner*, the Tuesday nearest after the feast of St Bartholomew, apostle, in the year of grace 1297. The sealing of the charter is therefore likely to have taken place on Tuesday 27 August 1297 (POMS, https://poms.ac.uk/record/factoid/73620/).

Five churchmen and 'many others' are listed as witnesses. Two of these witnesses have what sound like very local names. *Dominus* Andrew de Garuyach, named third in the list of witnesses, had become treasurer of the cathedral chapter by 1291 (Watt 1977, 215). The other person with a local name was *dominus* Thomas of Inuerowry (Inverurie).

The excommunication of the household heads of Formartine

In documents issued in 1382–1383, local and national affairs became entangled. A large group of men, who were collectively called the husbandmen (or household heads) of Formartine were excommunicated by Bishop Adam de Tyninghame. A document, which might have been written in the scriptorium at Fetternear, explains that the men were excommunicated in 1382 in the chapel of the bishop's manor of Rayne (*REA*, I, 163–6). After passing three term dates without paying a tax called the second tenths to the church, they approached Bishop Adam to ask for absolution, who seems to have been in residence at Fetternear.

Why did non-payment of taxes result in the severe punishment of excommunication? The punishable offence they committed seems trivial compared with Robert I's murder of his rival John Comyn before the altar of the Greyfriars' church in Dumfries, for which Pope Clement V excommunicated him in 1306, or for breaking a papal truce in 1318, when Robert I was excommunicated for a second time (Penman 2013, 1047). Bishop Adam, however, had previous experience in the legal customs of the papal court in Avignon, which had acquired a reputation for efficiency in the collection of taxes. During summer 1358, he served as sub-collector of papal revenues and in 1380, on another visit to Avignon, he secured his position as bishop of Aberdeen (Watt 1977, 553–4).

Robert II had previously granted the lordship of Formartine to his eldest son, John, earl of Carrick who, in turn, made a grant of the lands to his cousin James de Lindsay, lord of Crawford. It appears the earl of Carrick put pressure on James to persuade the householders not to pay the church the second tenths, which they had done previously when the lordship was under crown control. Bishop Adam petitioned Robert II, who was forced to instruct his son, the Earl of Carrick, and his nephew, James, now lord of Crawford and Formartine, to allow the householders to pay the tax. The householders were said to be 'more afraid of offending against human power than against the power of God' (*RPS*, Document A1382/6/1). Moreover, Robert II concluded, 'if the said lord bishop should proceed against the non-payers by ecclesiastical censure, we will endure this patiently' (*RPS*, Document A1382/6/1).

Bishop Adam then moved to collect the unpaid second tenths. On 9 March 1382, in his chapel at Old Rayne and in the presence of high-ranking churchmen from the chapter of the cathedral in Moray and from his own chapter in Aberdeen, he granted absolution to John de Camera who, in addition to being a farmer in Formartine, was the bailie and receiver of the lands of the lordship, from the sentence of excommunication pronounced against him for not having collected the second tenths. The bishop also absolved more than 50 men from the parishes of Fyvie and Tarves once they had pledged to pay the second tenths and shown their contrition and penitence. The document stated that Bishop Adam absolved them with his own hand and with a penitential psalm. He then admonished them for receiving Eucharist while they were excommunicated during the preceding Easter, for which they had fallen into grave suspicion of heresy. They were to present themselves before him in St Machar's cathedral on the forthcoming Thursday of Holy Week or another solemn holy day, in bare feet, head uncovered and wearing no girdle, each one of them bearing a candle so that before the whole congregation they might make their humble request for absolution. Bishop Adam added, however, on this occasion he would not seek to impose this punishment (*REA*, I, 164–5).

In Fetternear, on the 15th day of the same month, and in the same manner, Bishop Adam absolved four further men from the parish of Tarves and one from the parish of Fyvie, who all travelled from Formartine to Fetternear to obtain absolution (*REA*, I, 166).

James de Lyndsay, lord of Crawford and Formartine, issued an order in 1383 to instruct the households in his lordship to pay in perpetuity the second tenths to the church on the feast days of Pentecost and Saint Martin. He appended his seal to the document as a witness, to be shown at Aberdeen 'and to remain before the lord bishop' (*REA*, I, 166–7). Bishop Adam had succeeded in his aim to restore the church income.

Concluding comment

This study of places as loci of human activities demonstrates how places can shift through time – the Cot-town of Fetternear has disappeared from view – but also how they can persist in subsequent ages. Where places persist, their reuse through time constitutes an active process of reworking, adapting and modifying them for new purposes. Ancient places of assembly, such as the standing stones of Rayne, could be made to bolster authority in the administration of justice.

Some places were inalienable. To the leading churchmen of the medieval diocese of Aberdeen, Fetternear was one such place serving as the mensal church a mile from the bishop's palace to support episcopal activities, including those of the scribes who worked in the scriptorium-cum-counting house. In the complex interplay of ownerships, possessions and landholdings, Earl David of Huntingdon granted *c.* 1189 the two carucates of land in Ardlair to the church of Aberdeen and to Bishop Matthew in compensation for the loss of income from churches in the Garioch, including Rothkes (the Polnar Chapel) and Monkeigie (Keithhall). By the 13th century, the bishops of Aberdeen regarded these carucates as alienable and they granted them to non-churchmen, as long as the new holders of the land made their symbolic payments of a silver coin to the church on the feasts of Pentecost and St Martin in winter. The grants and confirmation made by bishops Hugh and Henry at Fetternear were underscored by the non-transferable status of Fetternear as church patrimony.

Scribal activities recording specific grants and taxation of lands were associated with perambulations and journeying to specific locations to convert the written record into publicly acknowledged deeds. Churchmen in the diocese of Aberdeen knew their lands through such journeys and many of them were moreover immersed in the Latin idioms of the papal chancery in Avignon, which they brought back to Scotland after spending periods of time there. Alexander de Kininmund and Adam de Tyninghame, mentioned above, both secured their appointment as bishop of Aberdeen in Avignon. The historian Geoffrey Barrow suggested that Alexander de Kininmund might have contributed to the writing of the Declaration of Arbroath because Alexander, as one of Robert Bruce's envoys who delivered the document to Pope John XXII, would have been accustomed 'to handling legal and political arguments, steeped in the rhythmic

Latin style of the papal chancery, having an interest in history and a sound knowledge of the bible and of at least one of the classical Latin authors' (Barrow 1984, 22–23). On his visits to Avignon, he might well have seen the building that John XXII was undertaking at Pont-de-Sorgues, 12 miles from Avignon (Plate 7.10). At Sorgues, the castle consisted of four ranges disposed around a courtyard with a tower at each corner, as well as a central gatehouse tower. It was surrounded by ramparts and probably a ditch (Baro *et al.* 2014, 167). Bishop Alexander used this architectural model when he built a residence at Old Aberdeen (Dransart 2016a, 70–71). Boece's account of Bishop Alexander's seasonal round of residences may be idealised but, because Sorgues served as the summer palace of the pope in Avignon, Bishop Alexander possibly did start the custom of using Fetternear as his summer residence.

Figure 7.11. The chapel in Spynie bishop's palace, diocese of Moray (Photograph: P. Dransart).

Fetternear, with its moat, already had the arrangement of a castle of enclosure. It does not appear to have acquired the imposing mass of Spynie Castle, in the neighbouring diocese of Moray, and its chapel was a single storey building, rather than being elevated on the first floor as at Spynie (Figure 7.11). Fetternear and the bishop's manor of Rayne were, nevertheless, suited to the theatrical performance involved in the absolution of the householders of Formartine. The householders would know when their second tenths became due from the setting point of the sun over a hill such as Whitecross. For four centuries, the bishop's palace of Fetternear played a key role in Bennachie's landscape. Its history and archaeology reveal how it was connected to trodden paths in a nexus of local and national events and seasonal change.

Sources

Legends of the Saints in the Scottish Dialect of the Fourteenth Century (1896) Metcalfe, W.M. (ed.), Scottish Text Society, Vol. II. Edinburgh and London.

London Museum n.d. Objects and stories. https://www.londonmuseum.org.uk/collections/v/object-36055/pen/

OSNB = Ordnance Survey Name Book (1848–1878). *Object Name Books of the Ordnance Survey (6 inch and 1/2500 scale)*. Edinburgh, Ordnance Survey. https://scotlandsplaces.gov.uk/digital-volumes/ordnance-survey-name-books

POMS = *People of Medieval Scotland 1093–1371*. https://poms.ac.uk/

REA = *Registrum Episcopatus Aberdonensis Ecclesie Cathedralis Aberdonensis Regesta que Extant in Unum Collecta* (1845), Innes, C. (ed.), 2 vols. Edinburgh, The Spalding Club.

RMSS = *The Register of the Great Seal of Scotland* (1882) *Registrum magni sigilli regum Scotorum A.D. 1424–1513*, Paul, J.B. (ed.), Vol. 2. Edinburgh, H.M. General Register House.

RPS = *The Records of the Parliaments of Scotland to 1707* (2007–2023), Brown, K.M. *et al.* (eds), St Andrews. https://www.rps.ac.uk/

Bibliography

Baro, G., Seriyes, M. and Carru, D. (2014) Le palais des papes de Sorgues (Vaucluse). Première approche archéologique. In *Archéologie du Midi médiéval* 32, 159–82. https://doi.org/10.3406/amime.2014.2078

Barrow, G. (1984) *Robert the Bruce and the Scottish Identity*. Edinburgh, Saltire Pamphlets: New Series, 4.

Barrow, G.W.S. (1992) *Scotland and its Neighbours in the Middle Ages*. London, The Hambledon Press.

Boardman, S. (2002) The burgh and the realm: medieval politics, *c.* 1100–1500. In Dennison, E.P., Ditchburn, D. and M. Lynch (eds) *Aberdeen Before 1800: A New History*, 203–23. East Linton, Tuckwell Press.

Boece, H. (1894 [1522]) *Murthlacensium et Aberdonensium episcoporum vitae*, ed. and trans. by Moir, J. Aberdeen, New Spalding Club.

Campbell, B.M.S. (2008) Benchmarking medieval economic development: England, Wales, Scotland, and Ireland, *c.* 1290. In *The Economic History Review, new series* 61(4), 896–945.

Cowan, I.B. (1972) The medieval church in the diocese of Aberdeen. In *Northern Scotland* 1(1), 19–48.

Cowan, I.B. and Easson, D.E. (1976) *Medieval Religious Houses Scotland*. London, Longman.

Davidson, J. (1878) *Inverurie and the Earldom of the Garioch*. Edinburgh and Aberdeen, David Douglas and A. Brown & Co.

Dransart, P. (2016a) Bishops' palaces in the medieval dioceses of Aberdeen and Moray. In Geddes, J. (ed.) *Medieval Art, Architecture and Archaeology in the Dioceses of Aberdeen and Moray*, 58–81. The British Archaeological Association Transactions XL. London, Routledge.

Dransart, P. (2016b) Trodden paths: evidence for bishops and trade at Fetternear, in the medieval diocese of Aberdeen, Scotland. In Ettel, P., Flambard Héricher, A.-M. and O'Conor, K. (eds) *Château Gaillard 27. Études de castellologie médiévale. Château et commerce*, 121–31. Caen, Presses universitaires de Caen.

Dransart, P. (2017) Bishops' residences, saints' cults, and the legacy of sacred authority in the medieval dioceses of St Andrews and Glasgow. In Rollason, D. (ed.) *Princes of the Church: Bishops and their Palaces*, 81–98. The Society for Medieval Archaeology Monograph 39. London, Routledge.

Dransart, P., Bogdan, N.Q. and Lindsay, W. (2001) Fetternear (Chapel of Garioch Parish). *Discovery and Excavation in Scotland* 2 (New Series), 9–10.

Kelly, W. (1910) St Machar's Cathedral. In *Transactions of Aberdeen Philosophical Society* 4, 169–89.

Leslie, C. (1869) *Historical Records of the Family of Leslie from 1067 to 1868–1869*. Three volumes. Edinburgh, Edmonston and Douglas.

Moir, G. (1845) The parish of New Machar. In Gordon, J. (ed.), *The New Statistical Account of Scotland* Vol. 12. Edinburgh, Blackwoods and Sons. Also University of Edinburgh, University of Glasgow (1999) The Statistical Accounts of Scotland online service: https://stataccscot.ed.ac.uk:443/link/nsa-vol12-p1026-parish-aberdeen-new_machar

Murdoch, K.R. (2008) 16. Glass. In Dransart, P. and Trigg, J. (eds) *The Bishop's Palace Fetternear 2005–2006, an interim report on the work undertaken under the Heritage Lottery Fund*, 41–55. Lampeter, Scottish Episcopal Palaces Project.

Murray, H.K. and Murray, J.C. (2012) *Excavations at the bishop's manor, Old Rayne, Aberdeenshire, in 1990 and 2008*. The Society of Antiquaries of Scotland, Scottish Archaeological Internet Report 52. Doi. 10.9750/issn.1773-3808.2012.52

O'Grady, O.J.T. (2014) Judicial assembly sites in Scotland: Archaeological and place-name evidence of the Scottish court hill. In *Medieval Archaeology* 58(1), 104–35.
Penman, M. (2013) 'Sacred food of the soul': In search of the devotions to saints of Robert Bruce, king of Scotland 1306–1329. In *Speculum* 88(4), 1035–62.
Robertson, J. and Grub, G. (1843) *Collections for a History of the Shires of Aberdeen and Banff.* Aberdeen, the Spalding Club.
Shepherd, C. (2016) Cartographic evidence for seventeenth-century 'cross-sites' in North-east Scotland: Robert Gordon of Straloch and the Blaeu maps of Scotland. In *Landscape History* 37(1), 69–85.
Shepherd, C. (2021) *The Late Medieval Landscape of North-Eastern Scotland: Renaissance, Reformation and Revolution.* Oxford, Windgather Press.
Simson, H. (1845) The parish of Chapel of Garioch. In Gordon, J. (ed.) *The New Statistical Account of Scotland* Vol. 12, 560–83. Edinburgh, Blackwoods and Sons. Also University of Edinburgh, University of Glasgow (1999) The Statistical Accounts of Scotland online service: https://stataccscot.ed.ac.uk:443/link/nsa-vol12-p560-parish-aberdeen-chapel_of_garioch
Stringer, K.J. (1985) *Earl David of Huntingdon. A Study in Anglo-Scottish History 1152–1219.* Edinburgh, University of Edinburgh Press.
Taylor, A. (2016) Written law and the maintenance of order 1124–1230. In Taylor, A., *The shape of the state in medieval Scotland, 1124–1290.* Oxford Scholarship Online. Doi. 10.1093/acprof:oso/9780198749202.001.0001
Youngblood, M. (1999) Whitecross equinox. In *Friends of Grampian Stones Newsletter* X(2) https://cleopasbe11.wordpress.com/tag/strathnatterick/
Ward Perkins, J.B. (1975) *London Museum Medieval Catalogue.* London: Her Majesty's Stationery Office.
Watt, D.E.R. (1977) *A Biographical Dictionary of Scottish Graduates to 1410.* Oxford, Clarendon.
Welfare, A. (2011) *Great Rings of Stone: The Recumbent Stone Circles of Scotland.* Edinburgh, RCAHMS.
West, S. (2006) *Prudhoe Castle.* London, English Heritage.

Chapter 8

Land for the landless: squatter encroachment in the uplands

Jeff Oliver

Introduction

The wild-looking uplands of north-east Scotland have a topographical secret: their windswept 'braes' – hillsides in this part of the world – are studded with the ruins of old cottages, tumbledown dry-stone dykes and overgrown trackways: places that have largely gone unnoticed, ignored, or forgotten. In the 18th and 19th centuries, when their lower-lying districts became the locus of celebrated agricultural transformations that swept away the old social order, uplands and other 'wastes' took on a less acknowledged significance: they became redouts for the displaced, the poor, and the landless. The scale of these cultural imprints in uplands is significant and form a previously unrecognised type of cultural landscape: squatter encroachment. Because they often fall outside the legal history of land ownership and tenancy, informal squatter encroachments represent one of north-east Scotland's least researched and least well-understood contributors to the history of the modern landscape.

This chapter builds on previous work on the historical archaeology of the Bennachie Colony, perhaps the most famous site of squatter encroachment in Scotland, located on Aberdeenshire's most iconic landform: the hill of Bennachie. The Bennachie colonists established a crofting way of life at arm's length from the influence of lowland lairds during the north-east's most intense period of enclosure. The collaborative efforts of our community partners, the Bailies of Bennachie, and colleagues at the University of Aberdeen have furnished us with a wealth of ideas about what life in the colony – on the so-called margins of rural society – was like; about its spatial history, about attitudes towards 'improvement', about the impact of the colonists on the local environment. The material remains of the Colony alongside the few archival sources we have at our disposal has provided an important degree of documentation to lives lived mostly outside of the historical record. For many years the Colony site was thought to be unique. But thanks to the eagle-eyes of our collaborators and vital documentary fragments, notably cartographic evidence on the division of uplands, it turns out that the Colony was not the only settlement, just the best remembered.

With the Bennachie Colony as a point of comparison, I set out here to provide an introduction to some of the landscapes of squatter encroachment that are slowly coming into view. The approach adopted is eclectic, focusing on three historic uplands – all 'commonties' – which became important sites for 'illicit' settlement. Drawing on the use of said cartographic sources, field visits, drone photography, along with supporting documentary records, I reconstruct the physical contours of their settlement patterns and the historical and geographical conditions that influenced their establishment and evolution. Many of these settlements were occupied for relatively brief spells. However, what they left behind – their landscape legacies – helped set the stage for later phases of development, from the plantation of tenants to commercial forests. The afterlives of these hillsides are not only diverse, but crucial for understanding the extent to which the history of squatting can be unpicked from the modern landscape. The chapter concludes with a number of reflections on how research into squatter encroachment might be further expanded.

Improvement and the new rural landless

To understand the history of squatting in the north-east requires a short detour into the wider context of agricultural improvements and the significant social and legal transformations they spurred. The end of the 18th and the early 19th century saw sweeping changes to land tenure and agricultural practice on older manorial estates. Small tenant farmers, many of whom continued to work fields laid out in run-rig, were largely replaced by a new breed of capitalist 'muckle' farmers (Dixon and Gannon 2007, 194–5). Lowland improvements were so thorough that, by around 1840 they had mostly obliterated the old order (Carter 1979, 21). Enclosed and consolidated farms run for profit replaced open fields focused more on subsistence farming. The reorganisation of the landscape over many decades resulted in a new landless demographic. Some stayed on estates as farm servants or wage labourers, while others left for growing cities like Aberdeen, industrial centres to the south or overseas to places like Upper Canada, Virginia, and New South Wales (Harper 1988).

Still others looked to the uncultivated 'frontiers' of the Scottish north-east. They sought to settle lands that fell within the hinterlands of estates, often uplands of moor or moss, places that had been mostly overlooked by the factor's accounting ledger (Plate 8.1). They can be divided into two types: crofters with tenancies and squatters without though, as we will see, they share many commonalities. 'Crofter colonies' were often actively promoted by lairds and their agents to establish settlements of smallholders who could expand the cultivated areas of estates along with their rent rolls (Kay 1962, 105; Carter 1979, 57). Their inhabitants became pioneers for transforming 'waste' into settled small holdings of productive economic activity. They also helped to check the tide of emigration, ensuring a labour pool for estates and

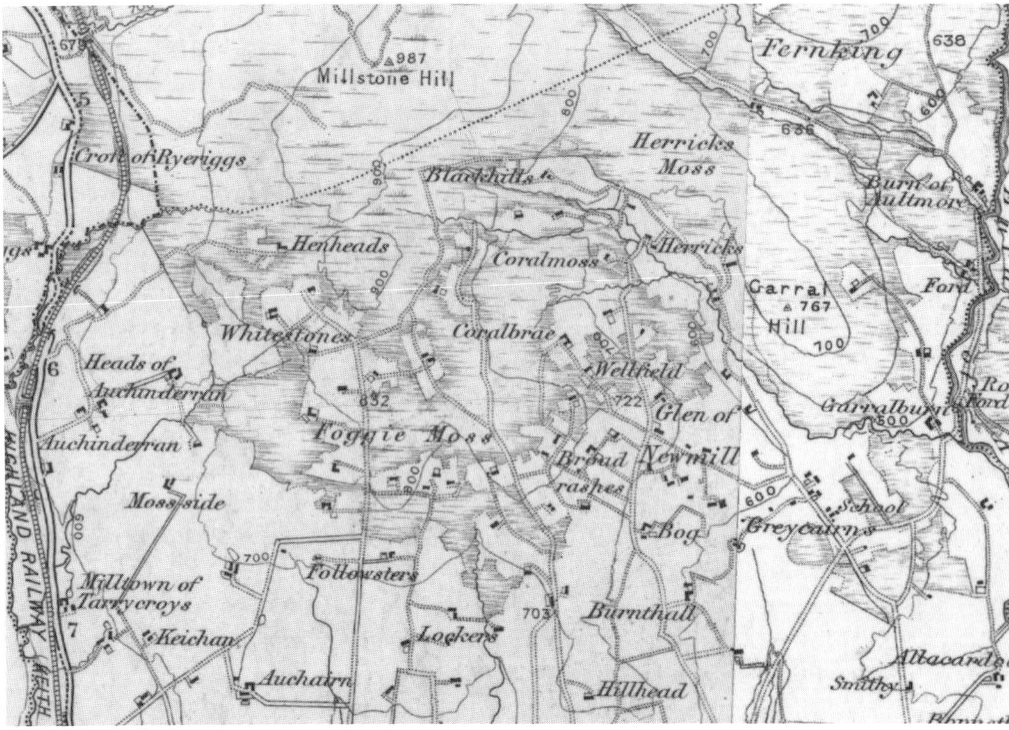

Figure 8.1. Ordnance Survey Map showing the Newmill crofter colony nibbling the edges of Millstone Hill near Keith in the council area of Moray, 1885–1900 (Provenance: One inch to the mile, 2nd Edition/National Library of Scotland, CC by National Library of Scotland).

larger capitalist tenant farms (Figure 8.1). Well-known crofting colonies or townships were established at Duthil and Rothiemurchus, in the watershed of the River Spey, where there was a policy of 'letting small improvements towards the skirts of the hills' (Turnock 2016, 236–8). Others were found at Rora Moss, near Peterhead, the level country known as the Betchach on the north slopes of Benrinnes, at Newmill, north of Keith and also in Bogmuchals, north of Knock Hill (Carter 1979, 57); and there are many other examples besides (see Caird 1980, 209). But it is the second type that concerns us here.

Less well known, but the principal subject of this discussion, are the informal settlements of 'squatters' – to use the pejorative term of the landlord. Squatters looked to settle 'off grid', or at least to select landscapes where their bold attempts to colonise and settle land were tolerated or even went unseen. Much of this activity appears to have evaded the interests or attention of 19th-century commentors, though occasionally it was the focus of their gaze. For example, a survey of the Sutherland estate in 1820 produced a list of 408 settlements that were not on the rent rolls (Given 2004, 148). Being able to evade the payment of rent and the sometimes-oppressive expectations of lairds is why most squatters chose to put down roots on undivided commonties, typically large areas of upland, which in the north-east can often be traced back to former royal forests (Shepherd 2024, 2). A commonty is a Scottish legal term for 'land possessed in common by different proprietors' (Adams 1967, 27; see also Wightman 2013, 66; Shepherd 2021, 109). They usually encompassed lands defined as 'wastes' situated beyond the infield and outfield of touns (Dodgshon 1981, 191). Their modern description as wastes betrays the fact that they possessed vital resources, like peat for fuel, stone for building and pasture for grazing, which were free to exploit by proprietors and their tenants. Because they were historically shared spaces, no single estate had a controlling interest, providing much needed legal ambiguity for those who wished to stake out and colonise ground. Like other parts of Britain, the erection of a 'one-night house' over the course of a single evening may have provided a degree of legitimacy to a squatter's claim (Sayce 1942), which up until the middle of the 18th century were rarely challenged (Adams 1967, 29). In the 19th century, travel writer Alexander Inkson McConnachie suggested the tradition had been alive and well at the founding of the Bennachie Colony: 'the neighbours joined together and in one day erected a house for a "squatter," celebrating the event by a supper in the same evening, in the newly erected building' (1985, 93).

The line between crofters and squatters in the north-east is a diffuse one. Both settled along the margins of established estates – places that could not only be considered physically peripheral, but socially peripheral as well. While the inhabitants of crofting colonies normally held a short tenancy, squatters normally did not. This lack of legitimacy likely fed into stereotypes about the status of their civility or morality. They could be othered as primitive 'mountaineers' (Anonymous, cited in Fagen 2011, 12), or worse, disparaged as a 'dishonest generation' of 'muggers and tramps' (Adams 1967, 63), if they were mentioned at all. And yet, in many places, the categories were easily elided because squatters could also be tolerated where they were seen to be economically useful, especially where they could be put to use by improving the wastes (Kay 1962, 105–6). To make it even more complicated, their status could change. A squatter could become a respectable crofter once their names were inscribed on the rent rolls. Crofters transformed what squatters had previously achieved under the radar into a respectable form of settler colonisation. At the same time, they shared a similar economic mode of production: they were tenanted smallholders focused on colonising the wastes to achieve at least a basic level of subsistence farming, but also sold their labour to wealthy tenants or landlords. Indeed, because of these similarities, the history of rural squatting in Scotland is largely masked by the abundant and superficially similar remains of crofting sites.

What we know about settlement patterns

North-east Scotland contains important areas of cultivatable land, especially along some of its coastal stretches. However, it is also a landscape of uplands, especially in the west where the landscape tilts upwards into glacially weathered hills: outriders to the Highlands. At the turn of the 19th century, much of this upland area – vast interfluves of moorland and bog – lay within undivided commonties situated between around 200 and 500 m above sea level (Caird 1980, 209). A variety of factors likely shaped which locations were preferred. The freedom of the commonty and land that was improvable for smallholders was certainly a draw, as noted previously, but so were the social and economic networks fostered by estate centres. Settlements tend to cluster around the edge of commonties where they butt up against the estate landscape of improving farms, where wage labouring abounded and where a market could be found for crafts and agricultural produce. Proximity to peat mosses, a vital heating fuel, was also a consideration.

Diffuse references to squatter encroachment on commonties are known from the 17th century (Shepherd 2024, 7; see also Dodgshon 1981, 191), but our best evidence about the scale and distribution of this phenomenon comes from the colourful surveyed schemes of division commissioned by surrounding landowners in the late 18th and first part of the 19th century. These would ultimately aid in their demise. The plans for commonties such as Bennachie, Corrennie, Cowie and those that covered places like Fortry Moss and the Hill of Kilbadie, to name a few of most important ones, provide the earliest systematic portrayal of their location and pattern of settlement.

The physical features that marked out upland colonisation share several characteristics. Settlements ranged from lonely cottages to scores of dwelling houses scattered among small, enclosed fields and from dispersed forms of settlement to highly aggregated ones. Cottages likely began life as simple turf structures, before being eventually replaced by stone (Plate 8.2). Occasionally these have developed into modern farm houses. Cottages typically sit alongside small dry-stone enclosures used as kailyards, small arable fields and animal paddocks. Trackways carved out of the commonty's moorland connected these piecemeal crofting landscapes with agricultural estates beyond. Their efforts at colonisation not only established a new built landscape, but fundamentally transformed upland ecologies by transporting plants and animal species from valley bottoms to new hillside locations (see Smith *et al.*, this volume). Where settlements are shown on historic maps and plans, especially prior to the division of commonties, they are often made conspicuous by their irregularity, in contrast to the sub-rectilinear and rectilinear conformity of the tenanted landscape, though it would be unwise to assume this was a hard and fast rule, as we shall see.

The Bennachie Colony

The best-known squatter encroachment in the north-east is the Bennachie Colony. Located on the lower flanks of the conspicuous hill of Bennachie, the Colony sat on the edge of one of the north-east's last remaining commonties, a short stroll downhill to the cultivated and tenanted lowlands of the Garioch. Unlike most settlements of its type, its historical status seems to be linked with the fact that it was one of the last

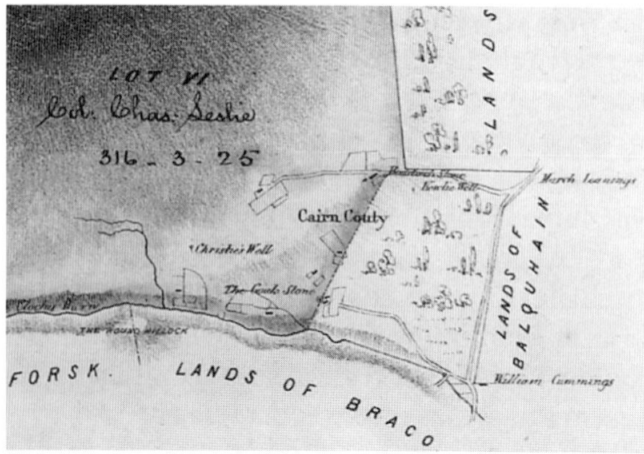

Figure 8.2. Detail of New Scheme of Division of the Commonty of Bennachie, showing the irregular settlement enclosures of the Bennachie Colony (Provenance: MS 3860/19614/ University of Aberdeen Special Collections).

to be divided in the north-east and its colonists became something of a cause célèbre at a time when landed interests were being increasingly challenged by an emboldened proletariat (Carter 1983).

Documentary evidence suggests the first settlers arrived during the 1830s. A plan of the division of the commonty, drawn by the surveyor Alexander Smith in 1845, depicts the enclosed ground of the settlement composed of small groups of haphazardly laid-out enclosures, each associated with at least one cottage, a kailyard and sometimes outbuildings. Each farm with its cottage and enclosures is separated by not more than a stone's throw of rough ground, while the colony as a whole is separated by a narrow strip of unimproved land from the enclosed and tenanted farms of the Balquhain Estate (Figure 8.2). As Silvester (2007, 57) has argued for Wales, this thin strip of common might have contributed to the feelings of difference sometimes accorded to the colonists. On the unregulated commonty, settlers established their encroachments according to preference and availability. Land that presented fewer obstacles for 'riving in' was attractive, but so were social factors like good neighbours. Census records suggest these kinds of relationships were significant and could result in ties of marriage. The settlement continued to attract landless migrants into the 1850s. The Ordnance Survey of 1866 shows at least two new cottages along with newly colonised ground. At its zenith, census records indicate 56 (counted) souls and at least 10 dwellings (Fagen 2011). The year 1859 was a watershed year for the Colony as the Commonty of Bennachie was divided among its surrounding estates. With this formal appropriation, the 'squatters' became rent paying tenants of the Balquhain estate. The following decades were not kind. A range of factors including unaffordable tenancies, difficult winters and better opportunities elsewhere, ensured the sapping of its strength, followed by its virtual abandonment in the 1870s. Today, the ruins of this fossilised mid-19th century landscape spread up the base of the hill, shrouded by stands of plantation: islands of rectilinear and curvilinear drystone enclosures, all askew, occupied by tumbledown cottages, some with the ruins of outbuildings, connected to the outside world by the vague outlines of overgrown trackways (Plate 8.3).

Corrennie Moor

A range of unremarkable, weatherbeaten hills runs from Bennachie south-west to the river Dee. Corrennie Moor, a massif of heather-clad hilltops with modern plantations and hill farms draped along its lower slopes, sits above improved and enclosed farmland. If the Bennachie Colony is conspicuous for its more aggregated character, squatter encroachment on Corrennie Moor is largely dispersed. A plan of the division of Corrennie Forest in 1834, by George Stephen, catches them out at a moment of transition: soon the settlers will be lease-paying tenants. Concentrating on Stephen's perambulation along the boundary of the commonty, the survey depicts at least 59 dwellings or other structures and their associated enclosures, mostly hugging the edge of the commonty, though a few farms are located deep inside it. The vast majority of these were likely the small cottages of squatters, though a small range of other building types are also depicted. Two improved farm houses with their surveyed fields, suggest that bordering estates were also taking liberties, nibbling away at its borders for their own economic advantage. The squatter dwellings sit within or alongside small, enclosed fields or kailyards, largely irregular in shape though a few are more squared. The survey also shows place-names. While hilltops, tors and burns are all named, so are many of the crofters whose homes dotted the slopes. Names like 'Charles Ewan' and 'James Ewan' in close proximity suggest the importance of familial chain migration, whereas names like 'Mary Thompson' and 'Mary Scott' indicate that some households were headed by women.

Corrennie Moor also demonstrates the transiency of much squatter encroachment. Writing about the state of agriculture in Aberdeenshire in the 1870s, Alexander Smith reflected on the remarkable changes seen on the common, observing that many of the current tenants, 'originally squatters', who had 'established themselves in huts, on small patches [with] Kailyards' had, since the partitioning of the hillside, developed 'substantial biggings [buildings] and no mean portions of land' (1875, 350). The 1899 Ordnance Survey map for Corrennie Moor shows that significant elements of the squatting landscape had either disappeared or been subsumed into the highly regular landscape of estate-sponsored crofter colonies, which pushed up the hillside in salients during the intervening decades. While the geometry of surveys has clearly had an impact on the modern landscape, the signature of squatter encroachment can still be detected in places. When not obscured by plantation, their tiny fields can be seen either as a residual pattern in later enclosure walls or are betrayed by conspicuous vegetation patterns of gorse and broom as revealed by drone photography. Like crop marks, they reveal the presence of improved, well-draining soils or hidden archaeology under their roots (Plate 8.4) (see also Oliver and O'Driscoll 2024). In other places, squatter cottages form the footprints of later 19th century 'pattern-book' houses.

Privileges of the Davoch of Grange

Not all squatter encroachment was seen as trespassing. While we often assume it is concerned with the illicit occupation of property, in certain contexts their presence was either tolerated or even actively encouraged. And where these attitudes prevailed, squatters could manage a degree of security, even within the boundaries of estates. This was particularly the case on marginal land, especially former commonties that had been divided. In a documentary survey of farms between the Moray coast at

Cullen and the highlands of Huntly, 20 miles north-west of Bennachie, Kay (1962, 107) has shown how landowners actively encouraged squatting because it expanded the cultivated lands of the estate and enhanced the rent rolls. Squatters could be enticed through being recognised as legal tenants, usually on short leases with an initial period of rent-free occupancy. While initially appearing as benevolent, this arrangement was often short-lived. No sooner had smallholders made tangible improvements then their reclaimed land was snatched from beneath them and amalgamated into larger capitalist farms – often termed 'engrossment' (Carter 1979, 54) – for the benefit of wealthier tenant farmers who could afford to pay higher rents.

A sketch of the 'Privileges of the Davoch of Grange' made around 1800 of the lands of Grange and Paithnick shows the extent of piecemeal squatter reclamation that numerous squatter farmers were making along the margins of mosses and moors outside the tenanted lands of the estate. The scale of reclamation is impressive: two principal reclamation fronts of intermittent activity at the edge of Fortry Moss and the Hill of Kilbadie are over 1 km long. Each front is composed of cottages and land undergoing transformation: clearing of peat, moss, and stone, building of consumption dykes, laying of drains and spreading of lime, all by hand (Kay 1962, 104–7). They likely represent an arrangement where landowners gave tacit approval to such developments and may be more akin to a form of licenced encroachment, an arrangement with a respectable pedigree in parts of Britain going back to at least the 16th century (Bowen 2014, 17). Here we might note that the difference between squatter and crofter begins to break down. With lease in hand the squatters begin to take on the trappings of legitimacy. Later 19th-century maps combined with satellite imagery clarify the durability of such settlement arrangements. The OS survey of 1902 demonstrates the virtual disappearance of the early 19th-century endeavours of squatter farmers. In place of their individualistic efforts, we find the modern landscape of large geometrically organised fields with ramrod straight field boundaries. Former cottages and kailyards wiped virtually clean from the landscape, remembered only by the subtlest of crop marks and field undulations, otherwise hidden by fields of pasture and white crops, such as barley and oats.

Squatter encroachment and its landscape legacies

So far I have made the case for the significance of squatting landscapes at select locations. I have also hinted at their demise. Despite their monumental efforts at reclamation, the labours of these smallholders would endure for mere decades; a metaphorical footnote in Scotland's story of human-environmental relations. A conspiracy of factors ensured their land claims were not to last. An agriculturally marginal environment, a profit-seeking landed elite in thrall to high rents, and the bright lights of Victorian towns and cities, eventually sapped their strength. And yet, many north-eastern hillsides have legacies worth reflecting on. In some cases they set the stage for more recent histories of land use. In turn, these recent histories are themselves implicated in whether the archaeology of squatting has endured into the present, and the extent to which they survive in memory, or have been forgotten (Oliver and O'Driscoll 2024).

It is tempting to hive off the history of squatter encroachment as a unique historical phenomenon; to deal with it in the abstract, defined by its cultural and chronological peculiarities. But attempting to unpick the squatting landscape from what went on around it, and after, creates a parcelling up of events and processes into a deceptive package, with little sense of how these connect with the world around it. Looking beyond the box sheds light on a range of other historical relationships that hint at both continuity and change.

Let us begin with the observation that squatters could became tenants. Clandestine farms were often provided with leases and encouraged to expand cultivation and enclosure further up the hillslope. We can see these continuities through the history of cartography discussed earlier – illicit cottages established by squatters become legitimate and orderly crofts with tenancies. Of course, alongside such changes in the landscape are changes in the social history of these hillsides as squatters became crofters; many ambitious, many with offspring born with the confidence that comes with greater security of tenure. Just because the freedom of the commonty had come to an end, doesn't mean we are dealing with different people. The thought experiment I evoke here has been written about compellingly by Sara Tarlow (2007; 2008). At Rhos-Gelli-gron in west Wales a squatting settlement known by outsiders for its so-called workshy and godless miners in the early 19th century became an established community of proud farmers by the century's end with the sorts of aspirations that characterised agrarian living elsewhere. Would crofters and their descendants eschew such legacies? As family biographers would certainly remind us, our status in life can change. It can shape how we remember and how others see us. We should therefore be attuned to the idea that the history of squatting could also be implicated in the history of crofting.

Persistence and legacy can be seen in other areas too. We have already seen how the material legacy of squatting is visible in later landscapes as a form of squatter fingerprint, such as irregularities in field shapes – sometimes diluted, sometimes not – within later enclosure schemes defined by their overall regularity. At the same time, the material endeavours of squatter encroachers and their relative success at transforming moor and bog into ambitious little farms also spelled out what Hauser and Amstrong (2012, 213) call 'geographies of possibility', which could be attractive to others. This was particularly so where improved smallholdings caught the attention of lairds and their lieutenants. A pattern that holds true for commonties like Corrennie and Cowie, north of Stonehaven, or the uplands above the Davoch of Grange is that squatter colonisation, followed by tenanted crofter expansions set the stage for the establishment of later 19th- and 20th-century capitalist hill farms. In many parts of the north-east, increasing commoditisation of land over the late 18th and early 19th centuries stimulated estates to see smallholders as an investment to increase the profit margins of their accounting ledgers down the road. So, nascent crofting communities – whether illegitimate or legitimate – were all too often incorporated through engrossment into an ever-expanding rentier economy.

Several north-east locations illustrate this evolution from piecemeal squatter colonisation to tenanted crofting colonies to the formation of capitalist hill farms, many of which dominate the higher ground. Let us return to Corrennie Moor, which preserves a particularly fine example. The headwaters of Culthibert Burn, on the north side of the moor in the shadow of Green Hill, shows a landscape in transition. The ruins of a crofting colony composed of regular dry-stone enclosures occupied by granite cottages and connected to the former Kincraigie Estate by a ramrod straight trackway is a testament to almost a century of 'riving in'; first by squatters, tidied and expanded by crofters, and finalised by capitalist farmers. Cartographic regression analysis of Ordnance Survey maps confirms a pattern initially of settlement, then followed by relentless abandonment. The abandonments begin after 1866, whereby less successful crofts are eventually deserted (either by choice or eviction) with their fields either left to rough grazing or absorbed by more viable neighbouring farms. The 1899 map shows about half of the crofts within the watershed had met this fate. The process is completed, inferred by standing archaeology, at some point early in the 20th century when a single cottage and associated steadings, located at the lowest point of the hill, now forms the focal point of a much larger farm taking in all the surrounding enclosures, which have largely fallen into ruin. It is only the maintenance of an external dry-stone dyke marking the edge of the improved moor, that signifies the unity of this much enlarged space of production; one no longer needed for small scale marginal arable but rather for the pasturing of lucrative livestock. Ironically, it is the modern focus on upland livestock pasturing that has helped preserve the former landscape of crofting (Plate 8.5). The ruins of these settlements and field systems survive well within modern pasture as they do in former pasture left to the earlier stages of rewilding. Areas with more productive soils would likely have seen the removal of enclosure walls and the ruins of cottages to allow for the cultivation of arable fields. As a coda to this narrative of transformation, field visits to the farm suggest it is no longer lived-in but simply used as temporary shelter for visiting farm workers. These workers return to the hillside on a temporary basis to manage livestock that are transported between a network of pasturing sites connected with a larger commercial farm operation located elsewhere.

Not all hillsides conform to this pattern. At the same time that many uplands were transitioning from crofter colonies to the current pattern of hill farms, others were sliding imperceptibly towards desertion – if they had ever been colonised – and devoted to other forms of land use (Plate 8.6). Grouse moors were encouraged, especially on hilltops, but it was forestry plantations that began to compete with crofters, in some places effectively silencing their existence altogether. The history of forestry plantations can be traced to the beginning of the 19th century when gentlemen farmers across north-east Scotland worked out that in some areas a tidier profit could be made by reserving stoney, unimproved land for plantations of

Scots pine and larch rather than smallholdings (Kay 1962, 107). In many cases they presented well-drained locations for saplings. As crofting in some uplands was on the edge of viability, many landowners cleared their crofters in favour of plantation. The first and second OS series documents the growing trend among landowners across the north-east for establishing and expanding plantations during the second half of the 19th century.

Returning to Culthibert Burn – but this time further down the hillside – shows us precisely how former crofting landscapes can be effectively erased from our collective consciousness. Although the evidence of crofter colonisation is easily visible in modern pasture as described above, the lower slope of the hill was, at some point in the 20th century, turned over to plantation. Satellite imagery shows that former fields, kailyards and even crofts were planted with conifers, that in the intervening years have produced a largely impenetrable canopy of conifers like larch, spruce and fir that repels even the best efforts of remote sensing. Attempts to navigate plantations like these are often met with a dense thicket of juvenile trees and deadwood that can make observation difficult if not impossible. The effects of giant roots on buried and standing archaeology can be catastrophic to dry-stone structures undermined by the effects of bioturbation. Only the geometry of a few standing dry-stone field walls and prominent trackways, not run through by forestry harvesters and forwarders, continue to provide important clues about the former structure of this historic landscape. The legacy of conifer plantations has not been kind to the archaeology of hillscapes. And once out of sight, they go quickly out of mind.

A similar story, but with a different outcome, is seen at the Bennachie Colony. In contrast to many other parts of the north-east where squatting spurred a wider process of crofter colonisation, the establishment of further smallholdings was effectively strangled after the Balquhain estate, which participated in the division of the commonty, made the decision to devote its slice of the hill to plantation. Plantations were initially established in the open ground around existing tenancies, and later within extinguished ones, until the remains of much of the settlement were hidden under a canopy of trees (Plate 8.7). By the time the plantation had begun to mature the Colony was virtually abandoned; a process that can be easily observed between the first and second Ordnance Survey series. After 1943 this land was transferred to the ownership of the Scottish Forestry Commission, which continued to plant the lower slopes with commercial timber (Cumberbirch 2013, 56). Why the Bennachie Colony has remained in the collective consciousness is an interesting question. It seems to be connected to the fact that its role as a 'squatter' colony persisted well into the mid-19th century – indeed, oral histories continue to circulate among its descendants (Vergunst 2013). Its memory was never diminished by being incorporated – and hidden – within a sponsored crofting settlement. What is more it stood on one of the last commonties to be divided among landed interests at a time when class consciousness was becoming realised among the working classes. The story it offered an emerging proletariat about dispossession at the hand of landed elites helped mobilise workers and their supporters (Carter 1983). The idiosyncrasies of place have their own affective qualities.

Reflections

What I have outlined above is a rough sketch based on a relatively small number of locations. If one can begin to generalise from this sample, a number of broader points emerge, each prompting questions and challenges for further research. The first is that squatter encroachment was a more important type of settlement than we have previously recognised in the north-east – and possibly within Scotland more generally. This is particularly so within the vast commonties that continued to characterise the region up until the middle of the 19th century when they were carved up by landed interests. As we have seen, squatter encroachment could produce a range of settlement patterns. At one extreme the Bennachie Colony represents a relatively aggregated form. At the other is the widely dispersed pattern around the edge of Corrennie Moor. Somewhere between these extremes is the piecemeal reclamation noted by Kay (1962) within the Davoch of Grange, each reclamation 'front' focusing its efforts on a single hill face. Just how significant their role in landscape formation was will require a more exhaustive survey than this. However, the examples described here begin to point to the kinds of activity that others have found for Wales (Ward 2002; Silvester 2007; Wiliam 2010) where both upland and lowland encroachment was both routine and extensive, as well as parts of England, notably places like Shropshire (Bowen 2014) and the New Forest (McDonagh and Griffen 2016; Moody 2016).

Commonties were clearly significant to the landless for a variety of reasons. I have already noted some of the principal attractions: land that was improvable for small-scale agriculture and freedom from onerous leases being central. Resources were also important: stone and turf for building, for example. But much better granularity could be achieved about the sorts of factors that made one so-called 'waste' more attractive than another. For example, the availability of peat as a heating fuel may have played an important role in the same way that access to forest resources in the New Forest of Hampshire was crucial to the survival and prosperity of squatters (Moody 2016, 138). In the 19th century, coal became a widely used heating fuel among rural populations facilitated by the spread of better transport networks. But for many, paying for coal required one to be yoked to the cash economy as wage labourer (Whittington 1983, 147). Freely accessible peat on the other hand may have enabled squatters with limited means to be less dependent on the emerging money economy. Equality, the attitudes of landlords, whether they were tolerant of colonists living outside of the tenanted landscape, likely played a role in which uplands were selected and which ones were not. Which sites were the most promising will require more focused work considering the balance of factors that made settlement viable.

Identifying the geography of squatter encroachment faces other challenges. Part of the problem is that we are guided by what is archivally visible. What entered the historical record was framed by a narrow set of historical interests. The selection and planning of particular uplands ripe for division at particular historical moments means that we are likely seeing a very partial view of the location of squatting sites. Can squatting sites be recognised outside of the historical record? As Silvester (2007) has shown for Wales, even without historical maps, squatter encroachment may be recognisable for its telltale characteristics within today's landscape, notably their diminutive scale and irregularity within modern field systems composed of mostly larger and more regular enclosures. We have seen in the examples of Bennachie and to a lesser extent Corrennie moor, that this is possible. But, at the same time, I have also shown how it could be rapidly supplanted by estate-sanctioned tenanted crofter colonisation, some of which could utterly reform the landscape. So while the physical characteristics of known landscapes may help us identify undocumented sites in areas with standing archaeology, where older forms of enclosure have been obliterated informal settlements may well be lost altogether.

A further and related challenge is related to the temporality of squatter encroachment and its wider distribution within the north-east. They are especially visible in the 19th century because landless populations were in the ascendant due to large-scale estate reorganisations and the fact that commonties and other upland areas were among the last 'frontiers' for the uprooted to settle. However, such places by this time were but vestigial remnants of formerly vast regions of unenclosed common land. Their much reduced, if still substantial, size was likely the product of a slow process of encroachment, much of it moving slowly if relentlessly uphill from the infields of surrounding estates. Colin Sheperd (2024) has analysed the various types of informal encroachment that took place largely within estate lands between the late medieval and early modern periods. The most historically visible can be seen in court records and mostly involved land owners and their tenants. However, the rural poor were also involved in encroaching on outlands and wastes. This form of encroachment seems to have been commonplace and represented an often tolerated means through which peasant communities dealt with issues of land scarcity. But, at some point in the 17th century, the value of such outlands changed from a more communalistic one defined by rights and obligations to an increasingly individualistic one measured in terms of profits that could be extracted by the landlord through productive exploitation and rents. At the same time, we see a shift from the more permissive form of encroachment, what Shepherd calls 'licit', to 'illicit' encroachment which was increasingly known as squatting (Shepherd 2024, 18). The broader point is that there is a much older and larger footprint of squatter encroachment. Some of this may well be located as older phases of settlement within the footings of 19th century sites. However, there is also a strong possibility that many will lie outside the boundaries of known commonties, on the lower approaches to these uplands within modern field boundaries, their preservation highly uncertain.

A fuller understanding of squatter encroachment in the north-east is still some ways off. The focus of this chapter has been squarely on identifying and outlining its settlement patterns, the factors that influenced its establishment as well as its legacies within the modern landscape. Work at this comparative regional scale will help to shed light on its magnitude with respect to Scotland, other parts of the United Kingdom and beyond. However, it is only the first step towards a fuller understanding of the phenomena. As our community archives and community archaeology efforts have established at the Bennachie Colony (Armstrong *et al.* 2015; Oliver *et al.* 2016; 2022), there is much that can be done to understand these sites and their inhabitants on their own terms. It would be a mistake to assume they conform to type. As Hechter (1975, 51) notes, hills tended to provide refuge for cultural dissidents and individualists of all kinds. The biographical quality to these places needs to be understood at a local scale. So, attentiveness to local histories and mixed methods is key to bring voices back to these mostly silenced hillsides. It is these unknowns that make the study of squatter encroachment so compelling.

Acknowledgements

I am indebted to colleagues in the Bailies of Bennachie who have helped point me in the direction of a number of key historical sources that have been foundational to my understanding of squatter encroachment in the north-east. Many thanks in particular to Alison Kennedy, Colin Miller, and Colin Shepherd. Additional appreciation goes to Colin for his kind invitation to speak at the mini conference 'Cultural Landscapes of North-east Scotland', which helped me to organise my thoughts into a new set of research questions. Finally, Josh Wright read the penultimate draft, which has helped to improve its consistency.

Bibliography

Adams, I.H. (1967) Division of Commonty in Scotland: The use of the eighteenth- and nineteenth-century estate plans held by the Scottish Record Office in a study of historical geography. University of Edinburgh, Unpublished PhD thesis.

Armstrong, J.W., Miller, C.H. and Oliver, J. (2015) Bringing archives and archaeology together: community research at the Bennachie Colony. In *Scottish Archives* 21, 18–29.

Bowen, J.P. (2014) Cottage and squatter settlement and encroachment on common waste in the sixteenth and seventeenth centuries: some evidence from Shropshire. In *Local Population Studies* 93(1), 11–32.

Caird, J.B. (1980) The reshaped agricultural landscape. In Parry, M.L. and Slater T.R. (eds) *The Making of the Scottish Countryside*, 203–22. London, Croom Helm.

Carter, I. (1979) *Farm Life in Northeast Scotland, 1840–1914: The Poor Man's Country*. Edinburgh, John Donald.

Carter, I. (1983) The raids on Bennachie. In Whiteley, A.W.M. (ed.) *Bennachie Again*, 119–25. Inverurie, Bailies of Bennachie.

Cumberbirch, J. (2013) The Forestry Commission's acquisition of Bennachie: a study of mid-20th century land acquisition and tenurial arrangements on the National Forestry Estate. In Shepherd, C. (ed), *Bennachie and the Garioch: Society and Ecology in the History of North-east Scotland*, 51–62. Chapel of Garioch, The Bailies of Bennachie, Bennachie Landscapes Series 2.

Dixon, P.J. and Gannon, A. (2007) The transformation of the rural landscape. In RCAHMS, *In The Shadow of Bennachie: A Field Archaeology of Donside, Aberdeenshire*, 215–44. Edinburgh, RCAHMS.

Dodgshon R.A. (1981) *Land and Society in Early Scotland*. Oxford, Clarendon.

Fagen, J. (2011) *The Bennachie Colony Project: Examining the Lives and Impact of the Bennachie Colonists.* Chapel of Garioch, The Bailies of Bennachie, Bennachie Landscapes Series 1.
Given, M. (2004) *The Archaeology of the Colonized.* London, Routledge.
Harper, M. (1988) *Emigration from North-east Scotland.* Aberdeen, Aberdeen University Press.
Hauser, M.W. and Armstrong, D.V. (2012) The archaeology of not being governed: a counterpoint to a history of settlement of two colonies in the eastern Caribbean. In *Journal of Social Archaeology* 12(3), 310–33.
Hechter, M. (1975) *Internal colonialism: the Celtic fringe in British national development.* London, Routledge.
Kay, G. (1962) The landscape of improvement: a case study of agricultural change in North-East Scotland. In *Scottish Geographical Magazine* 78, 100–11.
McConnochie, A.I. (1985[1890]) *Bennachie.* Aberdeen, James G. Bisset.
McDonagh, B. and Griffin, C.J. (2016) Occupy! Historical geographies of property, protest and the commons, 1500–1850. In *Journal of Historical Geography* 53, 1–10.
Moody, D. (2016) Godshillwood and Woodgreen: A Squatter Settlement on the Edge of the New Forest 1600–1840. In *Hampshire Studies* 71(1), 126–47.
Oliver, J. and O'Driscoll, J. (2024) Landscape Legacies of the Landless. In *Places Journal* https://placesjournal.org/article/landscape-legacies-of-the-landless/
Oliver, J., Armstrong, J., Curtis, E., Curtis, N. and Vergunst, J. (2022) Exploring co-production in community heritage research: Reflections from the Bennachie Landscapes Project. In *Journal of Community Archaeology and Heritage* 9(3) 196–215.
Oliver, J., Armstrong, J., Milek, K., Schofield, J.E., Vergunst, J., Brochard, T., Gould, A. and Noble, G. (2016) The Bennachie colony: A nineteenth-century informal community in Northeast Scotland. In *International Journal of Historical Archaeology* 20(2) 341–77.
Sayce, R.U. (1942) The one-night house, and its distribution. In *Folklore* 53(3), 161–3.
Shepherd, C. (2021) *The Late Medieval Landscape of North-east Scotland: Renaissance, Reformation and Revolution.* Oxford, Windgather Press.
Shepherd, C. (2024) Licit or Illicit? Encroachments on 'the Lord's Waste' in North-east Scotland, *c.* 1400–*c.* 1800. In *Rural History* 35(1), 1–21.
Silvester, R. (2007) Landscapes of the poor: encroachment in Wales in the post-medieval centuries. In Barnwell, P.S. and Palmer, M. (eds) *Post-Medieval Landscapes*, 55–67. Macclesfield, Windgather Press.
Smith, A.C.E. (ed.) (1875) *A New History of Aberdeeshire, Part I.* Aberdeen, Lewis Smith.
Tarlow, S. (2007) *The archaeology of improvement in Britain, 1750–1850.* Cambridge, Cambridge University Press.
Tarlow, S. (2008) Who are you calling marginal? A squatter settlement in upland Wales. In Rainbird, P. (ed.) *Monuments in the Landscape: Studies in Honour of Andrew Fleming*, 177–89. Oxford, Tempus.
Turnock, D. (2016) *The making of the Scottish rural landscape.* London, Routledge.
Vergunst, J. (2013) Oral history at Bennachie. In Shepherd, C. (ed.), *Bennachie and the Garioch: Society and Ecology in the History of North-east Scotland*, 11–23. Chapel of Garioch, The Bailies of Bennachie, Bennachie Landscapes Series 2.
Ward, C. (2002) *Cotters and Squatters: Housing's Hidden History.* Nottingham, Five Leaves Publications.
Whittington, G. (1983) Agriculture and Society in Lowland Scotland. In Whittington, G. and Whyte I.D. (eds) *An Historical Geography of Scotland*, 141–61. London, Academic Press.
Wightman, A. (2013) *The Poor Had No Lawyers: Who Owns Scotland and How They Got It.* Edinburgh, Birlinn.
Wiliam, E. (2010) *The Welsh Cottage: Building Traditions of the Rural Poor, 1750–1900.* Aberystwyth, Comisiwn Brenhinol Henebion Cymru/Royal Commission on the Ancient and Historical Monuments of Wales.

Chapter 9

Exploring the effects of post-medieval crofting on the modern hillside ecosystem: vegetation history as cultural legacy

Louise Smith, Jeff Oliver, Gill Plunkett, Kate Britton, and J. Edward Schofield

Introduction

Scottish uplands have been the focus of human activity for over 10,000 years (Guttmann *et al.* 2006; Wickham-Jones *et al.* 2020). While upland ecologies have been shaped by humans over much of this history, agricultural improvement in the late 18th and 19th centuries at the hands of crofter colonists – both legal tenants and opportunistic squatters – brought profound and previously unseen changes to the landscape. The colonists altered uplands in a variety of ways. The abiotic physical properties of soils, such as the texture, structure, and depth were permanently changed, as were biotic factors such as the seedbank, the amount and types of seed available, and the range of plant life growing on these sites. Today, many of these former smallholdings are abandoned and either lie fallow or have been turned over to forestry. With no one to maintain them, they are subject to secondary vegetation succession, the process by which new plants start to encroach onto sites, and eventually replace existing plant communities. Generally, ruderal herbaceous species appear first followed by shrubs and trees (Egler 1954; Flinn and Vellend 2005). Over time, this facilitates the replacement of earlier vegetation communities by new ones (Egler 1954). The speed and composition of emigrating species is dependent upon a variety of factors. This includes time since abandonment, the physical state of the site, climate, soil, and the presence of initial plant species (Myster 1993).

In this chapter we investigate the impact that crofter colonists had on the environment of Scotland's uplands and how the legacies of their actions continue to inform the ecological make-up of these places today. Two sites in Aberdeenshire that have lain fallow for more than 80 years form the focus for this pilot study: Boghead of Tullos, a croft located within the Bennachie Colony – a former squatter settlement – located on the flanks of the hill of Bennachie, and Baudyground Croft,

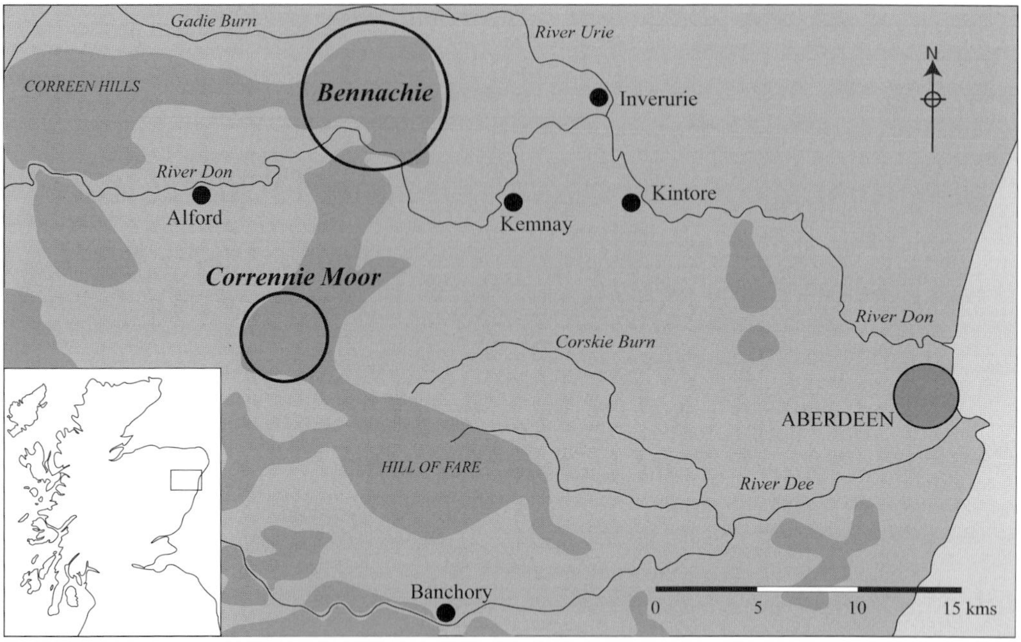

Figure 9.1. Map of northern Britain, with a closer look at Aberdeenshire showing the two study sites: Bennachie and Corrennie Moor.

located within an area of crofter colonisation on the slopes of Corrennie Moor (Figure 9.1). Both sites saw moorland and rough grazing transformed into small agricultural holdings beginning in the mid-19th century. To understand how these settlers modified these environments, our methodology draws on the use of historical details, including historical maps and plans, and standing archaeology, alongside the use of vegetation surveys. While the project is ongoing, in this chapter we present some preliminary qualitative observations on vegetation patterning based on our initial data, demonstrating that crofter colonisation resulted in lasting changes to the diversity of plant species found on the hillsides as well as the wider ecological context.

Background

The agricultural improvements of the late 18th and 19th centuries not only changed how agriculture was practiced, but it had major social effects as well. Prior to the improvements, multi-tenancy farms focused on subsistence agriculture were the norm. However, with the shift to 'improved' farming methods, agriculture was increasingly focused on capitalist production. Open fields worked in common were replaced by unitary farms orientated towards growing for the market. Many tenant farmers were displaced as larger capitalist farms swallowed up land, while high rents limited those who could afford to participate in the new status quo. Some migrated into growing towns and cities, but others chose to settle upland 'wastes' of moor, bog, and rough grazing (Kay 1962). The settlers can be separated into two types. Crofter colonists were attracted by token rents and the opportunity to develop a smallholding on marginal areas within landed estates. In contrast, squatters encroached areas beyond the direct influence of lairds, usually areas of commonty, which were by custom open to local tenants and their dependants for accessing resources like turf, peat, and stone, and grazing for stock. Despite differences in their legal status, both of these groups (crofters and squatters) fundamentally transformed uplands on a scale previously unseen (Oliver and O'Driscoll 2024). While the smallholders struggled to implement some of the larger scale improvements of wealthy tenant farms, they nevertheless enclosed and drained land, introduced cultivars, crop rotations and new fertiliser regimes to hillsides that had never before seen a plough or a hoe.

Over years and decades, settlers transformed upland ecosystems, often at altitudes of between 200 and 400 m, into small, and often piecemeal, parcels of agricultural land. Small granite cottages and outbuildings were often built, and small fields and kitchen gardens enclosed. Settlers were particularly industrious during the early and mid-19th century. However, by the later 19th and early 20th century, many of these places experienced eventual decline and abandonment. The reasons for this are complicated: sometimes it was a result of agricultural viability on land that was simply too marginal. In these cases, uplands were turned over to forestry plantations or have been left to be recolonised by nature. In other cases, smallholders could be victims of the value of land risen through their own efforts of improvement. No sooner had they made substantial investments than lairds would move to reorganise their holdings through 'engrossment' (Kay 1962; Carter 1992). This entailed the amalgamation of crofts to make larger capitalist hill farms that could be leased at market rates. Some of these holdings survive today as hill farms focused on the pasturing of sheep and cattle.

Locations and approaches

Identifying former crofting sites on the ground today can prove challenging and requires mixed methods. While some estate sponsored crofting colonies are known from the literature, others can only be recognised using historical maps and plans. Crofting colonies are often identifiable through their field shapes on Ordnance Survey maps, usually small rectangular enclosures of between two and four acres and are often part of a wider scheme of settlement. Squatter encroachment on the other hand is identifiable through their even-smaller and more irregular field shapes and can be found on surveyed schemes and plans designed to divide areas of commonty among surrounding estates (Oliver and O'Driscoll 2024). Many commonties in north-east Scotland were divided in the late 18th and early 19th centuries (being among the last major privatisations of common land in Scotland). Once candidates for potential sites have been located, field visits can help to assess the contemporary condition of these sites. Many have been subsequently planted over with forestry, others have been recolonised by successional vegetation and lay hidden under dense grasses and shrubland. Aerial photographs and satellite images, together with field visits can help to establish their contemporary condition. Two case studies have been selected for this study: Boghead of Tullos, a croft of 6.2 acres located between 180 and 220 m above mean sea level (amsl) on the hill of Bennachie, and Baudyground croft, 2.5 acres, situated at an altitude of 380–420 m amsl on the slopes of Corrennie Moor.

Until 1859, the hill of Bennachie, sometimes known as 'Free Bennachie' or the 'King's Forest of Bennachie', was a large commonty whose natural resources were considered a privilege for tenants and their dependants from surrounding estates (McConnochie 1890). Taking advantage of the legal ambiguity of the commonty, in the 1830s, an informal settlement of squatters was established on the lower flanks of the hill (Oliver *et al.* 2016). By 1851, at least 56 people were recorded as residing in the colony (Fagen 2011). 1859 was a watershed year because the commonty was legally divided by surrounding estates, making squatters into lease-paying tenants. Harsh winters and steep rents spelled decline. By 1881 there was a single remaining croft, Boghead of Tullos, and by the beginning of the 20th century a single crofter. George Esson continued to rent land in the former colony until his death in the 1930s (Bodgan *et al.* 1999). While the land has remained in private hands,

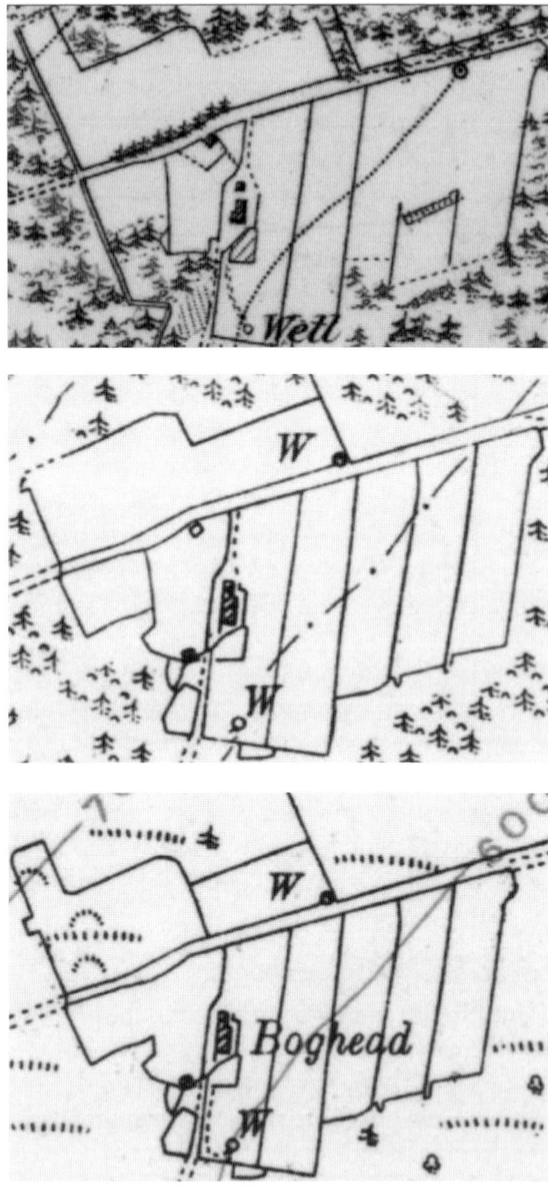

Figures 9.2–9.4. OS maps of Boghead of Tullos at Bennachie in Aberdeenshire, Scotland, for the years 1865–6 (9.2), 1899–1901 (9.3), and 1920 (9.4). The maps show enclosed fields representing the improved area of the croft as well as the cottage, well and a potential kitchen garden. A roofed and later unroofed outbuilding is also shown (Scale: 6 inches to one mile. Source: National Map Library Scotland, CC by National Library Scotland).

there are no records or other indications in the landscape to suggest that the land has been used for agriculture since this time.

Historical records provide additional details concerning the Boghead of Tullos croft. Figures 9.2 to 9.4 show the historical development of the area using Ordnance Survey (OS) maps. These maps reveal that the majority of the site was already well developed by the 1860s and that, by this point, a plantation had already been established surrounding the croft. Between the 1860s and 1920, only minor changes in the use of an outbuilding and the field layout are visible.

Site visits reveal that many of the features seen on the maps are still apparent in the landscape today. Archaeological features include the ruins of the cottage and the kitchen garden, along with surprisingly intact enclosure walls that separate the croft into multiple smaller fields. The croft is surrounded by forestry on three sides, with semi-natural woodland bounding it on the north-west. Today the site is open to wildlife, so grazing by deer is likely. New plant species may have invaded the site when the surrounding forestry was still young. However, as the trees are now tall and mature, presenting a significant barrier, this is less likely today. Old photographs can also be used to help further establish aspects of continuity and change. Figures 9.5

Figures 9.5 and 9.6. Two photographs of the cottage on Boghead, Bennachie, Aberdeenshire; one taken during the 1930s (Figure 9.5) (Bailies of Bennachie) and the other in 2023 (Figure 9.6) (Louise Smith).

and 9.6 show two images of Boghead of Tullos taken almost 100 years apart. One can see some of the trees planted back then have survived until today.

Less information is available about Baudyground. While there are no written records about this settlement, historical map evidence suggests it was established when the commonty of Corrennie was thrown open to settlement by crofter colonists, sometime after 1834. The site is located at an altitude of around 400 m and is therefore at the very edge of viability for agriculture if one considers frost-free days, and this may explain why it was abandoned at some point in the early 20th century. To the east of Baudyground lies a mature plantation. To the south, modern hill farms have swallowed up the remnants of what was once a larger crofting colony. Mostly hobbyists, sheep farmers continue to use the land for grazing today. Archaeological features include the ruins of at least one cottage along with a number of possible outbuildings, the walls of the former kitchen garden and a possible mill; the precise purpose of the latter is currently unknown. Some of the former enclosure walls are still visible, except on the croft's northern edge where the land runs steeply up to the edge of moorland.

The vegetation landscapes at Boghead and Baudyground appear to be in the early stages of plant succession. Both sites are primarily covered by grasses with a sparse cover of low shrubs and trees. Early stages of succession are typically marked by high levels of biodiversity and usually only last a decade (Myster 1993). However, since they have been abandoned for at least 80 years, the two locations appear to be experiencing a relatively slow rate of plant succession. This discrepancy makes them ideal candidates to investigate how the former settlers shaped the environment and the vegetation legacy this has produced.

Our study uses plant surveys to provide data about the current vegetation characteristics at each site (Harmer *et al.* 2001). These surveys provide different kinds of data. First, the general vegetation on the sites was assessed using quadrats. At least 30 squares, each measuring four square metres per site were placed according to a randomised grid. All vegetation species were identified within each square according to percentage. Additionally, species of interest – those with known culinary, cultural or medicinal relevance – were mapped to examine their relationship to recognisable archaeological features, such as enclosure walls, cottages and kitchen gardens. These species, in a number of cases, are likely to have been introduced by the crofters themselves and recording their presence can be helpful in better understanding whether artificial or natural introduction of these and other species at the sites are more likely.

Each croft was also paired with a control site. These locations have provided us with details about what plants are prevalent in areas without significant histories of settler interference. At Boghead (Plate 9.1) the comparison site is located less than 500 m from the croft and is primarily covered by heather and birch trees (Plate 9.2). Although OS maps suggest the control site has not been used for any recent agriculture or forestry, we cannot discount the possibility it was historically grazed by stock prior to the division of the commonty. At Baudyground (Plate 9.3) the comparison site is directly adjacent and supports a heathland ecology apart from a natural drainage line which is covered in grasses and herbs (Plate 9.4). Like the other comparison site, this has not been used for any recent agriculture or forestry. As with Bennachie, Corrennie Moor has, however, been a site of historical grazing.

Preliminary observations

Boghead

At Boghead, the vegetation survey revealed that the croft (Plate 9.1) is primarily covered by wild grasses. The enclosed fields are surrounded by active forestry and (semi-) natural woodland. None of the 19th-century cultivars that crofters are known to have husbanded, such as oats, barley, rye, and clover grass (Carter 1979, 22) were visible on the hillside and seem to have been displaced by wild grass species. One grass species identified, cock's-foot (*Dactylis glomerata*), was widely used for producing hay and featured within pastures.

Herbs also make up a large portion of the plant species identified during the survey. Four recorded herbs – foxglove (*Digitalis purpurea*), yarrow (*Achillea millefolium*), angelica (*Angelica sylvestris*), and common self-heal (*Prunella vulgaris*) – have uses that are either medicinal, culinary, or ornamental (Van den Eynden 2022). However, the vegetation survey showed no specific spatial patterns with regards to their location, making it difficult to say if they were planted purposefully or spread naturally onto the site. Foxglove, for instance, has both ornamental and medicinal uses (Brickell 2008; Goldthorp 2009) though how they were used locally in the north-east of Scotland historically is poorly documented. The species also occurs naturally and could have spread onto the site during or after abandonment. A third possibility is that the presence of foxglove is the product of both natural and cultural processes.

Larger plant species, shrubs and trees, can be categorised as introduced or naturally occurring taxa with more confidence. Two species of shrub at Boghead exhibit interesting patterns: gorse (*Ulex europaeus*) and raspberry (*Rubus idaeus*). Gorse grows primarily on or close to standing archaeological features such as enclosure and house walls, specifically where the ground has been disturbed (Jones 2021). Historically, this plant was used for hedging and for marking boundaries as well as for a variety of cultural, culinary, and medicinal uses. It was also used as fuel and to create dyes, and when bruised it provided winter fodder for livestock (Rotherham 2007). The latter is well attested at a range of lowland farms across the north-east (Brook 2024). In the uplands gorse was an important tool for controlling boundaries (Winchester 2000). Unfortunately, we do not currently have any clear idea whether such practices were in use within the Bennachie Colony. The vegetation survey has shown that gorse is growing disproportionately around edges of dry-stone walls, making ingress in some places towards the inside of fields. While its abundance along field boundaries could suggest an anthropogenic origin, it is more likely to be a legacy of the settler presence than the result of their deliberate planting. In other cases, gorse's presence is likely a result of it taking advantage of well-drained and disturbed ground associated with historic enclosures (Jones 2021).

Raspberry is and was an important food crop, can easily be grown in the uplands, and has many culinary uses. At Boghead, vegetation survey revealed an interesting distribution for raspberry plants. The majority are located close to the former kitchen garden and house and their frequency decreases with distance. Large parts of the croft do not have any raspberries. The tendency for raspberry to be located adjacent to kailyards and dwelling houses provides reasonably compelling evidence that these are the descendants of those introduced by the colonists. The Bailies of Bennachie, a long-standing community group, with close ties to the hill, have created a model 'kailyard', at Shepherds Lodge – another abandoned croft within the Bennachie Colony – and have included raspberries in their planting roster (as discussed by Chris Foster in this volume).

Of the tree species found on the site, of particular interest are rowan (*Sorbus aucuparia*), cherry (*Prunus avium*), and sweet chestnut (*Castania sativa*). All three species seem to have been introduced by the settlers and some of the trees that were originally planted still exist today. The longer lifespan of trees and the relative size of their trunks means we can estimate age. In Figure 9.2 a line of trees can be seen on the north edge of a trackway bisecting the parcel in the First Edition OS map dated to the 1860s. Field observations reveal a row of old rowan trees in the same location. This provides a compelling argument that they were planted by the residents. While we cannot discount their aesthetic appeal as a motivation for the choice of this tree, rowans also hold cultural significance (Kenicer 2020; Van den Eynden 2022). They were believed to ward off evil and to protect livestock from interference by witches. Their position at the edge of the property may therefore indicate that they were intended to fulfil a similar purpose at Boghead. Additionally, rowan had a culinary use. Their berries can be made into jelly, jam, chutney, and even wine. Future work into the folk history of the region may help us to understand whether such products might have been made on Bennachie.

In Figures 9.5 and 9.6, three trees can be clearly seen to the left of the cottage in both pictures. One picture was taken in the 1930s prior to abandonment. Two of the trees appear to be fully grown and decades old while the third may be younger. The vegetation survey has shown three trees growing in the same area today: two cherry trees and a sweet chestnut. They can also be seen in the photograph from 2024 (Figure 9.6). The old photograph provides evidence for the trees having been planted during the crofting era, possibly for aesthetic or culinary reasons.

At the comparison site adjacent to Boghead, the vegetation survey registered only a small number of additional species such as bilberry (*Vaccinium myrtillus*), cowberry (*Vacciniun vitis-idaea*), wavy hair grass (*Deschampsia flexuosa*), and sphagnum moss (*Sphagnum sp.*). There was very little evidence of overlap between the species found on the croft and those on the comparison site, which was dominated by birch forest and heath. Most importantly, plants with potential practical or cultural purposes were not found on the comparison site, emphasising that they probably did not originate from there prior to crofting activities.

Baudyground

The vegetation at Baudyground (Plate 9.3) shares many similarities with that described for Boghead and is also mostly covered by various grass species. The cover of grasses appears to be lower than at Boghead and broom and gorse are growing in larger quantities across the site. There are no extant crop plants growing on the site either (Carter 1979, 22). Cock's-foot was found, though it is not clear whether it was introduced by the crofters or if it occurs naturally in the area.

It is difficult to determine if any of the herb species observed at Baudyground were introduced by the crofters. However, one species is found only at Baudyground and not Boghead: the bluebell (*Hyacinthoides non-scripta*), which was located in the former kitchen garden. While bluebells are typically indicator species for ancient woodlands (Glaves *et al.* 2009), their kitchen garden location with its thicker soils provides a more compelling answer: they were probably planted for aesthetic purposes. They were a favourite in parks designed by the Victorians and were popular garden plants during that era (Hamilton *et al.* 2006). The plants that have survived until today are very probably the descendants of bluebells planted in the 19th century. The site also supports foxgloves but, as for Boghead, it is hard to determine if the species was introduced by the crofters or if it occurs naturally at these locations.

Several shrub species were found at Baudyground including bilberry, raspberry, elderberry, gorse, and broom. The distributions of bilberry and raspberry, both known for culinary purposes, are particularly interesting. Raspberries exhibit a similar pattern to their counterparts on Boghead, with the frequency of recorded plants decreasing with distance from the house and kitchen garden. Therefore, they were most likely planted by the crofters in their kitchen garden or around the house. Bilberries, on the other hand, are more frequent at a distance from the house and kitchen garden and are especially prevalent on and adjacent to the nearby moorland. They are most abundant at the comparison site and have probably encroached upon the crofting site from these areas. It is unlikely that the crofters planted these in the kitchen garden as there were likely plenty of bilberries growing nearby (see Foster, this volume).

The gorse and broom (*Cytisus scoparius*) on the site are also distributed slightly differently than at Boghead. While they are still covering the ruins of the house, they are absent from the kitchen garden and occur randomly across the wider site in larger patches. They are not correlated with any of the former enclosure walls as they are at Boghead. Most likely, they have spread onto the site since the abandonment and have no relationship with crofter occupation.

The last shrub species of interest at Baudyground is the elderberry (*Sambucus nigra*). Two individuals were identified during the vegetation survey, with the more mature of them found at the corner of the kitchen garden (Plate 9.5). This position, directly at the edge of this feature, may indicate that the plant was strategically planted there. The other is roughly 20 m away and appears to be a younger individual, based upon its smaller height and size. It may be a descendant of the older plant. Elderberries are known for culinary, medicinal, and cultural uses. Elderberries were seen as protectors and avengers within local folk tradition (Charlebois *et al.* 2010). Notably, they were thought to offer protection from malicious spirits and witches, as well as from lightning and thunder, which might explain why this taxon was planted at the edge of the kitchen garden. For centuries, the fruits of the plant have also been used as natural remedies against colds, fevers and the flu (Blochwitz 1677). They were, and are, also used to make jellies, jams and cordial, being particularly popular during the Victorian era (Langlands *et al.* 2008). The positioning, in combination with the usefulness of the plant, makes it very likely that it was planted by the settlers and that is has since produced at least one viable offspring.

There is only one tree species of interest on the site: rowan. These can be divided into two categories: mature trees and young saplings. The mature specimens are located at the upper edge of the property in a straight line, strongly indicating that they were planted here (Plate 9.6). They may have served a similar purpose to that postulated at Boghead, *i.e.* as an aesthetic barrier, spiritual protector or culinary resource. Across the north of the site, close to the mature rowan trees, are a large number of rowan tree saplings (Plate 9.7). They decrease in frequency with distance from the adult trees and are most likely their offspring. The comparison site had no unique species and the only species of interest that occurred at the comparison site was bilberry.

Conclusions: what plants tell us about the lifeways and legacies of crofting

The changes that crofters made to the uplands they settled are still very much visible today and have modified localised ecosystems for almost two centuries. In comparison to proximal 'control' sites without known crofting activities, the plant communities we have identified at sites settled in the past 200 years have been altered and enriched by species introduced by their human inhabitants. Several of the species identified provide insights into how plants were viewed and perhaps used by the colonists, ranging from practical to spiritual intent. Species identifications inform on culinary choices, animal foddering/provisioning and even building materials – including how they roofed their houses – and what they may have used to treat illnesses. Taxonomic diversity even hints at culturally important superstitions, despite living through a period often associated with 'enlightenment' and 'improvement' values. Analysis of the plants found at both sites also suggests that, in some senses, the settlers may have chosen what to grow no differently than other members of rural, Victorian society (Langlands *et al.* 2008). The species we have identified, such as raspberries and elderberries, show that their diet did not solely consist of the stereotypical brose (an oat-based porridge) and tubers like turnips and potatoes. It was probably enriched by fresh fruits, when in season, but possibly also by preserves, wines, and cordials (*ibid.*).

A number of steps can be taken to explore this phenomenon further. Firstly, the study area can and should be expanded beyond the small number of hills tackled here into other parts of the north-east, Scotland more widely, southern Britain and beyond. We know, for example, that the poor and landless were making similar kinds of choices in transplanting cultivars to crofting sites in Sweden (Williamsson 2024). Much might be learned about commonalities of small-scale agriculture and how local strategies varied through comparisons across these different regions. Other avenues of research may provide complementary evidence, such as further investigations of the pollen record. Pollen analysis (Moore *et al.* 1991) can be used to reconstruct vegetation histories for sites where suitable deposits (peats, lakes, muds, or acid soils) are available. Analysing pollen samples collected close to archaeological sites can help fill historical gaps in our understanding of vegetation history (see, for example, Jones and Noble, this volume; Shepherd and Ralston, this volume). Such research would help us to understand both the more recent period of abandonment as well as the deeper historical context prior to settler colonisation. The pollen record may help us understand more clearly the similarities and differences between upland squatters and crofters and lowland tenant farmers. Much more can be done to help us determine the range of species selected by crofter colonists and how these continue to shape upland ecologies today. The application of dendrochronological methods, such as the use of an increment bore to date mature living trees, would help to clarify, with greater precision, when they were planted and help in relating them to the chronology of upland settlement. With regards to further exploring the culinary (or other) uses of the different taxa identified, the analysis of plant macrobotanical remains from archaeological contexts at these sites may provide fresh evidence for how different plants were processed and thus utilised (see D'Andrea 2020 and Johnston 2023 for recent summaries of this approach). Evidence of material culture from the excavation of sites would also help determine the ways in which the different plants featured in the everyday lives of settlers. Such an approach might even be paired with the chemical analysis of residues on vessels, which can be used to analyse, amongst other things, the presence of alcohol, resins, and waxes (see overview in Pecci 2018).

From the evidence shared here, it is abundantly clear that there are significant legacy effects on vegetation and the ecological composition of Scotland's uplands as a result of the efforts of squatters and crofters. The built environment they created continues to have an impact on the hillside, even though natural recolonisation processes are clearly playing-out and decreasing the visibility of their efforts. More research is needed to investigate this phenomenon in order to bring emerging patterns into clearer focus. Crofting is an important, but often under-acknowledged, part of the historical ecology of uplands in the north-east. Continuing research into the vegetation legacy of crofting will not only increase our understanding of the lifeways of the poor and landless, but also help to improve our knowledge concerning what the future ecologies of hillsides might look like.

Acknowledgements

I would like to thank my team of supervisors: Jeff Oliver, Gill Plunkett, Kate Britton, and J. Edward Schofield. Additionally, I would like to thank Jackie Cumberbirch, Forestry and Lands Scotland, and the Bailies of Bennachie for their help and guidance. Lastly I would like to acknowledge QUADRAT and NERC for funding my PhD project and the research for this chapter.

Bibliography

Blochwitz, M. (1677) *Anatomia Sambuci, or, The Anatomy of the Elder Cutting out of It Plain, Approved, and Specific Remedies for Most and Chiefest Maladies: Confirmed and Cleared by Reason, Experience, and History*. London, Brome and Sawbridge.

Bodgan, N.Q., Dransart, P.Z., Upson-Smith, T. and Trigg, J. (1999) *Bennachie Colony House Excavation. An Extended Interim Report.* Unpublished report by the Scottish Episcopal Palace Project.

Brickell, C. (2008) *A-Z encyclopedia of garden plants*, 3rd edition. London, Dorling Kindersley (ed.) in association with the Royal Horticultural Society.

Brook, T. (2024) *The archaeology of whin mills in post-medieval northeast Scotland.* Unpublished Undergraduate Dissertation, University of Aberdeen.

Carter, I. (1979) *Farm life in northeast Scotland, 1840–1914: the poor man's country*. Edinburgh, John Donald.

Carter, I. (1992) Introduction. In Alexander, W., *Rural life in Victorian Aberdeenshire*, 5–28. Edinburgh, The Mercat Press.

Charlebois, D., Byers, P.L., Finn, C.E. and Thomas, A.L. (2010) Elderberry: Botany, Horticulture, Potential. In Janick, J. (ed.), *Horticultural Reviews,* Volume 37, Chapter 4 (Wiley Online Library), 213–80. Doi. https://doi.org/10.1002/9780470543672.ch4

D'Andrea, A.C. (2020) Paleobotany. In Richards, M.P. and Britton, K. (eds) *Archaeological Science: An Introduction*, 276–313. Cambridge, Cambridge University Press.

Egler, F.E. (1954) Vegetation Science Concepts I. Initial Floristic Composition, a Factor in Old-Field Vegetation Development. In *Vegetatio* 4, 412–17.

Fagen, J. (2011) *The Bennachie Colony Project: Examining the Lives and Impact of the Bennachie Colonists.* Chapel of Garioch, The Bailies of Bennachie, Bennachie Landscapes Series 1.

Flinn, K.M. and Vellend, M. (2005) Recovery of forest plant communities in post-agricultural landscapes. In *Frontiers in Ecology and the Environment* 3, 243–50.

Glaves, P., Rotherham, I.D., Wright, B., Handley, C. and Birbeck, J. (2009) *Field Surveys for Ancient Woodlands: Issues and Approaches. A Report to the Woodland Trust.* Sheffield, Hallam University.

Goldthorp, W.O. (2009) An Account of the Foxglove. In *British Medical Journal* 338:b2189. Doi. https://doi.org/10.1136/bmj.b2189

Guttmann, E.B., Simpson, I.A., Davidson, D.A. and Dockrill, S.J. (2006) The management of arable land from prehistory to the present: Case studies from the Northern Isles of Scotland. In *Geoarchaeology* 21, 61–92.

Hamilton, J., Hart, P. and Simmons, J. (2006) *The gardens of William Morris.* London, Frances Lincoln.

Harmer, R., Peterken, G., Kerr, G. and Poulton, P. (2001) Vegetation changes during 100 years of development of two secondary woodlands on abandoned arable land. In *Biological Conservation* 101(3), 291–304.

Johnston, P. (2023) Archaobotany: What Can Plant Macro-Remains Tell Us? In *Archaeology Ireland* 37, 36–40.

Jones, E.L. (2021) *Landscape history and rural society in Southern England: an economic and environmental perspective, Palgrave studies in economic history.* Cham, Palgrave Macmillan.

Kay, G. (1962) The landscape of improvement: A case study of agricultural change in North-East Scotland. In *Scottish Geographical Magazine* 78, 100–11.

Kenicer, G.J. (2020) *Scottish plant lore: an illustrated flora*. Edinburgh, Birlinn.

Langlands, A., Ginn, P. and Goodmann, R. (2008) *Victorian Farm* (London, Batsford Books).

McConnochie, A.I. (1890) *Bennachie*. Aberdeen, D. Wyllie & Son.

Moore, P.D., Webb, J.A. and Collinson, M.E. (1991) *Pollen analysis*, 2nd edition. Oxford, Blackwell.

Myster, R.W. (1993) Tree invasion and establishment in old fields at Hutcheson Memorial Forest. In *Botanical Review* 59, 251–72.

Oliver, J. and O'Driscoll, J. (2024) Landscape Legacies of the Landless. In *Places Journal*. https://placesjournal.org/article/landscape-legacies-of-the-landless/

Oliver, J., Armstrong, J., Milek, K., Schofield, J.E., Vergunst, J., Brochard, T., Gould, A. and Noble, G. (2016) The Bennachie Colony: a nineteenth-century informal community in northeast Scotland. In *International Journal of Historical Archaeology* 20(2), 341–77.

Pecci, A. (2018) Chromatography and Archaeological Materials Analysis. In López Varela, S.L. (ed.) *The Encyclopedia of Archaeological Sciences*. Wiley Online Library. Doi. https://doi.org/10.1002/9781119188230.saseas0092

Rotherham, I.D. (2007) Wild Gorse: history, conservation, and management. In *Farming and Wildlife Advisory Group Scotland* 7, 17–21. Doi. *https://api.semanticscholar.org/CorpusID:73529097*

Van den Eynden, V. (2022) Plants as Symbols in Scotland Today. In Pardo-de-Santayana, M., Pieroni, A. and Puri, R.K. (eds) *Ethnobotany in the New Europe*, 239–45. Oxford, Berghahn Books.

Wickham-Jones, C.R., Noble, G., Fraser, S.M., Warren, G., Tipping, R., Paterson, D., Mitchell, W., Hamilton, D. and Clarke, A. (2020). New Evidence for Upland Occupation in the Mesolithic of Scotland. In *Proceedings of the Prehistoric Society* 86, 13–42.

Winchester, A. (2000) *The Harvest of the Hills*. Edinburgh, Edinburgh University Press.

Williamsson, S. (2024) Three crofts in southern Sweden – a microhistorical approach to dwelling and agency. Paper delivered to a joint meeting of the Anthropology Society and Northern Archaeological Seminar Series, University of Aberdeen, 27th May (Unpublished).

Chapter 10

When the ice goes, the river flows: evidence of Mesolithic settlement from Deeside and the north-east

Sandra Davison

Mesolithic Deeside community archaeology group

Mesolithic Deeside is a community archaeology group of archaeologists, volunteers and students investigating the earliest periods of human occupation along

Figure 10.1. Melting ice (Photograph: Sandra Davison).

the River Dee and its tributaries in Aberdeenshire, north-east Scotland. Seed-funding from Aberdeenshire Council in 2016 enabled the group to become a formally constituted organisation and, in 2017, a National Lottery Heritage Fund grant provided funds for Mesolithic Deeside to pay for a project supervisor for a year, and for a lithic specialist to report on finds. The fieldwork and outreach work of Mesolithic Deeside has been acknowledged as bearing 'testament to the value of community archaeology' (Wickham-Jones *et al.* 2021, 7).

Figure 10.2. Mesolithic Deeside field walkers (Photograph: Alan Donald).

The River Dee

The Dee rises above 1200 m in the Cairngorm mountains at the Wells of Dee (approximate National Grid Reference NN 93798 98836) and flows east for 140 km to Aberdeen and the North Sea.

The Cairngorm mountains form 'the largest continuous block of high ground in Britain [with] a high-altitude plateau dissected by large valleys' (Fraser *et al.* 2020, 129). Through the 'Upper Dee Tributaries Project' (*ibid.*) and the 'Looking Up' project (Butler *et al.* 2024), Mesolithic sites and find spots have been identified at Chest of Dee (Aberdeenshire Historic Environment Record [HER] NO08NW0042), Caochanan Ruadha (Aberdeenshire HER NN98NW0004 and NN98NW0007), Glen Geldie (Aberdeenshire HER NN98NW0006), and Sgòr an Eòin (Aberdeenshire HER NN99SE0004). With the kind permission of Professor Graeme Warren from University College Dublin, volunteers from Mesolithic Deeside's Cairngorms subgroup have participated in the Sgòr an Eòin excavations in 2022 and 2023 and under the guidance of Daniel Rhodes (National Trust for Scotland Archaeologist), Professor Warren and Bruce Mann (Senior Historic Environment Officer, Aberdeenshire Council), the subgroup continue to plan and, outwith ground-nesting bird season, complete field prospection walks in the Mar Lodge Estate area of the Cairngorms.

The Cairngorms group field prospection approach replicates Mesolithic Deeside's own by which, with the permission of landowners and farm tenants, Mesolithic Deeside have fieldwalked ploughed and weathered fields along the more eastern part of the River Dee, concentrating on the area between Aboyne and Peterculter. In 2024 Mesolithic Deeside volunteers walked several fields along the Water of Feugh, a tributary of the Dee, close to Strachan near Banchory. All areas walked are shown in Plate 10.1, which covers the fieldwalking years 2021–2024, and is available for interactive browsing through the Mesolithic Deeside web page (www.mesolithicdeeside.org). Between 2017 and 2024 Mesolithic Deeside have walked 114 fields, covered 574 ha, and recorded 17,416 lithics. Fieldwalking methods and reports are discussed later in this chapter.

The Mesolithic world and culture

Before describing the Mesolithic Deeside methodology, it is worth reflecting on the potential environment adjacent to the River Dee during the Mesolithic period. The last Ice Age (not the late medieval 'Little Ice Age') ended in the area approximately 17,000 to 15,000 years ago. The complex geochronology of glaciers, ice-caps, ice-flow directions, and ice-streams makes it difficult, but not impossible, to hint at the rate of disappearance along the length of the River Dee. However, that is beyond the remit of this paper. Suffice to say, it was not a uniform disappearance, and there was a limited return of ice to the Cairngorms during the Loch Lomond Stadial/Younger Dryas (approximately 12,900 to 11,700 years ago; Bickerdike *et al.* 2018; Carter-Champion *et al.* 2022). The possibility of seasonal permafrost along parts of the River Dee highlights the significant value to be gained by bringing together knowledge from related disciplines, such as geology, geomorphology, palynology, and archaeology. This multidisciplinarity helps us to better understand the changing environment which Late Upper Palaeolithic, and then Mesolithic people encountered when they moved along the River Dee. (Helpful resources for learning more about the geology of north-east Scotland include Merritt and Leslie (2009). To learn more about the Palaeolithic and Mesolithic periods and regional research frameworks, a good starting point is ScARF [Scottish Archaeological Research Framework], available online.)

After the ice left, and the River Dee flowed from mountain to sea, the landscape most likely resembled what we would recognise today as Arctic tundra. Prevailing winds meant precipitation as rain or snow along the west side of Scotland, left the eastern side relatively arid (Carter-Champion *et al.* 2022). The peat-covered hills we see today required warmer, wetter conditions to enable vegetation to grow and, subsequently, rot to create the peat. The rich arable land along the coastline needed broadleaved trees to repopulate the area, with their annual fall of leaves helping to build the humus-rich brown soils over the glacial till left at the end of the Ice Age (Tipping 1994; Bishop *et al.* 2015; The James Hutton Institute 2023).

Plate 10.2 shows a soil map of north-east Scotland. It illustrates the soil types (A) and (B) along the River Dee, combined with the Historic Environment Records where the Finder has been entered as MDP (Mesolithic Deeside Project). Along the River Dee, meltwaters from the glaciers of the last Ice Age resulted in what would today be known as a 'braided river' (Tipping *et al.* 2022, 4, 10). Over several thousand years, the River Dee transformed from this into the more meandering, single waterway of today. The Mesolithic landscape would, therefore, have been different, yet the structure present in the coast, rivers, glens, and mountains would still be recognisable to us today. Mesolithic lives would also be different, yet recognisable. Food would be cooked – but not by microwave or cooker – instead over campfires (for evidence of hearths see Wickham-Jones *et al.* 2020; Murray and Murray 2021, 46). Food would be hunted and gathered. (Further insights about Mesolithic lifestyles are discussed in Warren 2010 and Biddulph *et al.* 2020.)

The Mesolithic culture has been well discussed in the archaeological literature (Warren 2010; Conneller 2022) yet, in north-east Scotland, the scarcity of actual settlement sites continues to be challenging. The Cairngorms sites, mentioned earlier, attest to movement into the area although, what the radiocarbon dates available tell us, is that the movement was sporadic. However, the large amounts of lithics found downstream by Mesolithic Deeside would indicate either a lot of lithic production sites, a lot of settlement, or a bit of both. Without locations where radiocarbon dates can confirm the presence of Mesolithic people, the search has to continue. We need to locate more sites where the lithic record is strengthened by evidence of shelters indicative of short-term or more permanent settlements. This will help us to understand better how and why the Mesolithic people may have moved along the River Dee and its tributaries.

Pollen records can also support the possibility of Mesolithic people using plant materials both for food and storage. Mesolithic Deeside are planning to use available pollen records to inform which plants were available for use. Products made from plants would have included baskets woven from osiers and, potentially, for the making of fish traps. Re-constructing a fish trap (Plate 10.3) proved to be a successful activity, attracting public engagement at the August 2024 Aboyne Highland Games.

The Mesolithic period is well known for the consumption of hazel nuts (Bishop *et al.* 2013; 2022), which were typically roasted and then presumably stored safely during the winter months. Shell middens at sites like Sands of Forvie attest to seafood consumption (Warren, pers. comm.; Canmore ID 165124 [https://canmore.org.uk/site/165124/sands-of-forvie]).

Finding the Mesolithic

The Mesolithic folk are an elusive people; they didn't build monuments that we can visit or homes that have survived until today. If we know what to look for, we might catch a glimpse of them in their flint tools at the side of a path, or the edge of a ploughed field. (We certainly channel our 'inner hunter-gatherer' with the enjoyment we get in walking outdoors or when we gather irresistible blackberries from the hedgerow, or even when seeking the best-looking bananas in the supermarket!). To discover more about the Mesolithic – where they lived, how they lived, and how they moved around north-east Scotland, we need to find more of the places where they camped and to understand how they travelled between those camps. This is why finding more of their distinctive microlith flint tools is very important. Historical records can help, giving us clues about where to look, based on previous finds. Work done to date by archaeologists and community archaeology groups like Mesolithic Deeside hints at a Mesolithic preference for river travel, and camps on river terraces in the sheltered valley of Lower Deeside. Yet, tantalisingly, microliths have been found in the glens and mountain passes of the Cairngorms, indicating that Mesolithic people travelled through these areas, perhaps seeking resources, intending to meet up with other groups, or perhaps simply to go exploring. Walk into the Cairngorms area, and you'll find paths through mountain passes like the Làirig Ghrù that can be used to walk from near Braemar to near Aviemore without needing to go up onto the exposed plateau. Based on historical records, known Mesolithic findspots are on flatter ground that was typically once broadleaf woodland close to rivers with terraced banks. However, that's because, to date, that is mainly where archaeologists and community groups have looked for them. Move away from the River Dee and what becomes of more importance is the way to, and through, a mountain pass. The recognition of landmarks as directional markers and for understanding how to live within the landscape is critical. Such knowledge as: where the waterfalls are; where to find shallower, safer places where animals can cross rivers and drink; where people can gather at certain times of the year. These will have been of fundamental importance.

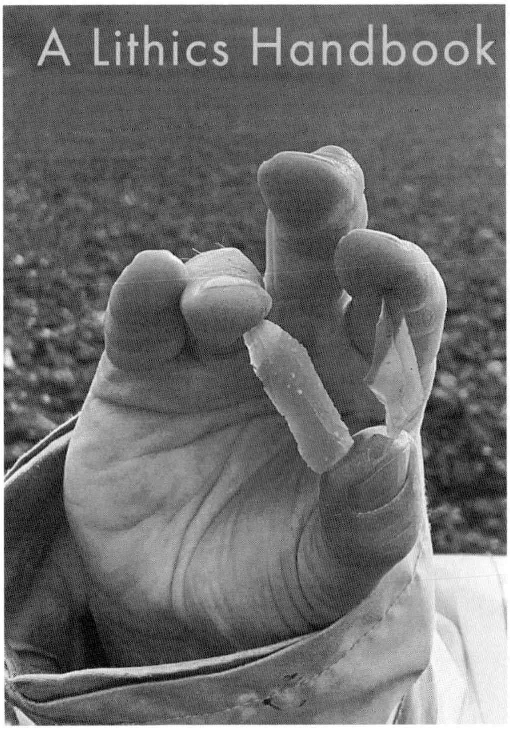

Figure 10.3. A Lithics Handbook, *published by Mesolithic Deeside in 2022.*

When fieldwalking along the River Dee, Mesolithic Deeside follow tried-and-tested methodologies, which have been refined over the years. These are documented in research papers (*cf.* Wickham-Jones *et al.* 2021) and in the group's own document *A Lithics Handbook* (Mesolithic Deeside 2022; Figure 10.3). These describe the methods used to categorise, catalogue, and, to some extent, analyse the lithic finds ahead of those discoveries being published.

Previous Mesolithic research along the Dee

Looking for evidence of the Mesolithic along the River Dee has, itself, a reasonably long history. It begins with Hilda Paterson of Birkwood, near Banchory. She found microliths in March 1906, in a molehill. Even today, in pastureland or rough ground, Mesolithic Deeside volunteers will eagerly look at the surface of molehills, hoping to find lithics. Paterson continued her research and in 1936, following excavations at Birkwood, co-authored a paper with Lacaille (Paterson and Lacaille 1936). The significant contribution made by Paterson in recognising that her microlithic finds were important evidence for the establishment of a Mesolithic presence in Scotland occurred at a time when such a thing was not considered possible (Wickham-Jones *et al.* 2021, 4).

Later, in the early 1970s, Dr John Grieve began walking ploughed fields between Maryculter and to the west of Banchory. He identified most of the large flint-scatters along this stretch of the River Dee, labelling the scatters as 'flint factories'. His hand-written notes, later typed up by Roger Daly, inform many of the Mesolithic Historic Environment Records. His collection of finds was donated to Aberdeen City Council Collections in 1975 (Object number ABDMS0235918 – see Aberdeen Archives, Gallery and Museum, nd) and has been more recently re-assessed by Torben Ballin and Caroline Wickham-Jones (Wickham-Jones and Ballin 2018; Ballin 2019) (see Plate 10.4).

The late James Kenworthy, a 'well-kent' local archaeologist, completed an excavation at Nethermills in the late 1970s. Approximately 30,000 lithics were collected in one part of a field now known as NM4 (Nethermills 4). Over Fifties Archaeological Research Society (OFARS) and, subsequently, North-east Scotland Archaeological Research Society (NESARS) began a detailed field-walking programme, which resulted in around 10,000 lithics being found in the fields between Milton and the east-end of Nethermills (for an analysis see Ballin 2017; Sabnis and Sabnis 2019).

In 2005–2006, Charles and Hilary Murray excavated Mesolithic pits at Warren Field, Crathes and later, as part of developer work prior to quarry excavations, found evidence of Mesolithic activity at Nether Park (Murray and Murray 2021). Excavation of more Mesolithic pits at Milltimber Brae were completed by Headland Archaeology (Dingwall *et al.* 2019).

Higher upstream along the River Dee, footpath work on the Mar Lodge Estate in 2013 revealed a Mesolithic site at Chest of Dee (Wickham-Jones *et al.* 2020). Lithics were found in the upper Dee glen at Carn Fiaclach Beag in 2006 and Sgòr an Eoin, and also along the Geldie, a tributary of the Dee, at Caochanan Ruadh (Warren *et al.* 2018; Butler *et al.* 2024).

Finally, in May 2016, Caroline Wickham-Jones organised a meeting at the University of Aberdeen. Her idea was that it would be interesting to research – and fieldwalk – the areas between the known find spots along the River Dee, and to join them up to get a more complete picture of Mesolithic activity along the river. This idea was taken up, and eventually led to Mesolithic Deeside being created and formally launched at Crathes Castle in October 2016. With Alison Cameron of Cameron Archaeology as the Chair, the community archaeology group has continued, supported in the early days by the National Heritage Fund Lottery grant.

In the years since then, with a temporary halt for COVID, and in addition to fieldwalking ploughed and weathered fields, the group has completed at least one test-pitting project per year. The original scope of the group has also expanded and now includes a Cairngorms subgroup who look specifically for lithics along the Mar Lodge Estate footpaths – a vast area to cover and very different conditions to fieldwalking lower down the river, which can often feel comparatively benign.

Fieldwalking does, however, remain the most important group activity (Plate 10.5). With a Fields subgroup deciding the most likely places to visit, typically between January to the end of March, permission to walk the chosen fields is obtained. Finds are bagged and labelled according to our *Lithics Handbook* (see Figure 10.3), and beginners are given friendly help and advice to ensure minimal mis-recording takes place. Field notes are kept for each field walked, and these are used as the basis for the annual reports and summaries. During the 2024 season, the field notes were supplemented by an online tool called 'StoryMaps' with the aim of making the results more widely available through the Mesolithic Deeside website. Figure 10.4 shows part of the Field Notes for Beltcraigs 3 (the third field to be walked at Beltcraigs) and Plate 10.6 shows part of the StoryMaps entry for the same field.

Field Walking Record 2024

Beltcraigs 3 – Field details

Field	**Location**	Beltcraigs
	Parish	Banchory-Ternan
	Field Code	BC3
	Central point	NO 7057 9493
	Field Size (hectares)	7.89
	Soil	The field had an undulating surface and had been rolled before seeding. LiDAR images show a terrace and towards the small wood adjacent to Bridge of Feugh car park the field dropped away steeply.
	Bedrock	Tarfside Psammite Formation - a metamorphic rock formed between 1000 and 541 million years ago.
	Superficial Deposits	The field contains both Banchory Till Formation and Alluvium. Banchory Till is a sedimentary superficial deposit formed between 116 and 11.8 thousand years ago. The Alluvium deposits are also sedimentary and were formed between 11.8 thousand years ago and the present. The Alluvium deposits are the furthest away from the river Feugh and river Dee. In the small wood at the north west end of the field, nearest to the Bridge of Feugh car park, the deposits are Lochton Sand and Gravel, which was formed the same time as the Banchory Till.
Field walking survey	**Date walked**	25 - 27 May 2024
	Volunteers	4 on 25 May 2024 3 on 26 May 2024 7 on 27 May 2024
	Weather	On all days the weather was dry, bright and sunny with occasional light cloud cover.
	Underfoot	The field had been rolled and sown. Apart from one slightly damp area the ground was dry.
	Lithics found	578 lithics (137 on 25 May, 173 on 26 May and 268 on 27 May.
History	**Canmore / Pastmap**	The farmstead at Beltcraigs was included in the OS First Edition map (see HER NO79NW0114) and a house nearby was included in the OS Second Edition (see HER NO79NW0193).
	Historic Environment Record	Mesolithic Deeside have previously walked two other Beltcraigs fields • HER NO79NW0200 (May 2023) - 983 lithics found (BC2) • HER NO79NW0191 (March 2021) - 622 lithics found (BC1) Nearby HER NO79NW0197 (compiled 2023) reports that worked flints had been found near the mouth of the Feugh.

Figure 10.4. Section of the Field Notes for Beltcraigs 3 (Written by the author).

Analysing the results of fieldwalking

Consistently accurate reporting enables good analysis and enables the group to share its findings with a wider audience. This sharing includes the online website, school visits, stalls at the Banchory or Aboyne Games, and in bringing along local schools to test-pitting events.

Recorded lithics are entered into Excel spreadsheets, and the grid references from handheld GPS enable the results to be displayed in QGIS software. This record sheet is illustrated in Figure 10.5. Plate 10.7 shows the QGIS plot for Beltcraigs 3 and Plate 10.8 shows a selection of the lithics gathered there.

The group are increasingly aware of the importance of recognising river terraces appropriate for Mesolithic use. These terraces were formed in the early years of

	A	B	C	D	E	F	G	H	I	J	K
1	ID	X	Y	Code	Location	Number of Lithics	Raw material	Condition	Survival	Type	SubType
2	BC3-1-2024	70571	94915	BC3	Beltcraigs	1	Brown flint	OK	Distal survives	Retouched blade	Inner
3	BC3-2-2024	70597	94892	BC3	Beltcraigs	1	Grey flint	Heat/frost shattered		Spall	Inner
4	BC3-3-2024	70499	94846	BC3	Beltcraigs	1	Grey flint	OK		Spall	Inner
5	BC3-4-2024	70518	94873	BC3	Beltcraigs	1	Grey flint	OK	Distal survives	Flake	Inner
6	BC3-5-2024	70489	94894	BC3	Beltcraigs	1	Brown flint	OK	Fragment	Flake	Inner
7	BC3-6-2024	70418	94903	BC3	Beltcraigs	1	Grey flint	OK	Proximal survives	Flake	Secondary
8	BC3-7-2024	70612	94824	BC3	Beltcraigs	1	Grey flint	OK	Complete	Blade	Secondary
9	BC3-8-2024	70422	94937	BC3	Beltcraigs	1	Burnt flint	Calcined		Small flake	Inner
10	BC3-9-2024	70409	94946	BC3	Beltcraigs	1	Mottled brown flint	OK	Fragment	Blade	Inner
11	BC3-10-2024	70628	94796	BC3	Beltcraigs	1	Burnt flint	Calcined		Spall	Inner
12	BC3-11-2024	70622	94801	BC3	Beltcraigs	1	?			Flake	
13	BC3-12-2024	70516	94876	BC3	Beltcraigs	1	Grey flint	OK	Proximal survives	Blade	Inner
14	BC3-13-2024	70592	94820	BC3	Beltcraigs	1	Burnt flint	Heat/frost shattered	Complete	Flake	Secondary
15	BC3-14-2024	70483	94885	BC3	Beltcraigs	1	Light grey flint	OK	Fragment	Flake	Inner
16	BC3-15-2024	70542	94766	BC3	Beltcraigs	1	Mottled brown flint	OK	Distal survives	Blade	Inner
17	BC3-16-2024	70463	94899	BC3	Beltcraigs	1	Grey flint	OK	Fragment	Flake	Secondary
18	BC3-17-2024	70430	94920	BC3	Beltcraigs	1	Mottled red flint	OK	Proximal survives	Flake	Secondary
19	BC3-18-2024	70441	94912	BC3	Beltcraigs	1	Grey flint	OK	Complete	Flake	Inner
20	BC3-19-2024	70465	94896	BC3	Beltcraigs	1	Mottled brown flint	OK	Complete	Flake	Inner
21	BC3-20-2024	70465	94896	BC3	Beltcraigs	1	Red flint	Heat/frost shattered		Spall	Inner
22	BC3-21-2024	70406	94935	BC3	Beltcraigs	1	Grey flint	OK	Complete	Blade	Inner
23	BC3-22-2024	70399	94941	BC3	Beltcraigs	1	Burnt flint	Calcined		Small flake	Secondary
24	BC3-23-2024	70421	94936	BC3	Beltcraigs	1	Mottled grey flint	OK	Complete	Flake	Primary
25	BC3-24-2024	70501	94805	BC3	Beltcraigs	1	Dark grey flint	OK		Spall	Primary
26	BC3-25-2024	70487	94865	BC3	Beltcraigs	1	Grey flint	OK	Distal survives	Retouched blade	Secondary
27	BC3-26-2024	70464	94911	BC3	Beltcraigs	1	Brown flint	OK	Complete	Flake	Secondary
28	BC3-27-2024	70696	94946	BC3	Beltcraigs	1	Brown flint	OK		Small flake	Inner
29	BC3-28-2024	70390	94957	BC3	Beltcraigs	1	Red/brown flint	OK	Complete	Blade	Inner
30	BC3-29-2024	70416	94899	BC3	Beltcraigs	1	Brown flint	OK	Distal survives	Blade	Secondary
31	BC3-30-2024	70405	94924	BC3	Beltcraigs	1	Burnt flint	Calcined	Segment	Blade	Inner
32	BC3-31-2024	70503	94885	BC3	Beltcraigs	1	Brown flint	OK	Distal survives	Flake	Inner
33	BC3-32-2024	70407	94945	BC3	Beltcraigs	1	Brown flint	OK	?	Flake	Inner
34	BC3-33-2024	70533	94788	BC3	Beltcraigs	1	Mottled grey flint	OK	Complete	Flake	Inner
35	BC3-34-2024	70522	94948	BC3	Beltcraigs	1	Red flint	OK		Spall	Inner
36	BC3-35-2024	70472	94982	BC3	Beltcraigs	1	Grey flint	OK	Fragment	Flake	Inner
37	BC3-36-2024	70427	94950	BC3	Beltcraigs	1	Brown flint	OK	Fragment	Flake	Inner

Figure 10.5. Beltcraigs 3. A sample of the Excel spreadsheet of the finds. Column B (X) and Column C (Y) become the grid references used to plot each lithic in the QGIS system managed by Mesolithic Deeside.

the Dee, immediately after the last Ice Age (Tipping *et al.* 2022) with some of their fields forming part of modern-day flood plains, which can lead to some interesting fieldwalking conditions (Figure 10.6)!

Plate 10.1 shows the spread of Mesolithic finds along the River Dee, as fieldwalked by Mesolithic Deeside. The 'hot spot' areas continue to be the lower, downstream reaches of the River Dee. However, through consistent recording, it is possible to begin to look at these foci in relation to places where Mesolithic blades have been found and where Mesolithic cores or scrapers are common. These differing types of finds may suggest the history behind these distinctive distributions. The presence of cores may indicate a preparation site where flint was being knapped for a specific purpose. Blades, on the other hand, may represent a possible hunting site, whilst the rarer scrapers might indicate a hunt-processing location.

Figure 10.6. Footwear after a few minutes fieldwalking (Photograph: Sandra Davison).

Irrespective of site usage, the spread of lithic findspots along the Dee hints at prolonged, regular, travel along the river. As the group begins to explore River Dee tributaries, such as the Water of Feugh at Beltcraigs, and into the fields of the Howe of Cromar, the links between river and its tributaries should become clearer. The gaps on the present QGIS maps indicate areas that require further fieldwork. The absence from the record may simply be a lack of arable fields in the area, in which case fieldwalking is not possible; or, the gaps may represent genuine blanks where, for one reason or another, Mesolithic people failed to go.

There are few sources of flint nodules in Scotland from which flint tools were made (Wickham-Jones and Collins 1977). Several deposits of flint gravels are known, including Den of Boddam in Aberdeenshire, where there is evidence of flint working during the Neolithic (see Aberdeenshire HER NK14SW0003, NK14SW0019, NK14SW0098). Elsewhere in Scotland flint nodule sources include Orkney and north Caithness. In north and east Orkney, Dr Hugo Anderson-Whymark has identified flint pebbles on beaches and in clay cliffs, and has begun analysing the flint colours used for particular tools during the Neolithic and Mesolithic (Anderson-Whymark 2023). Using the data collected through Mesolithic Deeside fieldwalking it will also be possible to see if similar – or different – patterns of tools and colours exist in the flint tools made by the Mesolithic of Deeside.

Rhyolite also features in the Mesolithic toolkit, as attested by tools excavated in the Cairngorms, where 'Rhyolite-bearing intrusive dykes are common' (Wickham-Jones *et al.* 2020, 25). As Mesolithic Deeside complete further fieldwalking and prospection along the Dee and more flint and rhyolite tools are found, it may be possible to begin building a pattern of usage and propose, through analysis, patterns of exchange of both materials and tools.

The exchange of tools could also indicate long distance travel and trade. Whilst it is not possible to directly connect the Mesolithic sites of Star Carr in Yorkshire with Balbridie near Banchory, the striking similarities between a flint blade found during fieldwalking and a flint blade found at Star Carr has been documented and prompt questions about 'how far the Mesolithic population would have travelled, where they went and who they met up with along the way' (Clarke, nd, 3).

Plotting the lithic assemblages found along the River Dee by Mesolithic Deeside makes geographical analysis and comparison of tools with other locations, such as Forvie at the Ythan estuary on the north-east coastline of Scotland possible. This remains an activity to be considered, together with comparisons with the lithic scatters found in the Cairngorms. Part of the challenge of such analysis is that, whilst the Mesolithic Deeside lithics have been catalogued to a consistent standard, that standard may be different for earlier collections gathered by different groups and collectors.

At Nethermills of Crathes, cross-discipline research has demonstrated that by combining the evidence of excavation, fieldwalking, flint typological analysis, geomorphological mapping, sedimentology, pollen analysis, AMS ^{14}C dating, and OSL (Optically Stimulated Luminescence) dating it is possible to conclude that Mesolithic people were attracted to the resources available in the lower reaches of the River Dee (Tipping *et al.* 2022). Here, several large lithic assemblages have been found on what is known as the Camphill Terrace. Similar work, to be published, is ongoing in the upper reaches of the Dee, in the Cairngorms. Eventually, a comparison along the length of the River Dee may be possible, linking the environmental changes Mesolithic people encountered with the tools and resources they may have had access to over several thousand years.

Also, in the Crathes area, at Warren Field, Hilary and Charles Murray (Murray *et al.* 2009) excavated a pit alignment with eventual carbon dates spanning the Mesolithic and Neolithic (see Aberdeenshire HER NO79NW0012). A search of the Aberdeenshire HER database reveals that a further 16 possible pit alignment sites exist in Aberdeenshire. Of these – excluding Warren Field – five are considered to be potentially Mesolithic in origin, based on their alignment similarities to those at Warren Field. Whilst completing a research dissertation for a Masters in Cultural Heritage the author plotted the pit alignments in QGIS. They are some distance away from the River Dee, with three situated in the Mearns area (NO67SE0012, NO66NW0028, NO77NW0029), one near Kintore (NJ81NW0039) and one along a small tributary of the River Dee, west of Banchory. Based on the carbon dating at Warren Field, the potential for pit alignments to indicate Mesolithic sites as precursors for Neolithic sites may be worth future research. Mesolithic Deeside, however, remains firmly focused on finding further evidence of Mesolithic people along the River Dee and its larger tributaries.

Conclusion

The research outlined here demonstrates that the existence of Mesolithic people along the course of the River Dee is informed by the presence of lithics, the particular typology of which includes the microliths mentioned earlier in this chapter.

However, the Mesolithic people of the River Dee and their lifestyles remain only dimly visible through the mists of time. Our work has only just begun. How did they navigate around the landscape of the River Dee? How often did they travel into the Cairngorms – and why? How did they communicate and what were the stories they told and the songs they sang at night by the campfire, listening to the crackling of the flames and the occasional pop or crack of a stray, burning flint flake? What other sounds did they hear? Whilst the lack of evidence from animal bones makes this difficult to prove – the acidic soils of the north-east being not conducive to their survival – there would have been animals, and the river would always be there: a sound of meltwater after the harsh winter, perhaps a faint murmur on a still, summer's evening. The lithics we have found are only the beginning of our own journey of understanding the Mesolithic after the ice went and the River Dee flowed once more.

Acknowledgements

The author would like to thank the following reviewers of this paper: from Mesolithic Deeside, Alison Cameron, Angela Groat, and Sheila Duthie, Bruce Mann (Senior Historic Environment Officer, Aberdeenshire Council), and Colin Shepherd (University of Aberdeen).

Mesolithic Deeside Funders and Partners

As a community archaeology group, Mesolithic Deeside appreciate the kind funding and support from our Funders and Partners:

Aberdeenshire Council, Kincardine and Mearns Area Committee, Marr Area Committee, Aberdeenshire Council Archaeology Service, National Lottery Heritage Fund, 'Bread of Life' of Torphins, King George V Wind Turbine Panel, Aboyne Highland Games, ScotMid Community Fund, Skinner Charitable Trust, Live Life Aberdeenshire, Arnold Clark Community Fund, Mid Hill Wind Farm, Leys Charitable Trust, Crathes, Drumoak and Durris Community Council, Cameron Archaeology, Universities of Aberdeen, St Andrews and Stirling.

Bibliography

Aberdeen Archives, Gallery and Museums (nd) *Grieve Collection Flints.* https://emuseum.aberdeencity.gov.uk/objects/189309/grieve-collection-flints

Anderson-Whymark, H. (2023) *Ness of Brodgar flaked stone assemblage* In Card, N., Edmonds, M. and Mitchell, A.6 (eds) *The Ness of Brodgar As it Stands*, 208–23. Kirkwall, The Orcadian.

Ballin, T.B. (2017) *Early Mesolithic, Late Mesolithic and other flint artefacts from Nethermills Farm, Banchory, Aberdeenshire.* https://www.academia.edu/35298813/2017_Early_Mesolithic_Late_Mesolithic_and_other_flint_artefacts_from_Nethermills_Farm_Banchory_Aberdeenshire

Ballin, T.B. (2019) *The Grieve Collection: Characterisation and discussion of lithic assemblages on the Dee, Aberdeenshire.* https://www.academia.edu/90365316/2018_The_Grieve_Collection_what_can_we_learn_from_legacy_assemblages_and_what_are_their_shortcomings

Bickerdike, H.L., Evans, D.J.A., Stokes, C.R. and Cofaigh, C.Ó. (2018) The glacial morphology of the Loch Lomond (Younger Dryas) Stadial in Britain: a review. In *Journal of Quaternary Science* 33(1), 1–54.

Biddulph, K., Ritchie, M. and Wickham-Jones, C. (2020) *Into the Wildwoods: Explore the Mesolithic in Scotland's Native Woodlands.* Inverness, Forestry & Land Scotland.

Bishop, R.R., Church, M.J. and Rowley-Conway, P.A. (2013) Seeds, fruits and nuts in the Scottish Mesolithic. In *Proceedings of the Society of Antiquaries of Scotland* 143, 9–71.

Bishop, R.R., Church, M.J. and Rowley-Conway, P.A. (2015) Firewood, food and human niche construction: the potential role of Mesolithic hunter-gatherers in actively structuring Scotland's woodlands. In *Quaternary Science Reviews* 108, 51–75.

Bishop, R.R., Kubiak-Martens, L., Warren, G.M. and Church, M.J. (2022) Getting to the root of the problem: new evidence for the use of plant root foods in the Mesolithic hunter-gatherer subsistence in Europe. In *Vegetation History and Archaeobotany* 32, 65–83.

Butler, M., Doughty, A., Lifton, N., Kelley, S., Moucheron, M., O'Brien, C., Mann, B., Skelton, R. and Warren, G. (2024) Looking Up for prehistoric hunter-gatherer archaeological sites in mountain landscapes in Europe: A case study from the Cairngorms, Scotland. In *Hunter Gatherer Research* 7(3/4).

Carter-Champion, A., Abrook, A.M., Pike, J.H., Matthews, I.P., Palmer, A.P. and Lowe, J.J (2022). Ice-sheet deglaciation and Loch Lomond Readvance in the eastern Cairngorms: implications of a Lateglacial sediment record from Glen Builg. In *Journal of Quaternary Science* 37(8), 1332–47.

Clarke, A. (nd) *The story of a flint blade from Aberdeenshire.* https://s3-eu-west-1.amazonaws.com/s3.spanglefish.com/s/37931/documents/balbridie-blade.pdf

Conneller, C. (2022) *The Mesolithic in Britain: Landscape and Society in Times of Change.* London, Routledge.

Dingwall, K., Ginnever, M., Tipping, R., van Wessel, J. and Wilson, D. (2019) *The Land was Forever: 15,000 years in North-East Scotland: Excavations on the Aberdeen Western Peripheral Route/Balmedie – Tipperty.* Oxford, Oxbow Books.

Fraser, S.M., Noble, G., Warren, G., Tipping, R., Paterson, D., Mitchell, W., Clarke, A. and Wickham-Jones, C. (2020) The Upper Dee Tributaries Project: Finding the Mesolithic in the mountains of Scotland. In Borić, D., Antonović, D., Mihailović, B. and Stefanović, S. (eds) *Holocene Foragers in Europe and Beyond: Papers Presented to the Ninth International Conference on the Mesolithic in Europe MESO 2015, Belgrade, Serbia*, 64–69. Serbian Archaeological Society, Belgrade, Ninth International Conference on the Mesolithic in Europe, Belgrade, Serbia.

Merritt, J. and Leslie, G. (2009) *Northeast Scotland: A Landscape Fashioned by Geology*. Perth, Scottish Natural Heritage. https://www.scottishgeologytrust.org/downloads/LandscapeFashionedbyGeology-northeastscotland.pdf

Mesolithic Deeside (2022) *A Lithics Handbook*. Deeside, Mesolithic Deeside. https://www.mesolithicdeeside.org/documents/lithicshandbook2022pdf.pdf

Murray, H.K. and Murray, J.C. (2021) *ARO43: Nether Park Quarry, Aberdeenshire: a small Mesolithic and Neolithic site on the banks of the River Dee*. Glasgow, GUARD Archaeology Limited. https://www.archaeologyreportsonline.com/reports/2021/ARO43.html

Murray, H.K., Murray, J.C. and Fraser, S.M. (2009) *A Tale of the Unknown Unknowns: A Mesolithic Pit Alignment and a Neolithic Timber Hall at Warren Field, Crathes, Aberdeenshire*. Oxford, Oxbow Books.

Paterson, H.M.L. and Lacaille, A.D. (1936) Banchory Microliths. In *Proceedings of the Society of Antiquaries of Scotland* 70, 419–34.

Sabnis, H. and Sabnis, D. (2019) *Stone Age Crathes – Lithic Analysis*. http://www.stoneagecrathes.com/lithic%20analysis.htm

ScARF (Scottish Archaeological Research Framework) (nd) *Palaeolithic & Mesolithic*. https://scarf.scot/national/palaeolithic-mesolithic-panel-report/

ScARF (Scottish Archaeological Research Framework) (nd) *Regional frameworks*. https://scarf.scot/regional/

The James Hutton Institute (2023) https://www.hutton.ac.uk/learning/natural-resource-datasets/soilshutton/soils-maps-scotland/download#soilmapdata. See also https://www.hutton.ac.uk/soil-maps/#soilmapdata Soil Survey of Scotland Staff (1981). Soil maps of Scotland at a scale of 1:250 000. Aberdeen, Macaulay Institute for Soil Research.

Tipping, R. (1994) The form and fate of Scotland's woodlands. In *Proceedings of the Society of Antiquaries Scotland* 124, 1–54.

Tipping, R., Bates, R., Cameron, A., Clarke, A., Duthie, S., Ewan, L., Kinnaird, T., Mann, B., Noble, G., Ross, I., Sabnis, H., and Wickham-Jones, C. (2022) Environmental reconstruction and formation processes in a large Mesolithic lithic scatter at Nethermills of Crathes, Aberdeenshire, Scotland. In *Journal of Archaeological Science, Reports* 45, 103605.

Warren, G. (2010) *Mesolithic Lives in Scotland*. Stroud, The History Press.

Warren, G., Fraser, S., Clarke, A., Driscoll, K., Mitchell, W., Noble, G., Paterson, D., Schulting, R., Tipping, R., Verbaas, A., Wilson, C. and Wickham-Jones, C.R. (2018) Little House in the Mountains? A small Mesolithic structure from the Cairngorm Mountains, Scotland. In *Journal of Archaeological Science*: Reports (Volume 18, 2018), 936–45. Doi. https://doi.org/10.1016/j.jasrep.2017.11.021

Wickham-Jones, C.R. and Ballin, T.B. (2018) *Grieve Collection, Interim report on the analysis of a lithic scatter.* https://www.socantscot.org/wp-content/uploads/2019/09/Grieve-Interim-Autumn-2018.pdf

Wickham-Jones, C.R. and Collins, G.H. (1977) The sources of flint and chert in northern Britain. In *Proceedings of the Society of Antiquaries of Scotland* 109, 7–21.

Wickham-Jones, C.R., Bates, R., Cameron., A, Clarke, A., Collinson, D., Duthie, S., Kinnaird, T., Noble, G., Ross, I., Sabnis, H. and Tipping, R. (2021). Prehistoric communities of the River Dee: Mesolithic and other lithic scatter sites of central Deeside, Aberdeenshire. In *Scottish Archaeological Internet Reports* 97. https://doi.org/10.9750/issn.2056-7421.2021.97

Wickham-Jones, C.R., Noble, G., Fraser, S.M., Warren, G., Tipping, R., Paterson, D., Mitchell, W., Hamilton, D., and Clarke, A. (2020) New Evidence for Upland Occupation in the Mesolithic of Scotland. In *Proceedings of the Prehistoric Society* 86, 13–42.

Chapter 11

The Shepherds Lodge kailyard: experiments in reconstructing a 19th-century upland rural garden

Christine Foster

Introduction

Brassica oleracea is a member of the cabbage (crucifer) family, more commonly known as kale. In Roman times kale was a significant crop and during the Middle Ages became a basic staple for peasants due to its easy maintenance and resistance to cold temperatures. The word 'kailyard' refers to a small plot of land, attached or close to a country dwelling, where vegetables are grown for the inhabitants' table, in other words a kitchen garden. As kale was resistant to cold temperatures and easy to grow, it became a valued winter vegetable in Scotland and a core diet of its country folk. Large amounts were grown by Scottish crofters and cottars in their small gardens, which were often referred to as 'kailyards'. The word kailyard can also refer to a genre of sentimental Scottish literature that became popular in the late 19th century and focused on rural domestic life.

Background

In 2013 an old croft site on Bennachie, known as Shepherds Lodge and built in the 19th century, was excavated under a joint initiative by the Bailies of Bennachie, Bennachie Landscapes Project, and the University of Aberdeen as part of a co-production programme. This croft was part of the 'Bennachie Colony' (Fagen 2011, 4) – a dispersed rural settlement established by squatters in the 19th century on part of the Commonty of Bennachie (land in the shared ownership of surrounding estates). The croft was occupied by the Littlejohn family who built the dwelling during the 1830s and lived there for over 40 years. The crofters on Bennachie had small acreages where they would grow their main crops of cereal, grass, potatoes, and turnips (Fagen 2011, 10). The smaller areas close to the dwellings would have been their kailyards containing such crops as carrots, peas, leeks, early varieties of potatoes, soft fruit bushes, and, of course, kale. Following the excavations at Shepherds Lodge one area of interest was the small stone-walled enclosure next to the croft. It showed soil depths far deeper than anywhere else, clearly demonstrating that this would have been used as the Littlejohns' kailyard. What then might have been grown here, how was it maintained, what issues might these people have faced and what influence did they ultimately leave on the land?

The kailyard project

It is hard to perceive exactly what the day-to-day life of the colonist would have been like without more evidence. Speculation kindled our desire to learn more, so in 2017 members of the Bailies of Bennachie and the Bennachie Landscapes Project steered an experiment to reconstruct part of the kailyard in an effort to discover more. We received funding from the Heritage Lottery Fund to cover the purchase of materials and members of the local community were also invited to join in. A plot approximately 5 m × 5 m within the original kailyard was chosen and prepared using methods we considered similar to those the colonists would have used. Unfortunately, little had been recorded by the crofters themselves, so we based our research on what the local crofting community in Aberdeenshire were growing, eating, and managing in their own gardens during the 19th century.

In 2017, trying to keep within the same parameters as the crofters proved difficult at times as a number of factors had to be taken into consideration, *e.g.* location – Shepherds Lodge is a 20-minute uphill walk and all tools, *etc.*, had to be carried up and returned at the end of the day; facilities – although the well at this croft still exists, the water nowadays dries up in the summer, so water would need to be fetched from further afield when conditions dictated; upkeep – unlike the colonists, there would not be the opportunity to keep a daily watch on the kailyard. Also, the drystone walls of the kailyard are now in ruins so this would leave it open to deer, rabbits, *etc.*, as well as many pet dogs, who are given a free reign on Bennachie during their walks. The decision, therefore, was to grow fruit bushes, due to their low maintenance, and to build a fence around our small plot. In time this took the form of a wattle fence made from brushwood arising from maintenance of the surrounding conifer plantation. We chose a rustic fence as this would not disturb the existing archaeology, could easily be maintained and was within the parameters of our objectives, even though deviating from the known facts.

Our next step then took us to researching varieties of fruit being grown in Scotland during the 19th century. With the aid of gardening catalogues, books, newspaper articles, *etc.*, and advice from the James Hutton Institute, Dundee, we were able to choose suitable heritage examples for our experiment. The fruit varieties chosen for the kailyard were:

Blackcurrants

Goliath* – Very old variety grown since before 1847.
Russian Black – Recorded in England in Royal Horticultural Society records *c.* 1826.
Baldwin – A very old variety of unknown origin.

Whitecurrant
White Versailles – Dates back to 1830s.
Recommended by Dr Rex M. Brennan, James Hutton Institute, Dundee.

Redcurrant
Red Versailles – This is the red equivalent to the white, which was raised in 1835.
Recommended by Dr Rex M. Brennan, James Hutton Institute, Dundee.

Gooseberries
Crown Bob*
Early Sulphur*
White Eagle*

(The Early Sulphur and White Eagle failed. These were replaced with a gooseberry cutting taken earlier from an unknown variety found growing on one of the old colony sites and a cutting taken from a modern variety 'Invicta' – claimed to be a heavy cropper and mildew free. This will be used for comparative purposes.)

Raspberries
Gaia – Mixed old parentage including Black Raspberry* (pre-1860).
Heritage Raspberry.

Rhubarb
Prince Albert – Advertised in *The Aberdeen Journal* 1848.
* Indicates varieties listed in *The Fruit Manual* by Robert Hogg (1884), which quotes varieties of fruit being grown in Britain at that time.

We also located a supplier who specialised in heritage varieties and was able to provide most of the varieties we needed. During our research other interesting facts from that period were also revealed, such as the gooseberry craze, as discussed below.

While the researchers were seeking out this information, the gardeners started on the kailyard plot. First they cleared the area of broom and herbage; then they dug and prepared the soil, much as the colonists would have done. We followed a strict procedure keeping as much as possible to the methods we believed would have been practised, such as using hand tools only and improving the soil with local animal manure. While this was in progress two small excavations (Foster, B. 2019, 47–52) took place to establish whether the garden paths noted on the 1st edition OS map of 1867, could be identified (see Figure 11.1). As nothing permanent was discovered, the conclusion was that the paths were nothing more than grassy baulks left in order to access the garden plot. Once the plot had been cleared and dug over, we carried out a standard soil test to check the pH condition of the soil within the plot. This was aided by pupils from nearby Oyne Primary School. The result showed quite a high acidity, which we reduced by adding lime, a method used by farmers at that time and still used today (Harper 2012, 14). By the end of November 2017, the garden had been well dug, fertilised with horse manure, tilled and planted up with our chosen

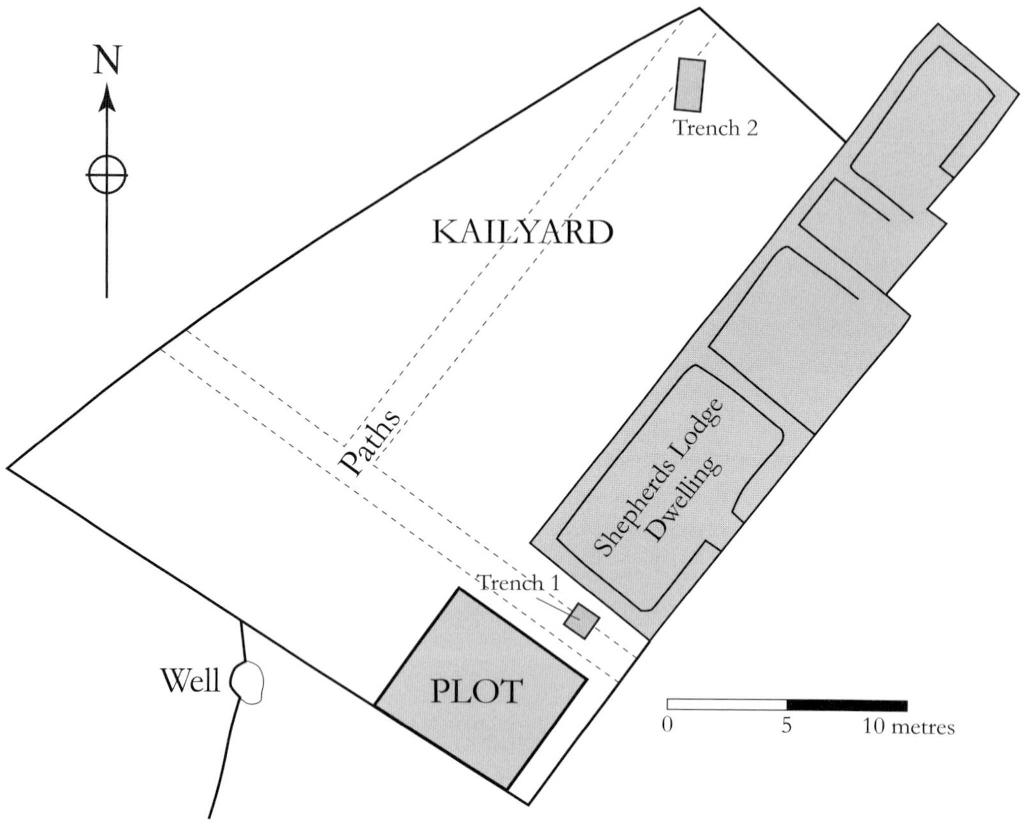

Figure 11.1. Plan of dwelling house and kailyard plot. Paths are as shown on 1st edition OS map surveyed 1867.

heritage fruit bushes in what we deemed to be a fair interpretation of a 19th-century style of croft gardening (Foster, C. 2019, 53–64) (see Plate 11.1).

Colony life

Some reports studied during our research were critical of the colonists and their way of life, but the evidence from the excavations and our studies showed that they were hard-working folk. When they first arrived, they would have needed to clear wasteland, predominantly consisting of stones, gorse and broom, build their own homes and turn the remaining area into arable land capable of growing crops, thus changing the landscape. Soil test pitting led by Aberdeen University (Oliver *et al.* 2016, 341–77) showed that their kailyards had a soil depth of up to 64 cm and field depths between 33–66 cm. Comparison with areas outside the fields, which were very shallow at 16–18 cm, clearly demonstrates the amount of hard work this would have taken each man and his family, while also working in other employments further afield. Over the years drainage systems were installed in their fields and the soil improved

Plate 8.5. Culthibert Burn. Orthomosaic of the former crofting landscape, created by stitching together hundreds of aerial photographs (Photogrammetry: 2024 by James O'Driscoll). Note the former enclosure walls and cottages of the abandoned crofts. Today this landscape is used for the pasturing of livestock.

Plate 8.6. A deserted colonist's dwelling on the moor of Corrennie, perched above a 'strype' (watercourse, burn) (Photograph: James O'Driscoll).

Plate 8.7. Vertical shot of the deserted dwelling of Burnside within the Colony of Bennachie (see also Plate 8.2). Its enclosed fields and garden have been swallowed by industrial woodlands and only the outline of the house is visible. The more subtle traces of outbuildings and domestic architectural design are no longer visible (Photograph: James O'Driscoll).

Plates 9.1 and 9.2. Showing the study area of Boghead (9.1 top) and the control site (9.2 bottom) (Top photograph: Jeff Oliver; Bottom photograph: Louise Smith).

Plates 9.3 and 9.4. Showing the study area of Baudyground (9.3 top) and the control site (9.4 bottom) (Photograph: Louise Smith).

Plates 9.5–9.7. Elderberry bush (9.5 top), line of rowan trees (9.6 bottom left) and rowan sapling (9.7 bottom right) at Baudyground (Photographs: Louise Smith).

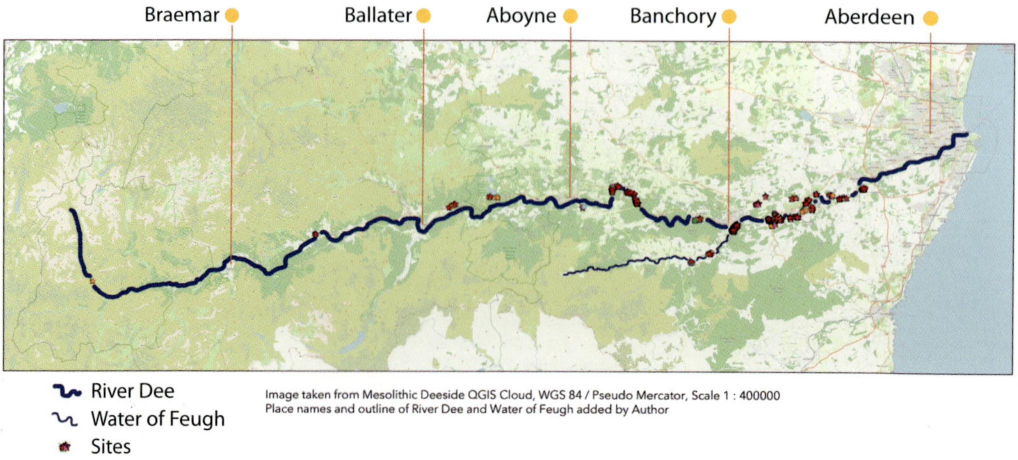

Plate 10.1. Locations of fieldwalking sorties (Artwork by Irvine Ross and Sandra Davison).

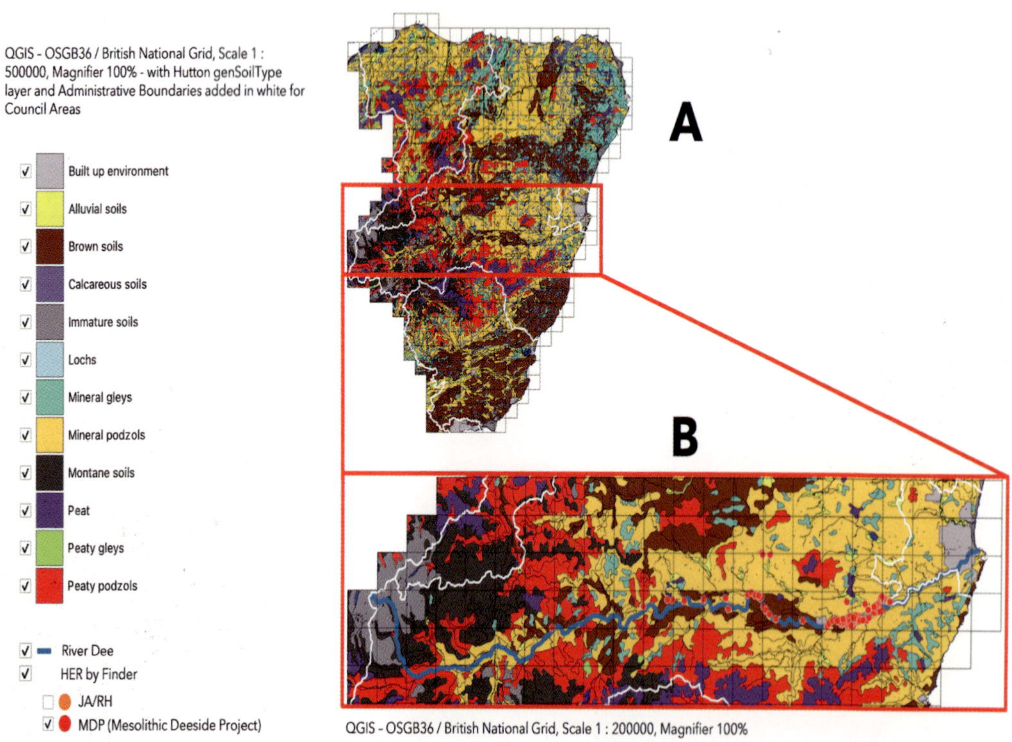

Plate 10.2. Showing a soil map of north-east Scotland (Artwork produced in QGIS by Sandra Davison. 'Shapefiles' courtesy of the Hutton Institute, used as per the terms of The James Hutton Open Data Licence of 5th December 2014).

Plate 10.3. Reconstruction of an early fishtrap (Photograph: Sandra Davison).

Plate 10.4. Display of the Grieve Collection of flints (Photograph: Sandra Davison).

Plate 10.5. *Fieldwalking opposite Normandykes Roman Camp (Photograph: Sandra Davison).*

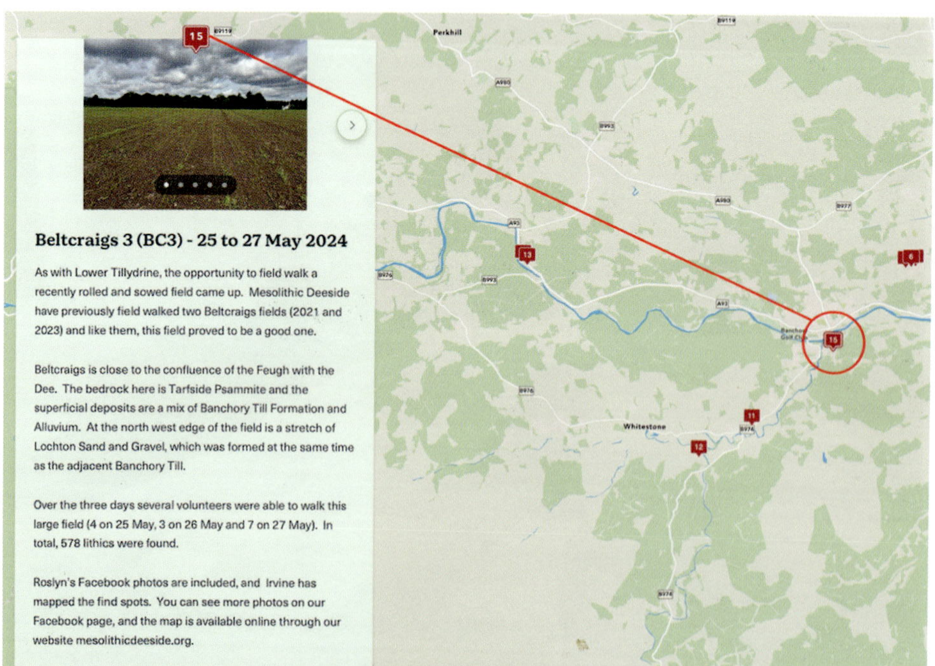

Plate 10.6. *StoryMaps interactive webpage showing entry for Beltcraigs 3 (Courtesy of Mesolithic Deeside).*

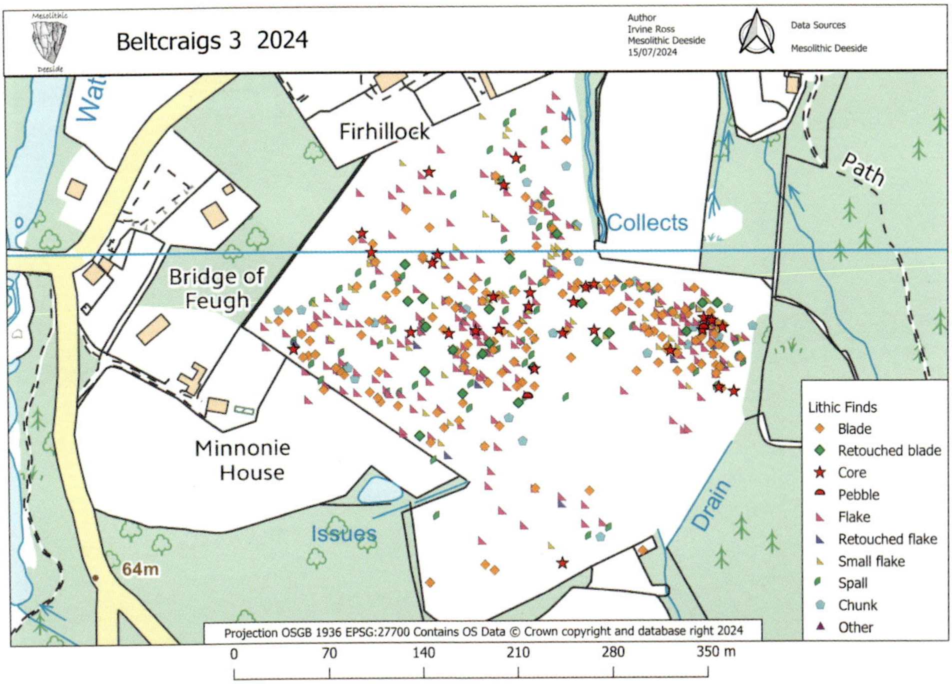

Plate 10.7. Showing the QGIS plot for Beltcraigs 3 (Created by Irvine Ross).

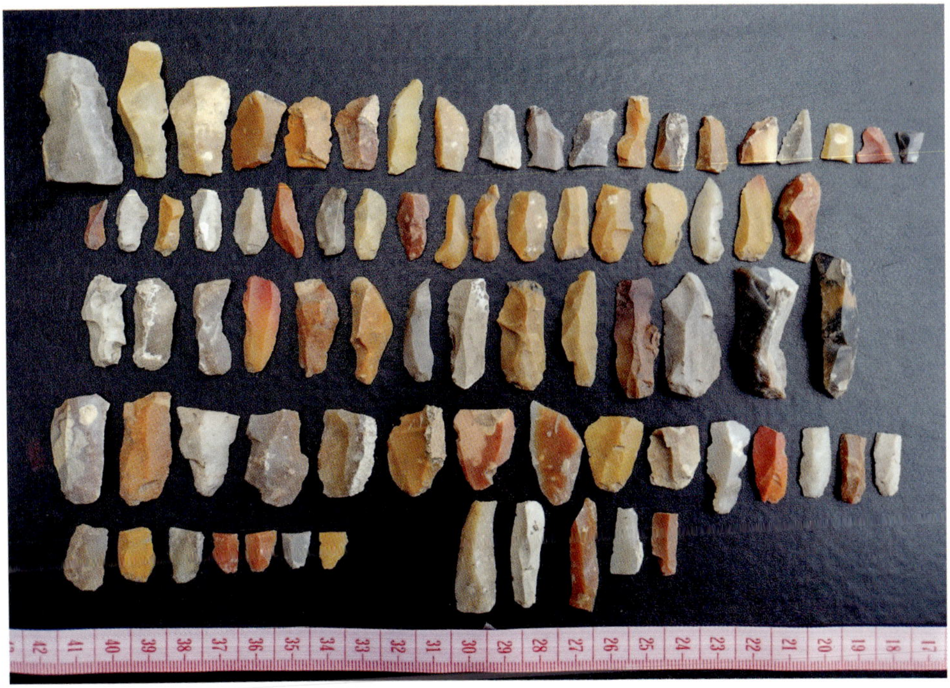

Plate 10.8. Showing a selection of the lithics gathered at Beltcraigs 3 (Photograph: Mesolithic Deeside).

Plate 11.1. Volunteers helping in the early stages of digging the kailyard plot (Photograph: Chris Foster).

Plate 11.2. Nineteenth-century pottery found within the Kailyard (Photograph: Chris Foster).

Plate 11.3. Summer 2018: Plants are thriving, despite a hard winter and dry spring, and well protected by the wattle fencing (Photograph: Chris Foster).

Plate 11.4. View from the Colony Trail across the kailyard to the landscape of the Garioch beyond (Photograph: Chris Foster).

Plate 12.1. View of the castle of Pittodrie and its manicured grounds seen from the edge of the wooded study area (Photograph: Iain Ralston).

Plate 12.2. View of Trench 9 with the large enclosure dyke ([AN]/[AJ]) to the left and the earlier stone feature ([AS]) lying between the baulks, halfway along the trench. The woodland, planted in the early 19th century as part of the policy landscaping, preserved this relict landscape. The conifer woodland beyond was initially planted in the 18th century, contrary to popular misconceptions (Photograph: Iain Ralston).

Plate 12.3. Two late medieval kilns seen side-by-side. The earlier, earth-cut kiln lies on the left with its successor – made of carefully-laid stones bonded by dense clay – to the right. The kilns were cut into the bright orange sand that appears to have been imported onto the site at a much earlier time (Photograph: Iain Ralston).

Plate 12.4. The entrance to the Bede House seen from within the building. The doorway, with fine, chiselled stones can be seen in association with a neatly laid threshold and path beyond. The path ran between the inverted ends of the garden dyke giving the approach to the house quite a 'grand' feel. The gap between path and dyke suggests a former grass verge or flower border (Photograph: Iain Ralston).

Plate 12.5. The interior, southern end of the house showing raised corner platform and possible later hearth in front. This may have been used by the workmen when taking the house down in the late 18th or early 19th century. Note how the roots of the sitka surround the wall. Had the tree blown down, all the archaeology would have been destroyed (Photograph: Iain Ralston).

Plate 12.6. Pollen sampling in the boggy area. The site of the kilns lies beneath the beech trees in the background and Mither Tap can be seen beyond them (Photograph: Iain Ralston).

Plate 13.1. The Young Archaeology Club of Aberdeen helping at the excavation. The older members in the nearest trench are discovering the top stones of the late medieval kiln. At the time, its existence and the purpose of those stones were unknown. Younger members are working through the upper layers of a further trench in the background (Photograph: Iain Ralston).

Plate 13.2. Two young students (archaeology and history) sharing a moment over a site survey (Photograph: Iain Ralston).

Plate 13.3. A convivial moment as Iain is noticed stalking his camera prey (Photograph: Iain Ralston).

Plate 13.4. Andrew, in the foreground, marshalling his band of bog enthusiasts (Photograph: Iain Ralston).

by adding turves dug from the peat beds on the hill. The large amount of pottery and artefacts found whilst digging the kailyard plot also shows the colonists were improving their soil partly by using domestic waste from their middens. The pottery has also given us a good indication of what utensils were being used and demonstrates that there would have been quite an assortment of different crockery on the table at any one time. It showed a wide range of varieties, colours, and patterns – some basic but others of a better quality (Taylor 2015, 105) (Plate 11.2). It is possible that some of these were items thrown out by the local estates where we know the colonists were often employed; others would have been bought from tinkers, pedlars, or at markets and fairs, while some could have been inherited. One can imagine a family going off to the annual fair and having a fun and enjoyable day out, meeting family, friends, and neighbours, then coming home with a new dish and/or trinkets purchased while there. Is this something our colonists did? One would certainly like to think so.

Unfortunately, there is no definitive documentation as to how the colonists worked their kailyards and what they grew, nor are there many written records of their day-to-day lives. But, with snippets of information from our research, evidence from excavations, and thoughtful experimentation on our part, we now have a somewhat better perception of their lives. In particular, it has underlined how essential a kailyard was to their existence, as it helped provide the extra food that was so important to their survival. They relied on good harvests and suffered when the weather or circumstances brought bad years. They would have worked long hard hours as, apart from caring for their own crofts, research has shown that many of the colonists had casual work on the local estates and larger farms (Fagen 2011, 52). The men were often employed as farm or general labourers and masons. Still visible on Bennachie today are some of the drystone dykes they built, proof that they were accomplished at their jobs. The women were employed for domestic work, taking in laundry, and knitting woollen stockings for merchants in the local stocking trade. The children too were expected to help with chores, even when attending school. If help was needed at home, they would not attend school and absenteeism was more noticeable during the summer when weeding and harvesting needed extra hands. The Education (Scotland) Act, providing for elementary education for all children between the ages of 5 and 13, was not passed until 1872, by which time the Colony was on the decline. Nevertheless, many of the Colony children had still attended the local schools where they received an education (Fagen 2011 13).

Climate

As mentioned, the weather would have played a significant part in the success of each year's harvest. Records of past weather patterns (https://premium.weatherweb.net/weather-in-history-1800-to-1849-ad/; https://premium.weatherweb.net/weather-in-history-1850-to-1899-ad/) show that there were some extreme weather conditions that severely affected crops, including snow in summer, with rain, wind, and severe cold for long periods. In particular, during 1834–8, there were notably severe winters and cold springs in north-east Scotland. John Dickie (Harper 2012, 15) writes of a very severe storm during the winter of 1837–8, which lasted for over two months. He recalls that he and his father had to clear snow off the whins (gorse/furze) and broom every day for over two months as the snow was lying too deep for their sheep to provide for themselves. In 1850, during an unseasonable cold-snap in mid-August, it was reported that there was snow on the Cairngorms nearly down to Braemar. The winter of 1852–3 in Scotland also was severe, particularly in February, with low temperatures and heavy snowfall, lasting well into March. The year 1867 rained all summer and by November the crops were still green and frozen producing small yields of an inferior grain. Conversely, the following year there was no rain from planting to harvest, making the straw very short and the ear of the corn under-developed (Allan 1983, 58). One wonders how the colonists managed to survive when the harvests were sparse and food short; a hard existence would have become even tougher.

Further research into weather patterns during the colonists' era might prove interesting in relation to the demise of the Colony. One fact we have noticed, since working at Shepherds Lodge, is that it is usually warmer there than a little further down the hill. The croft is on the south-east slope of Bennachie, thus sheltered to some extent by the hill itself and is open to the warmth of the sun. The vista from Shepherds Lodge is superb too, suggesting that this was no chance positioning for a home and may reflect part of the reasoning behind the choice of this location by the Littlejohns.

Plants and seeds

Because of their low maintenance needs, we chose fruit bushes that were popular at the time. During our research we discovered that the late 18th century saw the beginning of the gooseberry craze and by the mid-19th century there were over 170 clubs throughout the UK. The main competition was to see who could grow the heaviest gooseberry. Many new varieties were developed, and the craze even went to America. Unfortunately, some varieties grown in America and imported into the UK inadvertently contained the mildew disease and wiped out vast numbers of gooseberry bushes all over the UK. Some of the clubs never properly recovered owing to this disease and the early 20th century saw the popularity of the gooseberry fade. Today only a few gooseberry societies remain. There is still a bush surviving, seemingly from the 19th century, at one of the colony sites today, which supports our belief that gooseberries would have been grown. (The current world record for the heaviest gooseberry was set in 2013 at 64.49 g [2.27 oz]!) Blackcurrants were another fruit that was quite popular, and it has been said that it replaced the gooseberry in popularity because of its sharper taste. However, Bennachie today has vast quantities of blaeberries (bilberries) growing on its lower slopes, which may well have been the case in the 19th century and provided a further wild species. We did include some old varieties of blackcurrants in our kailyard but wonder if they would have bothered with these if they could pick bilberries so close to home. Raspberries were also planted and there were some wild canes still growing in the plot when we prepared it. We did, however, remove them in order to reduce the risk of compromising the genetics of the planted varieties. This prompted the question of whether the wild raspberries were growing prior to the colonists' time or whether they brought them onto Bennachie. Were the ones still growing at the kailyard ones left from the 19th century? There are a number of areas on Bennachie where raspberries can be found and are often close to where there was once habitation. Birds are also good distributors of raspberry seeds, so perhaps this question is unanswerable without more genetic research.

The Fruit Manual (Hogg 1884) assisted in providing us with types and varieties of fruit bushes available, as did suggestions from the James Hutton Institute, Dundee (see above). Searching records for the types and varieties of plants grown around the 19th century and wondering where we might find these varieties today, prompted questions as to where the colonists may have acquired their plants and seeds. There were seed merchants but how much could they afford to spend? The local tinker or markets may have been sources. Many of the colonists were employed by local estates for work on the land or in the house, so maybe there were surplus items here that might have come their way. Perhaps too, the odd cutting or seed found its way into their pockets! Some colonists were from local families, so there is a strong possibility they may have acquired items from them. Once their own kailyards were established, did they collect their own seed, passing on surplus to their neighbours, just as we do today? These questions will probably never be fully answered, and we can only assume that some or all of these methods were used. Our own acquisition of plants came from nurseries specialising in heritage varieties known to be available during the 19th century. A cutting taken from the old gooseberry bush still existing in one of the colony crofts is doing well. We have not yet discovered the variety, but the fruit is very tasty!

Garden pests and viruses

How did the colonists cope with pests and viruses, and what methods would have been used? We did not have long to find out! One of our first problems in the kailyard was the arrival of sawfly, the grubs of which soon started munching their way through the tender young leaves of the gooseberries and stripping them bare. We discovered one of the best methods, and one still used today, is to pick the grubs off and dispose of them, clean out the soil around the stem of the bush and replace with fresh soil. Keep a check for any new grubs appearing and remove immediately. This did the trick for us, and we have not seen any more in the last six years! It was often the female or older members of the household who took care of the kailyard, so one might imagine that the children were probably employed to collect the grubs. Maybe the colonists would have used this method for slugs, snails, or any other unwanted bugs as well. Chemicals (now banned today) were available during the period of the Colony, but were possibly too expensive for the crofters who no doubt had other methods of their own.

Produce from the kailyard

Following the November planting and despite a hard winter and dry spring in 2018, the plants were doing well in their first year and even produced a handful of fruit (see Plate 11.3). Over the years the amounts of produce from the Kailyard have varied depending on conditions and circumstances during any particular year. While a good harvest is always preferred, our main objective was to grow food in the same manner as the colonists and try to recapture their experiences. When harvesting time came around, how might they have used some of the fruit? The typical diet of a 19th-century crofter/farmworker in Aberdeenshire was very plain and consisted predominantly of oats and kale (Beaton 1915; Cameron 1980, 132–3). But, presumably, when the summer fruits were available, these would have been used to their best advantage, perhaps even throwing a handful into their porridge or brose! The colonists cooked on an open fire so their range of meals would have been limited. However, some of our volunteers looked-out old recipes and tried such things as: fruit vinegars, rhubarb and sweet cicely (young shoots picked from the hedgerows), cranachan and jams. Today cranachan is still a popular pudding and one that can be traced back to Scottish country folk. It is quite possible that this was made by the colonists, who would have had all the necessary ingredients on hand to make it, *e.g.* oats, cream, honey, raspberries, and even whisky. In the book *Bennachie* (McConnochie, 1890, 98), reference is made to the 'Malt Barn', which was used in connection with illicit 'whisky running'. Initially, we thought making jam may have been too expensive for them but, having researched the sugar trade of the 19th century, we found that sugar would have been quite affordable. It was said that by the 19th century, rather than only gracing the tables of monarchs and aristocrats, sugar was on almost every table in Britain and would have been stirred into pretty much every servant's cup of tea. Social historian, John Burnett, put annual consumption in 1801 at 13.87 kg (30.6 lb) per person, although this did fluctuate throughout the century, and went as low as 6.94 kg (15.3 lb) per person in 1840, before increasing again.

Health

This kailyard experiment has disclosed issues we had not previously considered, such as the effects of ill-health. Although illness was a feature of rural life, it was not such a major problem as in the cities, presumably owing to cleaner air and less population density. Child mortality was higher than today, and records report several such cases experienced by the colonists (Fagen 2011, 66–67). Doctors were far too expensive to be called unless in an emergency and no doubt some of the colonists would have been capable of providing a certain amount of remedial help. Herbs and berries from their gardens or the countryside would have made up their medicine chests, probably using recipes passed down from their ancestors to make suitable treatments. As an experiment, an old recipe for sore throats and colds was made with some of the blackcurrants from the kailyard. Its effectiveness remains unproven as no infections among the volunteers were being suffered at the time, but blackcurrants are known for their medicinal properties for soothing sore throats. Unfortunately, no specific herbs were discovered at Shepherds Lodge despite conducting a botanical survey before cultivating the kailyard, but there would have been a viable choice of wild plants growing locally and suitable for such purposes.

Landscape

When the colonists first arrived on Bennachie, the landscape would have been covered with stones, broom, gorse, and other herbage. Over the years the colonists built cottages, made gardens and reclaimed some of the land, turning it into cultivated fields. By the end of the 19th century only one family remained on Bennachie, most having departed by 1880 either by force or choice. The landscape then would have shown a small, abandoned settlement where around nine families once lived, with some of the homes razed to the ground. In the early 20th century Alex Mitchell (1911, 80–81), once a resident of the Colony, came back to visit. How the landscape then looked is best described in his own words:

> I now went by Ben[n]achie to see the old homes, or rather the place where they had been, for the houses had all been done away with and a well-grown plantation had taken their place. It was difficult to find the exact spot where the houses had stood. The pine trees had spread their branches across the path that led to the old well. The staid step of old age or the prattle of youth have no more messages along that path, it is obliterated from the knowledge of future generations.

If only Alex Mitchell could have seen into the future, hopefully, he would have been pleasantly gratified at the interest these 'old homes' now have for people today. The Bennachie Colony is well remembered and recorded for future generations both locally and around the world. I'm sure he would have been delighted to know that during 2024 relatives from the USA came to visit Shepherds Lodge to see where Alexander Littlejohn, their ancestor, had once lived. Changes in the landscape continue. The plantation conifers that once cloaked the moss-covered stones of Shepherds Lodge, with its kailyard and field, have been felled. The kailyard plot and the remains of Shepherds Lodge are open to the public and to the sky (Plate 11.4).

Conclusion

There is still more to be discovered from this experiment, so we are continuing to maintain the kailyard and try different crops, such as kale. Young plants were added earlier this year (2024) and were doing well, but unfortunately a deer managed to jump the fence and had itself a meal! Luckily, the plants were unharmed, so we added some protection, and they are now growing well again. Areas of research for further investigation could include weather patterns and the effects on the harvests, methods of treating garden pests and viruses, preparation of food and recipes, ill health and herbal remedies. Also, a comparative study of kailyards throughout Scotland would be of value.

Acknowledgments

The kailyard reconstruction could not have happened without the help and support from so many volunteers over the last seven years. Their hard work and enthusiasm in whatever field of assistance given has been constant and very much appreciated in making this project a success and giving us a better understanding of the colonists' lives. Volunteers have come from numerous organisations and areas of Aberdeenshire and beyond, including members of the Bailies of Bennachie, Bennachie Landscapes Project, Aberdeen University, Oyne School and the local community. Thanks also to Forestry and Land Scotland for allowing us to proceed with the project on Bennachie, and the Heritage Lottery Fund in providing the initial funds to start the project. Special thanks to Jo Vergunst and Colin H. Miller for reviewing this report and for their valuable advice and suggestions.

Bibliography

Allan, J. (1983) Agriculture in Aberdeenshire in the Eighteen-Sixties. In Gordon, D. (ed.) *Bennachie Again*, 58. Chapel of Garioch, The Bailies of Bennachie.

Beaton, H. (1915) *At the Back of Bennachie/Life in the Garioch in the Nineteenth Century*. Aberdeen, Central Press.

Cameron, D.K. (1980) *Willie Gavin, Crofter Man*. London, Victor Gollancz Ltd.

Fagen, J. (2011) *The Bennachie Colony Project: Examining the Lives and Impact of the Bennachie Colonists*. Chapel of Garioch, The Bailies of Bennachie, Bennachie Landscapes Series 1.

Foster, B. (2019) Shepherds Lodge Kailyard: Pre-Planting Excavation. In Shepherd, C. (ed.) *Bennachie and the Garioch: Society and Ecology in the History of North-east Scotland*, 47–52. Chapel of Garioch, The Bailies of Bennachie, Bennachie Landscapes Series 4.

Foster, C. (2019) Recreating a 19th-century Kailyard. In Shepherd, C. (ed.) *Bennachie and the Garioch: Society and Ecology in the History of North-east Scotland*, 53–64. Chapel of Garioch, The Bailies of Bennachie, Bennachie Landscapes Series 4.

Harper, M. (ed.) (2012) *Footloose in Farm Service: Autobiographical Recollections of John Dickie*. Aberdeen, Research Institute of Irish and Scottish Studies.

Hogg, R. (1884) *The Fruit Manual: Guide to the Fruits and Fruit Trees of Great Britain*. London, Journal of Horticulture Office.

McConnochie, A.I. (1890) *Bennachie*. Aberdeen, D. Wyllie & Son.

Mitchell, A. (1911) The Recollections of a Lifetime. Unknown publishing details.

Oliver, J., Armstrong, J., Milek, K., Schofield, J.E., Vergunst, J., Brochard, T., Gould, A. and Noble, G. (2016) The Bennachie Colony: a nineteenth-century informal community in northeast Scotland. In *International Journal of Historical Archaeology* 20(2), 341–77.

Taylor, S. (2015) Pottery Finds from the Colony Site: Some Initial Observations. In Shepherd, C. (ed.) *Bennachie and the Garioch: Society and Ecology in the History of North-east Scotland*, 105. Chapel of Garioch, The Bailies of Bennachie, Bennachie Landscapes Series 3.

Website

https://premium.weatherweb.net/weather-in-history-1800-to-1849-ad/; https://premium.weatherweb.net/weather-in-history-1850-to-1899-ad/

Chapter 12

'Colonising the margins': excavation and environmental analysis within a late medieval settlement area on the Pittodrie estate

Colin Shepherd and Iain Ralston, with contributions from Jackaline Robertson, J. Edward Schofield, and Tim Kinnaird

Introduction

According to the national Historic Land-use Assessment (www.hlamap.org.uk) of the area, the part of the Pittodrie Estate forming the present study area comprises a modern (19th-/20th-century) conifer plantation and an area of managed woodland of 17th or 18th century date, neither containing any historical sites. In fact, the modern 19th-/20th-century conifer woodland was planted in the 18th century and the managed 17th-/18th-century woodland not until the early 19th century. Within this woodland are upstanding remains of rig and furrow, house platforms, a large rectilinear enclosure cut by a hollow-way and various other lumps and bumps that included, when excavated, two late medieval grain-drying kilns. The modern conifer woodland contains the upstanding remains of a 17th-century 'hospital' – the 'Bede House' – with garden/enclosure that stands on a former major routeway linking powerful political centres of the region. Plate 12.1 shows the castle of Pittodrie surrounded by its 19th- and 20th-century landscaped grounds. The view is taken from the edge of the study area.

The sites (plural) at Pittodrie tell the story of low-status rural life through the medieval period. The 'authorised heritage discourse' (Smith 2006) for this period in Scotland is populated by castles and kings – the mass of the population sidelined as invisible puppets doing the bidding of their betters. Such folk are brought out of hiding in the 19th-century discourse and provide an idealised tapestry of hard-working 'sons of the soil' filling their leisure time with bothy ballads and whisky, all overseen by the paternalistic guardianship of the local 'improving' laird. In reality, little is known about the development of rural settlement, domestic architecture and social relations of the period between the end of the Pictish period and the beginning of the early modern one. We know far more about how Bronze Age people lived in the north-east than we do about 15th-century farmers. Not one 15th-century rural dwelling has so far been recognised. Before we can learn about that period, these sites have to be discovered.

As part of an ongoing collaboration between the University of Aberdeen and local community participants, members of the Bailies of Bennachie and the Bennachie Landscapes Project Group began studying the remains of what has been known locally, since the 19th century, as the Bede House. Described in more detail below, these investigations attempted to unravel some of the inconsistencies inherent in local traditions concerning this 17th-century hospital. However, prior to these investigations, members of the group had noted various other earthwork remains in the vicinity. These were compounded with further upstanding remains discovered through studying a LiDAR survey jointly commissioned by the University of Aberdeen, Aberdeenshire Council, and Forestry Commission Scotland (now Forestry and Land Scotland) in order to shed light on the landscape immediately surrounding the Pictish fort on Mither Tap. After a successful excavation of the Bede House in 2018 the focus of the group's studies moved downslope to these other anomalies. The archaeological excavations at the Bede House have been published by the Bailies (Ralston and Shepherd 2019). This, along with four interim reports covering the subsequent four years of archaeological work on the extended landscape can be accessed via the Bailies website (https://www.bailiesofbennachie.co.uk/).

The purpose of this paper is to assess the results to date and to place them in their wider regional and national settings by making use of palaeo-environmental evidence and dating carried out by Optically Stimulated Luminescence (OSL). These areas of landscape that exist outwith the 'authorised heritage discourse' are frequently ignored academically, fall outside development areas that become the subject of developer-funded projects, and are badly misunderstood by simplistic Historic Land-use Assessments.

An interesting corollary to the historic landscape considerations at Pittodrie is a positive social loop that is seeing an area of former commonty re-invigorated by community access and ecological management. The new owners and managers of the woodland in which the Bede House is situated (Foresight Group and RTS Forestry) are engaging with the Bailies to jointly plant and manage an area of broadleaf woodland in accordance with the palaeo-environmental evidence discovered on the site and using historically derived management strategies. The historical nature of the site has thus provided an impetus to re-imagine community participation in helping to create an enhanced biodiversity in keeping with the environmental history of the site. The strategy re-introduces the historic notion that community members can work with landowners to manage land for mutual benefit, in keeping with historic commons/commonty management traditions (Ostrom 1990).

Historical background

The study area (Figure 12.1) forms part of the historic estate of Pittodrie, formerly the western part of the larger estate of Balhagertie. The site sits on the eastern slopes of Bennachie overlooked by the Pictish fort on Mither Tap (Noble and Evans

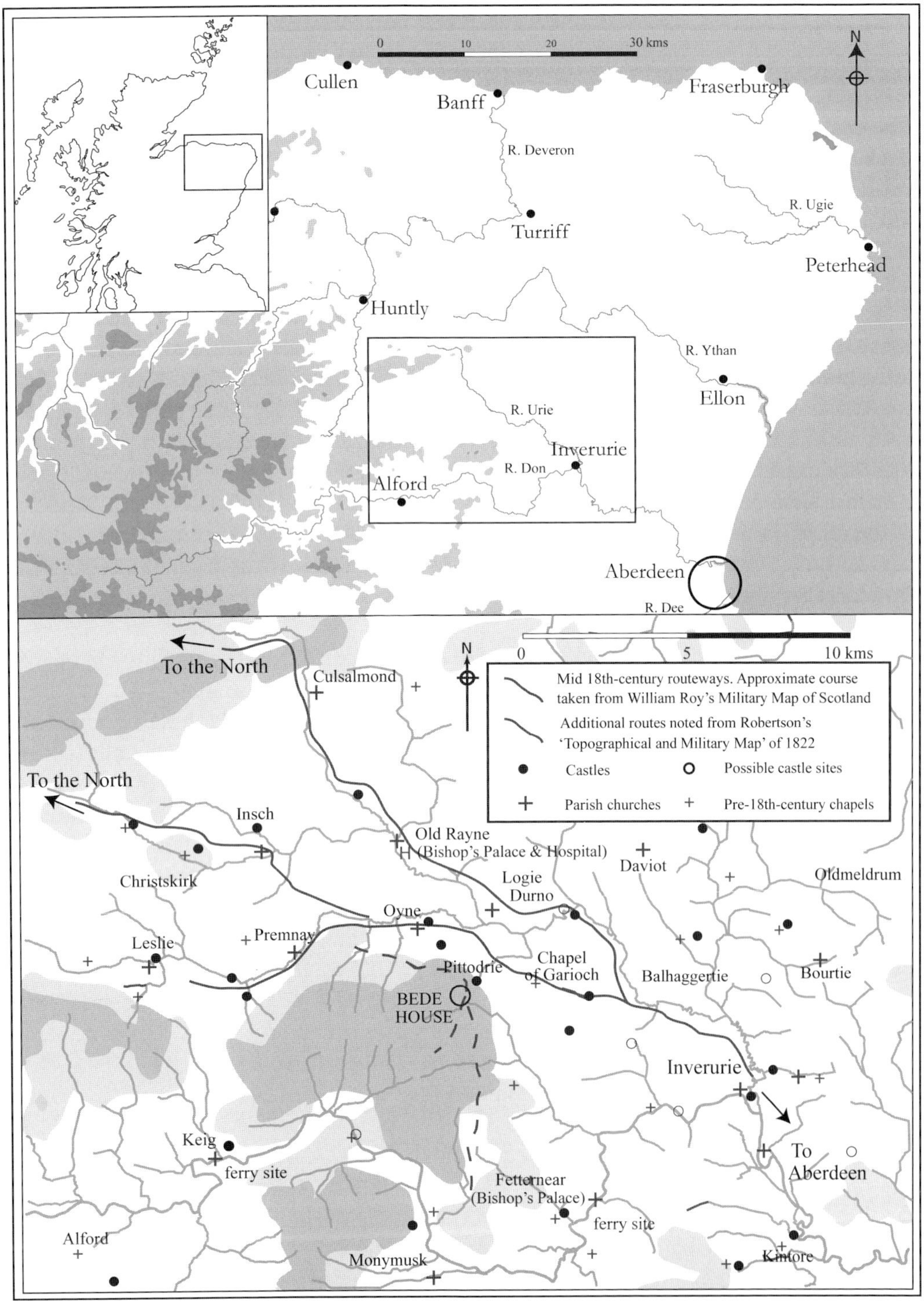

Figure 12.1. Site location. Upper plan shows simplified topography in tone. Lower map shows land considered suitable for only pasture and upland grazing shaded. This data derives from the Land Capability for Agriculture assessment (Data courtesy, Soil Survey of Scotland Staff, 2016 and the James Hutton Institute).

2022, 106–7) and close to another smaller Pictish fort, Maiden Castle (Cook 2011) to the north. South of the site is a series of roundhouses, also lying within woodland on the former commonty. Numerous charters grant rights of common access to the resources on the hill – rights of servitude – to resources such as peat, turf, grazing, and stone (see below). Bennachie was a 'Commonty' – owned by the surrounding estates, utilised by the tenants of those estates, but undivided. Some resources, such as certain peat mosses were, by tradition, considered to be reserved to specific estates.

These lands had formed part of the Barony of Balhagertie. Since at least 1355x7 this barony was held by the Erskines (AB Coll, 537–8) and included, at that time, Balhagertie, Inveramsay, Pitscurry, Pitbie, Pittodrie (Pettochery), and Newlands. The last indicates how old some 'new lands' can be. This portfolio creates a useful corridor from east of the River Urie, where it joins the Durno Burn, westwards up through Pittodrie onto Bennachie. Much earlier, sometime between 1185 and 1219, Earl David of Huntingdon (King William the Lion's brother) granted a 'davach' of the lands of Resthivet to David de Audri. This grant included the right to pasture his beasts either side of the Urie so far as they could return by nightfall (Stringer 1985, 223–4). This davach of land appears to form the central water-side holdings of the later Barony of Balhagertie.

A further grant by the Earl to Simon and Robert of Billingham, each of one ploughgate of Durnachechell may well relate to Drumdurno as David Audri's land was said to have run up against Robert's. (*ibid.*, 223–5). This place-name crops up again in a register of crown lands of 1463 and is there spelled 'Dornoschelis' (*RSRS*, 7, 161). This compound name appears to represent the 'shiels of Durno' though, by the time of the document it was clearly productive farmland, rather than upland pasture as indicated by the shieling name. Logie Durno was the parish core and still sits surrounded by a number of 'Durno' place-names on the north side of the Urie. It seems likely that Drumdurno/Durnoshiels was upland pasture associated with the core settlement zone, possibly supplying seasonal summer pasture or, at least, pasture 'outsets' where cows and sheep were milked (Winchester 2000, 90–93). Harold Fox has noted how many former shieling sites incorporate place-names associated with the young women usually tasked with minding the sheep and cattle and producing the butter and cheese to be taken down to the 'wintertown' (Fox 2012, 155–6). The 'maiden' place-names in the area – Maiden Castle, Maiden Stone – would not look out of place in this pastoral setting.

Rights of commonty were enshrined in the Erskines' mid-14th-century charter: '*et cum communi pastura in foresta de Benechkey, et in siluis de Aldeclochy*' ('and communal pasture in the forest of Bennachie and in the woods of the Clochy burn'). 'Auld' is a frequent mis-rendering of gaelic 'allt' stream. This charter usefully links the Clochy to the barony and, in a later charter of 1550 (*RMS*, 4, 434), Dorlethen – an adjoining farm – is noted as forming one of the farming units. In 1613 it was said to have been a 'manerie' (a 'manor') (*RMS*, 7, 863). A witness statement from an old indweller of Dorlethen taken during a spat over common rights between the Leslies and Erskines on one part and the Earl of Aberdeen on the other in the mid-18th century noted how their cattle had been taken up the Clochy Burn to pasture 'from time out of mind' (GD33/16). Clearly, local memory was not mistaken.

A document of 1572 (*RMS*, 4, 2072), signed and witnessed at Pittodrie, shows the castle's developing local importance and, in 1603, it was noted as the principal house of the estate – '*principale messuagium de Petathorie*' (*RMS*, 6, 1396). It's not presently known how long the woods lasted in 'Old Clochy', but they were still being noted in a charter of 1618 (*RMS*, 7, 1778), only 18 years before the first document directly recording the study area.

This earliest historical reference to the specific piece of landscape under study is a rental of 1636 (MS3043/70) and it lists a series of small farmsteads lying in and around the study area. A small group of holdings appears to run down the west side of the estate, starting with Firboggs in the north and progressing through 'Craig Wall', 'The Miln Croft', 'The ? ... Mound croft', 'The Wobsters (webster/weaver) croft', and ending with 'Dorlethen'. One of the names is now only partly legible in the 400-year-old and badly creased document. 'Craigwell' survived into the late 19th century and its well supplies the burn that runs adjacent to the large enclosure being excavated. 'Miln croft' suggests a mill somewhere in the vicinity, though there is no mention of such a mill in the rental, making it likely that it had fallen out of use by that time. 'The ? ... Mound croft' has been tentatively suggested as relating to the mound on which the kilns were found. The whereabouts of the 'wobsters croft' cannot be guessed, but a weaver's house on the skirts of upland pasture is to be expected. One of the crofts may relate to the longhouse discovered by the Linn Burn and it may be suggested that these small farming units had been responsible for the construction and use of the kilns on the mound. It should be noted that the Linn Burn is known as the Rushmill Burn above the Fog House – a 19th-century 'folly' – perhaps suggesting the former mill to have lain higher up the hillside.

Craigwell and the miln croft each paid 20 marks in rent – approximately £14. Wobsters croft paid £4.6s and 'The ? ... Mound croft' paid only 5 marks – about £3 – and was the least valuable. In fact, it paid the least rent across the entire rental, with the Wobsters croft second to last.

A later rental of 1771 (MS2392) suggests a wider area of settlement stretching south from this possible nucleus. After Craigwell the list contains Doubstown, Rush Miln croft, Saughen Waird croft, Wairdside croft, Guttertown, Craignathunder, Clubb, Muirtown, before reaching Dorlethen. Other parcels of land (five pieces) are just called 'Braeside' and it is not certain whether they held dwellings or were simply plots of land rented to nearby farmers. The latter seems most likely. With reference to the 1st edition OS (1867), we can see that Muirtown and Guttertown lay south of the study area. Also in this area are Hill croft and Braeside along with one small unnamed building in the plot north of Muirtown. Craignathunder might arguably be Hill croft – both named after the peak of Craignathunder. Clubb may also fit into this area, whether or not it had any relation to the un-named building. This does,

Table 12.1. Crofts along the braeside as described in estate rentals and shown on the 1st edition OS.

1636	*1771*	*1868 (north to south)*
Craigwell	Craigwell	Craigwell
	Doubstown	
The Miln croft	Rush Miln croft	
	Saughen Waird croft	
The ? ... Mound croft		
	Wairdside croft	
The Wobsters croft		
	Guttertown	Muirtown
	Craignathunder	Guttertown
	Clubb	Hill croft
	Muirtown	Braeside
Dorlethen	Dorlethen	Dorlethen

however, rest on the assumption, supported by the OS map, that the 1771 record progresses south from Craigwell.

That leaves Doubstown, Rush Miln croft, Saughen Waird croft and Wairdside croft to place. It is known that the enclosure under study was still in use in the early 19th century and may well have been the 'waird' ('ward') referred to. The use of 'ward' to denote a specialised enclosure is well known from estate plans across the north-east. Most frequently it is found in an associative form, such as 'Horse Ward'. 'Saughen' suggests the enclosure had been associated with willow trees at some point. A Miln croft, of course, is known from the 1636 rental and, arguably, might be seen to reflect the 1771 Rush Miln croft. One of the crofts may well be the Wobsters croft from 1636, suggesting that the enclosure dyke may have been breached prior to that. The excavations, discussed below, show the large enclosure to have been cut through on its northern side for the insertion of a cottage. Table 12.1 shows the named crofts from the various records.

The study area was quite capable of supporting the number of missing crofts from the list. Moreover, the 'waird' name may suggest the large enclosure being studied and, as will be seen below, there are two probable dwelling sites directly associated with the enclosure. If they are the 'Waird' crofts, only two recorded crofts remain unlocated: Rush mill croft and Doubstown. The longhouse beside the Linn Burn/Rushmill burn may be either, though there must be a strong suspicion that it is the Rush mill croft. Doubstown had the largest arable allocation of any of these crofts – 16 acres – and little pasture compared to many. This may indicate that it lay further down the hillside than some of the other crofts. At the moment, that is about as far as the documentary evidence can be pushed.

Sandwiched between these historical agricultural references is an Act of Parliament (*RPS* 1641) granting leave to build a 'hospital' within the grounds. This 1641 Act ratified the use of former revenues for the use of the 'Hospital of the Barony of Balhalgardy' (Miller 2019). This hospital, though it now sits all alone on the shoulder of Bennachie, would have been bordering a flourishing agricultural landscape and lay on the uphill side of a regionally important routeway.

The historical sources, therefore, suggest that in the 12th century, some of the Pittodrie lands were still used as open grazing. The place-name evidence suggests that, at some time, they had been shieling sites. David de Audri was able to lead his beasts as far as he liked on both sides of the Urie so long as they didn't over-night there. Two hours walking would easily have moved his cattle up to Drumdurno at first light and returned them as it was growing dark (personal experience, Penny Shepherd, who used to herd cattle that distance as a girl). By 1355, however, at least parts of Drumdurno were under the plough and by 1550 at the latest, Pittodrie, Newlands, and Dorlethen were functioning farming units, Dorlethen being described as a manor by 1613.

These changes in settlement pattern around this portion of the Commonty of Bennachie drive home the impression that the bounds of the Commonty ebbed and flowed up and down the hillside in tune with changing social, economic, and climatic forces. In effect, commonty lands started where rentable lands finished. In terms of the local infield/outfield husbandry – or 'convertible husbandry' as outlined for other parts of Britain by Rippon (2014, 130–6) – where the outfields were brought in and out of use, the boundary was never fixed. Compounding this with fluctuations in climate, population, agrarian practices etc., any permanence of boundary is impossible to conceive. This said, it is clear that the lands of Pittodrie along the line of the Commonty had become permanently fixed by about the mid-18th century at the latest and, in the area of the Bede House, by the mid-17th century.[1] The 1771 rental (MS2392) records the estate's plantations along the western edge of the estate and these seem to be shown on Taylor and Skinner's 1776 survey. At least one of these is depicted on William Roy's Military Map of the 1740s. The excavations considered here push the period of use of this small area of landscape much further back in time.

Site location, geography, and geology: the site in its regional setting

Figure 12.1 shows the study area in its regional setting. The lower map also shows castle sites and the few 18th-century routeways that are known. It can be assumed that the late medieval political centres and these routeways are not accidentally associated. The shading indicates a schematised view of the 'upland' zone that, with respect to modern agricultural perceptions, reflects poorer lands. This does not mean they were so-considered in other periods. Clearly, within this area are small pockets of high-quality arable land, though unsuited to the scale of modern production. Also, it should be remembered that in medieval times, meadow land was often considered more valuable than arable land and was still well protected by baronial courts in the area in the 17th century (*cf.* SHS, 1919). (In England, during the 14th century, when the best arable was valued at 2/6d per acre, meadowland was worth 3/- per acre [Bailey 2002, 71].)

Geologically the Bede House sits on the edge of the igneous granitic intrusion of 'Bennachie Pluton' (BGS, British Geological Survey, https://geologyviewer.bgs.ac.uk). The kilns and enclosure sit on a metamorphic bedrock of the Aberdeen Formation. These are overlain by a glacial till – the Banchory Till Formation – and superficial deposits of peat up the Rushmill Burn (*ibid.*). Overlaying these are localised mixes of peaty podsols, gleys and brown earths with even some aluvium lower down along the Linn Burn. It is worth noting that the three medieval manors in the immediate area – Pittodrie, Dorlethen, and Whitecross – all appear to be centred on patches of Brown Earths. The enclosure also sits on the edge of these same Brown Earths (Scotland's Soils, https://soils.environment.gov.scot).

The Pittodrie Estate excavations: 2018–2023

What follows is a brief review of the archaeology discovered through excavation and a limited amount of palaeo-environmental research. It is hoped that this research into the site will be expanded in the future. Figure 12.2 shows the site plans overlaying the LiDAR survey referred to above. Although no excavations have yet taken place there, the longhouse site has also been included in order to demonstrate the extent of the archaeology in this small area of relict landscape.

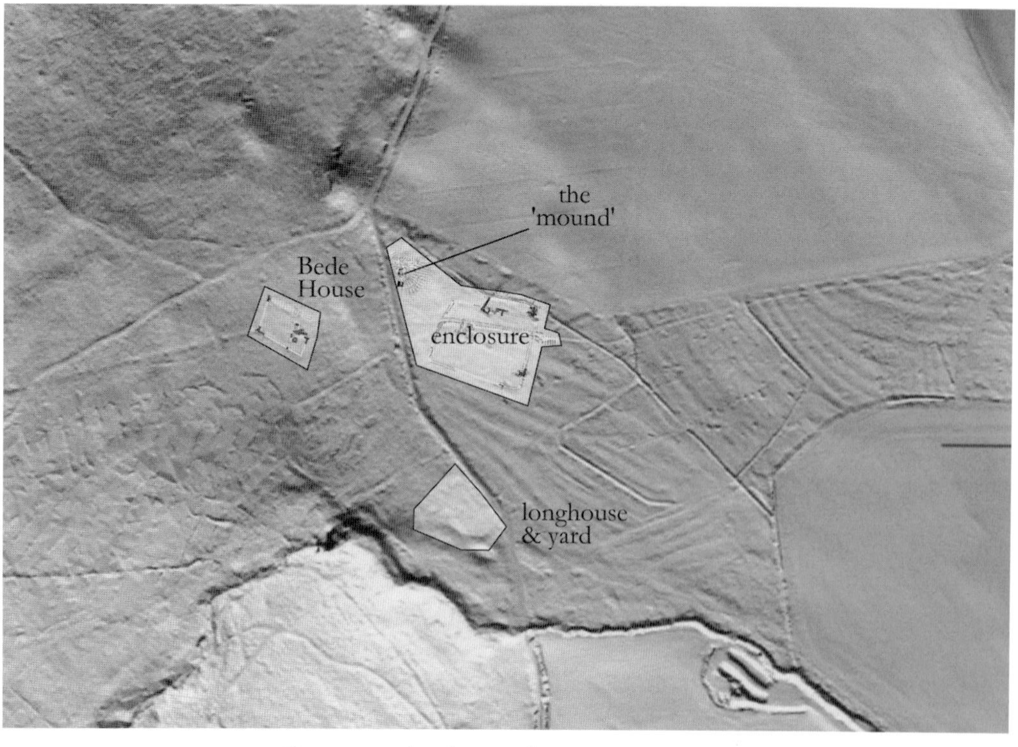

Figure 12.2. Site plan overlaying LiDAR image.

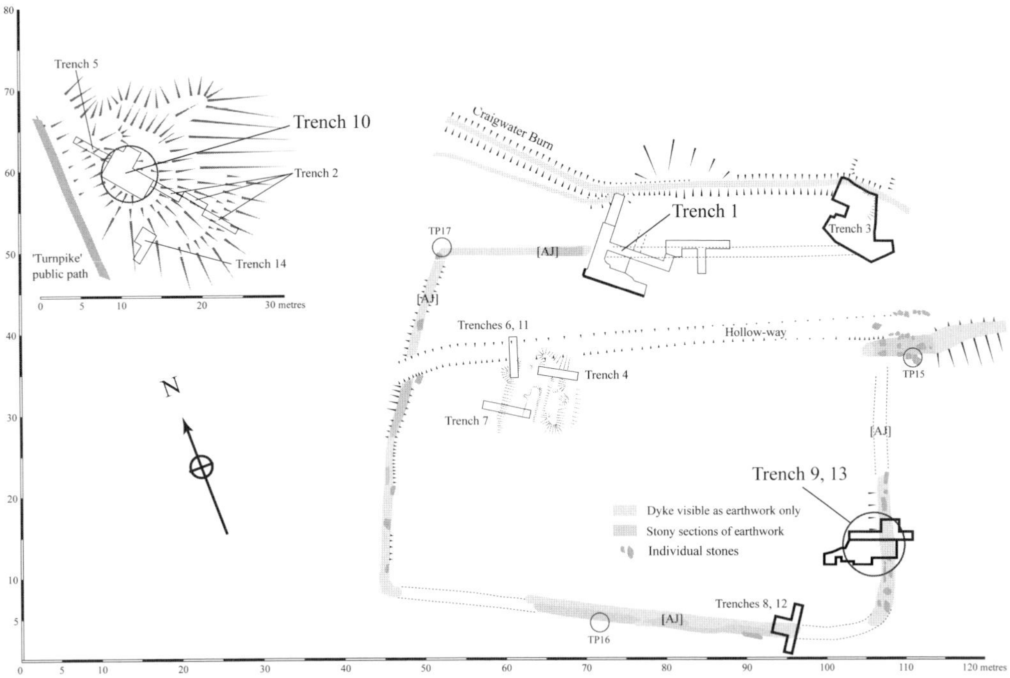

Figure 12.3. Plan of trenches.

Figure 12.3 shows the trenches as described in this account. The following description will concentrate on Trenches 1, 9/13, and 10, though not in that order. It can be seen that many other trenches have been dug and these have been described in the various interim reports (Bailies, nd; BLP, nd) The Bede House will also be considered, though this forms a separate site within the study area (see Figure 12.2). This account of the excavations will progress chronologically through the site, demonstrating the deep temporal nature of the remains within this very limited piece of landscape.

Neolithic/Bronze Age

The evidence for possible pre-Iron Age archaeology comes primarily from a single sherd of unstratified late Neolithic/early Bronze Age pottery, discovered on the side of a mound, adjacent to the 'Turnpike' routeway, during the initial trial trenching carried out in 2019. Further evidence appears to take the form of a large stone, also initially recorded in 2019 that, when fully investigated in 2023, appeared to have been set within a socket and to have been associated with a deep deposit of clean, orange sand (791). The orthostat, therefore, is considered to have stood upright. The use of such a clean 'bright' deposit in association with a late neolithic ceremonial site has also been noted by one of the authors (CS) at an unpublished site near Huntly (Aberdeenshire SMR ref NJ54SW0054).

This sand (791) had been cut into by the later kilns, which may suggest no intervening period of use. However, it was recorded as overlying as well as surrounding

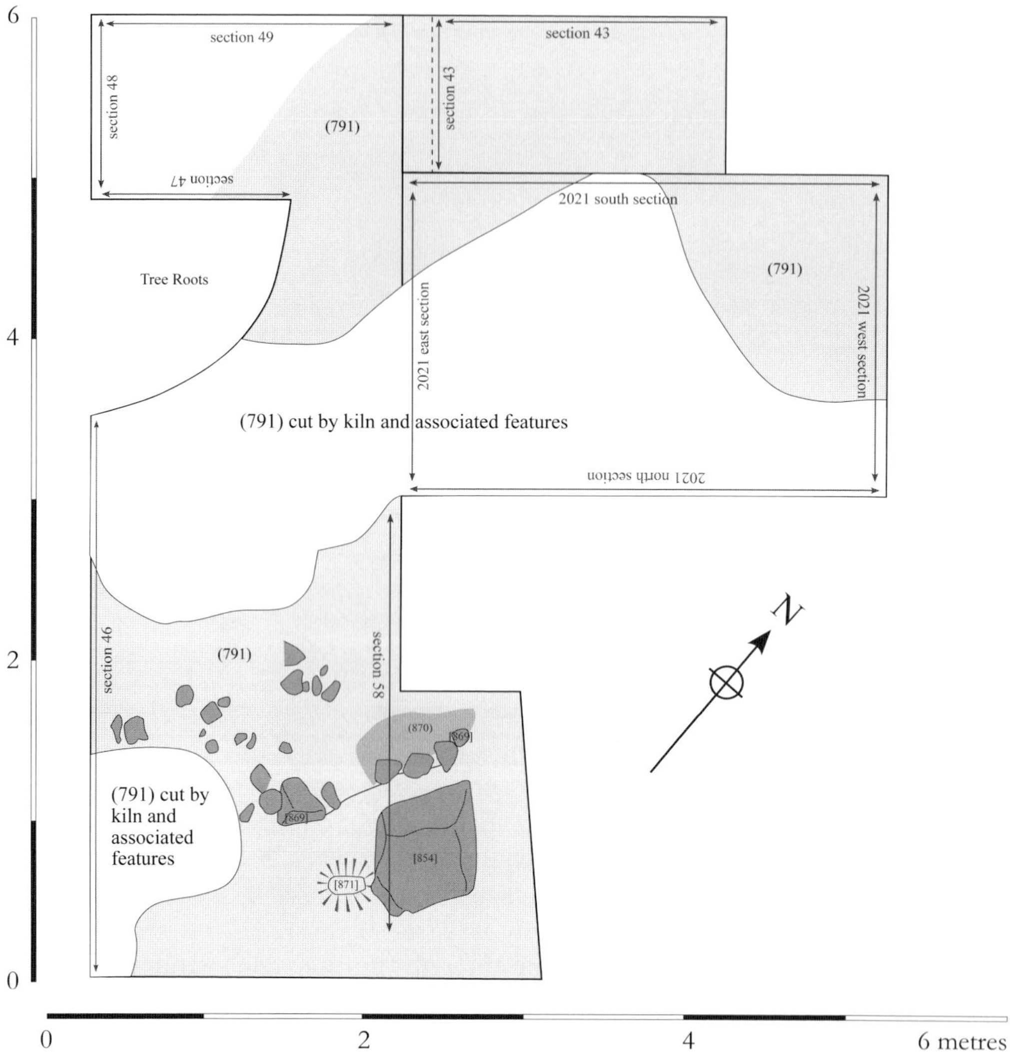

Figure 12.4. Trench 10 plan showing extent of the bright orange sand (791).

the stone, which may indicate a possible scattering of that sand after the stone was laid flat. Tim Kinnaird's optically stimulated luminescence dating (OSL) of context (791) gives a very wide window of 630 BC±1270 years. Sadly, this cannot at present be refined but, if the orthostat were contemporary with the early prehistoric sherd, the site may have been slighted at a later period.

A further possible prehistoric artefact may be the surviving half of an incised stone found in association with the flue of the later kiln (Figure 12.5). Though the engraving could have been made at any time up to the destruction of the kiln, there are certain similarities between this stone and a series of 'sun-stones' or 'spider stones' found

Figure 12.5. The possible 'sun-stone' found in Trench 10.

in Denmark, particularly on the island of Bornholm (Starr 2017). The 'spider' name refers to the web-like design found on many of them. However, no such stones have yet been recognised in Britain so any similarity may be simple coincidence.

Iron Age

Iron Age activity has been demonstrated by radiocarbon dating[2] and dating by OSL. A small piece of alder charcoal was discovered beneath the stones of a mangled feature [AS] in Trench 9/13 (Plate 12.2). The charcoal was radiocarbon-dated and most likely belongs to the period between 550 cal BC and 400 cal BC, though there is also a possibility that it could be earlier, between 750 cal BC and 650 cal BC (SUERC-101066 – GU59115). A bit further south and, perhaps, slightly higher in the stratigraphy, though still within the same context (805), an OSL sample returned a date of AD 130±330. The two pieces of dating combine to suggest activity in the vicinity in the earlier and middle Iron Age periods and possibly associated with feature [AS]. However, this might equally be later and associated with succeeding 11th-century dates from the site.

Early and later medieval

OSL has provided data for estimating the age of the enclosure and for some internal features. Of particular interest was Test Pit 16 (see Figure 12.3 for position) that

Figure 12.6. Trench 9 plan showing position of features, including linear stone feature [AS].

returned a date of AD 1380±100 years for the soil immediately underlying the dyke [AJ] (see Figure 12.7). This gives a date after which the enclosure was constructed. As the sample came from near to the pre-dyke surface, it might be suggested that the enclosure was built shortly after this date. However, the ± 100 years OSL calibration margin does present a very wide window for its construction.

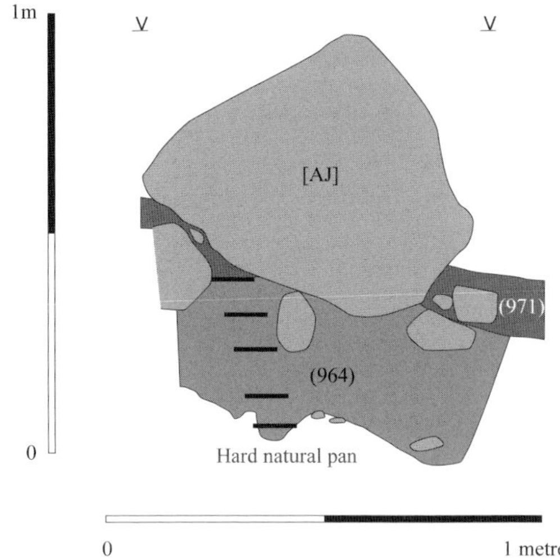

Figure 12.7. Section 52 showing the OSL sample points below the enclosure dyke [AJ].

A further date – AD 1090±50 years – was returned from near the base of context (792) in Trench 9/13 (see Figure 12.8). This soil appears to have built up after the construction of the stone feature [AS] and the OSL date may, therefore, indicate the initial phases of this accumulation. A piece of hazel charcoal, carbon-dated between cal AD 900 and cal AD 1020 (SUERC-91076 – GU53454R), also suggests activity in the area during the 10th/11th century. Sadly, the charcoal appears to have somehow been re-deposited on top of the mound and its context post-dates the construction of the kilns. It does still, however, support the notion of activity around the enclosure at that time.

It would appear that limited Iron Age activity (as evidenced by the alder charcoal (550 × 400 cal BC) and the OSL date (AD 130±330) deriving from shallow context (805) in trench 9/13), may have been succeeded by a long period of inactivity before a renewal of interest in this part of the site during the 10th/11th centuries. However, this apparent absence of evidence does not mean that evidence does not exist – only that we may not yet have found it.

The substantial build-up of soil behind feature [AS] that accumulated on top of (805) suggests a subsequent long period of use and probable ground enhancement in which context (792) was deposited. The preceding soil layer (805) is quite thin and the much greater depth of (792) suggests that the ground was being improved by bringing new 'feal and divots' to the site. This practice was still commonly carried out into the 17th and 18th centuries, though it drew frequent and vociferous condemnation from Lord Forbes who forbade his tenants to carry out such digging in the lanes and meadows of his lands (*cf.* SHS 1919).

The purpose of [AS] is unclear. The build-up of soil behind it suggests it is more likely to have been a linear feature than a building, though this must remain a possibility. Whether it lasted long enough to be re-designed into a component of the larger enclosure that still survives and may be, speculatively, dated to the earlier 15th century is one possibility. However, this is not supported by the sherds of Scottish redware found in context [780] that appears to have post-dated the feature

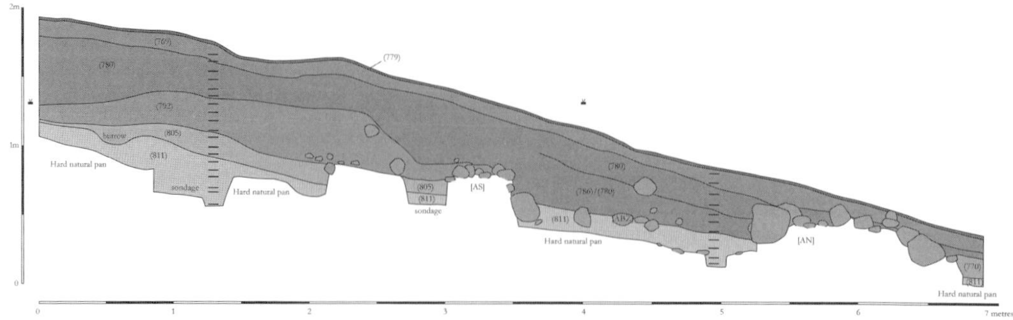

Figure 12.8. Section 56 showing OSL sample points as short horizontal lines and soil contexts in relation to feature [AS] and enclosure dyke [AN].

Figure 12.9. Possible plough-marks east of enclosure.

[AS]. Such pottery is sadly not very age-sensitive and can date anywhere from the 13th to the 15th centuries (Hall 1996, 126–7). At the moment, it may be suggested that the deep accumulation (792) occurred after *c.* 1090 but prior to the use of the redware pottery on the site, be that anywhere between the 12th and 15th centuries. In other words, it may be indicative of small-scale agricultural expansion onto higher lands during the medieval warm spell – the so-called 'Medieval Climate Anomaly' (*cf.* Oram 2021).

It can be seen from the LiDAR image that rig and furrow ploughing respects the enclosure and appears to be aligned parallel with it. At the extreme east end of the 2021 excavation of Trench 9/13 parallel marks were found in the subsoil that may represent gouges made by a plough/ard (see Figure 12.9). However, these appear to run at ninety degrees to the later rigs shown on the LiDAR image, but parallel to the east side of the enclosure.

At this point the documentary evidence should be recalled. It suggests that the area was unlikely to have been active arably on a large scale until the 1500s at the earliest. If the large enclosure predates that, as suggested by the OSL, it may be more likely to have had a pastoral function, perhaps later becoming used by the small farmsteads for growing crops. However, this does not explain its 10th/11th-century use, or the soil build-up – 'lynchet' – behind [AS] suggesting earlier arable use, though perhaps of only limited extent. This is a fairly mysterious period in the north-east countryside both historically and archaeologically and the accompanying settlement pattern is evasive. Fortuitously, this site does hold out the exciting prospect of discovering more.

Late medieval – the Pittodrie kilns

By the later 1500s and especially the 1600s the documentary record begins to shed a bit more light on the cultural history of the area. This is also beginning to be accompanied by a slight lightening of the archaeological gloom. However, virtually no evidence for rural housing has yet been discovered in the north-east that unarguably predates the 1600s. The likelihood is that the region was still tolerably well wooded into the later 1500s and most dwellings may well have been built of wood and/or other perishable materials. Clay-walled buildings are likely to have been built in areas of suitable, naturally occurring clay. The small deserted burgh of Rattray by the Loch of Strathbeg was meticulously excavated by the Murrays and the 13th-century dwellings of the ordinary burghers were timber-framed, with the later 14th-century examples using more clay and stones (Murray and Murray 1993, 137–42). None of those buildings would have survived as upstanding field remains.

Kilns – especially stone-built examples – survive better because of their robust nature and these are sometimes the only clue to settlement locations. One problem, however, is that kilns were usually positioned a little way from dwelling sites because of their fire risk. At Pittodrie two kilns have been discovered (see Figures 12.10 and 12.11; Plate 12.3), both cut into the orange sand on top of the mound. The first appears to have been a simple earth-cut bowl that would have been covered with a wattle and daub dome. This was replaced by a more robust stone-built structure, extremely well-bonded with clay. The floor was similarly very neatly made, also with stone and clay. It too would have been capped by a wattle and daub dome. (An earlier type of kiln has also been found during excavations at Druminnor [Shepherd 2018], also as part of the Bennachie Landscapes Project and a more full discussion of kilns in general can be found there via the Bailies website.)

Two further sets of kilns have recently been found as a result of developer-funded excavations along pipelines in Aberdeenshire. Two were found on a site at Dumyocher

(Johnson 2017) and a further one in the Glens of Foudland (Wallace forthcoming). They all comply with the same general size and shape as the stone-built one at Pittodrie, though Dumyocher 1 does have an additional, possible venting arrangement. None of them survived to the same height as the Pittodrie example and they appear to have had most of their superstructure removed before the site was cleared and back-filled.

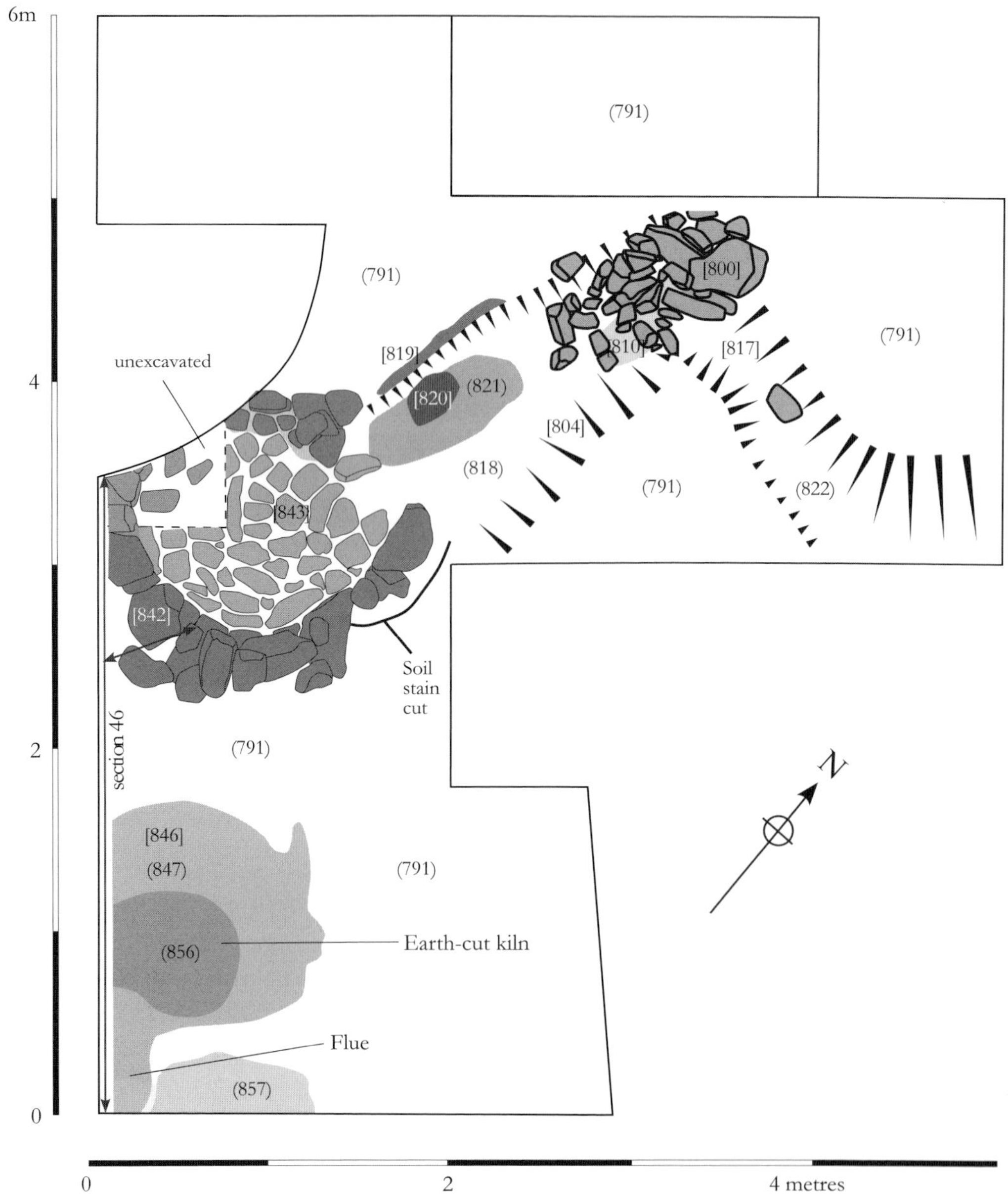

Figure 12.10. Excavation plan showing both kilns.

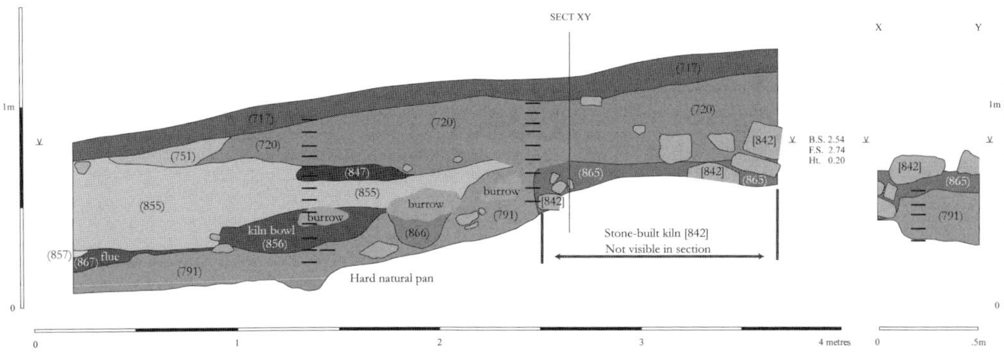

Figure 12.11. Section showing kilns in relation to soil contexts (Short horizontal lines are the OSL sample points).

The recognition of the earth-cut kiln at Pittodrie is probably due to its positioning next to the later kiln. Had it been found outside of that context, its very slight remains may well not have invited further interrogation.

One other example that was not stone-lined came from an 11th- to 13th-century context at Lhanbryde (Alexander 1997). However, like the Druminnor example of a similar age, the Lhanbryde kiln may have been part of a 'lordly landscape' – though ecclesiastical rather than lay. The Pittodrie, Drumyocher, and Foudland kilns are later and appear to have functioned as communal kilns built by the surrounding small farmers. The earlier ones probably formed part of an innovative technological suite incorporating mechanical mill, mouldboard plough and a revised open field system that was changing the face of local agricultural production in the 13th century across the north-east (Shepherd 2018, 26–28).

At the east end of the flue was a collection of stones embedded in clay. Amongst these were found the 'sun-stone' and four pieces of roughly shaped masonry, the latter seeming to have been dressed for architectural use. These occurred at the junction of the presumed end of the flue and a cut into the natural hard pan, running at ninety degrees to the flue. This was filled with a substantial amount of charcoal and was suggested to have been the cut for a sleeper beam supporting a timber structure. The assemblage seems impossible to understand, but attention might be drawn to the kiln found at Dunrobin, which lay in association with an 'open area delineated by a low wall' (Close-Brooks 1980, 340), running at ninety degrees to the flue. The worked masonry seems anomalous in the context of the kiln and may hint at a hitherto unknown structure lying in the vicinity. If so, this structure is likely to have been of quite high status.

The Pittodrie Bede House: a 17th-century 'hospital'

The 'Bede House' has been known to the local oral tradition, presumably since before its destruction. This is assumed to have occurred during the re-planning of the Pittodrie policies in the late 1700s or, more probably, early 1800s. Its stones and

Figure 12.12. Bede House plan showing house, garden and trenches.

those of its garden/enclosure dyke appear to have been removed and used for building the new landscaping dykes. A 'hospital' in the 17th-century, would have been more like a hostel than a modern hospital. Here, it was said initially to have been run by four 'poor men' who would have tended to travellers' needs and processed to church with the Erskine family on Sundays (McConnochie 1890, 27). In earlier times, such 'bedesmen' would have been required to say prayers for souls of their benefactors (Ralston and Shepherd 2019, 140–8).

The demolition of the building appears to have been a well-ordered affair with the intention of re-cycling material. Only fragments of roofing slate were found, suggesting the roof was removed for use elsewhere. Large amounts of mortar and plaster also attested the careful removal of most of the stone superstructure – no appreciable stones were left inside the building, apart from the large rocks forming the base of the stairs to the upper storey. These were probably considered too unwieldy for easy transportation. Figure 12.12 shows the Bede House with its garden and the positions of excavated trenches.

Much of the garden dyke had been removed, presumably when the house was dismantled, and the stones used to make the early 19th-century policy dykes. The earlier (18th-century?) plantation dykes had also been largely removed, probably because the plantations had been extended down to the 'turnpike' trackway by that date. An earlier long-distance trackway, shown on the Robertson map of 1822 (Robertson 1822), though not on the 1776 Taylor and Skinner map, ran past the Bede House and joined the 'turnpike'. The latter is shown by Taylor and Skinner as running from Monymusk to Old Rayne. A further spur from the Robertson road ran down the hill and dissected the large enclosure discussed above. The Robertson road can be found as a relict earthwork as it winds around Bennachie in the direction of Tillyfour and Castle Forbes. The Bede House, therefore, appears to have been sited with this wider communication network in mind.

Figure 12.13 shows some of the excavated internal features. It is difficult to determine which, if any, of the three areas of burning were original hearths. They may have been used by the workmen dismantling the house or by later workers on the hill. However, the eastern one, associated with a cobbled surface may well be original. Carved door jambs show the position of the rooms in relation to what must have been wooden room-dividing screens. These would have created two rooms, one at each end and an entrance 'lobby'. Having entered the front door, the visitor would have been faced by a set of stairs leading up to the second storey. Presumably these were wooden and supported by the large stones beneath (Plates 12.4 and 12.5).

Access to the front door was by a neatly cobbled path. The gap between this and the garden dykes on either side suggests either a flower or grass border. Steps ran from beside the front door giving access to the garden area. No external gate/entrance has been discovered elsewhere around its circuit. A worked stone with neatly cut holes (see Figure 12.14) indicates that the windows had bars and suggests the potential for limited lawlessness at the time.

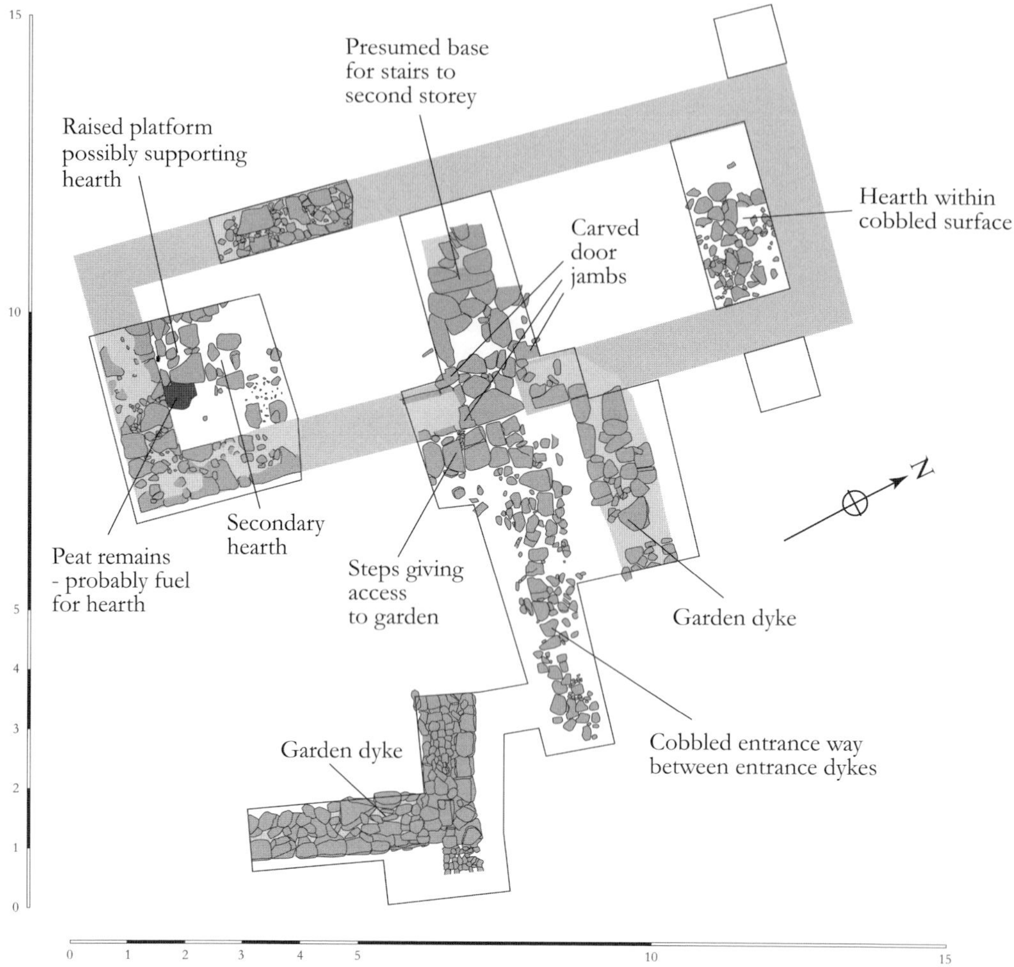

Figure 12.13. Bede House showing internal features.

The garden soil had been dramatically increased in depth in order to produce a rich loam over the rather thin natural soil of the area. This led to a good depth of preservation for the house itself, in contrast to some of the garden walls. The south-east corner of the garden dyke had been removed completely. However, the stone from the house was removed down to the level of the outside soil, leaving the interior preserved to three or four courses in places. The Leslies of Balquhain had their right to 'comon pasturage, foggage, fewall, peats, fail and divot in and throw the forrest of Bennachie' ratified by Charles II in 1670 (1670/7/43; rps.ac.uk). 'Fail and divot' would have provided the deep garden soil here. Intriguingly, there was some evidence for earlier linear features underlying parts of the garden enclosure, suggesting possible previous use. (Both the Leslies and Erskines had charters granting rights throughout the forest of Bennachie and the woods of 'Old Clochy', but it was the Erskines who were responsible for the erection of the Bede House.)

Figure 12.14. Window masonry showing holes made for iron bars.

Early modern

As discussed above, the cottage excavated in Trench 1 may be one of the 'Wairdside' cottages noted in the 1771 rental. It appears to have been removed when the new policies were being laid out, presumably contemporaneously with the demolition of the Bede House around the turn of the century. Given that timeline, it is difficult to imagine the cottage not having been there in 1771, if not earlier. Figure 12.15 shows some of the features associated with the cottage.

The large, rectangular enclosure had clearly changed use by the time the cottage was built, as it lay directly across the line of the enclosure dyke. During excavation, the back wall of the cottage, against the hill, was constantly waterlogged, even through the middle of summer. An internal drain lying along the length of this wall may have been associated with an attempt to keep the property dry or, possibly, may have had some other utilitarian function. Certainly, digging a channel behind the house would seem to have offered the more logical response to overcoming penetrating water. The water came from what appears to have been part of the pre-canalised run of the Craigwell Burn. This burn was canalised, probably as part of the new landscaping plan and its original course is largely unknown. The older channel above the cottage may have been dammed below the well but, over the years, water re-gained its former course (see Pollen report below). As a very outside possibility,

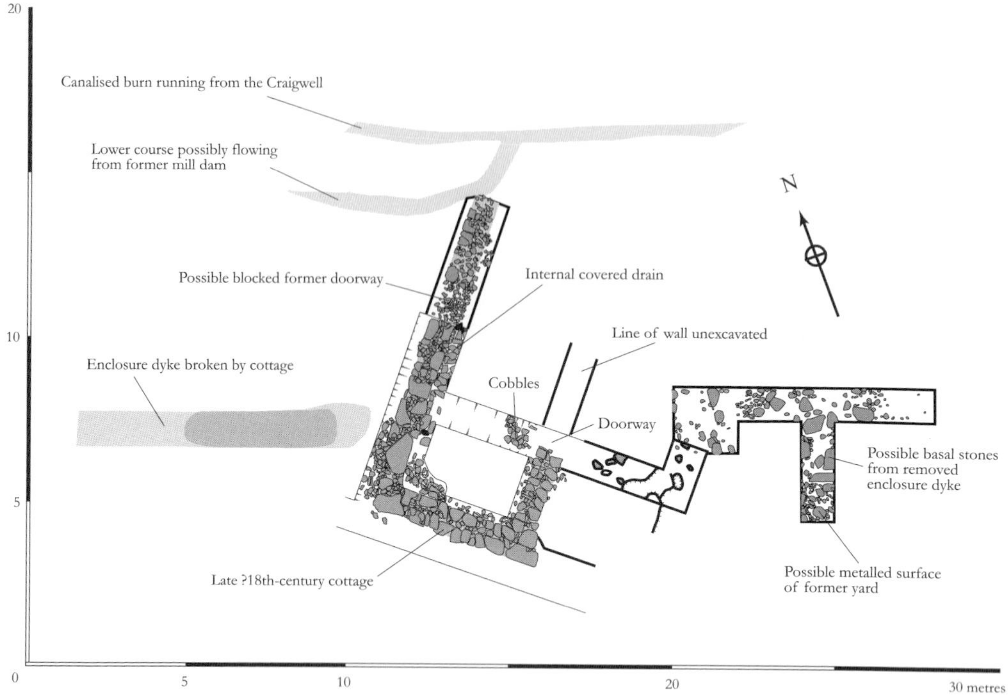

Figure 12.15. Trench 1 plan (cottage).

it may be worth considering a connection with the 1636 'Wobsters croft' and a possible use for water in the fulling process used in the finishing of cloth. Similar internal drains have reputedly been noted by NOSAS in other rural excavations in the highlands of Scotland.

The foundation walls of the cottage were made of substantial boulders and it is assumed that the upper walls were made of turf, in accordance with local building traditions prior to the late 18th and 19th centuries (Shepherd 2021, 141–50). The interior appears to have had a cobbled surface with a possible sunken area leading from the rear of the house to the door in order to aid sweeping out. A former, possible blocked entrance lay at the back of the house. East of the house lay the remains of what appears to have been a metalled surface that may have formed an external working surface for the cottage. Other slight features may well have been in use contemporaneously with the large enclosure, prior to the construction of the cottage.

The above offers a brief review of the major findings from the Pittodrie excavations to date. A more complete description of the individual trenches and sections may be found online at the websites noted previously. The full reports for the OSL, pollen and kiln ecofacts can also be found online there. However, a brief synopsis of those reports is included below.

Environmental analyses in brief

Kiln ecofacts

Jackaline Robertson (précised by Shepherd)

Bulk samples were taken from the two kilns that appear to date to the later 16th or early 17th centuries (see Kinnaird, below). Unfortunately, the folk using the Pittodrie kilns appear to have been annoyingly tidy and to have cleaned the kilns regularly, leaving little seed residue within the kilns. However, the charcoal remains from what seem to be these cleaning episodes are particularly helpful for indicating some of the local tree species present at the time. It is considered probable that they grew close to the kiln site in order to limit transportation.

Most of the remains came from context (847). This is presumed to derive from the cleaning and eventual destruction of the later, stone-built kiln. The wood species present were dominated by oak and hazel. Almost half of the latter was roundwood, possibly suggestive of coppicing. Also present were alder, birch, and cherry. Less evidence came from the earlier kiln. What did survive suggested that peat turf was the preferred fuel, whilst a mixture of turf and wood may have been used in the stone-built kiln. Some of the hazel roundwood may have been used in a wattle and daub superstructure sitting atop the stone walls.

Though meagre, this is the first evidence we have for the make-up of the woodland on this part of Bennachie in the 16th and 17th centuries and its findings appear to echo the pollen record described below. Of interest is the absence of willow here and from the early pollen record especially as 'willow' appears in the place-name 'saughen waird', discussed above. It is possible that willows were growing lower down the slope alongside the Craigwell and Rushmill Burns – perhaps around the boggy-sounding 'Doubstoun'. It's easier to carry wood downhill than uphill and the 'uphill' wood is likely to have been free for tenants to gather from the Commonty. The willows may have been on tenanted ground and, consequently, less accessible.

Pollen

J. Edward Schofield (précised by Shepherd)

A depressed area of boggy ground lying between the kiln mound and the canalised Craigwell Burn appeared to suggest its former use as a mill pond (Plate 12.6). In order to test this hypothesis, and in order to provide a vegetation reconstruction for the location, a sediment core for pollen analysis (Moore *et al.* 1991) was extracted from the centre of the feature, where the greatest depth of accumulation (*c.* 85 cm) could be found. The stratigraphy here (NGR NJ 69432 23619) comprises a hard base and a unit of sandy clay (*c.* 60–43 cm) intercalated between horizons of clay-rich peat (*c.* 85–60 cm, and from 43 cm to the surface). The concentration of pollen throughout the core is low (often <10,000 grains cm^3) with very little pollen present in the clay. The standard of preservation of the microfossils is poor, with many pollen grains exhibiting breakage and corrosion. However, the results shown in Figure 12.16 are adequate for some generalised observations.

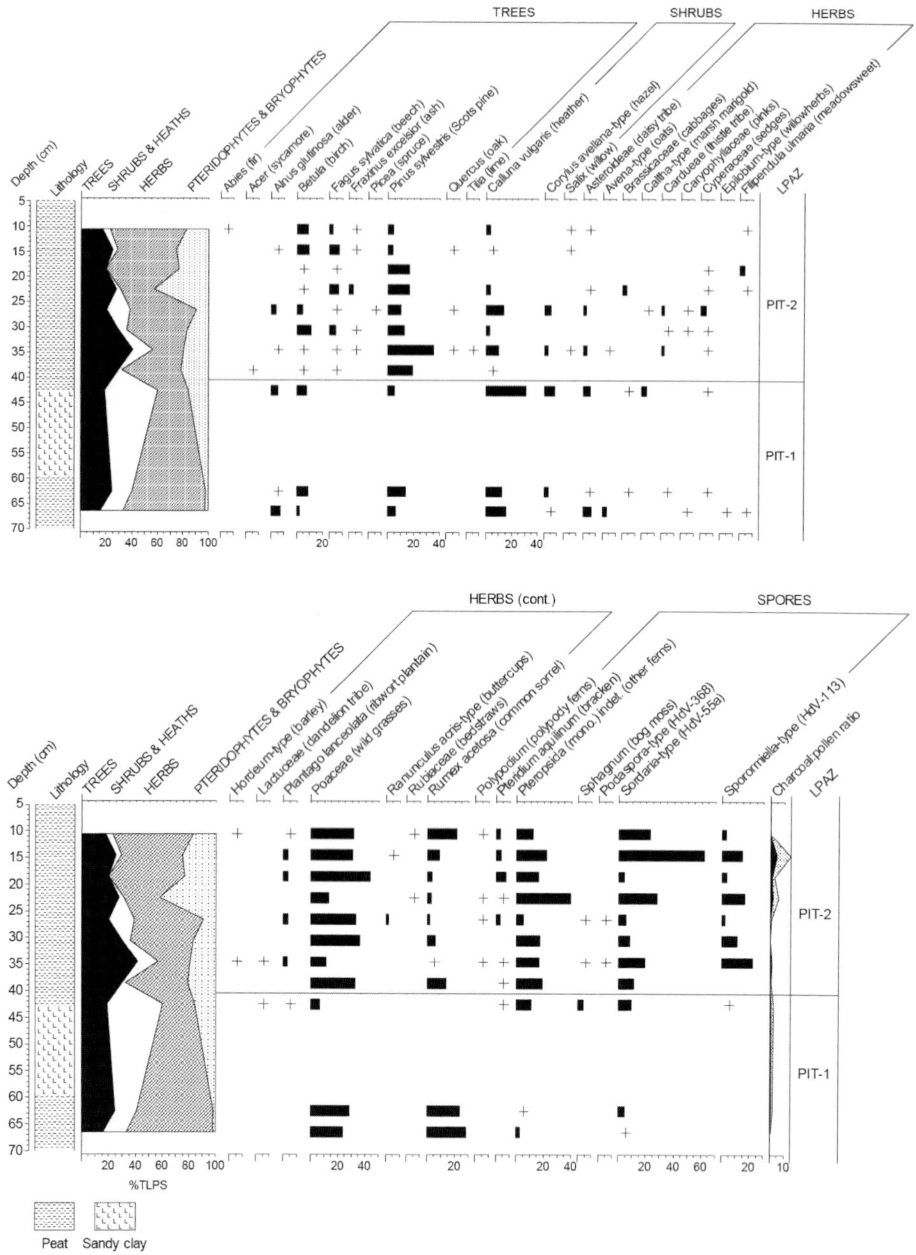

Figure 12.16. Percentage pollen diagram for Pittodrie showing selected taxa. Pollen samples were prepared and analysed following standard procedures (Moore et al. *1991). The percentages are based on a TLPS sum (i.e. the sum of total land pollen and spores; these collectively being trees, shrubs and heaths, herbs, pteridophytes and bryophytes). Due to the samples having low pollen concentrations, the pollen sum is relatively small in most cases (c. 75–150 TLPS) and therefore these data should be treated cautiously. The pollen diagram is divided into two biostratigraphic units or Local Pollen Assemblages Zones (LPAZs PIT-1 & -2). Plus (+) symbols indicate rare occurrences (<2% TLPS). Charcoal data are expressed as the ratio of charcoal fragments to pollen grains. Pollen was found to be near-absent from the sandy clay, which explains why there is no palynological data available from this sediment unit.*

The core comprises two biostratigraphic (or local pollen assemblage) zones, PIT-1 and PIT-2. In the earlier (lower) zone (PIT-1), the tree species in evidence are alder, birch, and Scots pine. Hazel – a small tree or shrub – is also recorded. This appears to echo the kiln remains except in the absence of cherry and oak and the presence of Scots pine. The absence of willow is particularly interesting, especially considering the place-name 'saughen' in the vicinity. However, willow is perhaps most likely to have occurred downslope from the coring area, away from the prevailing wind in a damper, lower zone. The large amounts of heather indicate an open grazing environment with heathland and grassland prominent before the development of the plantations. Heather was also noted as a possible fuel being used in the kilns. The absence of oak may suggest that these trees had already been removed from the immediate locality and that a possible trip to the woods of 'Old Clochy' were necessary to gather timber from that species.

The upper zone (PIT-2) shows a more wooded environment with tree pollen accounting for almost 50% of some samples. The trees present are those anticipated to be found within an 18th-century plantation, *i.e.* a number of recently introduced or re-introduced species, such as sycamore or beech (Smout 2002). This supports the cartographic evidence as discussed above that shows the slopes above the site being planted in that era.

Grass pollen is prevalent throughout the diagram alongside oats (mostly in PIT-1) and barley (most regular in PIT-2). Weeds of open farmland also occur, especially within the first half of that period, perhaps in accordance with the evidence for rig and furrow cultivation, prior to the enclosure and landscaping with beech woodland of the immediate area. Fungal spores from saprophytic fungi, indicative of dead wood and/or animal dung are very common, particularly so during PIT-2.

Direct evidence for arable cultivation comes in the form of cereal pollen (see above) and indirect evidence from the pollen of plants associated with agriculture or disturbed ground (*e.g.* common sorrel, ribwort plantain, and the daisy and thistle tribes). Interestingly, the saprophytic fungi (van Geel *et al.* 2003) present in the later period (PIT-2) are not well represented earlier (in PIT-1). This may suggest a greater interest in arable rather than pastoral agriculture during the earlier period, or it may mean that grazing occurred at greater distance from the sampling location, *i.e.* above the farms on the upland areas prior to their forestation. Otherwise, it may be that the fungi are more reflective of the presence of dead wood than animals. Charcoal is present throughout the sequence and its greatest concentrations near the top of PIT-2 may well record the early 19th-century burning that was so evident during excavation of the kiln mound.

A large gap in the pollen record is created by the impact of some ground-breaking occurrence that introduced a substantial depth of sandy-clay containing little to no pollen. One possibility is that this relates to the canalisation of the Craigwell Burn, although quarrying may provide an alternative explanation. Although the pollen diagram makes this appear to have been a serious hiatus on the site, the duration of this event is uncertain. The canalisation of the burn may have been carried out at the same time that the cottage in Trench 1 was built, in order to try to keep that building dry. However, after this event, the wider landscape remained largely unchanged for a while before the planting of the woodlands witnessed in PIT-2. No pollen from aquatic plants is recorded in the pollen diagram, which suggests that standing water was not present at the site. Other plants of wet soils (*e.g.* sedges) are also limited in frequency. This may indicate that this area was not used as a mill pond, as was initially suspected. To confirm this, it may be necessary to investigate other proxies such as diatoms (unicellular algae).

The evidence from the kiln ecofacts and the pollen analysis appear to support each other. The kiln evidence supplies a snapshot of aspects of the environment whilst the kilns were in use and this can be placed within the pollen record. The pollen record reveals the dramatic change that was wrought when the plantations were developed.

OSL dating

Tim Kinnaird (précised by Shepherd)

The results of OSL underpin the chronology of the site. Luminescence results from energy retained in quartz or feldspar, as a consequence of naturally occurring radiation in the environment. The luminescence is reset when the minerals are exposed to daylight: therefore it is possible to determine a 'time since last exposure'.

The samples from Trench 9 show a gradual increase in luminescence signal intensities with depth, suggesting an uncomplicated deposition of sediments through time. In all, four 'periods' can be recognised: glacial, Iron Age, medieval and post-medieval/early modern. Post glacial/earlier prehistoric is, presumably evidenced within the sediments but has not been independently dated here.

The Iron Age is represented by alder charcoal carbon-dated to around 500 cal BC from beneath the stone feature [AS], in context (805) (see above). From the same context, though from behind [AS] and further up the slope, OSL sample 13 returned a date of AD 130±330. Above context (805) in context (792), OSL sample 10 returned a date of AD 1090±50, marking a change to a medieval sequence. Above (792) was context (780) within which were found sherds of 12th- to 15th-century redware. Higher up (780) and into (769) these late medieval sherds were mixed with early modern ceramics.

Another sequence further east in Trench 9, from behind the enclosure dyke, shows an almost exact replication of the medieval and post-medieval sediments but without the Iron Age horizon, reflected in the lack of context (805). In fact, the soil from beneath the dyke [AJ] returned an OSL date of AD 1870±10, suggesting a complete reworking or robbing of this portion of dyke in the later 19th century. A similar situation was noted in Trench 15 where an OSL date from around the stones of [AJ] gave a date of AD 1830±30. That this 19th-century date does not reflect the original construction of the dyke is shown by an OSL sample from context (964) in Trench 16 that returned a date of AD 1380±100, suggesting the original enclosure dyke may date to the earlier 15th century.

Trench 10 provided a new sequence of sediments that were different to Trench 9 and has to be considered without reference to that. Both sections sampled – 46 and 48 – might be characterised as heavily disturbed. This can be seen by the frequent 'inversions' where older sediments appear to sit atop earlier ones. The process of digging-up such older soils, deposition, followed by rapid reburial, would negate the anticipated 're-setting' of the sediments' luminescence clock. Archaeologically, this process can be seen in the construction, use, and decommissioning of the two kilns. OSL dates from sealed contexts associated directly with the construction and use of those kilns gave dates of AD 1570±80 for the earlier one and AD 1600±120 for the later. A number of sediments from the final, overlying 19th-century landscaping context (720) provide older dates than for the kilns themselves. This would be characteristic of older sediments from elsewhere being brought onto the site for landscaping purposes. This process seems even more pronounced in section 48. It is suggested that the construction of the 19th-century dyke alongside the 'turnpike' routeway and the upgrading of that routeway itself may have introduced alien soils to this site. An anomalous ^{14}C date from context (752) – overlying the kilns – giving a date of cal AD 1076±24 – is also to be explained this way.

Context (791), through which the kilns were dug, provided a sampled OSL date of 630 cal BC, but with a very wide window of ±1270 years. At present this date cannot be refined further but does indicate much earlier activity on the site.

A combination of dating methods, contextualised by OSL sampling, has demonstrated settlement activity across the site from the Iron Age, through medieval and post-medieval horizons to the final landscaping event in the early 19th century. Earlier activity, preceding the Iron Age, has also been demonstrated but not categorised.

Conclusions

The multi-period landscape of Pittodrie is slowly coming into focus. No single feature is mind-bendingly exciting but from the temporal depth of the site, increasing amounts of new archaeological and environmental data are emerging. This especially applies to the 'non-elite' medieval rural landscape of the north-east about which so little is known. Of particular importance is the gathering of environmental evidence. At a time when so much deliberation is concerned with re-designing the rural landscape to be fit for future sustainability and biodiversity, the baseline ecologies of past north-east landscapes is bereft of appropriate data. This data is beginning to emerge at Pittodrie. The site is large and there is clearly much more to be discovered. Hopefully, this will slowly be brought to light by the doughty volunteers across the area.

But finally, to end where this began, on a particular warning note: don't always trust the Historic Land-use Assessment map (hlamap.org.uk) to be an accurate guide to below ground evidence and, unless it is updated and re-assessed regularly it is, at best, misleading and, at worst, injurious to the survival of the historic environment. HLA privileges the status quo in which the more obvious archaeological areas of known interest are highlighted and the low status rural archaeological sites, about which so little is known – like Pittodrie – become 'written-out' of the authorised heritage discourse (Smith 2006). As Rippon has previously warned (2013), there is a need to go beyond the superficial to gain an accurate view of a landscape. Sadly, HLA is considered by its sponsors to be amongst the first ports of call for site development and archaeological mitigation decisions, claiming to be used in 'Managing strategic landscape decisions' (hlamap.org.uk). However, as Pittodrie shows, it is not the 'comprehensive summary of landscape-scale information' those sponsors purport it to be (*ibid.*). There are no office-bound shortcuts to landscape assessment; it requires local knowledge and muddy boots.

Acknowledgements

Site supervision, palaeo-environmental research and OSL dating has been funded by the Bailies of Bennachie, radiocarbon dating organised by Bruce Mann of Aberdeenshire Council Archaeological Services and all other work has been carried out by volunteers, without whom the project could not have existed. The landowners, Macdonald Hotels, the Foresight Group and RTS Forestry have been most gracious in permitting these investigations to happen and, with the help of their hotel and estate managers, have provided much greatly appreciated support for the project. Grateful thanks to Jeff Oliver, Colin Miller, Andrew Wainwright and Jo Vergunst for their insightful comments and suggestions that have greatly helped this paper. All errors are down to the authors. Finally, many thanks to the three specialists – Jackaline, Ed, and Tim – for all their help and sound advice. Students from Alford Academy are especially thanked for their assistance with aspects of Ed's laboratory work linked to the pollen analysis.

Abbreviations

NLS, National Library of Scotland.
NRS, National Records of Scotland.
UoASC, University of Aberdeen Special Collections.

Notes

1 The Court of Sessions had firmly enshrined a narrow definition of private land ownership in Scots Law during the 1600s (Goodare 2013, 106, 115) that created a distinctive parting of the ways between Scottish and English land law from about this time (Shepherd 2021, 229). This then led to the Division of Commonties Act of 1695 (https://www.legislation.gov.uk/aosp/1695/69/contents) that may be considered not to have been paralleled in England until the 1845 Inclosure Act (https://www.legislation.gov.uk/ukpga/Vict/8-9/118/).

2 Detailed descriptions of the methods employed by the SUERC Radiocarbon Laboratory can be found in Dunbar *et al.* (2016). The radiocarbon ages given are calibrated to the calendar timescale using the Oxford Radiocarbon Accelerator Unit calibration program OxCal 4 (Bronk Ramsey 2009). Date ranges have been calibrated using the IntCal13 atmospheric calibration curve (Reimer *et al.* 2013).

Sources

AB Coll. = (1843) *Collections for a History of the Shires of Aberdeen and Banff*. Aberdeen, Spalding Club.
GD33/16 = Litigation concerning rights of commonty on Bennachie, NRS.

MS 2392 = (1771) Rental Book of the Pittodrie Estate, UoASC.
MS3043/70 = Rental of lands in the parish of Logiedurno, 1636, UoASC.
RMS = Thomson, J.M. *et al.* (eds) (1882–1914), *Registrum Magni Sigilli Regum Scotorum*, 11 vols. Edinburgh, H.M. General Register House.
Roy Military Survey of Scotland, 1747–1755, NLS.
RPS = Brown, K.M. *et al.* (eds) (1641) *The Records of the Parliaments of Scotland to 1707*, Act regarding the erection of the hospital of Balhalgardy. Ref. 1641/8/380. (http://www.rps.ac.uk)
RSRS = Burnett, G. (ed.) (1884) *Rotuli Scaccarii Regum Scotorum*, The Exchequer Rolls of Scotland, 7, 1460–1469. Edinburgh, H.M. General Register House.
SHS = (1919) *Forbes Baron Court Book.* Miscellany of the Scottish History Society 3, 2nd Ser. 19, 224–321.

Bibliography

Alexander, D. (1997) A medieval grain-drying kiln and earlier mill-lade at Lhanbryde, Moray. In *Proceedings of the Society of Antiquaries of Scotland* 127, 677–85.

Bailey, M. (2002) *The English Manor c. 1200–c. 1500*. Manchester, Manchester University Press.

Bronk Ramsey, C. (2009) Bayesian Analysis of Radiocarbon Dates. In *Radiocarbon* 51(1), 337 – 60.

Close-Brooks, J. (1980) Excavations in the Dairy Park, Dunrobin, Sutherland, 1977. In *Proceedings of the Society of Antiquaries of Scotland* 110, 328–45.

Cook, M. (2011) Maiden Castle, Insch, Aberdeenshire: choice and architecture in Pictland. In *Tayside and Fife Archaeological Journal* 17, 25–35.

Dunbar, E., Cook, G.T., Naysmith, P., Tripney, B.G. and Xu, S. (2016) AMS ^{14}C Dating at the Scottish Universities Environmental Research Centre (SUERC) Radiocarbon Dating Laboratory. In *Radiocarbon* 58(1), 9 – 23.

Fox, H. (2012) *Dartmoor's Alluring Uplands. Transhumance and Pastoral Management in the Middle Ages.* Exeter, University of Exeter Press.

Goodare, J. (2013) In search of the Scottish agrarian problem. In Whittle, J. (ed.) *Landlords and Tenants in Britain, 1440–1660. Tawney's Agrarian Problem Revisited*, 100–16. Woodbridge, Boydell Press.

Hall, D.W. (1996) Blind date – Scottish medieval pottery industries. *Tayside & Fife Archaeological Journal* 2, 126–9.

Johnson, M. (2017) Excavation of prehistoric roundhouses and post-medieval kilns at Drumyocher and Hospital Shields, Aberdeenshire. In *Scottish Archaeological Internet Reports*, 70. Doi: http://doi.org/10.9750/issn.2056-7421.2017.70

McConnochie, A.I. (1890) *Bennachie*. Aberdeen, D. Wyllie & Son.

Miller, C.H. (2019) Pittodrie Bede House Archival Research. In Shepherd, C. (ed.) *Bennachie and the Garioch: Society and Ecology in the History of North-east Scotland*, 87–105. Chapel of Garioch, The Bailies of Bennachie, Bennachie Landscapes Series 4.

Moore, P.D., Webb, J.A. and Collinson, M.E. (1991) *Pollen analysis*, 2nd edition. Oxford, Blackwell.

Murray, H.K. and Murray, J.C. (1993) Excavations at Rattray, Aberdeenshire. A Scottish deserted burgh. In *Medieval Archaeology* 37, 109–218.

Noble, G. and Evans, N. (2022) *Picts: Scourge of Rome, Rulers of the North*. Edinburgh, Birlinn.

Oram, R. (2021) Too much environment and not enough history: the opportunities and challenges in researching medieval seasonal settlement in Atlantic Europe. In Dixon, P. and Theune, C. (eds) *Seasonal Settlement in the Medieval and Early Modern Countryside, Ruralia XIII*, 193–201. Leiden, Sidestone Press.

Ostrom, E. (1990) *Governing the Commons. The Evolution of Institutions for Collective Action*. Cambridge, Cambridge University Press.

Ralston, I. and Shepherd, C. (2019) The Pittodrie Estate 'Bede House' Excavations. In Shepherd, C. (ed.) *Bennachie and the Garioch: Society and Ecology in the History of North-east Scotland*, 105–52. Chapel of Garioch, The Bailies of Bennachie, Bennachie Landscapes Series 4.

Reimer, P.J., Bard, E., Bayliss, A., Beck, J.W., Blackwell, P.G., Bronk Ramsey, C., Buck, C.E., Chenge, H., Edwards, R.L, Friedrich, M., Grootes, P.M., Guilderson, T.P., Haflidason, H., Hajdas, I., Hatté, C., Heaton, T.J., Hoffmann, D.L., Hogg, A.G., Hughen, K.A., Kaiser, K.F., Kromer, B., Manning, S.W., Niu, M., Reimer, R.W., Richards, D.A., Scott, E.M., Southon, J.R., Staff, R.A., Turney, C.S.M. and van der Plicht, J. (2013) Intcal 13 and marine13 radiocarbon age calibration curves 0–50,000 years cal BP. In *Radiocarbon* 55, 1869 – 87.

Rippon, S. (2013) Historic Landscape Character and Sense of Place. In *Landscape Research* 38(2), 179–202.

Rippon, S. (2014) *Beyond the Medieval Village; the Diversification of Landscape Character in Southern Britain.* Oxford, Oxford University Press.

Robertson, J. (1822) Topographical and military map of the counties of Aberdeen, Banff and Kincardine, London. (https://maps.nls.uk/view/74400182)

Shepherd, C. (2018) A 12th-century bowl-fired grain-drying kiln at Druminnor Castle, Aberdeenshire. Implications for social change, agricultural productivity and landscape development in north-east Scotland. In *Studia Celtica,* LII, 1–32.

Shepherd, C. (2021) *The Late Medieval Landscape of North-east Scotland: Renaissance, Reformation and Revolution.* Oxford, Windgather Press.

Smith, L. (2006) *The Discourse of Heritage.* Abingdon, Routledge.

Smout, T.C. (ed.) (2002) *People and woods in Scotland: a history.* Edinburgh, Edinburgh University Press.

Starr, M. (2017) *Hundreds of Mysteriously Carved Stone Age 'Sunstones' Have Been Found in Denmark.* www.sciencealert.com/vasagard-danish-island-300-mysterious-sunstones-sun-worship.

Stringer, K.J. (1985) *Earl David of Huntingdon, A Study in Anglo-Scottish History.* Edinburgh, Edinburgh University Press.

Taylor, G. and Skinner, A. (1776) Road from Edinburgh, by Brechine, Banchory & Monymusk, continued to Old Rain, NLS.

van Geel, B., Buurman, J., Brinkkemper, O., Schelvis, J., Aptroot, A., van Reenen, G. and Hakbijl, T. (2003) Environmental reconstruction of a Roman Period settlement site in Uitgeest (The Netherlands), with special reference to coprophilous fungi. In *Journal of Archaeological Science* 30, 873–83.

Wallace, K. (forthcoming) A Corn Drying Kiln at Glens of Foudland, Aberdeenshire. In *Tayside & Fife Archaeological Journal 30.*

Winchester, A.J.L. (2000) *The Harvest of the Hills. Rural Life in Northern England and the Scottish Borders, 1400–1700.* Edinburgh, Edinburgh University Press.

Websites

Bailies (nd) Bailies of Bennachie, www.bailiesofbennachie.co.uk

BGS, British Geological Survey, Contains British Geological Survey materials © UKRI [2024], https://geologyviewer.bgs.ac.uk

BLP (nd) Bennachie Landscapes Project, www.bennachielandscapes.scot

hlamap.org.uk, Scotlands Historic Land Use, https://hlamap.org.uk/

Scotland's Soils, https://soils.environment.gov.scot

Chapter 13

Thirteen years on: the Bennachie Landscapes Project experience. Learning from the past, shaping the future

Colin Shepherd and Jo Vergunst

Introduction

This book, *Cultural Landscapes of North-east Scotland*, originated in a series of presentations given in a conference of that name at the Garioch Heritage Centre in late September 2023. It seemed to be a suitable point at which to consider the Bennachie Landscapes Project in respect of other research being carried out across the area. A broad range of speakers were invited in order to share their work and to make us all more aware of each other. Although many of us knew, to some extent, of each other's research, it gave an opportunity to meet and discuss it in greater detail. The difficulty in retrieving all participants from convivial breaks throughout the two days attests to the success of that aspect of the conference! This 'conviviality' is a marked feature of 'community' research and deserves further reflection. Graham and Vergunst (2019) explored community heritage specifically as research, a form of inquiry that links past, present, and future in meaningful ways. They argued that for communities, 'what enlivens relations with the past is more an ongoing process of finding out, sharing, debating and undertaking small-scale acts of stewardship. These are stories that are worked on and pieced together collectively and with meaning for current circumstances, not simply uncovered.' These relatively small scale, localised projects (but not necessarily local in a parochial sense) do not just retell that past, but actively work on the present and future too. The purpose of this chapter is to try to gain a sense of how community-based and collaborative research works from the ground up, with a focus on social relations such as conviviality.

The first part of this chapter will consider aspects of the Pittodrie excavations. The substantive results of the research into this multi-phase site at the edge of Bennachie are presented in the previous chapter. Here, we explore its dynamics as fieldwork. Vergunst spent time on the dig during summer 2024 to learn about how it worked as a community heritage project and what perspectives participants had on their activities in it. He kept fieldnotes from conversations held with some of the participants and from other on-site observations. Shepherd has been a regular member of the digging team since work at the site began in 2018 and has helped place this material into a longer-term history of public engagement, delving briefly into the history, in British legal thought, of such tricky terms as 'ownership' and 'common property'. We seek to position the experiences of the Bennachie Landscapes Project in the evolving debate on collaborative working between and across disciplines, community groups, landowners and institutions. As was outlined in the Foreword to this book, the creation of the Bailies owed no small debt to perceptions of the conflicting notions of 'ownership' circulating at the time of the division of the Commonty of Bennachie.

Reflections on the 'Pittodrie dig'

Project determination

A feature of the Pittodrie dig is that it might be described as a 'Cinderella-site'. Apart from the Bede House, the other features across the site are the type of remains that are generally rather ignored and considered of no great historical value. Historic Land-use Assessment (www.hlamap.org.uk) appears dismissive of any potential archaeological interest in this area, which highlights the problems inherent in its utilisation of 'coarse-grained' and incomplete data (Rippon 2013). To local people, however, what is of interest may be very different from professionals, especially if they have no local connections. Notions of what are 'important' heritage assets are not neutral – different participants perceive 'importance' differently (Vergunst *et al.* 2017, 166–70).

The way the Pittodrie dig operates practically with the local community is important because, as with other community heritage projects, these social relationships are what enables the research to happen. Working in tandem with the Druminnor Castle site, Pittodrie is worked on two weekdays per week during the summer season, while Druminnor happens at the weekends. This means that community members have options depending on when they are free. There also is no fee for volunteers to join either dig and Iain Ralston, as the Pittodrie site supervisor, is supported by the Bailies of Bennachie.

Calls for volunteers are circulated around the Bailies membership, including by word of mouth, and posters are placed in local shops and on Facebook. All of this encourages people living locally to take part, and while access to the site generally requires either a car or a lift, a range of younger and older people take part. There are usually 10 to 20 volunteers on site each day of the dig. While the younger people are often keen to get practical archaeological experience as part of or a prelude to studying archaeology in higher education, for all volunteers there is a mix of practical learning and connection to their local landscape. A key point was expressed in conversation with one volunteer, who said that he was 'not just volunteer labour', and instead was caught up in the enthusiasm of the supervisor Ralston. The volunteer continued: 'I feel a bit more invested in it. When you're actually digging something up you can't help but learn about it. No better way of learning.' Volunteers are frequently asked for their opinions on the archaeology as it progresses and fully involved in conversations about possible interpretations and next steps. This all emphasises how local interest can be harnessed in what might seem to be an unpromising area, in order to develop a successful fieldwork project.

Other volunteers commented on the specific nature of the site as comprising the social history of the landscape. One said: 'I wouldn't have appreciated how populated this area was', noting that 'history is written by the well-off' and that here at Pittodrie, while excavating the early modern dwelling in Trench 1, the focus was on how ordinary people lived. Shepherd and Ralston, in their chapter on the findings from Pittodrie, note that there is a lack of evidence for pre-modern rural housing in north-east Scotland. This is relevant to the volunteers' interests too, as they explore local history from the perspectives of inhabitants whose lives are otherwise not well attested. Localising heritage in this way shows the significant value that even apparently unpromising sites can have.

Temporal constraints

A further feature of Pittodrie is how it demonstrates that small features, when considered in a broader landscape context, may hold far greater interest than the sum of their individual parts. This is in a large part determined by the slow pace at which community groups can operate. They can tease away at a site for years in a manner that is not easy for institutions to justify when constrained by project-funded mechanisms. Institutions operate in short bursts of high energy activity, regulated by university time constraints and project-funding agreements. A community group tends to operate at a lower energy level but over a sustained timeframe, unhampered by funding constraints as all labour is voluntary.

This is again reflected in our conversations with volunteers, who cover both 'stalwarts' who have been attending the Pittodrie and Druminnor digs for a number of years, and those who join during the season and may or may not return the following year. Longer term volunteers are able to immerse themselves in the detail of the site as it unfolds and take more responsibility for areas of the site, along with learning more advanced skills and helping less experienced diggers. To some extent, there is a dilemma for Ralston as site supervisor in the desire to help new volunteers learn and experience as much as possible for the days that they are present on the one hand, and ensuring the overall progress of the archaeological research on the site as a whole. A lot of newcomers necessarily means time spent introducing them and supervising their initial work at the potential cost of progress elsewhere, and yet enabling as many people as possible to join the dig is also one of the project's aims. This leads to a process of reflection for project leaders on how far the site's dual purposes are compatible – in other words whether it should function primarily as an introduction to local archaeology for the community, or as a more fully-fledged research operation. We argue that the community input is vital to how the research actually happens, and so there need not be a strict opposition here. For the site supervisor, decisions about the use of time and other resources are constantly being made. But the material presented here suggests that slow-paced but consistent research by a community group can achieve significant results.

Funding

The fact that the Pittodrie dig is driven by an almost totally voluntary structure is important. From the organisation and funding down to the individual day labour, volunteering is not just an economic aspect but the basis of social relations on site. But the economics of volunteering are significant, because they remove many of the constraints affecting institutions, in particular the long periods spent in grant preparation followed by expectations for specific results in a short timescale. On volunteer-run digs, the research happens more easily over the longer term and is responsive to the goals of the volunteers and the circumstances of the site, rather than having to follow pre-set research questions. Further gains from the slow pace of community explorations can be made with respect to specialist funding. At Pittodrie this has followed investigations rather than needing to be built in at the project planning stage. Consequently, specialist funding can be sought more appropriately in relation to what is actually found rather than what is expected. This has included funding for scientific dating as presented in Shepherd and Ralston's paper, and also for soil samples and pollen analysis as these needs have arisen and particular opportunities for funding pursued. On the other hand, decisions still need to be made about when and how to move into the post-excavation phase of writing-up and full dissemination of results, which will entail ending the fieldwork phase at some point. Project leaders are aware that as a research project, work at the site will need to end in order for the outcomes to be properly realised.

Community networks

Community groups such as the Bailies of Bennachie and the more informal grouping of volunteers at Pittodrie are, in a way, products of wide-ranging social networks. They exist because particular communities want them to exist. At Pittodrie and elsewhere around Bennachie, there is a ready-made, predominantly local, audience wanting to hear the results of research. This localism aids education and outreach opportunities; firstly, because of local interest and, secondly, because of 'the grapevine' that is already operational. As noted above, education has formed a central aim of the Bailies since their inception. Open days and guided walks around the landscape are an expected part of any Bailies project.

Such networks, gradually grown across 50 years and now stretching around the world, also produce funding opportunities and a ready pool of local expertise and knowledge. Many professionals on retirement use their skills for the voluntary benefit of the Bailies, with some specialists in geology a particular feature that draws on

Aberdeen's oil and gas industry. The challenge here is also to reach out to parts of the community less often associated with heritage and 'the local'. A number of young people are being integrated successfully into the work (see Plates 13.1 and 13.2), but the predominant volunteer base is, it seems, white and middle class. One volunteer also commented on what he sensed was a relatively low proportion of 'actual' local people volunteering, drawing a contrast between those born and bred nearby and those who have moved to the area from elsewhere in Scotland or the UK. Are these in-movers particularly concerned with making connections to their new landscape, perhaps? If so, this could be a way of reaching out to a broader range of communities too. Challenging the preconceptions of rural landscape history as simply the preserve of powerful landowners could also help – that the history of 'the people' lies in the mounds and dykes visible in our rural areas as much as it does in the city.

A key point from our volunteer conversations is that many people talked about the sociability of the dig itself, which is notably different from a standard research or contract excavation. Diggers are welcome and encouraged to find out what is happening elsewhere on the site and to take time to talk and learn from each other, often by simply wandering over to a different part of the site, or stopping to talk on the way to pick up a tool or piece of equipment elsewhere. Information was shared and opinions offered on the excavation in progress. Tea breaks are important for sharing insights and enjoying each others' company, leading to a better experience for all (Plate 13.3). Vergunst noticed that while the timings for starting the breaks were clearly set by way of a loud blow on a whistle audible all over the site, the breaks ended informally when people collectively felt it was time to go back to work. This contributed to a feeling of the volunteers being in control of their work rather than just following orders. Overall, these convivial social dynamics seem to be particularly important in a community-led, volunteer dig. These are the also the principles that could underlie a widening of the social make-up of the network.

'Ownership', 'commons' and 'community responsibility'

Our reflections point to a number of themes and conclusions arising from 13 years of growth in the Bennachie Landscapes Project as a whole. The project was created with a series of short-term aims in mind, but with the hope that it might become self-sustaining and cross-generational. Progress has been good though, obviously, there have been difficulties to overcome along the way. However, much of what has been achieved has been as a result of the local 'networking' mentioned above. Many things have been achieved almost unwittingly because of an apparent synergy between participants. The following discussion attempts to understand how that may have happened against the backdrop of historical developments that should have militated against such apparent good fortune. Within this discussion, the origin of the Bailies, developing from perceptions of the division of the Bennachie Commonty looms large. This was discussed in the Foreword and is now returned to here.

'Ownership'

'Ownership' is a weighty term that is frequently used without consideration of the baggage attached. Within conversations at Bennachie Landscape Project Group and Bailies meetings, the phrase, 'take ownership of' is frequently used in the sense of group members or individuals putting their collective hearts and souls into a particular project. Of course, what is not intended is a desire to legally 'own' any particular piece of property or intellectual property rights; it expresses a desire to 'take responsibility' for the project. However, it is interesting how the term 'ownership' is used in this regard. There remains a sense in which it suggests personal possession, thereby implicitly creating a sense of exclusion. As noted in the Foreword, issues of 'ownership' surround perceptions of rights of access to historic cultural 'assets', just as they accrue to perceptions of rights of access to land.

Reflecting on the history of 'ownership' in British jurisprudence is a worthwhile excursion at this point. Such matters were already exercising the minds of medieval thinkers of the 12th- and 13th centuries. It may be argued that the development of rigid property rights reflected the rise of 'Roman Law' over 'Customary Law' across Britain. According to Roman law, 'ownership' and 'legitimate use' could not be permanently separated (Spade and Panaccio 2019, 8.2). William of Ockham (d. 1347), however, defines two types of 'right' to goods: one was 'legal right', which amounted to ownership; the other was a 'natural right' of use (*ibid.*, 8.3). To the mind of the medieval church scholar Aquinas, all property was common in times of need (ST, IIb, IIae, 66, 7) and legal governance could only be communally sanctioned whilst it acted for 'common good' (Finnis 2020, 38–54). Faith notes that, in the peasant moral economy, rights to subsistence were embedded (2020, 60). In the 13th-century peasant economy this included a wide range of necessities to life: fuel, firewood, building materials, pasture, animal bedding, fodder and wild foodstuffs for human consumption.

Without going into how this psychological approach to property moved from a 'Customary' to a 'Roman' viewpoint, it led inexorably to the notion of 'enclosure' and exclusion of others. This is a theme at the heart of so much research on Bennachie and helped to inform the desire to found the Bailies. In 17th-century Scotland, the Court of Sessions delivered a judgement that codified the 'Roman' view of ownership. In 1626 the Court determined that a lease ('tack' in Scotland) could not contain 'perpetual obligations'; that is, a lease could not be hereditary (Goodare 2013, 105), otherwise 'ownership' of that leased land would be constrained by other 'rights', as had been the case prior to the court's decision. In 1695 the Scots Parliament gave permission for commonties to be enclosed (*RPS*, 1695/5/204) and by 1744 the Court of Sessions stated, 'It is the privilege of property that the proprietor can be put under no restraint' (Houston 2011, 45). In other words, land ownership was considered to be total, after the Roman fashion, and customary rights had been completely extinguished.

'Commons'

What has all this to do with community research? Interestingly, within a few years of the 'ownership' verdict of the Court of Sessions, Adam Smith was considering earlier forms of 'commons management' in order to re-imagine a 'non-mercantile' form of economy for the future. He drew attention to an imagined 'original state':

> In that original state of things which precedes both the appropriation of land and the accumulation of stock, the whole produce of labour belongs to the labourer. He has neither landlord nor master to share with him.
>
> Had that state continued, the wages of labour would have augmented with all those improvements in its productive powers, to which the division of labour gives occasion. All things would gradually have become cheaper.
>
> But this original state of things, in which the labourer enjoyed the whole produce of his own labour, could not last beyond the first introduction of the appropriation of land and the accumulation of stock (Smith, 1776, 36–37).

Smith was seeking a route back from 'mercantilism' to a fairer economy, seemingly closer to the ideals espoused by Aquinas: 'No society can surely be flourishing and happy, of which the far greater part of its members are poor and miserable.' (44) Two further quotes are worth comparing. Firstly, Smith's:

> the most absurd of all suppositions, the supposition that every successive generation of men have not an equal right to the earth, and to all that it possesses (209).

Secondly, John Calvin's view on the predestiny ordained for man by God:

> with regard to every man. All are not created on equal terms, but some are preordained to eternal life, others to eternal damnation (Beveridge 1846, 675).

The latter appears to have been utilised to formulate the baseline excuse for mercantile extraction: 'All for ourselves, and nothing for other people, seems, in every age of the world, to have been the vile maxim of the masters of mankind' (Smith 1776, 223).

More recently, economist Elinor Ostrom (1990) considered 'the Commons' (Common-pool Resources) in world-wide perspective and demonstrated their ability to withstand predatory overtures, given the collectives were able to maintain a suite of circumstances including, critically, that of being free from external governmental authority and that they adhered to their own strict set of rules (90). Such systems had been in place across Britain. Winchester (2000, 26–48) gives numerous examples of such 'byrlaw' courts and these find expression in the 'birlaymen' of the Forbes Court of Barony in the north-east (GD52/312). Bailey's studies of manorial court documents have shown the strength of those institutions, with cases brought and won by tenants against powerful manorial lords, even in their own manorial courts (Bailey 2014, 144).

Commons in England and Commonties in Scotland derived from the same background of shared customary rights and obligations (Shepherd 2021, 123–35) and these included the institutions used to run them and the rules governed by those institutions. Tine de Moor (2012) refers to these commonties as 'common property regimes', sitting somewhere between private and public property and the institutions running them as 'common-pool institutions'. Bennachie was 'owned' by the heritors, but others had rights to it – 'use and wont' in Scots legal parlance – that was as legally binding as the ownership itself. In fact, in earlier feudal times, those rights surpassed that of the landholders who only held their lands by right of the king as their overlord. Barnes and Williamson (2011, 102–3) have shown how commoners even planted and tended their own trees on similar tracts of common land.

This brief historical journey has considered the development of the notion of 'ownership', especially with regard to 'land', and we have argued that other forms of 'commons management' existed previously in Britain and still persist across the world.

Community responsibility

This returns us to the discussion at hand, relating to community responsibility with regard to the historic environment. It may be argued that the Bailies of Bennachie have been involved in a form of 'quasi-common-pool institution' with the landowners of Bennachie for the last 50 years. The Bailies have taken responsibility for maintaining some of the trackways around the hill in order to help maintain public access. More recently, for at least the last 12 years, they have helped to monitor and maintain the colony properties on Forestry Commission Scotland (now Forestry and Land Scotland) land. A recent Colony Management Plan has been devised by a small sub-group (piloted by Colin Miller) of the Bennachie Landscapes Project Group and passed to the Trustees of the Bailies and Forestry and Land Scotland for acceptance. The agreed document will form the basis of the future management strategy for the colony houses by the Bailies of Bennachie, even though they sit on Forestry and Land Scotland land. It is interesting to consider that the Roman legalistic notion of 'ownership' can fairly readily develop a few holes!

A similar, novel idea is presently being discussed with another landowner on Bennachie. This is for the Bailies to take on and manage an area of woodland as an 'outdoor laboratory' where different methods of woodland management, based upon historic models, can be tried and monitored. This will also enable the monitoring of ecological change as this former sitka woodland is returned to a range of traditionally managed pieces of broad-leaf woodland. The species to be used are those recognised from the pollen and ecofactual remains revealed by the ongoing archaeological work at Pittodrie. The development of this potential new project derives from a NERC-funded project 'Voices of the Future: Collaborating with children and young people to re-imagine treescapes' (NE/V021370/1) in which both authors and colleagues at the University of Aberdeen are involved.

Slowly, therefore, over the years, the collaboration of the Bailies, the University of Aberdeen, along with a host of volunteers – both academic and non-academic – have been able to demonstrate that 'ownership' can be permeable, provided partners share responsibility. 'Responsibility', therefore, would appear to be more important than legal 'ownership' in collaborative projects.

Collaborative research in history and archaeology

We have seen how different groups and individuals have come together to create a number of projects across the region. But, finally, we would like to consider in greater detail how complicated some of these webs of interaction have become.

Working through the list of contributors to this book may offer a way in. Bruce Mann is closely linked through his position with all of the archaeological projects that take place in his jurisdiction. Andrew Wainwright, as well as carrying out his own studies, digs and advises on the Pittodrie and Druminnor excavations. His input on the latter has been critical in understanding such a geologically challenging site (see Plate 13.4). Samantha Jones' and Gordon Noble's work on the 'Comparative Kingship' project has provided much needed ecological and historical data that has fed into the Pittodrie and Druminnor digs by helping to give a clearer understanding of the early medieval background of those areas. Nicholas Evans' work on the same project has similarly helped from a historical and place-name perspective.

Alex Forbes, as owner of Druminnor Castle, has contributed (as well as his grounds!) a great deal of later medieval detail, especially regarding the lordly families', which has been of use in understanding the contexts of the excavations. Charlotta Hilledal's work reminds us what is not recoverable from the historical and archaeological record and teaches us to be aware of the requirement to read between the lines of the evidence. She is also responsible for running the community engagement in archaeology undergraduate course at the University of Aberdeen – of critical importance in apprising students of that aspect of their discipline being discussed here.

Penny Dransart, as excavator of Fetternear, was also the first archaeologist to put a spade into one of the colony houses, Cairn Coutie, back in 1999 – well before the start of the Bennachie Landscapes Project. However, that excavation, sponsored by the Bailies, was instrumental in kick-starting a series of questions about the Colony that, ultimately, resulted in the larger project. The Bishops of Aberdeen, whose palace Fetternear was, were granted the rights of free forest on Bennachie, within which lay Cairn Coutie. The Colony questions prompted Jeff Oliver and the University of Aberdeen to become more involved and resulted in further excavations and environmental work on the hill. Louise Smith is now continuing his work, though concentrating on the ecological aspect.

Many volunteers who have worked on aspects of the Bennachie Landscapes Project have also worked on the Meso-Deeside project. Meso-Deeside's work has now led to the creation of a further group looking to extend their research further north into Donside and beyond. The impact of these fieldworking campaigns are giving us a much better understanding of the deeper archaeological landscape of the north-east. And, of course, Andrew Wainwright's suspicions about the glacial lake will be important for consideration of their Upper Palaeolithic finds, which seem to be becoming more abundant.

Chris Foster's experimental kailyard developed from the colony investigations and draws upon Jennifer Fagen's PhD looking at the squatters and their lifestyles (co-supervised by Jo Vergunst). Jennifer's book (2011), produced by the Bailies, was the first in the 'Bennachie Landscapes' series, presently numbering four. This story of the Colonists is important to the present-day psyche of many dwellers in the north-east who count squatter families amongst their ancestors. But, not only in the north-east. Numerous migrants from the north-east also number squatter families amongst their ancestors. The Bailies website has been instrumental in helping to gather together strands of this 'Bennachie diaspora'. Skype sessions have been held so that descendants from Australia, New Zealand and elsewhere have been able to share their family recollections of Bennachie with the Bailies and, this year, an American family, whose ancestral family was Littlejohn of Shepherds Lodge and kailyard fame, visited their ancestor's house and were shown around the Colony.

This Bennachie collaborative network is open-ended and ever-changing. Many people are involved without even knowing it! The conference, of which this book is a product, demonstrated that many of the participants – speakers and those observing – were working on related themes or on projects that overlapped, without knowing about each other's existence. In other words, the network was wider than realised. What is important is that it is growing and, it is hoped, this book will encourage others to engage with it and, for those in other places, learn from it. Our experience of collaborative working suggests that 'commons-based', egalitarian organisational structures (reminiscent of medieval manorial gatherings) are more productive than hierarchical 'top-down' strategies.

Sources

Beveridge, G. (trans.) (1846) Calvin, J., *The Institutes of the Christian Religion*. Edinburgh, Calvin Translation Society.

GD52/312 = (1663) *List of Birlaymen and duties in Clatt, Kearn and Auchindoir*, National Records of Scotland.

RPS = Brown, K.M. *et al.* (eds) (1641) *The Records of the Parliaments of Scotland to 1707*, Act regarding the erection of the hospital of Balhalgardy. Ref. 1641/8/380. (http://www.rps.ac.uk)

ST = *Summa Theologiae*, Thomas Aquinas, http://www.logicmuseum.com/authors/aquinas/Summa.

Bibliography

Bailey, M. (2014) *The Decline of Serfdom in Late Medieval England. From Bondage to Freedom*. Woodbridge, Boydell Press.

Barnes, G. and Williamson, T. (eds) (2011) *Ancient Trees in the Landscape, Norfolk's Arboreal Heritage*. Oxford, Windgather Press.

de Moor, T. (2012) What do we have in common? A comparative framework for old and new literature on the Commons. In *International Review of Social History* 57(2), 269–90.

Fagen, J. (2011) *The Bennachie Colony Project: Examining the Lives and Impact of the Bennachie Colonists*. Chapel of Garioch, Bailies of Bennachie, Bennachie Landscapes Series 1.

Faith, R. (2020) *The Moral Economy of the Countryside. Anglo-Saxon to Anglo-Norman England*. Cambridge, Cambridge University Press.
Finnis, J. (2020) Aquinas' Moral, Political, and Legal Philosophy. In Zalta, E.N. (ed.) *Stanford Encyclopedia of Philosophy*, https://plato.stanford.edu/archives/sum2020/entries/aquinas-moral-political/
Goodare, J. (2013) In search of the Scottish agrarian problem. In Whittle, J. (ed.), *Landlords and Tenants in Britain, 1440–1660. Tawney's Agrarian Problem Revisited*, 100–16. Woodbridge, Boydell Press.
Graham, H. and Vergunst, J. (2019) *Heritage as Community Research. Legacies of Co-production*. Bristol, Policy Press.
Houston, R. (2011) Custom in context: medieval and early modern Scotland and England. In *Past and Present* 211, 35–76.
Ostrom, E. (1990) *Governing the Commons. The Evolution of Institutions for Collective Action*. Cambridge, Cambridge University Press.
Rippon, S. (2013) Historic Landscape Character and Sense of Place. In *Landscape Research* 38(2), 179–202.
Shepherd, (2021) *The Late Medieval Landscape of North-east Scotland: Renaissance, Reformation and Revolution*. Oxford, Windgather Press.
Smith, A. (1776) *The Wealth of Nations*. 2014 edn, Middletown DE, Shine Classics.
Spade, P.V. and Panaccio, C. (2019) William of Ockham. In Zalta, E.N. (ed.) *Stanford Encyclopedia of Philosophy*, https://plato.stanford.edu/archives/spr2019/entries/ockham/
Vergunst, J., Curtis, E., Davis, O., Johnston, R., Graham, H. and Shepherd, C. (2017) Material Legacies: shaping things and places through heritage. In Facer, K. and Pahl, K. (eds) *Valuing Interdisciplinary Collaborative Research: Beyond Impact*, 153–71. Bristol, Policy Press.
Winchester, A.J.L. (2000) *The Harvest of the Hills. Rural Life in Northern England and the Scottish Borders, 1400–1700*. Edinburgh, Edinburgh University Press.

Website

hlamap.org.uk, Scotlands Historic Land Use, https://hlamap.org.uk/